T0349610

THE "COLORED HERO" OF HARPER'S FERRY

JOHN ANTHONY COPELAND AND THE WAR AGAINST SLAVERY

On the night of Sunday, October 16, 1859, hoping to bring about the eventual end of slavery, radical abolitionist John Brown launched an armed attack at Harper's Ferry, Virginia. Among his troops, there were only five black men, who have largely been treated as little more than "spear carriers" by Brown's many biographers and other historians of the antebellum era. This book brings one such man, John Anthony Copeland, directly to center stage. Copeland played a leading role in the momentous Oberlin slave rescue, and he successfully escorted a fugitive to Canada, making him an ideal recruit for Brown's invasion of Virginia. He fought bravely at Harper's Ferry, only to be captured and charged with murder and treason. With his trademark lively prose and compelling narrative style, Steven Lubet paints a vivid portrait of this young black man who gave his life for freedom.

A leading authority on African-American resistance to slavery and notable trials in American history, Steven Lubet is the Edna B. and Ednyfed H. Williams Memorial Professor of Law at Northwestern University School of Law. He is the award-winning author of numerous books, including *Murder in Tombstone: The Forgotten Trial of Wyatt Earp*; *Fugitive Justice: Runaways, Rescuers, and Slavery on Trial*; and *John Brown's Spy: The Adventurous Life and Tragic Confession of John E. Cook*. Lubet has been an award-winning columnist for *American Lawyer* magazine, a commentator on NPR's *Morning Edition*, and the author of many op-ed pieces in national newspapers and on *Slate* and *Salon*.

Charlestown Va. Octo 26th.
Listening to the Indictment & pleadings.
Copeland. 1859.

THE "COLORED HERO" OF HARPER'S FERRY

JOHN ANTHONY COPELAND AND THE WAR AGAINST SLAVERY

STEVEN LUBET
Northwestern University School of Law

CAMBRIDGE
UNIVERSITY PRESS

32 Avenue of the Americas, New York, NY 10013-2473, USA

Cambridge University Press is part of the University of Cambridge.

It furthers the University's mission by disseminating knowledge in the pursuit of education, learning, and research at the highest international levels of excellence.

www.cambridge.org
Information on this title: www.cambridge.org/9781107076020

First published 2015

Printed in the United States of America

A catalog record for this publication is available from the British Library.

Library of Congress Cataloging in Publication Data
Lubet, Steven.
The "colored hero" of Harper's Ferry : John Anthony Copeland and the war against slavery / Steven Lubet, Northwestern University School of Law.
pages cm
Includes bibliographical references and index.
ISBN 978-1-107-07602-0
1. Copeland, John A. (John Anthony) 2. African American abolitionists – Biography. 3. Brown, John, 1800–1859 – Friends and associates. 4. Harpers Ferry (W. Va.) – History – John Brown's Raid, 1859. 5. Antislavery movements – Ohio – Oberlin – History – 19th century. 6. Abolitionists – Biography. I. Title. II. Title: John Anthony Copeland and the war against slavery.
E451.L829 2015
326′.8092–dc23 [B] 2015002308

ISBN 978-1-107-07602-0 Hardback

To Sarah and Willard

CONTENTS

ACKNOWLEDGMENTS

Marcia Lehr, of Northwestern's Pritzker Legal Resource Center, provided me with outstanding support for many years. She recently retired, and I am deeply grateful that she was able to help me on one last project. Thankfully, Ann Miller is still at Northwestern, and she has enthusiastically continued to assist me in everything I have undertaken. None of this would be possible without Ann.

Special mention is due Louis DeCaro, whose vast store of knowledge and collegial generosity are unmatched in the field of John Brown studies. I cannot imagine a better editor than Deborah Gershenowitz, or a better agent than Katherine Flynn. And Molly "Meticulous" Abbattista deserves great thanks as well.

Sources concerning John Anthony Copeland are scattered among many archives and collections, but the two most important are at Columbia University and Oberlin College. I am grateful to archivists Eric Wakin and Thai Jones (Columbia University Rare Book and Manuscript Library) and Ken Grossi and Louisa Hoffman (Oberlin College Archives) for making their materials so readily available. Thanks also to Nicola Singleton Strathers, Thomas Thurman, Paris Gravley, Kim Baker, Linda Freeman, Diane Rapaport, Gloria Brown, Ceceile Kay Richter, Maribel Hilo Nash, Pegeen Bassett, Margaret Lynn Kincade, Mimi Katz, Caleigh Elizabeth Hernandez, and David Turk for research assistance. I am also grateful to Walter Stahr, Brian McGinty, Paul Finkelman, Robert Baker, Andy Koppelman, and Al Brophy for suggestions and encouragement.

Mornings at the Unicorn Symposium have sustained me throughout this project, and I have also been propped up as needed by Christel Bridges, Steve Simmons, Bill Haydasz, Ping Ng, Jeff Rice, Jim Foody, Rich Tye, Kurt Mitenbuler, Jim Ford, and Madhu Gorla.

I am grateful for the support of Dean Daniel Rodriguez and the Spray Trust Fund of the Northwestern University School of Law. Since

1975, my intellectual and professional home has been in Northwestern's Bluhm Legal Clinic, where I have benefited from the wise counsel and warm friendship of Tom Geraghty (for the entire forty years) and Bob Burns (since 1980). More recently, my corner of the legal clinic has been brightened by the good cheer of Shericka Pringle, Eraena Hart, Brianne Williams, Joe Hayes, George Geiger, Nancy Flowers, and many others. And also Ann Miller – who is mentioned above, but cannot be mentioned enough.

I still treasure every day that I spend with Linda. Natan and Sarah know what I mean.

AUTHOR'S NOTE

In 1859, Harper's Ferry was located in the Commonwealth of Virginia. The town is now in West Virginia, and the apostrophe has been dropped from its name. I have opted to use the original orthography, however, for the sake of consistency with antebellum sources, and I have done likewise with Charlestown (which is now known as Charles Town). Speaking of antebellum sources, I have retained original spellings, punctuation, emphases, and capitalizations in all quoted material, even though the results may at times seem jarring.

PROLOGUE

LOOKING OUT FROM THE BARRED WINDOW of his jail cell, John Anthony Copeland could easily see the rolling hills and agricultural lands that surrounded Charlestown, Virginia. There had been no opportunity for him to appreciate the beauty of the countryside since his arrival in the state only a little more than one week earlier. Now, in late October 1859, most of the abundant crops had been harvested, leaving the fields brown with rolls of hay and a few standing stalks of corn. The leaves on the native beech, oak, and ash trees, however, had already begun to turn red and gold, and the vivid colors might have cheered Copeland's spirit if he had not been facing death by hanging.

Copeland's home was in Oberlin, Ohio, over 400 miles to the northwest, where leaves had already fallen and his mother and father longed for news of their imprisoned son. In time, he would write to his parents, assuring them of his belief that "God wills everything for the best good."[1] But for now, he had no words to calm himself or to bring them comfort. There was little hope for a black man charged with murder in Virginia, and even less for one accused of inciting slaves to rebellion.

A mob had gathered outside the jailhouse, calling loudly for the blood of John Brown, whose abortive invasion of Harper's Ferry had lasted only three days – October 16–18 – while taking the lives of four Virginians and a U.S. marine. Brown was already notorious from his days on the battlefields of "Bleeding Kansas," but the four men captured with him – Copeland and three others – were unknown. That made no difference to the lynch mob, which wanted all of them dead. Nor did it matter to the Southern press, which dismissed all of Brown's raiders as "reckless fanatics" and "wanton, malicious, unprovoked felons."[2] In fact, Copeland's decision to join John Brown had been neither reckless nor unprovoked. Although only twenty-five, he had for many years been dedicated to abolitionism, having grown up among fugitives and freed slaves. As a child, he had evaded slave patrols in North Carolina and Kentucky; as a student, he had attended school with one of the former captives from *La Amistad*, who had been freed by order of the U.S. Supreme Court; and as a young man, he had confronted slave hunters and had spirited a runaway to freedom in Canada. In many ways, Copeland's enlistment under John Brown's command – far from an act of rash fanaticism – had been the culmination of his life's progress from idealism to militancy.

Copeland's motivation was also deeply religious. His parents had been known for piety in their native North Carolina, although the black churches they attended could never risk any open opposition to slavery. In Ohio, however, Copeland had been exposed to the evangelism of Reverend Charles Grandison Finney, the acknowledged leader of the Second Great Awakening and an avowed enemy of slavery. Finney preached in Oberlin's First Church, which was one of the few fully integrated congregations in the United States and by far the largest one. Sitting side by side with white children, Copeland came to understand that his "duty to both God and man" required him to fight slavery, even if that might take him to "the dark and gloomy gallows."[3] For any man "to suffer by the existence of slavery," he believed, was far worse than "the mere fact of having to die."[4] Copeland's determination was bolstered by his powerful faith in the afterlife. He warmly accepted Finney's promise that friends and loved ones would meet again in heaven.[5] As Copeland himself put it, "when I have finished my stay on this earth . . . I shall be received in Heaven by the Holy God [to meet those] who have gone before me."[6]

Like many Southern "mulattos," Copeland's mother traced her ancestry to a Revolutionary War veteran, in this case General Nathanael Greene.[7] And like many African-Americans in the North, Copeland himself idealized the revolutionary generation, believing that "those who established the principles upon which this government was to stand" intended the "right to life, liberty, and happiness" to belong "to all men of whatever color."[8] In Oberlin's integrated school, he had learned to revere George Washington as having "entered the field to fight for the freedom of the American people – not for the white man alone, but for both black and white."[9] That was a familiar story in abolitionist circles, made no less inspiring by the fact that it was not really true. Although Washington had sometimes expressed support for gradual emancipation, he had freed no slaves in his lifetime and, as president, he had signed the Fugitive Slave Act of 1793.[10] Still, Washington provided a convenient hero for a young African-American who was prepared to embark on a revolutionary course of his own. He held fast to the belief that "black men did an equal share of the fighting for American Independence," and the time had come for them to share the "equal benefits" they had been promised by the founders.[11]

If Copeland's veneration of George Washington was for the most part misplaced, his regard for another revolutionary era figure was fitting indeed. He identified closely with Crispus Attucks, who had been the first victim of the Boston Massacre in 1770. Copeland was proud that "the *very first* blood that was spilt" in the battle for American independence "was that of a negro," calling Attucks "that heroic man (though black he was)."[12] Attucks had been all but beatified by the black abolitionist movement, and Copeland shared the widespread admiration of his martyrdom.[13] In Copeland's words, Attucks had given his life for "the freedom of the American people," which also marked "the commencement of the struggle for the freedom of the negro slave."[14] As he contemplated his own death, Copeland turned time and again to Attucks's example of a black man whose memory endured long after his life's end. He prayed that his own sacrifice would be recalled as proudly by his family and friends.

But while he reflected on ideals of heroism, martyrdom, and immortality, Copeland's view of the outside world was bounded by the jailhouse walls. He could not even look in the direction of the Free states, as the only window in his cell faced cruelly to the south. With the shouts of the lynch mob in his ears, his thoughts turned to his years in Oberlin. It was the most thoroughly abolitionist community in America, where he had been nurtured, educated, and set on a path that led him to Harper's Ferry as a soldier in John Brown's insurrectionary army.

Professor James Fairchild had good reason to be proud of Oberlin College when he walked to the lectern on May 18, 1856, ready to present the Ladies Anti-Slavery Society with a "Sketch of the Anti-Slavery History of Oberlin." Like nearly all members of the faculty, Fairchild was an abolitionist and a pacifist, committed to ending slavery through peaceful means.[15] He could not have imagined, as he began his lecture, the bloody events that would occur only one week later in faraway Kansas, and how they would affect life in his own quiet community. On the night of May 24–25, John Brown would lead a sortie that has come to be known as the Potawatomie Massacre, slaughtering and dismembering five pro-slavery settlers and changing – at a literal stroke – the terms of the abolitionist struggle. Nor could Fairchild have envisioned how deeply Oberlin would become entangled in Brown's war, much less that one of its own recent students – a young African-American named John Anthony Copeland, Jr. – would become, as a soldier in Brown's army, one of the "colored heroes of Harper's Ferry." On that spring day, however, the violence still lay in the future, and Fairchild's only intention was to expound on Oberlin's pacific and honorable past.

For over two decades, Oberlin had been a beacon of abolitionism, sending ministers to preach against slavery in the pulpits of countless churches, providing teachers to the impoverished "negro schools" of Ohio, and, most notoriously, offering a haven to fugitive slaves. Fairchild had been at Oberlin virtually since its founding, first as a student (in the inaugural freshman class) and then as a teacher of theology, philosophy, classical languages, and mathematics.[16] In his late thirties at the time of the lecture, Fairchild had sunken eyes, a bulbous nose, and a weak chin, and he was already beginning to develop the heavy jowls that would become more pronounced as he aged. Despite his unimpressive appearance, Fairchild's erudition and animation ensured that he would have no trouble holding the attention of his audience. He was broadly versed in academics, but his great passion was to oppose "the intrinsic wrongfulness of Slavery, and the obligation to undo at once the bands of wickedness and let the oppressed go free."[17]

As Fairchild reminded the assembled ladies, the trustees of Oberlin had resolved in 1835 to admit students "irrespective of color" and, although the motion had passed by only a single vote, the college had since become the most integrated educational institution in the United States.[18] By 1856, there were forty "colored students" at Oberlin, both men and women, in a student body of 800. The town of Oberlin itself had an even larger African-American population, comprising both free blacks and runaway slaves. So common were the latter that the signposts on the road to Oberlin were said to show "a full length picture of a colored man, running with all his might" to reach sanctuary. Nor were the fugitives unwelcome. Oberlin prided itself as "a sort of general depot for various branches of the under-ground railroad," and residents readily either sheltered fugitives or helped them escape onward to Canada.[19]

Needless to say, Kentucky slave catchers were often attracted by the highly visible presence of so many runaways, and attempts at recapture were not uncommon. Fairchild was certain that no self-respecting Oberliner would ever "interrupt or expose a fugitive," but he realized that "there were those in every neighborhood who would undertake the odious work for the reward which was offered." Many Oberliners consequently became adept at thwarting slave hunters, using various ruses and deceptions. In one well-known instance, a wagonload of citizens disguised themselves as fugitives and lured a band of slave hunters to follow them out of town. Meanwhile, the real runaways were dispatched in the opposite direction, where they rendezvoused with a Lake Erie steamboat captain who had agreed to carry them to Canada.[20]

Thus, Professor Fairchild was able to boast, without exaggeration, that "no fugitive was ever taken here and returned to slavery," and yet there had been "no instance of bloodshed or personal harm" to a slave catcher.[21]

Fairchild's lecture – transcribed and published by the *Oberlin Evangelist* – was greeted with much satisfaction by the local citizens, one of whom was John Anthony Copeland, Jr. Then only a month shy of his twenty-second birthday, Copeland had been born free in North Carolina to parents of mixed background. The Copeland family – headed by John, Sr., and Delilah – had moved to Oberlin in 1843, seeking relief from the racism that plagued free blacks in the South. John, Sr., found work as a carpenter and cabinetmaker, and he arranged for his oldest son to attend Oberlin College's preparatory department (equivalent to a high school) in 1854–55.[22] The young Copeland – known to his family as John Anthony – was a respectable student, especially in theology and history.[23] Nonetheless, he left without matriculating – perhaps because his family could not afford the $18 annual tuition or perhaps because he needed to help support his six younger siblings – and joined his father in the carpentry trade.[24]

John Anthony had grown up surrounded by abolitionism. He attended his first anti-slavery meeting at age nine, when his parents stopped in New Richmond, Indiana, en route to Oberlin, and he continued his involvement for the rest of his life.[25] In Oberlin, John Anthony became active in the Anti-Slavery Society, and he was especially attuned to the plight of fugitives. At one meeting, he listened intently to the story of a runaway, "signifying often by the deep scowl of his countenance, the moist condition of his eyes, and the quivering of his lips, how deeply he was moved by the recital of wrong and outrage."[26]

Copeland's intensity was not reserved for abolitionist meetings. His arched eyebrows, high cheekbones, and piercing eyes gave him an appearance of settled purpose, as though his thoughts were keenly fixed on a distant objective. A bushy and well-trimmed mustache made him look slightly older than his years. His light complexion and wavy hair would later prompt the Southern press to describe him as a "bright mulatto," meaning that he could almost pass for white. Nearly fifty years later, however, Copeland's sister would deny that he was "bright," perhaps to emphasize that he had always identified as a black man.[27]

As he reached adulthood, Copeland began to abandon the tenets of nonviolence as preached by Fairchild and accepted in most of the Oberlin community. He eventually took up arms, beginning with a stout wooden staff that he employed to knock a hapless slave catcher to the ground. Copeland soon switched to a rifle, however, when the kidnappers themselves became more daring and combative.

In his 1856 lecture, James Fairchild had been able to brag that no fugitive had ever been seized in Oberlin, but most of the slave hunters until then had been amateurs who were not very hard to intimidate. They had been a nuisance, to be sure, but they were fairly easily repelled or diverted and were regarded almost humorously by the Oberlin gentry, who sometimes referred to foiling slave hunters as a "confidence game" and even "a lark."[28] The fugitives themselves were in no position to make light of their situation, however, and they felt quite differently about their pursuers. The Oberlin memoirist Milton Clarke wrote that the anxiety of being hunted "was beyond anything I ever felt in my life."[29]

Oberlin had been a thorn in the side of slave owners for many years, but it was also isolated and remote, and therefore relatively tolerable. By 1848, efforts to seize runaways in Oberlin had all but ended, thanks to the ever-alert work of the local "vigilance committee," which patrolled the town for signs of slave catchers.[30] The Fugitive Slave Act of 1850 shifted the responsibility for slave catching to the national government, on the theory that it would lead to more effective recaptures. But federal authority was virtually nonexistent in Oberlin – other than the local postmaster – and therefore useless to slave hunters. Besides, there were plenty of fugitives elsewhere in Ohio – or vulnerable free blacks, for that matter – who could be captured without opposition from vigilant fanatics.

In 1858, however, political intrigues in far-off Kansas and Washington, D.C., would combine to focus the attention of the federal government on Oberlin. The existence of such a brazen sanctuary became unacceptable to the administration of President James Buchanan for political reasons that stretched far beyond Ohio. Thus, the slave hunters of Kentucky were suddenly able to call on the power of the federal government, which emboldened them to strike deeply into the heart of Oberlin. What had once been a near idyll was quickly becoming a true battleground.

Force would be met with force, with John Anthony at the center of the fighting. His struggle against slavery would not stop in Oberlin but would reach all the way to Virginia at the side of John Brown.

IN 1857, THE U.S. SUPREME COURT decided the *Dred Scott* case, now most often remembered for Chief Justice Roger Taney's infamous pronouncement that a black person had "no rights which the white man is bound to respect."[31] Taney's disdain for African-Americans ran deeply. As historian Margot Minardi has observed, the chief justice was making not only a legal point but also a historical claim about the black experience in the United States.[32] The predicate for Taney's opinion was his insistence that blacks in the revolutionary era "had for more than a century before been regarded as beings of an inferior order, and altogether unfit to associate with the white race, either in social or political relations."[33] Thus, in Taney's view, African-Americans were a people who lived in a state of absolute subjugation, without historical agency, who were "never thought of or spoken of except as property."[34] He was wrong in terms of legal precedent, of course, as was pointed out in the dissents of Justices Benjamin Curtis and John McLean, but he was also intellectually and factually wrong. African-Americans – whether free, slave, or fugitive – had always been historical actors in America, from the time of Crispus Attucks to the time of John Brown. They had never acceded to their presumed status as property.

African-Americans in the antebellum era engaged in three main forms of active resistance to what was then known as the Slave Power (meaning the governmental and economic forces beholden to slavery that dominated political life in both the North and South). Many thousands escaped the Southern land of bondage, either as fugitive slaves or free black emigrants. In the Northern states, black communities came to the assistance of runaways, sometimes surreptitiously spiriting them to Canada and sometimes wresting them quite openly from the grasp of slave hunters. And some brave souls, both free and enslaved, joined armed insurgencies.

John Anthony Copeland was one of the few people who took part in all three. At age nine, he fled North Carolina in a wagon train of fourteen adults and children who, although legally free, were still at the mercy of roving "pattyrollers" who might disregard their papers and reenslave them at any moment. As a young man in Oberlin, he was active in the defense of fugitives – once clubbing a deputy U.S. marshal to the ground – and he played a crucial part in the momentous Oberlin Rescue of 1858. Ultimately, he joined John Brown at Harper's Ferry, where he gave his life in the cause of freedom.

As with most of Brown's men, Copeland's story has seldom been told, and never at book length. Brown's towering persona has understandably tended to overshadow all of his followers, but there is still much to be said about Copeland and the other black men who participated in the historic insurrection. Although all of Brown's many biographers have mentioned Copeland, none have paid more than passing attention to his background in the abolitionist movement, and most have gotten at least some of the details wrong.[35]

In this book, we will see how and why John Copeland's actions intersected with John Brown's at a critical moment in history. Far from incidental to his involvement at Harper's Ferry, Copeland's experience in Oberlin – including his earlier confrontation with slave hunters – turns out to have played a key role in Brown's own planning for, and execution of, the historic raid. Along the way, we will address three long-standing, and interrelated, questions about the Harper's Ferry raid. Why did Brown suddenly decide to launch his attack on October 16, 1859, while many of his close associates were expecting it to come at least a week later? How is it that Brown's greatest success in attracting black troops had come in Oberlin? When did John Anthony Copeland first learn of Brown's plans, and why did he enlist in the insurrectionary army when so many others demurred?

Perhaps needless to say, there is no simple way to recapture the life of a man who was obscure until eight weeks before his death at the age of twenty-five. Fortunately, there are many newspaper articles, letters, reminiscences, memoirs, and court documents that address various aspects of Copeland's life, although nearly all of them were created following the events at Harper's Ferry. Beyond that, we must pursue a complex process of reconstruction, using a combination of primary sources, the documented experiences of Copeland's friends, family, comrades, and contemporaries, and, of course, the context of the times in which he lived. I have done my best to flag those instances in which I found it necessary to make deductions or suppositions about relationships or events, relying in such cases on reasoned conclusions from the known facts. When assessing a balance of probabilities, I have taken care to explain the various alternatives. Gap filling is sometimes unavoidable, even if seldom ideal, although to do otherwise would allow stories such as Copeland's to remain untold.

It was John Brown's destiny to have grandiose plans but few men. Throughout his long war on slavery – from the battlefields of Kansas, to his brief incursion into Missouri, to his historic invasion of Virginia – he never attracted more than three dozen soldiers to his side, and a good many of those were his own sons and sons-in-law. Although he intended to lead a servile rebellion that would shake the foundations of Southern slavery, Brown was especially unsuccessful at attracting black troops. His important Chatham conference, for example, was attended by thirty-four black men who endorsed Brown's plan to assemble a "provisional army" of liberation, but only one of them eventually came to Harper's Ferry. Notable African-American leaders – including Frederick Douglass and Harriet Tubman – refused to join Brown's ranks. When Brown finally launched his armed attack on the U.S. armory at Harper's Ferry, he had only five black men in his small army. One of them was John Anthony Copeland.

Historians have treated most of John Brown's foot soldiers as loyal spear carriers in the operatic sweep of the events at Harper's Ferry – quite literally with regard to the black men who were assigned the task of distributing pikes to liberated slaves. This book will bring one of the "colored heroes" directly to center stage.

ONE

THE FROZEN RIVER

JOHN PRICE WAS ONE OF THE FEW KENTUCKIANS who welcomed the exceptionally cold winter of 1855–56. As a slave, he was pleased that the frigid weather would slow local work to a standstill, requiring masters and servants alike to remain indoors as much as possible. But even more than that, John realized that the enforced idleness and isolation in the area – with the country roads deserted and even village shops empty of customers – would afford him the long-awaited chance to bolt for freedom. And so he did, eventually reaching the abolitionist stronghold of Oberlin, Ohio. In Oberlin, Price fatefully crossed paths with John Anthony Copeland. Together, they set in motion a series of events that would culminate at John Brown's 1859 raid on Harper's Ferry, Virginia. It is likely that John Price never learned of his unintended impact on Brown's plans. He only knew that he wanted to be free. As it turned out, that would be enough to shake the nation.

The winters in northern Kentucky tend to be mild, but temperatures fell below freezing in mid-December 1855 and remained locked in place – even on sunny days – for weeks without letup. The landscape soon came to resemble New England more than the border South, as snow covered the fields and streams and ponds iced over. Even the Ohio River froze solid, blocking the riparian commerce that was usually the region's main activity in the winter months. With farming at an end until spring, and trade at a near standstill, humble families simply huddled for warmth around their fireplaces and stoves as they waited out the unaccustomed cold. More prosperous families traveled by sleigh to visit relatives, where they, too, huddled for warmth around their more substantial hearths.

There was one group of Kentuckians, however, for whom the uncommon weather promised much more than days of dull seclusion. Kentucky was slave country, as it always had been since Daniel Boone led the first colonial settlers from Virginia through the Cumberland Gap. The

Commonwealth of Kentucky was admitted to the Union in 1792, with a constitution that prohibited the legislature from "pass[ing] laws for the emancipation of slaves without the consent of their owners."[1] (Vermont was admitted as a Free state in the same year, in what was the first of many post-Constitution political compromises between slavery and freedom.)

By the 1850s, nearly a quarter of Kentucky's population was enslaved, with the heaviest concentration in the center of the state. Although less numerous, the slaves in Kentucky's northern counties had a distinction of their own: they were the most likely to run away. The northern slaves were not necessarily more restless or rebellious than those in other parts of the commonwealth, but they lived within reach – sometimes even within sight – of Ohio, where the temptations of freedom were ever present. Slavery had been banned in Ohio since its earliest days as part of the Northwest Territory. Ohio, admitted to the Union in 1803, had a constitution that provided "There shall be neither slavery nor involuntary servitude in this State, otherwise than for the punishment of crimes."[2]

The Ohio River formed the political and geographic boundary between Kentucky and Ohio while at the same time enabling strong commercial and social ties between the two states. Ferries made regular crossings from towns large and small, and riverboats and barges – which used the waterway as the nation's principal east–west thoroughfare – made frequent stops on alternating sides of the river. Affluent Kentuckians shopped in Ohio cities and read Ohio newspapers, and the most ambitious conducted business in both states. Some laborers and artisans more or less commuted, especially those who followed seasonal work.

Slaves, too, often made the trip from Kentucky to Ohio and back again. Although Ohio was a Free state, its laws and customs, as elsewhere in the North, afforded slave owners the "right of transit," meaning that they could travel comfortably without risking the loss of their human property. The scope of transit was flexible, as the privilege of slaveholding was often extended to slave masters who, with their servants, had all but taken up residence in cities such as Cincinnati. As one Ohio observer complained, "a transient resident, during a sojourn [to Kentucky], purchases a servant, and on removing hither, brings him along."[3] Relying on their property rights, some Kentucky masters went so far as to hire out their slaves for work in Ohio, assuming the power to reclaim them once the jobs were finished. There was nothing surprising, for example, when, in 1841, several slave musicians traveled by steamer from Louisville to Cincinnati to play "at balls or public entertainments," with the expectation that they would return with their earnings to their Kentucky master at the end of the party season. (The slaves, however, had other ideas; they absconded to Canada and were never heard from again.)[4]

More common were the short outings when masters or mistresses would spend a day, and perhaps a night, visiting friends or shops in Cincinnati or other river cities, with their personal servants in tow. Even while attending to the needs of their owners, the slaves were inevitably exposed to the substantial free black communities of Ohio, including merchants, barbers, tradesmen, porters, coachmen, and teachers – all of whom enjoyed freedom of movement and the right to keep the fruits of their own labor. Thus, stories of free black life would filter back to the slave quarters of northern Kentucky, where they spread as rumors and myths.

To most slaves, the very idea of freedom must have seemed like an unachievable fantasy. To others, however, it was an inspiration. One such slave was John Price.

BORN IN THE MID-1830S, John Price was the "property" of the Bacon family of Mason County, whose substantial farm – worked by as many as twenty-five slaves – was about six miles south of the county seat of Maysville, which in turn lay sixty miles upriver from Cincinnati. The elder Bacon died in 1846, leaving most of his property, both human and agricultural, to his widow. Two slaves, however, were devised to his son John Parks Glenn Bacon – John Price and his cousin Dinah. The younger Bacon owned a much smaller farm, also in Mason County, operating it with the assistance of only his two inherited slaves and a hired hand.

Like many slave owners, Bacon considered himself a benevolent master. He treated his slaves indulgently, by his own lights, and he entrusted John Price with much of the daily management of his tidy farm. Of course, a slave owner's humanity extended only so far. Upon receiving his inheritance of human property, Bacon had not hesitated to take the adolescent John Price away from his mother and family. In all likelihood, it had not even occurred to Bacon that slaves would consider that a hardship, although in fact such separation was among the worst of their misfortunes. Another Kentucky slave explained that other "bitter and cruel punishments . . . were as nothing to the sufferings I experienced by being separated from my mother, brothers, and sisters. . . . In ten long, lonely years of childhood, I was only permitted to see them three times."[5] We do not know how often John Price was able to see his family. Perhaps he was allowed a visit at Christmastime, when work was slow and Kentucky slaves were routinely given five or six days of rest.[6]

Nor did Bacon hesitate to beat his slaves when they disobeyed him, although he considered such punishments to be acts of paternal benevolence. Other masters were far more cruel, often whipping defiant slaves and then washing their wounds in salted water until their mortified "flesh would crawl and creep, and quiver."[7] Bacon disdained such savagery, employing only a belt or switch to discipline his slaves, and then only when he truly believed they deserved it. With the moral blindness so typical in the South, Bacon therefore had no idea that John and Dinah were dissatisfied with their life of bondage. He routinely left them alone on the farm, confident that they had neither reason nor inclination to decamp.

No matter how benign the master, however, the slave system ultimately rested on physical coercion. Even if John and Dinah themselves had seldom been beaten, they were surely aware of the brutality visited on other slaves in the region. By the 1850s, Kentucky had become a significant source of slaves for relocation to the Deep South, and Maysville was a major transfer point. Riverboats would regularly stop at the Maysville wharf to unload chained slaves, who would then be sold to brokers from the deltas of Tennessee, Mississippi, and Louisiana. To men like Bacon, the auction houses were nothing more than successful businesses, but the cousins John and Dinah would have been acutely aware that every coffle represented human misery – physical abuse, sexual exploitation, families divided, children lost. Even in the best of circumstances, all slaves realized that their lives could never be secure. The master's death or indebtedness, or whim for that matter, could at any moment lead to a downriver sale into malevolent hands.

At some point, the cousins began to plot their flight. Perhaps one of them had been badly or unfairly punished, perhaps they became fascinated by the stories of free blacks in Ohio, or perhaps they saw one too many weeping figures headed for the Maysville auction platform. The slaves did not need a single reason to escape, but they did need a plan if they were going to succeed. The greatest challenge was the Ohio River, which united white people on both banks while creating a difficult barrier for fugitive blacks. No ferry or riverboat captain would take a black person to Ohio without convincing papers, and a stolen skiff or makeshift raft could too easily be spotted on the heavily traveled river. There were Quakers and other abolitionists in Ohio – especially in the riverfront town of Ripley – who would sometimes help runaways make the crossing, but it was nearly impossible for slaves like John and Dinah, isolated on a small farm, to make such contacts before they fled.[8]

For John and Dinah, opportunity came in the wake of an arctic wind, sweeping south over Lake Erie, across all of Ohio, and finally turning the Ohio River into a sheet of ice. Bacon's farm was less than a mile from the river, so the plotting slaves were well aware that their moment would soon be at hand. They would leave as soon as they could elude their master's attention.

Another stroke of luck arrived in early January 1856, when John Bacon announced that he was taking his family to visit his wife's parents, who lived about four miles distant. Given the cold weather and the lack of activity on his farm, Bacon was planning to stay with his in-laws for several days. He locked his house and instructed his slaves to remain in their cabins until he returned. That night, after the hired man had gone to sleep, John and Dinah stole a pair of horses from Bacon's barn. They rode to a nearby farm, where they joined up with a slave named Frank, who had been part of their conspiracy to flee to Ohio.

It was an act of extraordinary courage for the three slaves to make their midnight escape. Their entire lives had been circumscribed by slavery, binding them to their masters' service and depriving them of any experience with the outside world. None of them had ever ventured far from the farms of Macon County, and they had no idea what life might be like for a fugitive in Ohio. They did know that a successful escape would almost certainly mean lifelong separation from their friends and families, and that failure – nearly all runaways were eventually captured – would mean a whipping or worse. They could not have carried more than a few days' worth of provisions, and after that, even if they reached Ohio, they would have been reduced to begging or stealing in order to keep from starving. Did they think at all about the danger of life on the run, or did they just plunge onward with the reckless confidence of youth? Whatever their emotions, the hope for freedom overcame fear as they first stepped into the frigid night.

In less than an hour – with Dinah riding double behind one of the men – they were at the river bank, where they released their mounts. They were runaways but they were not thieves, and they expected the horses to return, as they did, to Bacon's farm. And besides, there was no telling whether the ice could bear the horses' weight or, indeed, whether the unaccustomed sight of three black people on horseback would draw undue attention in Ohio.

There, in the dark of that uncertain night, they clambered across the frozen river until they reached the outskirts of Ripley, where they somehow survived until daylight. Once in Ohio, they were able to make contact – perhaps through sheer luck – with a Quaker family, who provided them with food and blankets. The kindly Quakers sheltered the runaways for a week or so and then provided them with directions to the next safe house along the underground route toward Canada.

For reasons unknown, Dinah at some point parted ways with John and Frank. She vanished from the historical record – disappearing among the free blacks of Ohio, or perhaps finding her own way to Canada – leaving only her master's description of her as tall, slim, and unusually self-possessed for a slave. Her skin was "dark copper," she "walked straight," with her head high, and she was "very quick spoken."[9]

The two men continued heading north together, traveling mostly at night and ultimately covering over 250 miles, either on foot or hidden in the wagons of anti-slavery Ohioans. The trip was fraught with discomfort and peril. Food was hard to come by in the winter, and contacts with sympathizers were always risky. There were no maps to follow from safe house to safe house, and illiterate slaves – it was illegal in Kentucky to teach a slave to read – could not even benefit from written directions. They might on any evening stumble into the wrong barn or woodshed, alarming a sleeping family and prompting a visit from the local sheriff. Apparent friends might at any moment turn out to be bounty hunters. Kentucky fugitive Lewis Clarke described his own flight, along with his brother, fearing that "if we got upon the wrong road, it would be almost certain death for us, or something worse." Even on the right road, there were moments of utter despair:

> Travelling through the rain and mud . . . we suffered beyond all power of description. Sometimes we found ourselves just ready to stand, fast asleep, in the middle of the road. Our feet were blistered all over. . . . We were so weak, before night, that we several times fell upon our knees in the road. . . . Our limbs and joints were so stiff that, if we took a step to the right hand or left, it seemed as though it would shake us to pieces.[10]

Worst of all, Kentucky slave hunters ranged across Ohio, armed with the authority of the Fugitive Slave Act of 1850. They were known to waylay black people, with little regard for their status as slave or free, and to ransack the homes and search the carriages and wagons of any white farmers who drew their suspicion. Lewis Clarke described his own revulsion at the thought of slave hunters:

> They are the offscouring of all things; the refuse, the fag end, the ears and tails of slavery; the scales and fins of fish; the tooth and tongues of

> serpents. They are the very fool's cap of baboons, the echo of parrots, the wallet and satchel of polecats, the scum of stagnant pools, the exuvial, the worn-out skins of slaveholders . . . they are the meanest, and lowest, and worst of all creation. . . . They get up all sorts of pretences, false as their lying tongues can make them, and then whip the slaves and carry a gory lash to the master, for a piece of bread.[11]

Fortunately, John and Frank evaded capture, reaching Oberlin by early March. Fugitive slaves were welcomed in Oberlin, almost uniquely among all Northern communities, and John Price soon found a home and work. Abandoning plans to reach Canada, he no doubt hoped to spend the rest of his life in quiet anonymity. There is no reason to think that John Price had any familiarity with the sort of militant abolitionism practiced by John Brown, and he surely had no intention of playing a role in the drama that would lead to civil war. Brown, on the other hand, would eventually learn of Price's escape and attempt to use it to his own advantage.

TWO

A GOOD ABOLITION CONVENTION

LIKE JOHN PRICE, JOHN BROWN was freezing during the winter of 1855–56, which he spent huddled with family members on the plains of Kansas. He had arrived in October, just a few months ahead of the "bitterly cold and cutting winds" that would keep everyone "shivering over their little fires" until spring.[1] Five of Brown's sons had arrived earlier that year, among the thousands of Free-state emigrants who moved to Kansas in order to resist the imposition of slavery on the newly created territory. Once the brothers had established themselves in a settlement dubbed Brown's Station, not far from the town of Osawatomie, John Brown, Jr., wrote to his father about the virtues and challenges of life in Kansas, emphasizing both the beauty of the prairie and the depredations of the Missourians who were determined to spread slavery by violent means. John, Jr., was discouraged by the passivity of the other Free-staters, calling them "abject and cowardly."[2] He asked his father to provide the five brothers with arms, including two revolvers, a rifle, and a bayonet for each man. "Every day strengthens my belief that the sword . . . will soon be called upon to give its verdict," he wrote.[3]

In the words of biographer Oswald Garrison Villard, the appeal for arms was one that "Brown could not have resisted had he desired to."[4] In the company of another son and a son-in-law, he headed west with, as he put it, a wagon load of "Guns[,] Revolvers, Swords, Powder [and] Caps" that he obtained from supporters in Ohio.[5] The overland journey took the better part of two months, much of it covered on foot in order not to overtax his "nice young horse." In Kansas, he found his sons and their families sick with fever and nearly destitute, living in tents and makeshift cabins. Of the eight adult men in the settlement, only one was in good health. Brown had intended to be "active among the emigrants" as a militia organizer, but instead he was compelled to devote himself to the care of his family.[6]

Late autumn brought restored health to the Brown camp, and conflict to Kansas. The first significant engagement was the so-called Wakarusa War, when a small army of Missouri's pro-slavery "border ruffians" gathered on the banks of the Wakarusa River in preparation for a raid on Lawrence, the Free-state capital. Learning of the threat, Brown and his sons rushed to the defense of the town, where they set to work building fortifications. Meeting for the first time with Free-state leaders, Brown proposed a preemptive attack on the Missourians' encampment. He was appointed captain of the anti-slavery Liberty Guards – a militia rank he would carry for the rest of his life – and he set about assembling a company of about twenty militiamen, in addition to his sons. At the last moment, however, the Missourians relented – either from second thoughts or drunkenness – and the impending battle was never joined.

Early spring saw ever more skirmishes. Many of the Free-state leaders "proved tepid in their resistance to the slave power," but the Browns, including the women, became increasingly militant. Wealthy Brown, the wife of John, Jr., wrote to her family in New York that they had "Military Companies formed and are ready and determined to go forward and defend their rights even if it must be by bloodshed."[7]

Both sides in Kansas were indeed well armed, but the pro-slavery militias – such as the Kickapoo Rangers and the Westport Sharpshooters – were more brutal and for that reason often more effective. They had terrorized Free-state settlers for months in a campaign that culminated with the sack of Lawrence on May 21, 1856. Missouri Senator David Atchison, a leader of the pro-slavery cause, had crowed that his men would soon drive all of the Free-staters out of Kansas. "We have entered that damn town, and taught the damned abolitionists a Southern lesson that they will remember until the day they die.... Kansas shall be ours."[8]

It was widely believed in the South, and feared in the North, that Free-staters could not match Slave-staters in either audacity or violence. Then, almost overnight, John Brown changed the terms of the engagement. His willingness to make "bloody reprisals" took the Missourians by surprise, and soon his "fame was established among the border ruffians" as a man who would fight and defeat them on even terms. In short, Brown introduced "Southern tactics to the Northern side."[9]

Not all of Brown's efforts in Kansas were noble. His determination to "strike fear in the hearts of the proslavery people" at one point led to carnage as frightful as anything ever perpetrated by the Kickapoo Rangers.[10] Upon hearing the news of the sack of Lawrence, Brown declared that "something is going to be done now" and vowed to take revenge.[11] On the night of May 24–25, 1856, Brown and seven others, including four of his sons, abducted and killed five pro-slavery settlers who lived along Pottawatomie Creek, literally hacking them to pieces with broadswords.[12] Appalling as it was, the "Pottawatomie Massacre" had the desired effect, terrifying the supporters of slavery while bringing Brown to the very center of the battle for control of Kansas.[13] Most abolitionist leaders in Kansas distanced themselves from Brown's brutality, but they still expressed relief that he had "given an immediate check to the armed aggression of the Missourians."[14]

Brown remained in Kansas through the summer, encouraging and participating in further raids against pro-slavery settlers. There were no further massacres, but Brown authorized his troops to execute captured enemies following trial (although no such trials were held and no one was ever executed), and to freely appropriate enemy property (which did lead to the plundering of many settlers' cabins and farms). The war came to a head on August 30, when an army of over 300 Missourians advanced on the Free-state town of Osawatomie, not far from Brown's Station, intending to destroy it en route to Topeka and Lawrence.

Realizing that they were vastly outnumbered, most of the settlers fled to safety, but Brown chose to stay and fight. He gathered a force of about thirty-eight men – many fewer than the border ruffians but in fact the largest contingent that Brown would ever lead – and shrewdly deployed them in the dense brush along the banks of the Marais des Cygnes River. As the Missourians marched along the road to Osawatomie, Brown commanded his men to open fire, shredding the ranks of the pro-slavery force. The Missourians were eventually able to regroup, and they ultimately succeeded in razing the abandoned town, but not before Brown's attack took a heavy toll. As many as thirty Missourians were killed and another forty wounded in the fighting, amounting to the heaviest single-battle losses in the entire Kansas war. At least six Free-staters were also killed, including Brown's son Frederick, who was shot hors de combat before the battle had even begun.

Remarkably, the fighting in Kansas ended, at least for the time being, within weeks of the Battle of Osawatomie. A new territorial governor – the deeply principled John Geary – arrived in mid-September, and he quickly ordered the disbandment of the pro-slavery militias. Against all apparent odds, the Missourians complied, even as their army was poised again on the outskirts of Lawrence. John Brown was quick to take credit for the demobilization of the enemy, but in fact their commanders were influenced at least as much by concern over the approaching presidential election. Republican John Fremont, representing his party in its first national election, presented a serious challenge to Democrat James Buchanan, and no Missourian wanted to risk tarnishing the image of the pro-slavery candidate.

With no one left to fight, John Brown left Kansas in late September, ultimately heading for the East Coast. James Fairchild and John Anthony Copeland had surely by then read of Brown's exploits, no doubt with approval and perhaps even with pride. There were hundreds of Oberliners among the Free-state settlers, and "people in Oberlin followed the unfolding events in Kansas with a watchful eye" as they were regularly reported in the *Oberlin Evangelist*.[15] John Brown's exploits were of particular interest, given his deep connections to Oberlin. His father, Owen, had been a trustee of the college in its early years, and he had cast one of the votes in favor of admitting students "irrespective of color."[16] Brown's sister and brother-in-law, both Oberlin graduates, had themselves emigrated to Kansas, and like many other settlers, they remained in constant contact with friends and family in the East. As an illiterate fugitive, John Price would not have known of Brown's Ohio connections, if he was aware of him at all. Still, he might well have heard about the fighting in Kansas, perhaps at a church service or from the underground communications network among runaway slaves.

Brown reached Massachusetts in early January. His stalwart reputation among the literati had preceded him, and he was greeted warmly in the parlors of Boston and Cambridge. Brown spent the rest of the winter raising funds among wealthy Easterners, traveling back and forth from Boston to New York. As a hero fresh from the Kansas battlefields, he was well situated to make his pitch. He was, after all, the commander who had defeated an army of Missourians and who had defended the village of Osawatomie when others counseled retreat.

Brown's ostensible objective was to supply arms to the Free-state settlers in Kansas, a cause that had unquestioned support among the transcendentalists of New England, including most of the otherwise "nonresistant" followers of William Lloyd Garrison. As to Potawatomie, the less said the better. Brown had disingenuously denied his involvement, and his enthusiasts were disinclined to interrogate him closely. That was just as well, because Brown was even less inclined to provide forthright answers. Asked whether he intended to attack the Slave states, Brown replied cryptically, "You know what I have done in Kansas. . . . I have no other purpose than to serve the cause of liberty."[17] In fact, Brown did have a secret purpose in mind that would take him far from Kansas. Although he said nothing of it to his new supporters, Brown had resolved to give the Southerners "something else to do than to extend slave territory."

"I will carry the war to Africa," Brown had vowed. He was already planning to invade the South.[18]

AN INVASION WOULD REQUIRE AN ARMY, and John Brown intended to enlist both black and white troops. There were many abolitionists in the antebellum North but few true egalitarians. John Brown, however, was as committed to racial equality as he was to emancipation. He envisioned a world free of color lines, and he attempted to live his life in keeping with that principle. Even other abolitionists were surprised – and in many cases shocked – at Brown's respectful treatment of his black friends. Author and anti-slavery lawyer Richard Henry Dana once enjoyed a meal at Brown's home, and he afterward expressed astonishment that his host had seated black and white guests at the same table while calling "the negroes by their surnames, with the prefixes of Mr. and Mrs." The black guests appeared to be runaway slaves, who evidently "had not been treated or spoken to" so politely before, as they had "all the awkwardness of field hands on a plantation." Dana was therefore further taken aback when Brown formally "introduced us to them in due form, 'Mr. Dana, Mr. Jefferson.'"[19]

Brown also believed in arming African-Americans for liberation and self-defense. In an era when "servile rebellion" was a nightmarish threat in the South and nonresistance was the dominant tenet of abolitionism, no position was more provocative than a demand to put weapons in the hands of black people. Brown therefore stood out as one of the few white men who actively encouraged a violent struggle against slavery. As early as 1851, he had organized the United States League of Gileadites in Springfield, Massachusetts, a band of forty-four black men, including fugitives, whom Brown convened to resist the Fugitive Slave Act of 1850. Brown named his recruits for the biblical Mt. Gilead, the site where Gideon was directed by God to raise an army in defense of Israel. Drawing on that story, he exhorted his Gileadites to defend their rights "to the last extremity" and to "hold on to your weapons, and never be persuaded to leave them, part with them, or have them far away from you." When confronting a slave hunter, the Gileadites were to strike the first blow and then "do not do your work by halves; but make clean work with your enemies."[20] In the words of biographer David Reynolds, that was the first time in American history that a white person openly promoted "preemptive armed warfare to be waged by blacks against proslavery forces."[21]

Thus, from the moment he conceived of the Harper's Ferry campaign, Brown was determined to recruit black soldiers to his cause, and not only as a matter of egalitarian principle. Brown hoped that hundreds, or even thousands, of slaves would join his uprising, and he pragmatically believed that highly visible black combatants – especially in leadership positions – would help draw those slaves to his side. And perhaps even more importantly, Brown recognized that the specter of black fighting men would terrify Southerners far beyond his field of operations, thus dramatically furthering his goal of destabilizing the entire slave system.[22]

Beginning in early 1857, Brown worked intently on his plan to invade Virginia, including the recruitment of black soldiers. His efforts would take him from the East Coast to Kansas and back again, to Canada, into Missouri, across the Midwest, and then through Ohio and Pennsylvania, with multiple trips to New England and New York. He was eventually able to assemble a small corps of twenty-one men at a Maryland farmhouse in the environs of Harper's Ferry, but his search for black comrades would yield painfully few results until John Anthony Copeland arrived on the very eve of the insurrection.

In autumn 1857, for example, Brown established camp near Tabor, Iowa, where he gathered ten veterans of the Kansas wars – only one of whom was black – promising to train them for further operations in Kansas and Missouri. The men nearly rebelled when Brown disclosed that he actually intended to invade Virginia. They had agreed to fight against the extension of slavery into Kansas but not to attack the peculiar institution in one of its home states. Nonetheless, Brown ultimately persuaded them to stay together over the winter while he returned to the East for yet more fund-raising. Six of the ten would eventually join Brown at Harper's Ferry, but the sole African-American – Richard Richardson, a fugitive slave from Missouri – would not be among them.

The following spring found Brown in Chatham, Canada West (today's Ontario), where he convened what he called "a good Abolition convention." It was in Chatham that Brown fully revealed his proposal to raise an army – in large part a black army – that would establish a liberated zone in the mountains of Virginia. To that end, Brown had drafted a "provisional constitution" to govern the enclave, which he presented to the conference for approval.

Brown had invited many prominent abolitionists to the Chatham conference, including Harriet Tubman and Frederick Douglass, who did not attend. Still, the assembled delegates included thirty-four black men and only twelve whites, all of whom voted to approve Brown's provisional constitution and, implicitly, his plan to create a self-governing, anti-slavery redoubt in the South. Brown was heartened by the militant unanimity, which gave him "the impression that the Negroes of Canada would assist him en masse upon call"[23] while providing "many black recruits for his invading army."[24] One of the Chatham delegates was a black Oberlin graduate named James Monroe "Gunsmith" Jones, who had been a childhood friend of John Anthony Copeland's. Jones worked on some of the weapons that would be used at Harper's Ferry, and Brown believed that the gunsmith would also join the coming insurrection, perhaps as armorer-in-chief. To Brown's disappointment, Jones ultimately demurred, but his relationship to Copeland may well have played a key role – more important than mere rifles – in gathering troops for the insurrection.

As it turned out, however, the convention vote would be the high-water mark in Brown's efforts to enroll black soldiers. Of the thirty-four black signatories at Chatham, only one man – Osborne Perry Anderson – would actually arrive to fight at Harper's Ferry.

Brown left Chatham in May 1858, believing that he would soon lead an insurrection in Virginia. As it happened, his plans were delayed for over a year while he dealt with defections, logistical snags, funding shortfalls, and one outright betrayal. (He also conducted a practice run in Missouri, where he successfully freed a dozen slaves, whom he then escorted to Canada.) During that entire time, Brown continued to importune African-Americans – both prominent and obscure – to join his command. Harriet Tubman declined, and Frederick Douglass famously refused. Brown might well have approached John Price if he had known of the humble fugitive's existence. By the time Brown departed Chatham, Price had been living quietly in Oberlin for over two years. Having turned down funds to finance a permanent escape to Canada, he was content with his life and had no apparent intention ever to attract the attention of outsiders, abolitionist or otherwise.[25] That was not to be. Within months, Price was going to play an unknowing role in pushing Brown's plans forward.

It was only natural that John Brown would eventually turn to Oberlin, Ohio, as the source for the black troops he so desperately wanted to enroll.

THREE

THE COLONY AND THE COLLEGE

THE OBERLIN COLONY WAS ESTABLISHED IN 1833 as part of the "grand scheme" of John Jay Shipherd, a young Presbyterian minister in Elyria, Ohio. Similar to other religious idealists in the early nineteenth century, Shipherd aspired to create a utopian community of "selected, consecrated souls, founded in the virgin forest far from the taint of established and sin-infected towns." The settlement, in his vision, would include a school for the education of the "hopefully pious," who, once educated, would serve as missionaries and educators throughout the western states.[1] Shipherd shared his ideas with a childhood friend named Philo Penfield Stewart, a former missionary to the Cherokees, and the two men set about locating suitable land in the northern Ohio district known as the Western Reserve.

Providence, as they put it, brought them to a remote location in Lorain County's Russia Township, which they determined to be an "eligible spot for a colony and school."[2] Most important was the region's isolation. It was separated by nine miles of "impassible roads" from Elyria, the county seat, and the growing city of Cleveland was a nearly insurmountable forty miles distant across a sea "of almost bottomless mud." Any place closer to civilization would have risked marring their "great educational work" by attracting "manufacturers and large establishments ... with many workmen" and the accompanying "saloons and other nuisances."[3] Shipherd and Stewart convinced the owners of the property – some 7000 acres – to donate a portion of the land and sell them the rest. Thus was born Oberlin, which they named after the German pastor John Frederic Oberlin, whose "benevolent social work and interest in Sabbath Schools" were thought to set a fine example for the new colony.[4]

The first Oberlin settlers arrived from the East in spring 1833, eager to clear the land – it would have to be "hacked out of a dense, unbroken wilderness" – and begin a new life of devotion, temperance, and prayer.[5]

By June, the first streets had been laid out, lined by the first ten homes. Construction continued throughout the summer and fall – a church, a school, log cabins, and even frame houses – and by December a true town had taken shape. December also saw the opening of the Oberlin Collegiate Institute, as it was then called, with forty-four students, including James Fairchild, who lived and studied in the newly built and aptly named Preparatory Hall. In a sharp break with tradition, the college was committed to "the opening of higher education to women," although under the aegis of a separate "female department."[6] The students and the settlers of both genders were all required to sign the Oberlin Covenant, committing them "to strive to maintain deep-toned and elevated personal piety." They promised to abstain from liquor (and even "tea and coffee, as far as practicable"), to eat only plain and wholesome foods, to dress modestly, to forsake "all the world's expensive and unwholesome fashions of dress, particularly tight dressing and ornamental attire," and to renounce all bad habits.[7]

As aspirational is it was, the Oberlin Covenant said nothing about opposition to slavery except, as James Fairchild later explained, to the extent that "such an element [was] necessarily implied in the very idea of a Christian colony and school in a land where Slavery exists." In fact, any such anti-slavery sentiment was not implied very strongly, if at all. There was agreement among the founding settlers that slavery was evil and a curse, but they also believed that there was no practical solution to the problem apart from "transporting to Africa a few thousands of freed colored people." It would prove embarrassing in later years, but it could not be denied that the early residents of Oberlin generally indulged "the general prejudice of the white race against the colored." But even then, there were three or four students who openly advocated immediate emancipation, and a few others who had begun to question the existence of slavery itself. The latter group included Shipherd, who considered himself a moderate abolitionist. Still, at Oberlin's first commencement, in 1834, not one speaker said a single word about slavery. That would turn out to be "a remarkable circumstance for an Oberlin Commencement," as Fairchild later observed.[8]

Change came quickly, and from an unexpected quarter. While the Oberliners were carefully avoiding the subject of slavery, students at Lane Seminary in Cincinnati were confronting the issue head on. Under the leadership of young Theodore Dwight Weld, who later became a leading abolitionist, a group of students at the seminary began a series of discussions of slavery in spring 1834.[9] Meeting in the college chapel, they debated the principles of William Lloyd Garrison, who only a few years earlier had initiated the movement for immediate abolition. Although Garrison advocated nonviolence – or nonresistance, as he put it – his call for "unconditional emancipation" was nonetheless extremely controversial, even among opponents of slavery. No doubt owing to Weld's extraordinary eloquence and powers of persuasion, most of the Lane students, including some from the South, eventually embraced abolitionist views, even at the predictable cost of alienating family and friends. The students formed an anti-slavery society devoted to "immediate emancipation [although] not by instigating the slaves to rebellion."

Modest as it was, that declaration was too much for the pro-slavery civic leaders of Cincinnati, ever alert to anything that might damage their commercial relations with slaveholding Kentucky and Virginia. Weld and his colleagues were accused of attempting "to organize a wide-spread revolution; to alter the constitution of their country; to upset the internal policy of a dozen independent states; and to elevate a whole race of human beings in the scale of moral dignity."[10] The latter was the most serious charge, and it could not be ignored by the trustees of the seminary, most of whom were themselves "men of commerce [who] understood better the pork market than the management" of a theological institution.[11]

All might have ended well if the seminary's president, Reverend Lyman Beecher, had been in constant residence. Beecher himself was a critic of slavery – he was the father of Harriet Beecher Stowe and Henry Ward Beecher – and a leader of the Second Great Awakening.[12] He had initially granted Weld and his confreres permission to meet in the college chapel, although he considered the resulting anti-slavery resolution unnecessarily provocative. Nonetheless, he was the person best positioned to prevent a clash between the students and the outraged businessmen.

Fatefully, however, Beecher departed Cincinnati for the summer, undertaking a tour of pulpits in the East.[13] With Beecher absent – along with almost the entire faculty – the Lane trustees adopted a resolution banning the discussion of slavery, even in private, and firing Professor John Morgan, who had been the students' strongest supporter. In response, a majority of the students withdrew from the seminary and established their own school a short distance away. Beecher returned and attempted to undo the damage, but it was too late. The aggrieved students – by then known as the Lane Rebels – refused to reenroll.[14]

Later that year, Shipherd found himself in Cincinnati on a fundraising tour. Despite its promising start, Oberlin was sinking in debt, without a sitting president and with only a few teachers. Fortunately,

Shipherd encountered Reverend Asa Mahan of Cincinnati's Sixth Presbyterian Church. Mahan had been a trustee of the Lane Seminary, but he resigned in protest over the decision to prohibit the discussion of slavery. The two men discovered that they had much in common. Mahan was the spiritual advisor to a group of students who lacked a true school; Shipherd ran a school in need of students, faculty, and even a president. Even better, Mahan had a potential benefactor in the person of Arthur Tappan, a wealthy silk merchant and devoted abolitionist in New York.

A tentative deal was quickly struck, under which Oberlin would establish a Theological Department, to be populated by the seceding scholars from Lane. It was still necessary, however, to convince the students to leave the familiar comforts of Cincinnati for the "inaccessible and forbidding" wilderness of Oberlin.[15] That would require a moral commitment to support their newly organized Anti-Slavery Society. They would not, as one Rebel put it, "swerve one hair from the great principles which have been the basis of all our operations in regard to Slavery."[16]

The full terms of the arrangement were therefore proposed with the Lane Rebels in mind. Asa Mahan would be appointed president of Oberlin, the fired Professor Morgan would be hired to teach mathematics, and freedom of speech would be guaranteed "on all issues of reform." In the final provision of the Lane compact, Mahan and Morgan demanded a resolution "that students shall be received into this Institution *irrespective of color*."[17]

Shipherd strongly endorsed the admission of black students, believing that it was "right in principle, and God will bless us in doing right." He suspected, however, that mere principle might not be enough to convince the trustees to take such a radical step. He therefore argued to the trustees, with Tappan in mind, that the resolution would gain for Oberlin "the confidence of benevolent and able men, who probably will furnish us some thousands." And if that were not enough, he hinted at his own resignation: "If our board would violate right so as to reject youth of talent and piety, because they were *black*, I should have *no heart* to labor for the upbuilding of our Seminary, believing that the curse of God would come upon us, as it has upon Lane Seminary."[18]

To Shipherd's surprise, the promise of money and threat of damnation were at first insufficient to persuade Oberlin's constituents to "receive black men into their idealistic haven."[19] The students voted against the resolution by a margin of 32–26, and the trustees – while unanimously voting to hire Mahan and Morgan – pointedly tabled the admissions resolution on the shamelessly spurious ground that they needed "other and more definitive information" about how such things were handled at other colleges.[20] Morally undeterred and fiscally needy, Shipherd insisted that the resolution come up again, calling a meeting at his own home in early February 1835. As the trustees debated, Shipherd's wife convened a parallel meeting of her lady friends, who prayed through the day for a favorable decision.

A vote was finally taken, but the trustees were evenly divided. The chairman of the board, Reverend John Keep, then cast the determinative ballot in favor of admitting black students. As Fairchild later put it, "the invitation and welcome to the colored man [was] decisive and unequivocal."[21] Dissention continued, however, as some trustees and students feared the possibility of "amalgamation" – meaning racial intermarriage – and thus could not quickly reconcile themselves to the prospect of black students. Nonetheless, the die was cast. From that day forward, Oberlin was officially committed not only to the education of African-Americans but also to the eradication of slavery.

The news would in time reach North Carolina, where John Anthony Copeland was not yet one year old.

FOUR

"A MOST WELL DISPOSED BOY"

JOHN A. COPELAND, SR., was born into slavery near Raleigh, North Carolina, in 1808, the son of a white man who was also his owner. Nothing is known of Copeland's mother other than that she was a slave whose pregnancy was likely the consequence of implicit coercion if not outright brutality. Little more is known about the elder Copeland's interactions with his father, although the relationship was common knowledge in their community. There must have been at least some bond between them, because Copeland was emancipated in his master's will, which set him free at the age of seven or eight. The slave owner left his mulatto son no additional funds or property, however, so the young boy was placed in the care of a prominent neighbor named Gavin Hogg, who owned a large home in Raleigh and extensive lands in Bertie County, as well as at least seventeen slaves.[1] As a free Negro, John was not allowed to attend school, so Hogg apprenticed him to a carpenter. The young man became adept at his trade – earning a reputation as a "most well disposed boy" – and he attracted regular work from both blacks and whites.[2]

On August 15, 1831, Copeland married Delilah Evans, a "most respectable woman of color" who had been born in Hillsborough, North Carolina, in 1809.[3] Delilah was from a well-established family of unusually mixed background, none of whom had ever been slaves. She and her two younger brothers, Wilson and Henry, were extremely light skinned – so much so that photographs of Wilson, in later years, were often mistaken for Henry Wadsworth Longfellow – and they claimed descent from General Nathanael Greene of Revolutionary War fame.[4]

Delilah was employed as a domestic for members of the wealthy Devereux family – related by marriage to the Hoggs – who considered themselves enlightened on race issues. They set aside funds for "Negro education" and supported a Presbyterian mission in Ceylon, but that did not prevent them from exploiting the many slaves on their properties. Their house servants enjoyed some measure of stability – with promises that they would not be sold out of state – but the Devereux field slaves could count on remaining with their families only until they "secured the crop on the ground" at the end of each growing season. Once the harvest was in, they might be auctioned or traded at will.[5]

The Devereuxes prized Delilah for her fair complexion and her evident piety, and especially for her free status, which made it "convenient to take her to the New England states as a nurse for [their] children." The Devereuxes evidently believed that a free woman would have little incentive to run away in the North, or perhaps would be less likely to attract the meddlesome attention of Boston's abolitionists. Delilah always returned willingly to North Carolina, although her exposure to life in New England may have had an impact on her family's later decision to abandon the South. In keeping with the treatment of free Negro women, Delilah received no regular pay during her years of service with the Devereuxes. As was common in North Carolina, she was expected to work "for allotments of food and clothing" and occasional small amounts of cash while her wages "accumulated" in the hands of her employers to be disbursed as they saw fit.[6]

Like all "masterless blacks," John and Delilah were required to accept the supervision of white guardians, who assumed considerable control over the lives of their wards.[7] It may well be that the couple was introduced, and perhaps affianced by arrangement, in the course of their work for the interrelated Hogg and Devereux families. In any case, their marriage met with "the approbation of those to whom the parties looked up to for protection," meaning their white patrons, whose permission was necessary for the wedding to proceed.[8] The Devereuxes further signaled their approval by paying Delilah her long-withheld wages. The couple set up a household, and John continued to work as a carpenter. His skills were much in demand during Raleigh's expansion in the 1830s, and he worked for several years on the reconstruction of the statehouse following a devastating fire in 1833.[9]

John Anthony Copeland, Jr., was born in Raleigh on August 15, 1834, exactly three years to the day after his parents' wedding.[10] Another son, Henry, was born to the Copelands in 1840. Their home was a happy one – John and Delilah would remain married for over fifty years – but it was not free from stress.

Life was always precarious for free African-Americans in the South. They were subject to a constantly shifting array of legal restrictions, economic disadvantages, and social disabilities that came to be known collectively as the "Free Negro Codes." Typical provisions included the prohibition of gun ownership, residency restrictions, registration requirements, curfews, enslavement for petty debts, and limitations on the practice of trades and occupations.[11] Laws against "seditious publication" were applied with special force to free blacks, and a free Negro who was caught teaching reading to slaves would be "fined, imprisoned, or whipped at the discretion of the court."[12] Even a period of unemployment could lead to trouble. A violation of the law against "idleness" could result in imprisonment or indenture "for a term of service and labor."[13] Industrious labor brought its own difficulties. The ban on providing testimony against white persons made it nearly impossible for a black artisan to collect legitimate debts from defaulting white customers.

North Carolina had once been liberal in its treatment of free Negroes – even extending the franchise to free men of color – but the situation changed dramatically in the early 1830s. Like every other Southern state, North Carolina fell into a panic over Nat Turner's 1831 rebellion in Southampton County, Virginia. Although no free Negroes had been implicated in the violence that took the lives of about fifty white people and one hundred or more blacks, terror-stricken Southerners were in no mood to draw fine distinctions among people of color.[14] Many new laws were quickly passed that led "to the further circumscription of free Negroes," including limitations on church services, funerals, and even visits between families and friends.[15] In that bitter spirit, North Carolina adopted a new state constitution in 1835 that further diminished the legal autonomy of emancipated African-Americans, eliminating the right to vote and throwing them deeply into a condition that, if not chattel bondage, was in no sense fully free.[16] As John and Delilah Copeland understood, they were not even permitted to marry without the consent of their white sponsors. One British visitor observed acidly that the members of such a "poor degraded class" were virtually "still slaves."[17] Or, as it was put by historian Ira Berlin, they were "slaves without masters."[18]

Legal disabilities were vexing to families such as the Copelands, but they could be endured. Far more worrisome was the constant threat to freedom itself. In the words of the great historian John Hope Franklin, "it was by no means enough to have been manumitted, or even to have been born free." Rather, "the free person of color had to maintain a strict vigil over his status lest it be reduced to that of a slave."[19] Freedom might be questioned at any moment, with a disastrous result. The necessary papers might have been lost, stolen, or destroyed, and a deed of emancipation could be challenged even decades after it had been granted.

There was a legal presumption that every black person was a slave, and the burden of proving the right to freedom fell on individuals whose total "ignorance of procedures" often made it impossible to assert their rights.[20]

The greatest danger of all, however, was vulnerability to abduction. Daring to venture even a few miles from home might raise the suspicion that one was a fugitive, a presumption that "was all but conclusive in some quarters." And, of course, not every slave patroller – or "pattyroller," as they were called in North Carolina – was scrupulous about claiming ownership of human property.[21] Thus, the risk of being sold back into slavery "hung over the heads of adults and children alike."[22] It was no small matter that the Copelands were able to call on the protection of the Hoggs and Devereuxes, but how long would it last and how far could it extend? Eventually, the uncertainty became more than they could bear.

SOMETIME AFTER THE BIRTH OF THEIR SECOND CHILD, the Copelands resolved to leave North Carolina in order to "escape the persecution" they experienced as free blacks.[23] They may have been impelled by a frightening incident, perhaps a near kidnapping or some other sort of abuse. They certainly wanted to provide a good education for their children, which was nearly impossible in the South.[24] John Anthony, who turned nine that year, was prohibited from attending the "common schools" of North Carolina, and a school for free black children had been repeatedly destroyed by white vigilantes. Then again, the Copelands might simply have been worn down by years of hardship and adversity. No record remains of their specific motivation or reasoning, but it is clear that their overriding purpose was to flee the South rather than attraction to a particular location in the North. Although they ended up in Oberlin, they had no ultimate destination firmly in mind when they departed Raleigh.

Whatever the cause or provocation, the Copelands' decision to abandon their home could not have been made lightly. Under the law of North Carolina, their departure would have to be permanent. A statute passed in the wake of the 1835 state constitution provided

> That if any time hereafter any free negro or person of color, who may be a resident of this State, shall migrate from this State . . . and shall be absent for the space of ninety days or more, it shall not be lawful for such free negro or free person of color to return to this state.[25]

Complementing the state law was a local ordinance in Raleigh requiring a constable "to go over the whole city and suburbs at least two Sundays in every month and search every suspect house and alley to prevent free Negroes from moving into town" or returning from the North.[26] Those caught were subject to a $500 fine, to be worked off as an indentured servant, and multiple fines could be imposed repeatedly until the "migrant" again departed the state.[27]

John, Sr., was an orphan with no acknowledged blood relatives. It is quite possible that he had white half-siblings by his owner-father – and he may or may not have harbored some residual affection for the Hoggs, who had raised him – but there appear to have been no significant family ties holding him in Raleigh. Delilah, on the other hand, was part of a large extended family, and it must have grieved her sorely to think that she might never again see her elderly mother or her brothers and cousins. Even correspondence would be difficult. Delilah and her mother were illiterate. The younger Evans boys may have been able to read and write – they were certainly literate by the mid-1850s – but all letters to and from free African-Americans were strictly monitored by the local post office.[28] Any hint of an anti-slavery sentiment would lead to suppression of the mail, and perhaps a visit from the sheriff.

The Copelands' decision was only the first step in a difficult journey. Free African-Americans in North Carolina could not even move from county to county without permission, and it required the approval of their white patrons for authorization to leave the state. The departure of free Negroes, however, was controversial among the Southern gentry. Some believed that free blacks should be encouraged or compelled to emigrate because their very existence in the state "demonstrated to slaves that blacks could be free."[29] Thus, statutes requiring emigration were enacted at various times, and in varying severity, in the slaveholding states.[30] Others, however, considered it "impolitic . . . to allow free negroes to go north from slave states," for fear that they would afterward conspire to assist fugitives.[31] In one more instance of their awkward and demeaning status, free blacks were at once encouraged to depart and prevented from leaving at will.

The Copelands were able to secure the consent of the Devereuxes, although it came with a warning that "abolitionists in the North were accustomed to capturing colored men and selling them into slavery."[32] Such myths were frequently spread as a means of demoralizing the black population and, in the hopes of the slaveholders, persuading free blacks to avoid associating with abolitionists.[33] The Copelands, while in Raleigh, had never been in contact with the anti-slavery movement – which would have been life threatening if it had not been impossible – and the story of treacherous abolitionists did cause them at least momentary hesitation.

The real threat of reenslavement, of course, came not from Northern abolitionists but rather from the slave patrols they would encounter as they traveled through the South. The Copelands were secure only as long as they remained in the environs of Raleigh, where they were well known to be free and where they enjoyed the protection of important white families. Their route north, however, would take them through distant parts of North Carolina and at least two others Slave states where itinerant blacks were always under suspicion as runaways.[34] The Copelands could be called on to prove their free status at any moment, with disastrous consequences if they failed. That is just what had happened to a black North Carolinian named Joshua Lee, whose freedom had been challenged in Beaufort County. Although Lee was eventually able to prove that he was not a slave, he spent twelve months in jail awaiting a decision, and even then he was released only upon posting a bond for good behavior.[35]

DOCUMENTATION WAS A CONSTANT PROBLEM for all free African-Americans in the antebellum South, including the Copelands. John, Sr., would have had a deed of manumission, as provided in his father's will, but Delilah and the two children had never been slaves and would therefore have lacked emancipation papers. Delilah may have had registration papers, which were issued to free Negroes subject to frequent renewal, but such documents were often questioned by suspicious whites as either inadequate or out-of-date. In Raleigh, of course, the Copelands were known to be free, but that would have done them little good in Virginia or Kentucky. The solution was to obtain a declaration of their status, either from a court or another government official, which again required the endorsement of white patrons.

Delilah obtained a glowing letter from Francis Devereaux, who commended her as an "intelligent, discreet, and sober-minded" woman who had "uniformly conducted herself with the utmost propriety." John's reference was if anything even more effusive, praising his skill as a carpenter and his reputation as "a fair, honest, and industrious character in this community." It would not do, of course, for John to be seen as an upstart or complainer, much less to acknowledge that free blacks had any cause to object to their treatment in North Carolina. Thus, John's sponsors noted that his reason for moving was attributable solely to "the recent hard times" in Raleigh, adding that he had "wisely, in our opinion [decided to] look for a new home in a more plenteous and populous country." John had no doubt provided the unthreatening explanation himself, not wanting to be thought of as a malcontent. Whatever resentments he harbored – from the destruction of the colored school to the sexual exploitation of his own mother – had to remain unspoken. The approach worked, as the letter of endorsement was signed by twenty-seven white citizens, most of them slaveholders, including the postmaster, sheriff, and secretary of state, all of whom noted their approval of John's "quiet, humble, and Christian-like manner."[36]

Even the most extraordinary letters of transit, however, provided no defense to kidnappers, who might waylay the travelers at any time.[37] Against that danger, the only safety was in numbers. To that end, the Copelands wisely arranged to travel in a caravan, joining forces with John Lane and Allen and Temperance Jones. A blacksmith by trade, Lane was an unmarried man of whom little more is known. The Joneses, however, made a great impact on the lives of the Copeland family.[38]

Allen Jones was born a slave of the Jeffreys family in 1794. Trained as a blacksmith, he shod horses as extra work in the evenings and on Sundays, including "all the stage-horses on the routes" in and out of Raleigh.[39] Jones was allowed – as was a common incentive – to keep a portion of the money he earned. He labored diligently until he had accumulated the $685 needed to purchase his freedom. He was, however, swindled by his owner, who, upon receiving the payment, claimed that the slave "could not possibly have earned that much unless he did it on his master's time," meaning that the money was not rightfully Jones's.[40] "You are my nigger yet," said Jeffreys, "and I have the money too." Undeterred, Jones kept working and, with the help of white friends, he again saved enough money to buy his own freedom, which his master could not deny a second time. Continuing to work, and now able to keep all of his earnings, Jones managed by late 1829 to gather the small fortune – perhaps as much as $3000 – necessary to free his wife and three children.[41]

This time, however, Jones took no chances on the slave owner's honesty. Rather than simply handing over the cash in exchange for a promise of manumission, he insisted on purchasing his wife and children, who therefore became his own slaves.[42] With the assistance of several well-connected lawyers, Jones then petitioned the county court for an order of emancipation. The court papers recited his ownership of "several negro slaves to wit: Tempe, Munro, Betheny, and Burnham," explaining that they were his wife and children, and vouching for Tempe's "upright character." The petition added that Tempe's service toward her former owner had been "dutiful, faithful, and highly meritorious."

Obsequiousness was not in Jones's nature, but the circumstances left him no choice but to "humbly pray . . . for the liberation of his said slaves."[43]

The deferential wording, of course, was not Allen Jones's. Then as now, clients played little role in drafting legal papers, and a white attorney would have been surprised to learn that a former slave like Jones could even read and write. Thus, the petition was prepared in the law office of Thomas Ruffin, with minimal input from Jones, to be presented in the November term of the Superior Court. Ruffin was no particular friend of African-Americans – he owned two plantations with over 100 slaves – and it is one of history's not infrequent ironies that he once represented the freedom-seeking Allen Jones. At the time, Ruffin was among the most prominent lawyers in the state, representing landowners, merchants, and other members of the Carolina gentry. He had twice served as a trial judge on the Superior Court, and had resigned from the bench only a year earlier in order to accept the presidency of the State Bank of North Carolina, which had been on the verge of collapse owing to a series of improvident loans to slave dealers. He engaged in law practice in Raleigh, in association with George Badger and Henry Seawell, while successfully reorganizing the bank's affairs to the great relief of the state's commercial and financial interests.[44]

Ruffin was rewarded for his efforts with an appointment to the North Carolina Supreme Court, which was confirmed by the legislature on November 24, 1829.[45] He took his seat in December, and within weeks he issued one of the most profoundly pro-slavery decisions of the antebellum era. In *State v. Mann*, Ruffin held that a master could not be prosecuted for shooting a disobedient slave. As he explained for the court, "the power of the master must be absolute, to render the submission of the slave perfect." Ruffin did express sympathy for unprotected slaves, who could be subjected to "incidences of cruelty and deliberate barbarity" at the hands of harsh owners, but he concluded that such "uncontrolled authority" was nonetheless "inherent in the relation of master and slave."[46] Although Ruffin remains best known today for his absolutist view of slavery, it was not out of character for him to have accepted a fee for pursuing Allen Jones's right as a master to manumit his own wife and children.[47]

The petition was duly granted, finally emancipating Temperance Jones and the three children, but the indignity of the ordeal must have been wrenching. Allen later gave interviews to journalists in which he proudly recounted his determined efforts to free his family. It appears, however, that he never revealed – even to his children and grandchildren – the humiliating fact that Temperance had once been his slave and that he had been forced to plead to a white judge for his children's manumission.[48]

In every other aspect of his life, Allen Jones was indomitable – the very sort of African-American whose "insistent drive for independence and respectability shook the ideological foundations of the slave society."[49] Having somehow learned to read, he boldly subscribed to the *National Intelligencer*, a Whig newspaper published in Washington, D.C.[50] That act of effrontery drew scowls from the white citizenry, but it was nothing compared with Jones's daring involvement in building a Quaker-led school for free black children. The school was burned to the ground several times, and the teacher threatened with tar and feathers, which led Allen and Temperance Jones to realize that there was no future for their family in North Carolina.[51] It does not appear that John Copeland, Sr., had any connection to the school. It was never mentioned in his later reminiscences or in interviews with family members, and Thomas Devereux's 1859 description of him – as a "most well disposed boy" – indicates that he was not viewed as a troublemaker, even in the wake of Harper's Ferry. The arson and terrorization, of course, would certainly have motivated John and Delilah as well as the Joneses to flee North Carolina.

In all likelihood, Jones was the organizer of the exodus. He was older than Copeland, with a larger family and more acute reasons to depart the South. The Joneses' exit papers have not survived, so we can only speculate as to what their sponsors said about their reasons for leaving Raleigh, or whether they described Allen as humble and quiet. The leading white citizens were most likely pleased to see him go, not only to be rid of an agitator but also because he had accumulated several thousand dollars' worth of property, which he was forced to "sell to white folks" at distressed prices in order to finance the trip.[52]

Allen Jones also had an aptitude for leadership, while John Copeland, Sr., was generally unassuming. In later years, Jones and his children would become important figures in several Northern communities, while the elder Copelands remained reticent and only had notoriety thrust on them in the wake of their son's involvement at Harper's Ferry.

Once assembled, the small wagon train headed across North Carolina, into Tennessee, and then northward through Kentucky to Cincinnati. They could have traveled a shorter distance by going immediately north into Virginia, which also would have enabled them to make part of their journey by river, a much easier means of transport in the days of dirt roads and creaking axles. We cannot know why the travelers chose the longer, more taxing overland route. It might have been a question of resources, or they simply might not have known better. Then again, they might have wanted to avoid even skirting Southampton County, Virginia, where scores of black people had been murdered in the wake of Nat Turner's uprising in 1831. At least eighteen innocent black lives had also been taken in spillover hysteria in Duplin and Sampson counties in North Carolina, which bordered Southampton.[53] True, the lynchings were more than a decade in the past, but stories of the Virginians' indiscriminate vengeance would have circulated ever since in the black communities of North Carolina. Times changed slowly in the antebellum South, and the risk may have been more than the families chose to undertake.

THERE WERE INITIALLY FOURTEEN PEOPLE in the party when the wagons departed Raleigh in March 1843: the Copelands and their two children; the Joneses and their seven children, including four who had been born free; and John Lane. Allen Jones's father, who had been born in Africa and survived the Middle Passage, had died some time earlier, and Delilah Evans Copeland's siblings and their families would remain in North Carolina for another decade.[54] The Copelands also adopted a young orphan named Reuben Turner at some point in Tennessee.[55]

Two of the Jones children were especially important in the life of John Anthony. Elias Toussaint Jones was born the same year as John Anthony, and the two developed a close friendship that continued as they grew up in Oberlin. "Toussaint" was a dangerously provocative name for a black person in North Carolina, evoking as it did the slave who led the 1791 Haitian Revolution. It may be that Allen and Temperance added their son's middle name only after they safely reached Oberlin, but it was certainly in keeping with their generally defiant outlook. Their oldest son was named after a much less controversial figure. James Monroe Jones – called only "Munro" in the petition for emancipation – was born in January 1821, making him thirteen years older than John Anthony and twenty-two at the time of the journey to Ohio.[56] As a young man, he would have been expected to help the other adults with their work – such as managing the two-horse teams and repairing the wagons – rather than spend much time with the children as the families made their way toward Ohio. Still, it would have been inevitable for John Anthony to look up to an older companion during their 600 miles of difficult travel in close quarters – especially one as exceptional as the oldest Jones brother. James Monroe was a gifted artisan who would later serve briefly as a gunsmith for John Brown. More than that, he was extraordinarily charismatic. For the rest of his life, friends and colleagues would remark on Jones's outgoing nature and dynamic personality. Of all John Brown's associates, James Monroe Jones was the one whom John Copeland knew longest and best.[57]

FIVE

"I HAVE FOUND PARADISE"

LIKE ALL REFUGEES, the members of the Copeland–Jones party were eager to reach safe harbor. Consequently, they headed to Cincinnati – their first stop on free soil – where they intended to consider their options for permanent settlement. Cincinnati had a substantial free black population, but the Copelands and Joneses were wary of living so close to slaveholding territory, and they found "that colored folks fared in Cincinnati about as in Carolina."[1] They were advised that New Richmond, Indiana, might be a safer and more welcoming place, so they soon continued their journey onward to the west.

Reaching the outskirts of New Richmond, they encountered a farmer named Tibbets, who told them he was "a friend of the colored man." Because it was already Saturday, Tibbets invited the travelers to rest at his home over the Sabbath, and he invited them to attend an anti-slavery meeting in town that evening. The Copelands at first were hesitant, recalling the stories they had been fed about the perfidious abolitionists who would sell them into slavery. They overcame their misgivings – reassured by Tibbets and no doubt prodded by the more venturesome Joneses – and attended the meeting, which was probably their first exposure to abolitionism. With Devereux's disingenuous warning still haunting them, however, the Copelands insisted on taking seats by the door "where they could escape if indications of danger appeared." To their great relief, they realized that their fears were unfounded, and they soon made friends with the white people in attendance. In later years, the Copelands would make light of their naiveté, but the experience was bracing at the time. Their guardians in Raleigh had been untruthful to them, and they had much to learn about life in the North.[2]

Among the attendees at the New Richmond meeting was an Oberlin theology graduate named Amos Dresser, who had once done missionary work among slaves and free blacks in Tennessee. Having been arrested himself and whipped by vigilantes, Dresser well understood the Copelands' trepidation about living anywhere near a Slave state. He suggested that they locate in Oberlin, "where the slave-holders would not kidnap their children as they were in the habit of doing along the Ohio River."[3]

Leaving the wagons and families behind, the three men set off on horseback to investigate "the colored man's land of promise." Following directions provided by Dresser, they got within about twenty miles of Oberlin when they decided to stop at a tannery "to inquire the way." The response was not encouraging, although it did give them an indication that Oberlin was indeed an oasis. The tannery workers cursed at the black men and sneered that Oberlin had "sunk" and no longer existed. Recalling the lies he had been told in North Carolina, Copeland replied that "he would go on and look into the chasm."[4]

Arriving in Oberlin on a Sunday, the travelers were surprised to see two young men – one white and one black – walking arm in arm to church. There were no such easy interactions, and certainly no integrated churches, in North Carolina. The Oberliners were also surprised, but for a different reason. They asked why the newcomers were riding on the Sabbath. Either Copeland or Jones explained that they were seeking a home for their families. The Sabbath violation was immediately forgiven, and the black men were placed in the charge of a prominent citizen who would help them explore the town.

After that, the decision was easy. Copeland and Lane returned to New Richmond to retrieve the women and children while Jones remained in Oberlin to continue making arrangements for their resettlement. He sent word that he "had found a paradise and was going to stay."[5]

COMPARED WITH RALEIGH, Oberlin was indeed a paradise for free black families. There were no curfews, housing restrictions, random searches, threats, whippings, occupational limitations, or any of the countless other humiliations regularly inflicted in the South. In Oberlin, as Allen Jones observed from the very first day, blacks and whites lived as neighbors, shopped in the same stores, worked in the same businesses, and worshipped together in the vast First Church, which, with over 1000 seats in the pews, had the largest sanctuary west of the Alleghenies.[6] As one African-American congregant observed, "every Sunday colored persons could be seen seated in conspicuous eligible places," where they were "made welcome as equals."[7] It was a scene that could hardly be imagined anywhere else in the United States.

The college was integrated, as the Lane Rebels had demanded, but that would not yet have mattered to the Copelands and Joneses. More important was the availability of basic education for their children. Ohio provided no public schools for black children until 1848, when the state established a dual system separated by race, in which the "nigger schools" were underfunded and poorly maintained.[8] In Oberlin, however, there was a single public school, located on Main Street, attended by both black and white students in a spirit of robust equality.

There was also a separate "adult colored school" – better known as the "Liberty School" – where adult refugees and fugitives were taught to read and write during the day, and where anti-slavery meetings were frequently held in the evenings.[9] It was a unique institution, where former slaves "felt entirely free to express their opinions" and even to challenge their instructors. So fervent was the "interracial dialog, discussion, and debate" – laced with both abolitionism and patriotism – that the Liberty School became known as the black man's "Faneuil Hall, in which the negro made his most eloquent and effective speeches against his enslavement."[10]

Abolition organizations were woven deeply into Oberlin's social structure. There was an Anti-Slavery Society that was open to everyone, as well as a Young Men's Anti-Slavery Society and a Female Anti-Slavery Society – the lack of originality in their names was evidently less important than the opportunity to associate within one's age or gender group. Public events – in those days almost always accompanied by oration – inevitably included condemnations of slavery. Commencement exercises, as James Fairchild later noted, routinely featured anti-slavery speakers, as did the frequent lectures by visiting notables.

Reverend Charles Grandison Finney commanded the pulpit of the First Church, where his sermons reliably touched on the evils of slavery and alcohol, and the relationship between free will and salvation.[11] Finney insisted that other Evangelicals give their testimony against slavery, arguing that silence on the subject was a "sin of the church."[12] His own congregation in Oberlin had voted that "no slaveholder could preach, serve, or commune in it," and Finney drove the point home with rare eloquence.[13] The most prominent apostle of America's Second Great Awakening, Finney had been the pastor of the huge Broadway Tabernacle Church in New York City until 1835, when he was recruited as a professor of theology in the same arrangement that brought the Lane Rebels to Oberlin. He later served as president of the college, and he led

Oberlin's denominational switch from Presbyterian to Congregational. Born in 1792, Finney was a thin man with a high forehead, gaunt cheeks, a round chin, and a heavy brow. He kept his wavy hair cut short in his youth, but he allowed it to grow longer as his hairline receded over the years, eventually raising a thick beard to match. It must have been a revelation – if not an absolute shock – for the Copelands and Joneses to encounter such strongly pro-equality sentiments in a man as eminent as the revered Professor Finney. No such person existed in Raleigh, or perhaps in the entire South, where the religious figures and community leaders were united in their determination to maintain the subjugation of black people.[14]

THE COPELANDS AND JONESES LIVED FIRST IN ROUGH CABINS that were set up quickly to accommodate them. Soon, however, they were able to occupy sturdy houses – built by John Copeland, Sr. – each featuring a deep root cellar and large attic, with latched doors and puncheon floors, and "beautified with trees and flowers."[15] The men, as skilled artisans, had no difficulty practicing their trades. Allen Jones maintained a smithy at the site of his original cabin, where he labored "early and late, pounding out the dollars to pay for educating his children." Jones had a fine voice, and he could usually be heard singing at the forge while keeping time with his hammer and anvil. Fittingly for a refugee from the house of bondage, his favorite song was "Canaan, O Canaan, bright Canaan, I am bound for the land of Canaan."[16]

John Copeland, Sr., worked on the construction of the many houses and shops needed to accommodate Oberlin's rapidly growing population. Copeland may also have worked on the last stages of the First Church, which was not finished until 1844. Although the building was constructed primarily of masonry, its roof rested on a wooden frame with traditional mortise-and-tenon joints that were already out of fashion at the time. (The decision to forego iron bolts would contribute to a small disaster in the 1870s, when half of the roof was blown away in a severe storm.)[17]

James Monroe Jones, already in his early twenties, entered the preparatory department at the college, and the younger children enrolled at the one-room common school, also located on Main Street. John Anthony attended class with three of the Jones boys – Elias, William, and John – with whom he was close in age. Their teacher was Mr. Merrell, who had a reputation as a fine instructor and a vigorous disciplinarian.

He "never spared the rod for the child's crying," explained one former student.[18] Nor did he draw distinctions of race. The Joneses excelled in school – having inherited their father's acumen and love of reading – while John Anthony did well enough, giving "more or less attention to his books." He learned penmanship, spelling, and grammar, but he showed no strong desire to pursue education for its own sake. He was at least as interested in religious education as he was in secular subjects, but he was most attentive outside the classroom when learning carpentry from his father.[19]

Children being children, there were the predictable fights among the students, and occasionally they had "quite a time of it." On one occasion in winter 1845, the fisticuffs were between two of the Jones brothers and two white boys, one of whom was the son of an Oberlin founder. Mr. Merrell investigated the scrap and "concluded that the white boys were most to blame." Despite the pioneer status of the prime instigator's family, Merrell determined that significant punishment was in order, and he called on the young man to take off his coat for a whipping. The boy refused and defiantly buttoned his coat up to his chin. "Well," said the teacher, "I will whip it off, then," and he applied such an energetic beating that he wore out his switches and had to send a student to the woods for more. The offender "had lots of pluck, and never shed a tear," but he left school that day and did not return for the rest of the term.[20]

The incident was unremarkable to the white students, who were accustomed to Mr. Merrill's chastisements, but the Copeland and Jones boys would never before have seen any white person get in such serious trouble for striking a black. There had been no integrated schools in the South, and any scuffles between white and black children would inevitably result in punishment for the blacks. In Oberlin, however, the students were treated as equals, both when they fought and when they made friends. John Mercer Langston expressed astonishment at such egalitarianism, remarking that before he came to Oberlin he "had never before had a young white friend who was willing to treat me as a friend."[21] Mr. Merrill's unrelenting corporal punishment seems extremely harsh today, but it was strictly delivered with an even hand.

As WELCOMING AS IT WAS, Oberlin was not immune from the ambient racism of the times. With only a handful of exceptions, John Brown chief among them, even the most ardent abolitionists harbored predictable biases against black people – which Edward Henry Fairchild referred to as the "caste feeling which prevailed throughout the north"– and not all the people of Oberlin were ardent abolitionists.[22] From the very beginning, there had been fevered opposition to the enrollment of Negroes in college, much of it on the assumption that they would thereafter inundate both the school and the town. A majority of the student body voted against admitting black students, and several trustees and benefactors – including cofounder Philo Stewart – threatened to withdraw support if the proposal was accepted. A New England fund-raiser cautioned against placing "black and white together on precisely the same standing." Indeed, he ominously predicted that "as soon as your *darkies* begin to come in any considerable numbers . . . the whites will begin to leave – and at length your institution will change colour."[23] The matter became so heated that Finney had to disclaim any intention to "hang out an abolition flag," and Shipherd felt it necessary to reassure his colleagues that Oberlin would not "fill up with filthy, stupid Negroes." Rather, he explained, the college would welcome only "promising youth who desire to prepare for usefulness . . . in the proper exercise of their freedom."[24]

The fearful flood of black folks never happened, but that did not allay all concerns. A greater worry all along had been anxiety over "amalgamation," meaning the "often unexpressed sexual fear . . . that undergirded all of American racial prejudice."[25] A number of Oberlin's female students from New England, considering themselves "young ladies of unquestioned refinement," announced that they would return home upon the admission of colored students, even if they had to "wade Lake Erie to accomplish it."[26] There was no aquatic evacuation, as it turned out, even after the black students began to arrive. Nonetheless, the "caste feeling" lingered among some for decades. In 1852, a young Massachusetts woman felt compelled to reassure her family that they could "tell anybody that asks that we don't have to kiss the Niggars nor speak to them without we are a mind to."[27] That sentiment appeared to run in both directions, as the black students at Oberlin showed no interest in intermarriage (they were all too familiar with the amalgamation that had routinely been forced on slave women in the South). For the most part, however, social relations between the races were comfortable, if not always warm. In 1843, Lucy Stone (later a pioneering suffragist) wrote to her parents that "colored gentlemen and ladies sit at the same table with us, and there appears to be no difference."[28] Some white students continued to express concern about being forced to "mingle with the colored population," but the administration's position was clear:

> In this college colored and white students of the same sex, walk together when both are agreed to do so – not otherwise. They eat together if both prefer it, or if neither chooses to eat elsewhere. They meet in the same classes for recitation if they happen to be studying the same branches, at the same stage of progress. They worship together before the same common Father – that is, if they both have the heart to worship at all.[29]

As it was in the college, so it was in the town. Allen Jones enjoyed a reputation as "a remarkable man, industrious and intelligent, and rather above the average colored people." Known as "the North Carolina emancipationist," he was active in Oberlin's anti-slavery movement and maintained his habit of newspaper subscription, now without limitation or fear of pattyroller reprisal.[30] In Oberlin, he subscribed to the anti-slavery *National Era*, which would have been impossible to obtain – and dangerous to be seen reading – in Raleigh. When Jones opened his newspaper in early June 1851, however, he was able to read the first installment of *Uncle Tom's Cabin*, which was banned throughout the South.[31] Although more reticent, John Copeland, Sr., was also esteemed as "a bright, intelligent colored man," whose carpentry work was highly valued by all who employed him.[32] When work and family obligations allowed, he attended the Liberty School with other illiterate adults, eventually learning to read and sign his name well enough for commercial purposes.[33] In other words, as the Copelands and Joneses perceived it upon their arrival in 1843, paradise.

SIX

"MY OBJECT IN COMING TO OBERLIN"

FUGITIVE SLAVES AND FREE BLACKS MADE THEIR WAY to Oberlin throughout the antebellum era, engendering great pride in the colony while drawing the wrath of many pro-slavery Ohioans. Pro-southern Democrats in the state legislature made four attempts to revoke Oberlin's charter between 1837 and 1843 as undisguised retribution for the school's opposition to slavery. As one antagonistic state senator put it, Oberlin had become "the great national manufactory of ultra-abolitionists" who lured slaves from the South for the purpose of "secretly conveying them through the state of Ohio, and transporting them to Canada."[1] The charge was true, if exaggerated on all sides. According to Professor James Harris Fairchild, the proposed revocations were based on "a thousand unfavorable rumors in relation to amalgamation, fanaticism, harboring fugitive slaves . . . without any evidence of their truth before the legislature."[2]

In fact, the number of fugitives was never as great as the Oberliners boasted or their adversaries feared, but it was sufficient to draw the attention of slave hunters, both Southern and domestic.[3] The "man-stealers" had a relatively free hand elsewhere in Ohio, seizing uncounted victims annually in reliance on *Prigg v. Pennsylvania*, a decision of the U.S. Supreme Court that gave slave owners the "positive, unqualified right" to recapture their slaves anywhere in the Union.[4] Although the Supreme Court had been unequivocal that no one could "be permitted to interfere with, or to obstruct, the just rights of the owner to reclaim his slave," people in Oberlin saw things differently. And although a steady stream of slave catchers did attempt to ply their trade in Oberlin, they were always rebuffed, to the great delight of the collegians and townsfolk. The stories of thwarted slave hunters became legendary, including one documented incident in 1841 that was reported in the febrile pro-Southern press as the "Oberlin Negro Riot." The event itself was far from a riot, involving at most a roadblock accompanied by "yelling, threats, and imprecations" before the slave catchers were diverted, but it made a strong impression in Ohio that helped to build Oberlin's reputation as an impenetrable haven for fugitives.[5] It is impossible to tell just how many confrontations actually occurred in that period, although diaries and memoirs suggest that there had been at least ten or twelve attempted abductions in and around Oberlin, and very likely more. The recollected incidents overlap, but, tellingly, not one of them appears to have involved pursuit by a federal marshal or deputy. By 1848, the frustrating attempts to capture runaways in Oberlin had been abandoned, and they would not be resumed for a decade.

The Copelands arrived in Oberlin in 1843, in the midst of the first wave of slave hunting. They were no strangers to kidnappings – having left Raleigh in part out of fear of child-stealing pattyrollers – and they would have been heartened by the resistance of both whites and blacks to slave catchers. Oberlin memoirist Milton Clarke, himself a runaway slave, wrote movingly about an incident that occurred in the same year involving nine fugitives from Kentucky. Their master, a plantation owner named Benningale, was in pursuit, "impiously claiming that he had property in these images of God." Needless to say, as Clarke put it, that was "not the doctrine taught by a great many good men" in Ohio. Benningale discovered that his slaves were hiding in Oberlin, and he "threatened to burn the town" if that was necessary to retrieve them. The fugitives, however, remained concealed under guard. After night fell, Benningale sent two spies into town, seeking the location of the runaways. To their chagrin, the would-be informants were identified and surrounded by colored men who "told them, if they caught them out again, they should be hung right up, as spies against liberty."[6]

The nine slaves were taken safely to Canada, but that was not the end of the story. Benningale learned of the light-skinned Clarke's role in the rescue, and he was determined to capture the man he called the "white nigger of Oberlin." The Kentuckian sent four slave catchers after Clarke, and they successfully waylaid him as he was riding in a carriage on the outskirts of town. "We are going to carry you back, and whip you, on the public square in Lexington," they told their captive. Fortunately, Clarke was able to sound an alarm, and "a large company" of Oberliners "left their ploughs and jumped upon their horses" to intercept the kidnappers. They insisted that the prisoner be brought before a local magistrate, who ruled that the slave catchers had insufficient proof that Clarke had ever "owed service" to his alleged master.[7] It was not uncommon for judges in Ohio and other Northern states to order the release of fugitives, which is one reason that Congress included an enhanced Fugitive Slave Act – giving authority over fugitives to federal officers and commissioners – as part of the Compromise of 1850.[8]

Stories of Clarke's recent liberation would still have been circulating when the Copelands arrived in Oberlin. Nine-year-old John Anthony could not have understood the nuances of fugitive slave law, but he surely understood the jubilation that accompanied the rescue of runaways. Those triumphs – usually quiet, but sometimes celebrated – continued throughout John Anthony's youth, as fugitives steadily arrived in Oberlin for transit across Lake Erie to Canada.

Even in the most peaceful times, slavery was a constant presence in the town. There were too many former slaves in Oberlin – each with a story to tell – for the issue to be ignored, even by children. One of John Anthony's schoolmates, for example, was a female student known as Sarah "Margru" Kinson. A short girl, with dark skin, cropped hair, widely spaced eyes, and an oval face, Margru – as her parents named her – had been born in the Mende country of West Africa in about 1832. The child of a large family, she was sold into slavery at the age of six or seven as payment for her parents' debt to an unknown creditor. Margru was taken to the slave fortress on Lomboko Island, located in what is now Sierra Leone, where she was brought aboard a Portuguese slave ship named *Tecora.* One of only three children on the ship, Margru survived the Middle Passage, arriving in Cuba in June 1839. Sold at auction in Havana, she was transferred to the schooner *La Amistad,* to be transported to the far end of the island with fifty-two other Mende slaves. Midway through the short voyage, one of the slaves, later known as Cinque, led a rebellion. He and his comrades took control of the ship, killed the captain, and futilely attempted to set an eastward course toward Africa. For nearly two months, *La Amistad* drifted up and down the Atlantic coast, until its timbers creaked and its sails turned to rags.

As a child, Margru did not participate in the *Amistad* rebellion, but she was taken into custody along with the other slaves when the ship was finally detained in August by a U.S. revenue cutter in Long Island Sound. At first mistaken for a pirate ship, *La Amistad* was brought to port in New London, Connecticut, where the truth of the mutiny was discovered. Competing claims were made for the ownership of the human cargo. Should they be treated as salvage, as slaves, or as free persons?[9]

Margru remained in custody in New Haven until March 1841, when the U.S. Supreme Court ordered all of the captives freed. The historic ruling did not end their ordeal, however, as no provisions had been made to restore the Mendeans to their homes. Instead, they were taken to Farmington, Connecticut, where they lived for nearly a year while abolitionists raised the necessary funds for the return voyage across the Atlantic. In Farmington, Margru came to the attention of wealthy merchant Lewis Tappan, whose brother Arthur had so generously endowed Oberlin. Tappan took an interest in Margru's education – he gave her the biblical name "Sarah," although she later added "Kinson" on her own – and he was instrumental in arranging for missionaries to accompany the Mendeans back to Africa.

Two of the Tappan-funded missionaries were from Oberlin, and their goal was more than merely to chaperone the voyage. Arriving in Freetown, Sierra Leone, in January 1842, the two Oberliners set about establishing a church and school that became known as the Komende Mission, where Sarah Margru Kinson soon became the star pupil. One of the missionaries reported back to Tappan that Sarah had excelled in her studies and that "she ought to go to America to be educated."[10]

Arrangements were made, and in August 1846 Sarah arrived in Oberlin, where she was enrolled in classes in the one-room school. At age fourteen (or so), Sarah was a contemporary of John Anthony and several of the Jones brothers. Unlike the occasionally unruly boys, she was a model student. In May 1847, Sarah reported her progress to her benefactor, Lewis Tappan. "I am now studying very diligently so as to be qualified to do good in the world as this was my object in coming to Oberlin."[11] She remained in the school until the end of 1848, when she entered the female department of the college. Sarah's harrowing and redemptive story must have had a strong impact on John Anthony, who was her schoolmate, demonstrating to him how resistance and survival could change the lives of the enslaved. Sarah Kinson would return to Africa as a teacher and missionary, still hoping to do good in the world. John Anthony shared her intentions, although he would choose a very different course of action.

In the meantime, John Anthony attended to his own formal education, although that would not be his passion. Upon completion of the common school curriculum, he enrolled in Oberlin's preparatory department for the 1854–55 session, joining his friend Elias Toussaint Jones. Copeland did well enough in school, but his heart lay elsewhere, and he did not continue his studies beyond that year.

If John Anthony had returned to the preparatory department in autumn 1855, he might have been seated next to Anthony Burns, who was then one of the most well-known former slaves in the United States. Burns had escaped from Virginia to Boston in 1854, only to be tracked down by his master's agents and arrested under the Fugitive Slave Act. Burns's capture ignited a firestorm in Boston, especially when he was imprisoned in the Suffolk County courthouse, which local abolitionists angrily declared had been turned into a "slave-pen." A hastily organized rescue attempt failed to free Burns, although it resulted in the death of a man who had been deputized to guard the building.

Burns was brought before a federal commissioner for a rendition hearing, which drew nationwide attention. Despite a spirited defense – led by attorney and author Richard Henry Dana – the commissioner ruled in favor of the slave owner and ordered Burns returned to Virginia. It took hundreds of state and federal troops to effect the rendition. An angry mob lined the streets between the courthouse and the dock, but they were held away at bayonet-point under the direct orders of President Franklin Pierce, while Burns was transferred to a southbound schooner. Upon Burns's arrival in Richmond, his owner had him whipped and chained in a windowless jail for months. Remarkably, he was able to smuggle a note to his supporters in Boston, who had not forgotten him. Burns's friends eventually succeeded in purchasing his freedom, and a benefactor then paid for him to study theology in Oberlin, where he arrived in time for the 1855–56 school year.[12] At least one of the Jones brothers was in Burns's class, and John Anthony was certainly aware of the renowned former fugitive's presence in Oberlin. Burns's harrowing story – of escape, freedom, capture, trial, rendition, whipping, and freedom again at last – would have been both chilling and inspiring to every young man in Oberlin.[13]

More impressive to John Anthony than even the most famous classmate would have been the presence of prominent African-Americans in the ranks of Oberlin's elite. Even prosperous and highly skilled African-Americans were marginalized in the South, where they were subjected to curfews and other limitations and required to accept the guardianship of white "protectors." Although free blacks faced withering discrimination elsewhere in Ohio, Oberlin for the most part encouraged individuals to achieve whatever station their native gifts allowed. Among the most accomplished were the Langston brothers, John Mercer and Charles.

Like Delilah and John Copeland, Sr., the Langstons had been born in slave country, the sons of a Revolutionary War veteran named Ralph Quarles and a mixed-race woman named Lucy Langston. But the similarity ends there. As far as we know, Copeland's white father had never shown any actual affection for his enslaved mother, which, like most antebellum sexual encounters between owners and their slaves, would have differed from rape only in name and legality. As one former slave put it, "Plenty of the colored women have children by the white men. She know better than to not do what he say.... Then they take them very same children what have their blood and make slaves out of them."[14] The liaison between Ralph Quarles and Lucy Langston, however, was far from that norm. Their relationship was known to be "permanent and open," and it might easily have been recognized as a marriage if that had been lawful in Virginia.[15] Quarles freed both Lucy and their children in his lifetime, taking an active interest in the "intellectual and manual training" of his mulatto sons, for whom he engaged private tutors. He also provided for them generously in his will, devising his estate to the "children of Lucy, a woman whom I have emancipated." Most important, Quarles arranged for his children to relocate to Ohio upon his death, so that they could be raised in a free environment. He passed away in spring 1834, just as Oberlin was becoming established, when Charles was sixteen years old and John Mercer was only four.[16]

Charles Langston spent a year in Chillicothe, living with a Quaker family, as arranged by his father. In 1835, he came to Oberlin, where he was one of the first African-American students enrolled in the preparatory department. Charles went on to the collegiate department and then to a career as a teacher and journalist. Short and slight, with a trim vandyke and neatly parted hair, he was already professionally established by the time the Copelands and Joneses arrived in Oberlin, and well on his way toward becoming a leader in Ohio's anti-slavery movement. He lived in Columbus, where he served as a school principal and briefly edited an anti-slavery newspaper, but he was a constant presence in Oberlin, where he remained a well-known and much admired figure.

In 1853, when John Anthony was nearing twenty and was well aware of the world around him, Charles Langston was named executive secretary of the Ohio State Anti-Slavery Society – a pathbreaking position for a black man in an organizational world dominated by whites. Charles was also a delegate in 1853 to the National Black Convention in Rochester, organized by Frederick Douglass, and he worked as an incognito organizer for the Free Soil Party, and later the Republicans, during the 1850s. Abolitionist political figures – including Joshua Giddings, Philemon Bliss, Salmon Chase, and Benjamin Wade – frequently consulted with Langston, which must have astounded the Copelands and Joneses, including young John Anthony. No white politician in Raleigh would ever have considered seeking the opinion of a black man.

Charles set a militant example for young black men in Oberlin. In 1851, he praised as "patriots" the fugitive slaves in Christiana, Pennsylvania, who had killed a pursuing slave owner. He openly carried a pistol and dared racists to confront him, although his audacity sometimes backfired. Once, while on a lecture tour promoting Frederick Douglass's newspaper, he was threatened by a gang of white toughs who menacingly surrounded his hotel. Langston was forced to flee through the back door in the middle of the night, wisely choosing to pocket his firearm and live to fight another day.[17]

John Mercer Langston was twelve years younger than his brother, and considerably more circumspect. He lived for ten years with the Quakers in Chillicothe before moving to Oberlin in the mid-1840s to enter the preparatory department. John Mercer had a long face and fine features. As a young man, he was clean shaven, with narrow muttonchops that ran nearly to his jawline, and in his later years he sported a well-groomed beard. He earned a bachelor's degree at Oberlin, and then a master's degree in theology, before deciding to become a lawyer. Denied admission to law schools in Ohio and Michigan, John Mercer instead studied as a law clerk in the Cleveland office of Philemon Bliss, who would later be elected to Congress as a Republican. John Mercer was only five years older than John Anthony, and he would have provided a fine role model if young Copeland had been academically inclined. That was not the case. John Anthony was far more interested in action than in words or books. If he took a cue from either Langston, it surely was Charles.

THE "COLORED CITIZENS OF OBERLIN" held a mass meeting at the Liberty School on February 12, 1849, for the purpose of claiming their "rights under the United States Constitution, and in having the laws oppressing us tested." John Anthony was too young to join the adults, but John Copeland, Sr., and Allen Jones would have been in attendance. In a set of published resolutions, the assembled African-Americans urged "the slave to leave immediately with his hoe on his shoulder, for a land of liberty," and they pledged to "keep a sharp look-out for men thieves and their abettors, and to warn them that no person claimed as a slave shall be taken from our midst without trouble."[18] They meant what they said, although at the time they had only vigilante slave hunters in mind. That assumption would be shattered the following year, when the U.S. Congress determined that the federal government would play a leading role in slave catching.

Although they may have lacked prescience, the colored citizens were forthright in their call for resistance to "the monster, SLAVERY."[19] Their declaration made a great impression on John Anthony, who missed no opportunity to attend anti-slavery meetings at the Liberty School.[20] He would quote from it on the last day of his life.

SEVEN

NOT A FUGITIVE WAS SEIZED

THE NATION WAS IN CRISIS IN 1850, with the Southern states threatening to secede over the question of slavery in the Mexican Cession. Henry Clay, and later Stephen Douglas, brokered a compromise to save the Union, in which California was admitted to the Union as a Free state, Texas relinquished its claims to New Mexico and other territory in exchange for the assumption of its debts by the federal government, and the slave trade was abolished in Washington, D.C. One further element of the Compromise of 1850 stuck much closer to Oberlin. In a major concession to the South, Congress enacted an amendment to the Fugitive Slave Act of 1793 – in reality, a completely new law – that virtually federalized the rendition of runaway slaves.

The Fugitive Slave Act of 1850 was deeply unpopular in the North, and not only among abolitionists. Its central feature was the authorization of U.S. commissioners – a class of part-time subjudges whose powers were otherwise very limited – to preside over all fugitive slave proceedings and to issue "certificates of removal" at the request of slave owners. The goal of the Act was to override the jurisdiction of state courts in the North, which were thought to be too protective of runaways. That was bad enough, but other aspects of the law made it even more objectionable. Alleged fugitives were prohibited from testifying in their own defense, could not demand jury trials, and were denied the right to appeal. The certificate of a Southern court – obtained ex parte by a slave owner – was deemed conclusive proof of slave status and escape. The commissioner was left to decide only the question of identity, which could be based on "a general description of the person so escaping, with such convenient certainty as may be." Moreover, the commissioner was to be paid a fee of $10 for allowing rendition, but only $5 for denying the certificate of removal. The penalty for interfering with the lawful capture of a fugitive was a fine of $1000 and six months imprisonment, and, worse still from the Northern perspective, all citizens were required upon the command of a U.S. marshal to aid "in the prompt and efficient execution of this law." Mere refusal to assist the marshal was itself a violation of the statute, subject to fine and imprisonment.

Signed by President Millard Fillmore on September 18, 1850, the "Monster Act," as Senator Charles Sumner called it, brought terror to the African-American population in the North.[1] The most panicky reaction, as would be expected, was among the many fugitives who had been living underground lives within the larger black communities. But free blacks were also in jeopardy. They had always lived in apprehension of abduction – even in cities far from the South – but the new law for the first time placed the power of the federal government firmly on the side of the would-be kidnappers. True, the Act required a hearing prior to rendition, but the proceedings were intended to be perfunctory. With no right to testify or appeal, even free-born black people would be treated as presumptive property by the U.S. commissioners who would determine their fates.

For many African-Americans, free and fugitive alike, the natural response was to leave the country. The *Pennsylvania Freeman* reported, with some evident exaggeration, that over a third of the black people in Boston fled to Canada immediately after President Fillmore signed the Act into law. The reaction was similar in other Northern cities, as shops closed and church congregations became noticeably smaller. A hotel in Pittsburgh, for example, complained that it had to close the dining rooms because most of the waiters and other staff had departed for Canada.[2]

It would not take long for the worst fears to be confirmed. On September 26, 1850, a young black man named James Hamlet was arrested in New York City by two deputy federal marshals acting on behalf of a Baltimore woman who claimed to be his owner. Brought before U.S. commissioner John Gardiner, Hamlet attempted to protest that his mother had been freed before his birth, which made him a free person as well. Commissioner Gardiner, however, would not allow Hamlet to testify, and instead accepted the testimony of Mrs. Brown's son and son-in-law, who claimed that she was "entitled to [Hamlet's] services as a slave for life; she never parted with him voluntarily; she came into possession of him by the will of John G. Brown, her deceased husband." The commissioner ruled in favor of Mrs. Brown, which led the *Baltimore Sun*, a newspaper not known for its friendliness to alleged fugitives, to observe that the proceeding had "been marked with a peculiar degree of promptitude and despatch – the arrest having been made, the examination held, and the prisoner on his way to Baltimore, within the space of three hours."[3] There would be twenty-one more proceedings under the Act before the end of 1850, with nineteen rulings in favor of claimants and only two dismissals.[4]

United States marshals continued to be crucial to the enforcement of the Fugitive Slave Act, pursuing runaways in Massachusetts, New York, Pennsylvania, and other Northern states.[5] They were not always successful. In September 1851, a deputy federal marshal from Philadelphia was enlisted by a Maryland slave owner for the pursuit of four runaways who were believed to be hiding in nearby Christiana. The posse found their quarry, but they could not make an arrest. Instead, they were routed by gunfire from the fugitives and several dozen more African-Americans, who had come to their assistance. The slave owner was killed, and the deputy was sent running for his life. News of the resistance spread quickly, drawing furious condemnation across the South and measured approval from Northern abolitionists. Some supporters were less restrained than others. Frederick Douglass extolled the resistance as "Freedom's Battle" and declared that "the only way to make the Fugitive Slave Law a dead letter is to make a half a dozen or more dead kidnappers."[6] In Oberlin, Charles Langston was equally unequivocal, applauding the actions of the "Christiana patriots [as] worthy of the imitation of every colored man in the country, whether bond or free, when his liberty is assailed."[7] The "Christiana Slave Riot," as it came to be known by allies of the Fillmore administration, led to the indictment of forty-one men – thirty-six blacks and five whites – on charges of treason. The case was premised on interference with the lawful actions of a U.S. marshal, which was undeniable, but the prosecutions failed in large part because of strategic blunders by the overzealous prosecutors.[8] Nonetheless, the gravity of the case – treason carried the death penalty – and the vigor of the administration's efforts, made it painfully clear that the resources of the U.S. government would thereafter be at the disposal of slave owners.

Charles Langston's call to emulate the Christiana heroes stood as an open challenge to the federal government. His defiant stance was broadly cheered in Oberlin, although it was not quite as bold as it might have seemed to seventeen-year-old John Anthony. No colored man's liberty had been "assailed" in Oberlin for several years, and the power of the U.S. government was far away. The only federal official in Oberlin was the postmaster, and local law enforcement was under the control of

Lorain County, which was by then dominated by abolitionists such as the magistrate who freed Milton Clarke.

In the early 1850s, there was a single federal judicial district covering all of Ohio, which meant there was a single federal marshal, based in Cincinnati. In 1853, President Franklin Pierce named Jabez Fitch to that position, which came with the authority to appoint deputies in other parts of the state.[9] The marshal's ambitions were modest, however, and he never assigned a deputy to Oberlin or its environs. Fitch was a mild-mannered functionary who had devoted himself to cultivating friends and connections. His principal attribute was a knack for making himself "generally useful," which had been sufficient for him to be named Cleveland's city solicitor at the precocious age of twenty-five. He held that post for five years, eventually "developing considerable ability" without achieving any particular acclaim or notoriety, while establishing himself as an uncontroversial choice for the federal appointment that would follow. (He later served as Ohio's lieutenant governor, another position that required more affability than tenacity.)[10]

By an act of Congress in 1855, Ohio was divided into two judicial districts, with the new Northern District headquartered in Cleveland, thus potentially bringing a new marshal – and possibly new deputies – within forty miles of Oberlin.[11] For the first time, there was reason to think that federal authority might reach the abolitionist colony, despite its founders' hope to remain apart from the "taint of established and sin-infected towns."[12]

Fortunately for Oberlin, the statute provided that the incumbent marshal – meaning Fitch, who was a Cleveland native – would become the marshal of the Northern District, presumably so that the more desirable Southern District position (headquartered in Cincinnati but also covering Columbus) could then be filled by a new appointee. In Cleveland, Fitch devoted himself more to record keeping than to law enforcement. He took great pride in the neatness and accuracy of his books, which he considered his greatest professional accomplishment. He was commended by the U.S. comptroller for submitting "the most perfect of any accounts that come to this desk," and by the First Auditor's Office in the Treasury Department for the "unequaled accuracy in the statements of your accounts."[13] That was high praise from an office famous for its "merciless auditing."[14]

The scrupulousness of Fitch's accountancy evidently left him with little time or energy for slave hunting. During his entire term in office, reported the *Cleveland Leader*, "not a fugitive was seized in Northern Ohio . . . although fugitives resided there during the whole period," and "no efforts were made in these parts, in a business so odious to the people, and so disreputable to the actors therein."[15] The new marshal in the Southern District of Ohio, Hiram Robinson, was far more accommodating to slave catchers, most famously assisting in the tragic seizure of Margaret Garner and her family in January 1856. Robinson had directed his deputies to break down the door of the cabin where the fugitives were hiding, leading Garner to slit the throat of her daughter and attempt to kill her sons rather than see them returned to slavery.[16] Fitch had no evident enthusiasm for Robinson's tactics and no stomach for the dreadful consequences, and he was heard to say with manifest relief that such cases "had been most adroitly dodged [within his] official beat."[17] The marshal of the Northern District was quite content to do his job – serving writs, assembling juries, managing court funds, collecting fines, auctioning confiscated property, and impounding the schooners of Lake Erie smugglers – without endangering the lives and freedom of desperate fugitives.

Fitch's term was scheduled to end in mid-March 1858, and the easygoing marshal hoped to keep his job under President James Buchanan, who had been elected on the Democratic ticket in November 1856. Although not a zealot, Fitch was a loyal Democrat, and he therefore applied for reappointment in early 1857, expecting it to be a formality.[18] To Fitch's surprise and dismay, several of Ohio's Democratic congressmen petitioned the president to delay the appointment for as long as a year in order to consider other candidates.[19] Thus, the pressure to oust Jabez Fitch began within weeks of Buchanan's inauguration, as other office seekers, and their sponsors, sensed the possibility of patronage under the new president.[20] Fitch might have been able to outlast the rapacity of the local spoils seekers, but he could not survive the political intrigues that originated far from Ohio.

The winner of the competition for Buchanan's favor would be a Toledo businessman named Matthew Johnson – a cunning operator, who, for insidious reasons of his own, would instigate a slave-hunting invasion of Oberlin in summer 1858. Resistance naturally followed, and many militant Oberliners would find themselves in Marshal Johnson's custody. Copeland was among Johnson's targets but would elude the marshal for over a year, traveling first to Canada, then through Pennsylvania to Maryland, and finally to Virginia. In the end, Johnson would follow John Anthony for nearly 400 miles to confront him in a Southern jail cell.

EIGHT

THE NEW MARSHAL

FROM THE INCEPTION OF THE OFFICE, every new president had been besieged by office seekers, virtually all of whom appealed for jobs by virtue of political loyalty. James Buchanan was more attuned to such claims than most. He had devoted his life to the Democratic Party – or "The Democracy," as its adherents preferred to call it – serving in the House of Representatives, the Senate, the Cabinet (as secretary of state), and as ambassador to Russia and Great Britain.[1] Finally elected president at age 65, Buchanan's friends called him "Old Buck," although he was known to his detractors as "Old Public Functionary."[2] Given his background, no president had ever been more familiar with the time-tested approach to distributing rewards and emoluments. Regional political leaders would assign major offices, lesser posts would be dispensed at the state level, and so on down the line – with favors allotted in proportion to electoral debts.

On inauguration day in 1857, no person appeared to have a greater claim on Buchanan's largesse than Stephen A. Douglas of Illinois. Douglas had been Buchanan's most significant rival for the Democratic nomination in 1856, but he was not a resentful loser. Instead, he had thrown himself into the campaign and had played a leading role in defeating the Republican, John Fremont. After the election, Douglas expected that he or his friends would have considerable control over offices in what were then known as the western states, from Ohio to Wisconsin. The marshal's position in the Northern District of Ohio therefore would ordinarily have gone to someone from the Douglas wing of the party, to be chosen by his ally Ohio Senator George Pugh, if not by Douglas himself.[3]

The relationship between Buchanan and Douglas had never been easy, however, and it was not helped by the president's failure to provide the Illinois senator with a "just proportion of the federal patronage," as Douglas frankly put it.[4] Eventually, their differences would become irreconcilable, aggravated by the near civil war in Kansas. In September 1857, a contrived constitutional convention – called by pro-slavery legislators and boycotted by Free-staters – met in the town of Lecompton, where a vote was taken to adopt a new, pro-slavery constitution. The Lecompton Constitution sought Kansas's admission to the Union as a Slave state, declaring that "the right of the owner of a slave . . . is the same and as inviolable as the right of the owner of any property whatsoever." It also barred free blacks from entering the territory and prohibited any future amendments that would "affect the rights of property in the ownership of slaves."[5] As cover for the blatantly one-sided constitution, the convention called for a referendum to be held the following November, but the ballot question was rigged to ensure that slavery would be included in the constitution no matter how the populace voted. Again there was a Free-state boycott, and the Lecompton Constitution was adopted on the basis of thousands of fraudulent votes. So egregious was the sham election that even territorial governor Robert Walker – a pro-slavery Democrat appointed by Buchanan – denounced it as "a vile fraud, a bare counterfeit." Walker resigned in protest and, along with a significant number of northern Democrats, urged the president to reject the Lecompton Constitution out of hand.[6]

Buchanan disregarded Walker's counsel. Bowing to pressure from the Southern wing of his party, the president announced his support for the Lecompton Constitution in December 1857, proposing to submit it to Congress as the basis for Kansas's admission to the Union as a Slave state. Many northern Democrats were outraged at the perfidy, none more so than Senator Douglas, who had built his career on the ideal of popular sovereignty. Douglas was more than willing to tolerate slavery in the territories, but only when it was endorsed by a majority of white citizens in a free election. The Lecompton Constitution satisfied neither condition: the election had been a farce, and a majority of legitimate settlers in Kansas – excluding Missourians who crossed the border for the sole purpose of casting illegal ballots – were clearly opposed to slavery.

Douglas now faced a crisis of conscience. His political future was linked in the near term to the Buchanan administration, as was his access to patronage. On the other hand, acceptance of the Lecompton Constitution would violate his most pronounced principles. Douglas could be a cagey operator when the situation called for it, but this time principle won out.

Douglas obtained a meeting with Buchanan at which he informed the president that he would lead the opposition to the Lecompton bill. Buchanan retorted that Douglas would pay a price for breaking with his party's leadership, reminding him of the fate of senators who had defied Andrew Jackson. "Mr. Douglas," said the president, "I desire you to remember that no Democrat ever yet differed from the Administration of his own choice without being crushed."

"Mr. President," replied Douglas defiantly, "I wish you to remember that General Jackson is dead."[7]

Neither man was thinking about the new marshal for the Northern District of Ohio in the midst of their quarrel, but the impact of the bitter rift between Douglas and Buchanan would soon be felt on the shores of Lake Erie. Senator Douglas and his ally Senator Pugh would lose any hope for influence over patronage appointments, while Buchanan would use every means at his disposal in his attempt to round up pro-Lecompton votes from the Democrats in Ohio's congressional delegation.

Applicants for the Northern District marshal's position had been lining up throughout 1857, but the open rupture between Buchanan and Douglas turned the queue into a parade.[8] At least a dozen aspirants pled their cases – both on paper and in person – each one producing glowing testimonials from Ohio's Democratic luminaries. Buchanan must have been frustrated, or at the very least bored, by the numbing sameness of the applications and letters of endorsement. Every man was touted from beginning to end as a loyal Democrat whose appointment would unify the party.[9] One applicant included a petition from Democratic members of the state assembly;[10] another had the support of a group of state senators;[11] a third countered with the signatures of a diverse group of party leaders and office holders;[12] and a fourth, more creatively, pointed out that his key rival was already a probate judge who, if given the marshal's job, would be replaced on the court by a "Black Republican" to be appointed by Governor Salmon Chase.[13] One hapless applicant was able to enlist but a single supporter, who happened to be his own daughter. It was most unusual in that era – perhaps unique – for a woman to write a candidate endorsement, but apart from her graceful handwriting, the young lady's letters were indistinguishable from the others in appealing to party unity.[14]

In most circumstances, a president would not have been bothered by the uniformity of the candidates, as he would simply take the counsel of a local political leader who knew the aspirants either personally or by reputation. In Ohio, that ordinarily would have been Senator George Pugh. But Pugh had broken with the administration on Lecompton – he was one of only four Democrats in the U.S. Senate to oppose the bill – and he was therefore exiled from the president's circle of advisors.[15] President Buchanan would make this appointment strictly by his own lights.

Matthew Johnson was an unlikely prospect to stand out in such a crowded field. A former businessman from Toledo, he had only a modest background in Democratic politics and was unknown to many party leaders, even in the northern part of the state.[16] Worse, his major business venture, the Commercial Bank of Toledo, had collapsed in bankruptcy, leaving many depositors "in ruin and disgrace."[17] Johnson denied malfeasance or irresponsibility in the bank's insolvency, claiming to have been duped by his partners. That may have been true, as his associates were described as experts at making "their bank appear so clean, while at the same time it was so very foul."[18] But even as a victim of others' chicanery, there was no way for Johnson fully to escape the aura of failure – as a "broken down banker" – that surrounded him.[19] With a thin résumé and a flat wallet, how could he hope to obtain a position so eagerly pursued by others with rich and influential backers? As it happened, he had a plan.

Among the office seekers, only Matthew Johnson departed from the narrow path of party cohesion and instead boldly entered the Lecompton swamp. It is possible that he sincerely believed in Buchanan's position on the admission of Kansas as a Slave state, but it is more likely that he was shrewdly trying to distinguish himself among a gaggle of otherwise indistinguishable contenders (as well as overcome his inability to gather much support among mainstream Democrats, most of whom had endorsed other applicants). To be sure, Johnson produced the predictable attestations to his "consistent and strong support of the Democratic Party," as well as several more finely tailored letters that vouched for his probity in the wake of the failure of his Commercial Bank of Toledo.[20]

Ultimately more important to Johnson's cause, however, was his strategic decision to stake out a position as the only identifiably pro-Lecompton candidate for the job. Rather than appeal to party unity – and no doubt aware of Buchanan's threat to crush internal dissenters – Johnson took advantage of the rift among Ohio Democrats by submitting a petition from "supporters of the wise and patriotic Kansas policy of the Administration." While others attempted to play both sides, or at least remain on good terms with the Douglas–Pugh wing of the party, Johnson argued that his appointment was "most earnestly desired by the friends of the Administration in Toledo [because] it would materially strengthen their hands" in dealing with the anti-Lecomptonites. The petition was signed by fifty-eight men – none of whom appear to have been notable officeholders – who unapologetically identified themselves as "Administration Democrats," in sharp distinction to supporters of the "Douglas Democracy."[21]

Johnson submitted other letters to the same effect, leaving no stone unturned in his efforts to convince Buchanan of his unique loyalty on the Kansas question. He even included one letter from an Ohio Republican congressman who, having defected from the Democrats over the expansion of slavery into the territories, confirmed that Johnson "remained steadfast, & I am sorry to add, seems hopelessly unconvertible."[22] No candidate other than Johnson appears to have taken such an outspoken position on the Kansas issue, siding openly with Buchanan at the risk of alienating the local grandees of his party.

THE SIGNATURES OF THE TOLEDO DEMOCRATS had been collected at a public meeting in support of the Lecompton bill, but Johnson was a talented conniver, and not all of his efforts were in the open. In early March 1858, Johnson obtained a private meeting with Buchanan, at which he proposed a remarkable deal. In exchange for appointment as marshal, Johnson promised to deliver the vote of Democratic Congressman Joseph Burns, who was known to be wavering on Lecompton. Johnson followed up the meeting with a letter to President Buchanan in which he reiterated his offer, while reassuring the president that Burns would vote as requested. "We have a distinct confidential understanding," Johnson explained.[23]

Buchanan's response, if any, is unknown. But Johnson characteristically decided to take no chances. He spread rumors about his most prominent opponents, Abner Dickinson and William Gill, both of whom had been supported at various times by Senator Pugh.[24] The whispering campaign intimated that Dickinson had "professed to be anti-Lecompton," and, more scurrilously, that Gill had "seduced a mason's daughter and had been expelled from a Masonic Lodge." Dickinson discreetly withdrew "for the harmony of the party."[25] Gill, however, had been stung by the accusation, and he felt compelled to respond by producing a letter from his pastor and a certificate of good standing from his lodge.[26]

Johnson's trickery was not yet exhausted. He informed Buchanan, and evidently leaked word to others, that Gill was willing to concede the marshal's position to Johnson in exchange for his own appointment as secretary for Nebraska. Gill angrily denied making any such deal, and he informed the president that Johnson had "no authority" to engage in any bargaining on his behalf. Gill's fury was palpable on the page as he denounced Johnson's chicanery in a letter to Attorney General Jeremiah Black. "*Such* a concession," Gill wrote, "would certainly be dishonorable not only to myself but to my friends." He asked Black to inform the president that he would "prefer a defeat to dishonor."[27]

Defeat was exactly what William Gill received. Relying on the help of his weighty political backers, Gill had remained confident that the job was his. But the rumors had taken a toll, and his most prominent supporters deserted him, as many feared that any continued endorsement of Gill would be seen as support for the "renegade" Senator Douglas and a disavowal of Buchanan's own "Kansas-Nebraska Democracy."[28] Poor Gill had personally importuned the president for over a year, visiting the White House so often that he was said to have "lived in Washington, constantly, since Old Buck was inaugurated," on the assumption that the official announcement would come any day. Instead, Gill was "strangled in the meshes of the executive net" when Buchanan chose Lecompton loyalty over broader party bona fides.[29]

Johnson was appointed marshal, and Representative Burns voted with the administration on the Lecompton Constitution – which was nonetheless defeated narrowly in the House of Representatives. But that was not quite the end of it.

Word spread of Burns's possible vote trading, which led to accusations of misconduct in the press and on the floor of the House of Representatives.[30] Burns angrily defended himself, admitting that he had lobbied Buchanan on behalf of Johnson but denying any "collusion . . . in regard to the promise of office, or official patronage."[31] A motion was presented for an investigation by the House, but it died on a party-line vote. Burns's political fortunes, however, were fatally damaged. Despite a later apology, his Lecompton vote led to a split in the local Democratic organization, and a Republican subsequently defeated him for reelection.[32]

Matthew Johnson, to his good fortune and to Oberlin's chagrin, was unaffected by the Burns contretemps. He received his commission and assumed office in Cleveland, determined to support administration policy with vigorous devotion. The defeat of the Lecompton Constitution, however, still resonated over northern Ohio, where the "Douglas Democracy" continued to claim the loyalty of many voters and party stalwarts.[33] As Buchanan's man on the ground, it was therefore Johnson's job to enforce policies that were overtly pro-Southern and pro-slavery.

Dozens of runaways were passing with near immunity through Cleveland and other Ohio towns, headed for Lake Erie ports such as Ashtabula, Lorain, Sandusky, and Conneaut, where they would be ferried safely across to Canada. That situation was becoming intolerable for Buchanan, who greatly needed the continuing support of slave owners in order to maintain his control over the national Democratic Party. And nothing would make the southern Democrats happier than enhanced enforcement of the Fugitive Slave Act, especially in the abolitionist counties of northern Ohio. Early on, therefore, Johnson decided to extend his authority right into the heart of Oberlin. If the Lecompton Constitution could not bring slavery to Kansas, the U.S. marshal could at least squelch abolitionism in the most defiant corner of his newly acquired fiefdom. Escaping Negroes, and their underground friends, would have great reason to fear the presence of a federal law officer regularly staked out near the middle of town, Johnson figured.

It was a perfect strategy for a schemer like Johnson, combining surveillance with intimidation and occasional force. The marshal lacked only one element to make his "war on Oberlin" a success.[34] He needed an enthusiastic deputy.

NINE

"RECITAL OF THE WRONG AND OUTRAGE"

Anson Dayton held a grudge against the African-Americans of Oberlin, which made him the perfect cog for Matthew Johnson's rumbling machinery of justice. Dayton had moved to Oberlin sometime in 1854 or 1855, attracted by the building boom in the rapidly growing town. He was a capable mason, and he initially went into business with his brother-in-law, Benjamin Pierce. Their firm, Pierce & Dayton, found plenty of work in Lorain County, laying the foundations for homes and stores.[1] Dayton eventually found that labor too strenuous, however, and insufficiently remunerative to support his growing family. He therefore changed professions, reading law in the office of an Elyria attorney, which allowed him to become one of the first lawyers to establish an office in Oberlin.[2] Dayton's skills as an attorney, however, proved deficient, even in a locale without much competition. In a characteristic demonstration of charity – although one that was soon regretted and ultimately rued – the village fathers installed Dayton as the township clerk, a position in which he was responsible for collecting fees and dispensing funds to paupers and the "transient poor," the latter being a euphemism for fugitive slaves.[3]

Unlike the Oberlin colonists, nearly all of whom followed Finney's First Church Congregationalism, Dayton was an Episcopalian who had no commitment to the abstemiousness of the Oberlin Covenant or the anti-slavery principles of the Lane compact. He was one of the founders of the Christ Church Episcopal Parish, which was established in late 1855 to counteract the "wild ultraisms" and "politico-religious teaching" that otherwise dominated town life. The objectionable "politico-religious teaching," of course, was abolitionism.[4] The Episcopal Church spanned the Free and Slave states, with many important congregations in Virginia and throughout the South. The denomination therefore condoned, or even tacitly supported, slavery, with most leaders either silent on the subject or strongly in favor of enforcement of the Fugitive Slave Act. To be sure, many individual Episcopalians resolutely opposed slavery – in the tradition of the great Anglican abolitionists, such as William Wilberforce and Granville Sharp – but the American church was in no position to denounce slaveholding as a sin, much less deny Communion to slave owners.[5]

His religion notwithstanding, Dayton identified himself as a Republican during his early days in Oberlin, which was necessary if he was to fulfill what was later called his "greed for office."[6] Perhaps he was even sincere, although events would soon cause him to change his affiliation in the sharpest possible way.

In 1857, Dayton was removed as town clerk, as well as from a position as school manager, to be replaced in both jobs by John Mercer Langston, who had recently been admitted to the bar.[7] Oberlin took great pride in having elected the first black public official in the United States, but Dayton did not take the outcome graciously. Not only had he endured the ignominy of defeat by a black man, but he also suffered the loss of the town's legal business, which was one of the principal benefits of the clerkship. As Langston later put it, "these were important positions in the township, and were of special advantage to a lawyer needing popular endorsement and advertisement in establishing himself in his profession."[8]

Clearly "jealous of his colored successor," Dayton switched party allegiance and joined the "little squad of Locofocos who hang around the Post Office," where he could commiserate with the only federal official – and thus the only Democratic officeholder – in town.[9] Dayton briefly returned to the practice of law, but he was unable to succeed in Oberlin, where his inconstant political affiliations caused him to be dismissed as a "pettifogger."[10] He was rescued from penury by his new allies, who, comprising the majority in the Ohio House of Representatives, appointed him clerk of the state legislature for the 1857–58 session.[11]

Dayton's legislative term passed uneventfully, and he returned to Oberlin in 1858, again seeking employment. He and Marshal Matthew Johnson soon found one another, united by their disdain for abolitionism and their complementary needs – one political, the other financial – to enforce the Fugitive Slave Act. Anson Dayton thus became the first deputy federal marshal ever assigned to patrol Oberlin.[12] His only duty was to track down runaway slaves.[13]

JOHN ANTHONY TURNED TWENTY-FOUR IN 1858, the year of Dayton's return, having grown to young manhood in the abolitionist environs of Oberlin. He had withdrawn from the preparatory department three years earlier, parting company with the Jones brothers, four of whom would eventually go on to graduate from the college.[14] He did remain close friends with Elias Toussaint, who was, ironically, the least adventuresome of the many Joneses. John Anthony worked with his father, becoming skilled as a carpenter and joiner, and contributing his earnings to the family's support. In the winter, when business was slow, he sometimes taught school in Logan County, where the Negro schools were in such constant need of teachers that lack of a high school certificate was not disqualifying.[15] John Anthony's parents had been raised in the Protestant faiths common among African-Americans in North Carolina – his father a Methodist and his mother a Presbyterian – but in Oberlin the family attended the Congregationalist First Church, along with nearly all of the other black residents.[16]

John Anthony was devoted to his family, diligent at his work, and serious about his religion. He was also deeply moved by the plight of slaves in the South, as well as the "transient poor," as runaways were known in Oberlin. He was recognized as "one of the most efficient and prominent members of the Oberlin Anti-Slavery Society "speaking frequently at meetings and exerting a calming influence when discussions "would wax warm." He did not defer to his white friends when they attempted to dominate the debates. Instead, he would strike a pose, with a wry smile and his hands in his pockets, while explaining that "colored men were capable of self-expression and self-government" and were not in need of white leadership. His participation was evidently memorable for both his posture and his eloquence. At one meeting, he was said to have condemned "the lamentable fact that in the American nation, under its flag of liberty and independence, four and a half millions of human beings are to-day crushed under iron-shod oppression."[17] The language may seem ornate coming from a young man who did not complete high school, but Copeland's surviving letters, written from a Virginia jail cell, include similar rhetorical flourishes. Of course, recollections of Copeland became more idealized in the decades following his martyrdom, with

John Mercer Langston's 1894 memoir as perhaps the most profuse exemplar. In his own characteristic verbosity, Langston extolled Copeland's "manly nature," saying that the "highest and best testimonial may be borne to his character and name, as well as to his devotion to those principles of liberty and equal rights of which he had learned at home." In a similar vein, Langston described a speech of Copeland's at a Liberty School meeting, including his "recital of the wrong and outrage" of slavery "and how glad he would be to see the institution under which such abuse was tolerated, overthrown and destroyed."[18] One might wonder whether the ornate language was Langston's rather than Copeland's, recalled as it was over thirty years later, but the more contemporaneous reminiscences of Copeland make it entirely believable that he would have used just such words. One friend remembered his heated condemnation of the Fugitive Slave Act: "We are all regarded in the eye of an impious enactment, as mere things. Consequently, we are subject to the basest wrong and violence."[19]

At least one of Langston's observations was unembellished. He attributed much of Copeland's devotion to the "principles of liberty and equal rights [to] the teachings which he had received in the school and the church of Oberlin."[20] Every black emigrant from North Carolina would naturally be opposed to slavery, as Langston of course realized, but the Oberlin environment gave John Anthony a broader perspective on organized resistance.

In summer 1847, for example, when John Anthony was turning thirteen, William Lloyd Garrison and Frederick Douglass arrived together for Oberlin's commencement ceremony, after which they engaged in a public debate with the college's president, Asa Mahan, over principles of abolitionism. Garrison and Douglass condemned the U.S. Constitution as pro-slavery and disdained all political activity (Douglass later changed his mind and broke with Garrison on the issue). Mahan, in contrast, advocated electoral politics – and, in particular, support for the Liberty Party – as the best means of ending slavery under the Constitution. The debate continued for four sessions, spread over two days, and it was attended by over 3000 people. Nobody in Oberlin was unaware of the significance of the debate, and most citizens were proud that Mahan had performed so well against such esteemed opponents.[21] As a young teenager, John Anthony would not have been alert to the nuances of antislavery philosophy, but he must have been impressed that such serious and important men were devoting so much attention and energy to the abolition of slavery. Nor could he have missed the presence of Frederick Douglass on the platform. No African-American youngster would have passed up an opportunity to see the most famous black man in the United States.

Douglas and Garrison would have had no reason to notice John Anthony, but they did take time to meet with a number of Oberlin students. The latter included Lucy Stone, a member of the class of 1847 and one of the first women in America to obtain a college degree. Stone went on to become a famous suffragist and abolitionist, her egalitarian and anti-slavery views having been sharpened at Oberlin. In 1856, she drew national attention when she attended the trial of the fugitive Margaret Garner, whose master was attempting to obtain her removal to Kentucky. When first captured by slave hunters near Cincinnati, Garner had killed her daughter, and had attempted to kill her sons, rather than see her children returned to slavery. Stone was rumored to have offered Garner a knife, with which she might commit suicide, while visiting her in jail. When questioned in court by an unbelieving U.S. commissioner, Stone's reply made headlines:

> I did ask her if she had a knife. If I were a slave, as she is a slave, with the law against me, and society against me, and the church against me, and with no death-dealing weapon at hand, I would with my own teeth tear open my veins and send my soul back to God who gave it.[22]

Lucy Stone's rebuke to the court drew rapt attention in Oberlin, as did every other victory or defeat for abolitionism throughout the turbulent 1850s: the passage of the Kansas-Nebraska Act; the ensuing war in Kansas, which drew scores of recruits from Oberlin and elsewhere in northern Ohio; the rescues of fugitive slaves (in New York and Massachusetts) and the rendition of others (in Massachusetts and throughout the North); and the infamous 1857 *Dred Scott* case, in which Chief Justice Roger Taney opined that black men had "no rights which the white man is bound to respect."[23] The *Dred Scott* decision elicited unbounded scorn in Oberlin, where it was denounced as "repugnant to the plain provisions of the constitution and subversive of the rights of freemen and free States."[24] Taney's pronouncement about the rights of black men rang in John Anthony's ears, and it would resound to him in an unexpected way as the decade neared its end. In the mid-1850s, however, John Anthony was still influenced more by his friends and relatives than by the Supreme Court.

When Delilah Evans Copeland departed Raleigh in 1843, she left behind her two younger siblings, Wilson and Henry. The two boys grew into adulthood in North Carolina, eventually marrying two sisters from the Leary family, Sarah Jane (who married Wilson) and Henriette (who married Henry). The Leary girls were much younger than their husbands, and they had a brother who was even younger. Lewis Sheridan Leary was born in March 1835, making him about a year younger than John Anthony Copeland.

Like many other free blacks in North Carolina, the Learys traced their ancestry to a white man who had served in the Revolutionary War, in this case Jeremiah O'Leary, who was of Irish and Croatan Indian background. Jeremiah married Sarah Jane Revels, a free woman of mixed black and Native American descent. The marriage might have been prohibited in North Carolina save for the fact that husband and wife both claimed Croatan ancestry, and Sarah Revels had always held herself "entirely aloof from Negroes."[25] The mulatto son of Jeremiah and Sarah, Matthew Nathaniel Leary, became a prosperous saddle maker and landowner in Fayetteville. In 1825, Matthew married Juliet Anna Meimoriel, a French woman who had been raised in Guadeloupe. The daughters of Matthew and Juliet were born shortly afterward, and they later married the Evans brothers.[26]

The Learys' youngest child was Lewis Sheridan, who, in common with his siblings, was sometimes thought to look "like an Indian, not a negro."[27] He was named after a local plantation owner – Lewis Sheridan – who had freed his slaves. According to Leary family lore, Mr. Sheridan had once courted Juliet Meimoriel, which adds an intriguing note to her story. There were few white women in the antebellum South who would have turned away a prosperous white suitor in order to marry a colored man, even one with Croatan lineage. Lewis Sheridan is also said to have moved to Liberia with his manumitted slaves, perhaps as a brokenhearted gesture to the woman who rejected him.[28]

The Leary family's comfortable life often seemed to transcend racial lines in Fayetteville. Matthew expanded his business with the aid of both free and enslaved laborers, and he later employed a white overseer to manage his affairs.[29] The Learys lived in a fine home, their children were educated by private tutors, and they were waited on by black servants, including slaves, whom they treated with the hauteur typical of the bourgeoisie everywhere. Henriette recalled an incident from her youth in which she was going to be the bridesmaid at a neighbor's summertime wedding. One of her duties was to bring flowers to the ceremony, and she feared they would wilt in the heat of the day. She therefore placed them in a box to protect them from the sun. On her way out of the house, she stopped in the drawing room "to show herself to her mother."

"Turn around – Let me see you," said Juliet. "Yes – you do very well. – But what is that in your hand?"

"A box," answered Henriette. "I thought I would carry my flowers & put them in there."

"A box!" exclaimed Juliet in horror. "Matthew Leary's daughter walk through the street with a box in her hand! Call one of the niggers!"[30]

The Learys' respectable standing was also acknowledged by their white neighbors. Thus, when North Carolina abolished free black suffrage in 1835, Fayetteville's *Carolina Observer* protested against such "total disenfranchisement of the free coloured people" on the grounds that "eight or ten" of the local African-Americans, certainly including Matthew Leary, possessed "every qualification of intelligence, respectability, usefulness, and property to entitle them, fairly, to exercise this high privilege."[31] Class distinctions aside, the Learys were nonetheless well aware of the oppression inherent in slavery. Matthew often hired slaves to work in his harness shop, paying them wages that could then be used to buy their freedom. Less admirably, he bought slaves at auction, afterward allowing them to "work out their purchase money" toward manumission.[32] Both practices were well intentioned, although the outright ownership of slaves obviously contributed to the attitude of privilege that pervaded the Leary household.

Young Lewis inherited his parents' independence but not their sense of caution. In the manner of a biblical prince, he was said often to have gone "among the slaves on the plantations around Fayetteville & preaching to them insurrection." Perhaps oblivious to the risk, as much to his listeners as to himself, he urged the field hands to rebel, declaring that "I would be no man's slave." There must be considerable exaggeration in the descriptions of Leary's mission to the slaves, which come from the interviews given many years later by his sister and his widow. No colored person in antebellum North Carolina – indeed, no white person of any station – could have openly preached rebellion and survived. Nonetheless, it does seem clear that Leary was perilously outspoken on the subject of slavery and that he was not always careful about his choice of audience. The family interviews were conducted separately, and the two women had been out of touch for decades, yet their recollections were quite consistent.[33]

We can only wonder how the plantation workers reacted to Leary, given that neither he nor anyone in his family had ever been a slave. It was one thing to profess resistance before returning to a comfortable life in a fine home but quite another to endure a whipping for disobedience. A more thoughtful man might therefore have worried about the usefulness of his message to the field hands, for whom insurrection would be suicidal, or the danger he was creating for his entire community. Leary, however, had a rashness about him that was born of his youth and good fortune. His family urged restraint, but "nothing could prevent him" from continuing to agitate for freedom.[34] Nearly to the end of his life, he would continue to disregard the impact of his actions on others.

Fayetteville eventually became "too hot" for Leary.[35] In one questionable story, again echoing Exodus, he was said to have intervened when he saw a master brutally whipping a slave. As told by a niece, "he immediately reversed the situation by taking the slave's part and soundly thrash[ing] the white master." Such an encounter, if it happened, or even if it came close to happening, would have been enough to endanger the life of any colored person in Fayetteville, no matter how well born.[36] It would have endangered his family as well – which makes the story even more unlikely, given that Matthew Leary continued to live and prosper in North Carolina throughout the antebellum and Civil War eras. In any case, Leary's sisters and their husbands decided to leave Fayetteville for Oberlin in 1854 and, as Henriette explained to a researcher many years later, "Matthew Leary thought it best for Sheridan to go with her, for his safety." Lewis's widow – who had also grown up in Fayetteville and was still living there in 1854 – put it more bluntly. He was "forced to fly," she said.[37]

There is another possible explanation for Lewis's departure, in which he was just as headstrong but not so foolish as to openly challenge the white power structure in Fayetteville. The imperious treatment of slaves in the Leary home must have been grating to a freedom-minded youth such as Lewis, especially given Matthew Leary's constant professions of abolitionism. If young Lewis had indeed urged slaves to claim their freedom, he might well have started with those in his own household. In doing so, he would not have been the first rebellious teenager to charge his father with hypocrisy, nor would Matthew have been the first parent to resent the arrogance of an overprivileged son. It is thus plausible that Lewis left Fayetteville in the wake of a falling out with his uncompromising father rather than in fear of retribution from slaveholders. That account is speculative, of course, but it does avoid the highly improbable story that Lewis had publicly beaten a white slave owner. Moreover, there is strong evidence of long-standing discord within the Leary family. Years later, when drawing up his will, Matthew Leary took careful measures to virtually disinherit all of his relatives who fled to Ohio, while bequeathing significant amounts to those who remained in North Carolina. Although he had accumulated a sizable estate, he pointedly left only $2 to his children and grandchildren in Oberlin. That was the action of a man who was bitterly estranged from members of his family, not of a solicitous parent who had urged his son to flee for his own safety.[38] Perhaps Lewis Sheridan Leary had no urgent reason to leave Fayetteville other than to get away from his father.

DESPITE THEIR STATUS AND THEIR NEARLY white backgrounds, the Evans–Leary families were not free to leave North Carolina at will. Both Wilson and Henry were obliged to enlist white sponsors to petition the governor for authorization to depart. Henry's patrons sought permission for the party to "pass by public conveyance from the Southern States without interruption," describing them as "entitled to as much respect and regard as any Colored family in our state." Wilson's request likewise sought "such a paper writing from your Excellency as will enable [the party to travel] without delay or hindrance."[39] Unlike the Copeland–Jones party ten years earlier, the Evans brothers were bound for Oberlin from the start, no doubt having been in touch with their sister Delilah Copeland. They were also able to make much of the trip by "public conveyance," traveling by rail through Virginia and then by river to Cincinnati, eventually reaching Oberlin in summer 1854.

Lewis Sheridan Leary had turned nineteen just before leaving Fayetteville. He might have known John Anthony Copeland as a child, and he was no doubt eager to meet him again as a young man. Some historians have erroneously referred to Leary as Copeland's uncle, although in fact their family relationship made them much more like second cousins.[40] Within a few years, they would be comrades in arms.

TEN

WACK'S TAVERN

JOHN SHIPHERD'S VISION FOR OBERLIN could not long endure. Despite his intention to establish an isolated colony exclusively for the "hopefully pious" and free from worldly distractions, the town's growing population and prosperity eventually attracted the "manufacturers and workmen" that the founders had hoped to avoid. As Oberlin expanded, so did the opportunities for commerce, thus leading merchants, jobbers, brokers, artisans, teamsters and haulers, and others to set up shop around the central square. Some of the businesses, of course, were run by faithful Oberliners, but many were run by outsiders who had no particular interest in Congregational salvation. The newcomers, needless to say, required services that the Oberliners themselves could not provide, especially alcohol and diversion, which were scorned by Reverend Finney's temperance-minded followers. It was therefore inevitable that there would be "saloons and other nuisances," as James Fairchild once put it, if only to serve the many travelers, craftsmen, and others who found themselves in Oberlin for reasons other than piety.[1]

Thus came Chauncy Wack's establishment, located on South Main Street not far from the Episcopal Church, and variously described as an inn, a hotel, and a tavern. The proprietor was a native of Vermont who had inherited none of New England's abolitionist spirit. Wack was out of place in Oberlin in many ways. He smoked, he drank, he voted for Democrats, and he was favorably inclined toward slavery. If that was not enough to make him an outsider, it was even said that he danced with his wife. But Wack had also identified an important niche in Oberlin's business community by offering food and lodging to those who were not satisfied by the plain fare and spartan conditions provided at the college-owned Palmer House, which was the only other hotel in town.

By the time Anson Dayton returned to Oberlin in 1858, with his deputy marshal's commission in hand, Wack's tavern had long been recognized as a gathering place for Oberlin's Episcopalians, misfits, and eccentrics. It was also the preferred haunt of local political dissidents – including representatives of the hated Buchanan administration, such as Postmaster Edward Munson and Deputy Anson Dayton. On warm evenings, the front porch was filled with coarse-looking men, joking and drinking ale, while the more modest locals did their best to avoid associating with the disreputable crowd. Youngsters were well advised to give the place a "wide berth," and children were even cautioned against playing quoits with Wack's children, for fear that they would pick up frivolous habits.[2]

Anson Dayton had more in mind, however, than simply passing time in the company of Chauncy Wack and his bibulous friends. His boss had gotten the marshal's job by pledging zealous adherence to President Buchanan's policies – including enforcement of the Fugitive Slave Act – and Dayton was likewise appointed for a reason. During his term as township clerk, Dayton had been responsible for dispensing funds to the "poor transients" who made up Oberlin's fugitive population. Consequently, he was familiar with many of Oberlin's black residents, and he was able to identify the ones most likely to be runaways. Capturing fugitives would be personally gratifying to Dayton, who still resented the elevation of John Mercer Langston at his expense, while fulfilling Matthew Johnson's obligation to the president.

But petty as he was, Dayton had a motive greater than revenge. Deputy U.S. marshals received no salary in the 1850s but depended instead on emoluments that were paid out on a per job basis. Even so, the sums were meager, and payment depended on approval by the First Auditor's Office in Washington, D.C., which was notoriously tight fisted. A typical disbursement might be as little as $15, although deputies were allowed to accept additional fees from third parties.[3] Dayton was one of thirty-eight deputies commissioned by Johnson in 1858, all of whom had to generate their own income. For some deputies, in larger cities such as Toledo and Cleveland, the position could be lucrative. In Oberlin, however, there was almost nothing remunerative that Deputy Dayton could do other than hunt fugitives. Consequently, there was no disguising his mission. Everyone in Oberlin realized exactly what their former clerk intended to do when he showed up with his new badge.

ANSON DAYTON'S ARRIVAL IN 1858 marked a pivotal year for John Anthony Copeland, who had quit school three years earlier to work in his father's carpentry shop. He remained on friendly terms with the younger Jones brothers – Elias, William, and John – all of whom continued their studies, while also serving on the Vigilance Committee that patrolled the environs for signs of slave hunters. John Anthony's contact with the oldest Jones brother was more sporadic. James Monroe had graduated from Oberlin College in 1849. He soon married and moved away, living for a few years in Cleveland before settling in Chatham, Canada West, where he established himself as an engraver and gunsmith.[4] Despite the distance, "Gunsmith" Jones stayed in close touch with his friends and family in Oberlin. He corresponded with his brothers, attended reunions, and contributed regularly to the Oberlin alumni directory. Jones was a staunch supporter of the Underground Railroad, which had a major terminus in Chatham. He sheltered many fugitives, including those who had traveled by way of Oberlin, and welcomed other anti-slavery visitors from the United States, always adhering to a "cosmopolitan" faith and believing that "all men are my brethren." As 1858 unfolded, he would serve as one of several important links between the Oberlin abolitionists and John Brown.[5]

Lewis Sheridan Leary was intelligent but not bookish. Unlike the Jones and Copeland children, and other enterprising emigrants from North Carolina, he had not been enrolled in school upon settling in Oberlin, perhaps because his parents remained behind in Fayetteville.[6] In his childhood, Lewis had attended a school for black children, paying more attention to music than to spelling or composition. His father was his "singing master," and he took instruction in several musical instruments as well. Leary also learned harness making from his father, who specialized in intricate stitching that turned the craft into a near art. Fortunately, one of Matthew Leary's apprentices, a mulatto named James Scott, had settled in Oberlin some years earlier. Scott took young Lewis into his shop, and they worked together making and repairing harnesses and saddles for the Oberlin trade.[7]

By 1858, Lewis Sheridan Leary and John Anthony Copeland had become friends, connected both by family and their mutual interest in the anti-slavery movement. Like John Anthony, Lewis Sheridan attended the evening meetings at the Liberty School, where he expressed his dedication to abolitionism and his willingness to use "any means which he could control and wield, to overthrow the institution which so thoroughly wronged" enslaved persons in the South.[8]

Otherwise, the two men were not much alike. John Anthony had grown up in Oberlin, as unaffected by racism as an African-American could be in antebellum America. Lewis Sheridan, in contrast, had come of age in Fayetteville, where his comfortable circumstances conflicted sharply with the treatment he and his family often received from white neighbors. It could not have escaped Lewis's attention that, despite his respectable and privileged background, he needed the intervention of white sponsors in order to depart North Carolina. He was, in the words of John Mercer Langston, acutely aware of the oppression that had "ruined the class with which he and his kin were identified." Nonetheless, Leary could be disdainful of those whom he did not consider among the "more advanced class of his people."[9]

John Anthony was deeply spiritual and religious, but Lewis Sheridan was far more worldly and aggressive than his friend. While John Anthony counseled consensus at meetings of the Anti-Slavery Society, Lewis Sheridan threw down challenges to everyone he considered less committed or less capable than himself, leading some of his friends to call him "a desperate fellow."[10] At Liberty School debates, Leary was known to admonish other African-Americans to "quit dancing and frolicking" and instead devote their time to self-improvement.[11] That was unexpected advice from a musician, but Leary was never one to worry over incongruity.

Of medium height, with broad shoulders and a muscular build, Lewis was an avid horseback rider and a fine athlete. He had light skin, high cheekbones, straight black hair, sharply arched eyebrows, and dark eyes. He favored a broad-brimmed hat, which he wore at an angle, sometimes tilting his head to make the contrast even more pronounced. John Mercer Langston described Leary's appearance as reflecting "manly determination," but a modern observer would have to call his affect rakish. There was a proud self-awareness about Leary – bordering on vanity – that would have great consequences for his family in the following year.

On May 12, 1858, Leary married Mary Simpson Patterson, whom he had known as a child in Fayetteville.[12] Mary was "an interesting and intelligent young colored lady" who, like Leary, claimed French and Native American ancestry.[13] She had come to Oberlin to enroll in the 1857–58 term of the preparatory department, but she left after only one year, perhaps because she had become pregnant.[14] Whatever the reason for ending her studies, early the following spring Mary gave birth to a daughter named Lois.[15] Fatherhood and married life appear not to have weighed heavily on Leary. He did not share confidences with his wife, and, in spectacular fashion, he soon would place his "manly determination" ahead of his family's welfare. Others would later tell stories of Lewis's devotion to Mary and baby Lois, but those accounts for the most part seem apologetic and contrived. But whatever the situation in his marriage, Lewis Sheridan's relationship with John Anthony remained close, as it would for as long as they both still lived.

IT WAS NOT LONG BEFORE the "official war on Oberlin commenced."[16] Deputy Dayton's first target was the Wagoner family, a husband, wife, and son who had escaped from slavery some two years earlier. As their friends later put it, the Wagoners had decided that "they owed more service to themselves than to a Kentucky master." Mr. Wagoner found work in Oberlin and Mrs. Wagoner took in laundry. Together, they were able to purchase a home and secure "the respect and sympathy" of the community.[17]

Unfortunately, Dayton's previous position as town clerk had allowed him to identify the Wagoners as fugitives, and he shared that information with slave hunters who were operating in the area. Shortly after midnight on a warm summer night, Dayton led a posse to the Wagoners' house. Rapping at the door, he succeeded in waking Mr. Wagoner, who demanded to know who was disturbing his sleep. "Mr. Johnson," replied Dayton, claiming that he was in need of clothes washing. Wagoner refused to open the door, and Dayton repeated his request. "Mr. Johnson, down here," he said, again claiming to have clothes for washing in the middle of the night. "Come out and get it."[18]

Mr. Wagoner may have been illiterate, but he was nobody's fool. He immediately "smelt a rat" in the interloper's rude insistence on late-night laundry. "I'll give you washing," he shouted, while calling loudly for his son to fetch his gun. Intentionally making a racket, Wagoner opened his door, only to see Deputy Dayton "lumbering over the rail fence" and running into the street. Dayton's two cronies, who had been stationed at the edge of the property, quickly joined him in flight. Showing more fury than prudence, Wagoner gave chase. "Robbers, Kidnappers," he yelled, as he "rushed after the invaders of his rest and his rights." Dayton and his men jumped into a waiting carriage while firing pistols into the air. The noise awoke the Wagoners' neighbors, most of whom were African-Americans, and "nightcaps and woolly heads popped out in all quarters." Wagoner and his friends – likely including the Jones and Evans brothers, who lived nearby – continued to give chase, shouting "stop that carriage" until the slave hunters vanished in the distance. Thus, according to the abolitionist press, was "the United States negro kidnapping *posse commitatus* put to ignominious flight by Sambo in his shirt-tail, armed with a broken, unloaded old blunderbuss."[19] Soon a comic song was making the rounds in Oberlin, taunting Dayton for his hasty retreat:

> Who was the first to break and run,
> Though strongly armed and four to one,
> From Wagner [sic] with his lockless gun?
> Our Marshal.[20]

The Wagoners themselves were not able to see any humor in the situation. Despite assurances of safety from Oberlin's leading figures, the family soon departed for Canada, having decided to "escape from the talons of the Eagle" by seeking protection under "the claws of the Lion."[21] They were wise to decamp. Dayton had been easily intimidated by a black man with a shotgun, but he was not yet finished hunting slaves. He had been appointed Johnson's deputy for the sole purpose of seizing fugitives, and his need for income somehow overcame his fear of retribution.

Shortly after the Wagoner fiasco, Dayton struck again. This time, he brought four men with him in an attempt to capture a black woman and her two children. Forewarned by the attack on the Wagoners, however, the woman recognized the slave hunters before they could seize her, and she began shouting for help. Her screams aroused the neighbors, who came rushing to her assistance. As before, Dayton and his men were in no mood for a confrontation, and they fled at the first sign of resistance. But that was not the end of it. Oberlin's commencement exercises were held only three days later, and Dayton shrewdly figured that most of the citizens would be busy at the ceremony, thus making it a perfect time to renew his attack. He figured wrong. Once again, he attempted to arrest the woman and her children, and once again she began calling for help. Her cries carried all the way to campus, where the assembled students and spectators – John Anthony and his friends likely among them – quickly jumped into action. They set off the village fire bells and, together with the fire company, went racing to the source of the screams. Thwarted once more, Dayton retreated to reconsider his tactics.[22]

The frontal assaults had failed, but Dayton also had other means at his disposal. Well before his three failed raids, the deputy had been angling to entrap another runaway, this time by stealth. James Smith was a mixed-race fugitive from North Carolina – "so bleached by Democratic amalgamation that he could almost pass for a white man" – who had been working in Oberlin as a stonecutter. Having had access to the town records in his former position as clerk, Dayton suspected that Smith was a runaway and set out to prove it. On the pretext of friendship, Dayton visited Smith's workshop and "wormed from him his slave history." Dayton then wrote to the slave owner in North Carolina – who appears to have been Smith's father as well as his master – "promising the return of the prodigal son as soon as the necessary documents should be received."[23] Fortunately, Smith still had friends in "The Old North State," who caught wind of the scheme and alerted him to the danger of apprehension. The upshot would lead to John Anthony's first battle against slavery, which was both efficient and successful.

Realizing Dayton's treachery, Smith gathered a few friends, including John Anthony, who armed themselves with hickory staves and set out to teach Dayton a powerful lesson. Confrontations with slave hunters had by then become relatively familiar occurrences in the Free states – often through passive resistance and sometime by violence – but they usually took the form of interception or rescue. That is what had happened a few weeks earlier in Oberlin, in the case of the Wagoners, when Dayton and his posse were frightened away by the mere sight of a shotgun. Once the slave catchers were thwarted, they were allowed to retreat with no further damage. Even the most aggressive rescuers in other places had drawn the line at protecting fugitives from capture and had stopped fighting once their immediate objectives were achieved.

John Anthony could have hidden James Smith or acted as his bodyguard. Or the two of them could simply have waited for Deputy Dayton to strike, confident that their fellow Oberliners would have helped protect Smith from the clutches of the federal law. Instead, however, they boldly tracked down the marshal, confronting him in broad daylight. That was an audacious tactic, seldom if ever seen before in any part of the country, but somehow almost to be expected in Oberlin. Unlike the situation in other abolitionist strongholds – such as Boston and Syracuse – there was scant divided sentiment in Oberlin. Almost everyone was opposed to slavery, and almost no one deferred to the Fugitive Slave Act for the sake of law and order. Having grown up in the South, a fugitive such as James Smith might nonetheless have been reticent about openly challenging authority, but John Anthony had been raised from boyhood in Oberlin, where "every man, woman, and child" had long before sworn "between clenched teeth to recommit themselves to emancipation."[24]

African-American journalist William Watkins had fretted over the apathy of Northern blacks in the face of slave hunting, and called for greater willingness to fight against anyone "who would rob him of his God-given rights."[25] In sharp contrast, he held up the African-Americans of Oberlin as his example of those "who were not afraid of the white man."[26]

It was therefore rousing, if not wholly surprising, when Smith and Copeland accosted Dayton on the street and "caned him until he ran bellowing for help." No one was willing to intervene on the despised deputy's behalf, however, and Dayton was forced to flee for refuge in the college-owned Palmer House, where he hid until his outraged pursuers departed. Dayton's beating was grist for another mocking verse,

> Who, bearing his revolvers twain,
> Fled from a boy but with a cane,
> And bawled for help with might and main?
> Our marshal.[27]

As delighted as Oberlin was by Dayton's humiliation, the authorities could not completely ignore the brazen assault on a white deputy by colored men. Copeland and Smith were therefore arrested on perfunctory charges of battery. The prosecution was placed in the sympathetic hands of attorney Samuel Plumb, one of Oberlin's leading abolitionists, who simply allowed the matter to drop upon the payment of a minimal fine. Copeland and Smith do not appear to have begrudged the small expense, the latter remarking that he had, thanks to the fight, "become a really free man."[28] So ended John Anthony's first violent confrontation with the long arm of slavery, as well as his first encounter with the law.

ELEVEN

A BRACE OF PISTOLS

Anson Dayton had not managed to catch any slaves, but his efforts had certainly succeeded in putting the entire town of Oberlin on edge. Tensions only mounted when several rowdy strangers showed up on the front porch of Wack's tavern in late August, laughing loudly and speaking in the immediately recognizable accent of rural Kentucky. Even children realized that the rough-looking men were out of place in Oberlin. Ten-year-old William Cochran learned what they were up to when he accompanied his uncle, a farmer named Stephen Cole, on a visit to the forge of Augustus Chambers, an African-American blacksmith.

Between the hissing of the fire and the crash of the hammer, William at first had to strain to hear the conversation between Chambers and his uncle. Soon, however, the blacksmith raised his voice, almost to an excited shout. "How long are you going to let these man stealers lie around Oberlin? I don't call them *slave-catchers*; there are mighty few *slaves* around here. I call them *man-stealers* – devilish thieves!" In fact, there were nearly always slaves in the area, hiding in the forest and swampland that stretched between Oberlin and Elyria. Chambers was in touch with the fugitives, whom he would often bring to Cole's farm for a brief respite before they continued onward to Canada. Now, however, Cole was concerned that Chambers was in danger, and he suggested that the blacksmith himself "go into hiding for a few days."[1]

"No, Sir!" the black man thundered, "*I stay right here.* And if any of those men darkens my door, he is a dead man." Chambers showed the astonished boy and his uncle an array of weapons that he held at the ready – a hammer, a sharpened poker, a "double-barrel shotgun loaded with buck," several knives, and "a pistol hung on the siding near his bed." Over and over again, Chambers shouted that he would kill a man stealer

"Quicker'n a dog. As God as my judge, the man who tries to take my life will lose his own."[2]

Cole attempted to assure his friend that there was no need for mayhem. Chambers had free papers, and Oberlin's well-organized Vigilance Committee would come to his defense. Besides, there would have to be a hearing before slave hunters could remove a captive from the state, and Chambers's neighbors would all testify for him. The blacksmith could not be calmed. "They will take me way off somewhere where you-uns can't come and more'n likely they won't try me at all. They'll slip me over the Ohio River if they can and say nothing to nobody." Even if there were to be a hearing, it would be before "a Commissioner appointed by a Democratic judge," he continued, his voice breaking with emotion. "When you pick up a negro worth $1000 or $2000, there is *money to divide among all concerned.* There is *nothing coming* to anybody if you set him free."[3]

Self-employed artisans were the backbone of Oberlin's free black community. The Langston brothers were professionals – a lawyer and a teacher – but Oberlin's other leading African-Americans were blacksmiths such as Augustus Chambers and Allen Jones, carpenters such as the Evans brothers and John Copeland, Sr., and harness makers such as James Scott and Orindatus Wall (who was also the Langstons' brother-in-law). Like burghers the world over, the successful black men and women of Oberlin frequently discussed their shared hopes and fears. If Augustus Chambers felt comfortable venting his anger in front of white men such as Stephen Cole, we can only imagine the fury he must have expressed to Allen Jones and John Copeland, Sr. Unlike fugitive slaves, many of whom would wisely depart for Canada in the face of trouble, most of the prosperous black Oberliners were in firm agreement with Chambers's defiant stance: "*I stay right here.*" They were equally determined to protect the actual runaways, who mostly worked as laborers or domestic servants, recognizing that the stability of their entire community depended on vigorous self-defense.

Thus, Chambers was speaking for Oberlin's entire black establishment – including the Copelands, the Evanses, the Joneses, and the Langstons – when he denounced the inequities of the Fugitive Slave Act and rejected full faith in the processes of the law. Although their white neighbors could shrug off the sudden resurgence of slave hunting – laughing at the buffoonish deputy marshal and relying on the probity of the courts – African-Americans knew better. "Any white man who wants to make a few hundred dollars can swear away my rights," Chambers fumed. All they need to do is "spot a likely negro, get his description [and] then get some fellow down south to claim him" by executing a power of attorney.[4] Fortunately for James Smith, Deputy Dayton had been thwarted before such documents had arrived from North Carolina, but there was no telling when the next slave hunter, papers in hand, would locate a victim.

John Anthony and his friends had already taken a stand when they caned Anson Dayton on the steps of the Palmer House, but the newcomers at Wack's tavern were not the sort who could be intimidated by mere hickory staves. Even as Augustus Chambers was fulminating in his smithy, the Kentuckians were conspiring with Dayton over plans to catch fugitives unawares and unprotected.

THERE WAS NO MISTAKING ANDERSON JENNINGS for anything other than a "fine specimen of a Kentucky slave hunter." Standing over six feet tall, Jennings had a thick beard, a muscular frame, and the forceful gait of a man who was accustomed to overpowering others. He carried a brace of pistols that he did not bother to conceal and a bowie knife on his belt that he fondly called an "Arkansas toothpick."[5] As Professor James Fairchild later recalled, professional slave hunters were not generally drawn from among "the select and cultured of southern society," and they conducted their business "with no apprehension of its repulsiveness." A slave hunter's natural bearing, according to Fairchild, embodied "the bull-whip, the pistol, and the Bowie knife," and Jennings fit the stereotype of a low-class brute.[6]

Jennings was carrying papers for the arrest of a Mason County runaway named Henry, whom he suspected might be living in Oberlin. Upon arriving at Wack's tavern, the slave hunter sought the assistance of Deputy Dayton. The two men huddled together, comparing Henry's description to those of known fugitives in Oberlin, but Dayton was not able to put the finger on anyone. His initial mission thwarted, Jennings asked Dayton if there were any other likely prospects in the area. Dayton readily complied, ticking through the list of those he could identify from his term as township clerk. Soon he got to John Price, whom Jennings believed he could identify as the property of John Bacon, his Mason County neighbor. Delighted at the unexpected chance to take a prisoner, Jennings wrote to Bacon with the information that he had "discovered a nigger near Oberlin answering to the description of his runaway, John," and requesting a power of attorney that would authorize him to make the arrest.[7]

Jennings had not yet given up on finding his original quarry, and he was determined to search other known refuges in the Western Reserve. He asked Dayton to accompany him to Painesville, about thirty miles east of Cleveland, where he thought Henry might be hiding. Always eager for a fee, Dayton agreed to make the trip, even though Painesville was well outside his assigned jurisdiction. Arriving in the morning, the two men began to make what they thought were discreet inquiries. Of course, they were mistaken about their supposed anonymity. The two strangers were immediately conspicuous, as they were seen "prowling about the houses and working places of the colored folks."[8]

Soon an angry crowd gathered, demanding to know the strangers' business. Jennings and Dayton "evaded as much as possible, but still said sufficient to satisfy [the] citizens that they were in quest of colored men." Unfortunately for the slave hunters, anti-slavery sentiment was as strong in Painesville – which had been founded by the "red-hot abolitionist" General Edward Paine – as it was in Oberlin.[9] The crowd – including both whites and blacks – became threatening, and the slave hunters were given only twenty minutes to leave town. Badly shaken, Jennings headed for the railroad station, grumbling that he had "never seen so many niggers and abolitionists in any one place in my life." "Might as well try to hunt the *devil* there as to hunt a nigger," he later added.[10] The citizens of Painesville agreed with the sentiment, if not the language. The local press observed ominously that "we don't know what the colored men here would have done [to the slave catchers], but we do know that self-preservation is the first law of nature." In Painesville, at least, the colored men were not alone. "A slave cannot breathe our air," declared one journalist, "nor can one who breathes it be reduced to slavery."[11]

The trip to Painesville had been a disaster for both men. Jennings was forced to depart empty-handed, but the situation was even worse for Dayton. He had been recognized as a deputy marshal, and word of his excursion had been sent back to Oberlin. "We should think that Oberlin would be a warm place for such a kind of man to live in," came the not so subtle warning. Dayton's days as a would-be slave catcher were not quite over, but the expedition to Painesville was the last one he would ever lead in person.

Meanwhile, Jennings's letter had reached Kentucky, where Bacon immediately set about assembling the necessary documents. The slave owner proceeded to the Mason County courthouse, where he executed a power of attorney appointing Jennings as his lawful agent "to capture and return the negro, John, now at large in the state of Ohio." The fugitive slave was described as "about twenty years old, about five feet six or eight inches high, heavy set, copper colored, and will weigh about 140 or 50 pounds."[12] Rather than trust the mail, Bacon handed the document to another slave hunter, a Mason County neighbor named Richard Mitchell, who was instructed to deliver it to Anderson Jennings in Oberlin. Bacon gave Mitchell either $50 or $100 for expenses (accounts vary) and promised him a reward of $500 for the successful capture of John Price.

Mitchell and Jennings rendezvoused at Wack's tavern on September 8, 1858. They attempted to recruit Dayton to join them in the hunt, but the wary deputy had by then endured his full share of close calls. Having been twice threatened at gunpoint and beaten with staves, and with nothing to show for it in the way of emoluments or fees, Dayton sensibly concluded that Oberlin was indeed becoming too "warm" for him to continue as the local face of the slave-hunting Buchanan administration. He was still willing to assist slave catchers with advice and information – as much out of indignation and resentment as from any sense of duty – but he did not intend any longer to risk his hide in the pursuit of some other man's property.

EVEN BEHIND THE SCENES, Dayton was extremely useful to Jennings and Mitchell. He first advised them to obtain a warrant from a federal slave commissioner in Ohio. Although a warrant was not technically necessary – the Fugitive Slave Act allowed the slave catchers to proceed solely under the authority of the papers issued by the Kentucky court – Dayton was adamant that the posse needed to produce as much documentation as possible. Following his own failures, the local press had already predicted that it would be a "lively spectacle" if anyone attempted another slave seizure in Oberlin, and Dayton astutely reasoned that manifest legality – originating at every conceivable level – would be the best protection against forcible interference.[13]

Dayton further counseled the slave hunters to obtain their warrant in the Southern District of Ohio, located in Columbus, rather than the Northern District in nearby Cleveland. Jennings and Mitchell must at first have balked at the suggestion. Not only was Columbus farther away than Cleveland, but it was not even on a direct rail line from Oberlin, thus making the trip considerably longer and much more inconvenient. Dayton, however, had convincing reasons for the advice. Cleveland was an abolitionist stronghold, and the Kentuckians might as easily be recognized there as they had been in Painesville. Warrant or no warrant, their mission would become immediately endangered once word leaked out that they had visited the commissioner's chambers. Although he probably did not tell his new comrades, Dayton also had his own interests in mind. He had already become "*persona non grata*" in Oberlin owing to his "espionage on the colored population," and he hoped if at all possible to keep his fingerprints off the next attempted arrest.[14] A warrant from Columbus might at least appear as though it had been obtained without his assistance – or that of his boss, Marshal Matthew Johnson – thus providing an early example of what has since come to be called plausible deniability. That strategy would ultimately fail very badly, but Anson Dayton could hardly be blamed for trying.

The round trip to Columbus took two days, but it was even more productive than Dayton had anticipated. Jennings had no difficulty convincing Commissioner Sterne Crittenden to issue a warrant identifying John Price as "a person held to labor in the State of Kentucky [who] has escaped and is now a fugitive slave," and authorizing any law officer to seize John and bring his "body before some United States Commissioner . . . there to answer the said complaint, and be further dealt with according to law."[15] Equally important, Jennings had been able to enlist two more henchmen, having recruited Jacob Lowe, a deputy federal marshal, and Samuel Davis, a part-time jailer and deputy sheriff. Both men were experienced slave catchers who were eager to take the job for $50 apiece.

The four-man posse reconvened at Wack's tavern for dinner on September 10. If their intentions had been obvious before, they must have been glaring by that Saturday evening. Two Kentuckians and two out-of-town deputies could not possibly hope to pass unnoticed in a town as small as Oberlin. Jennings well understood that it was going to take more than muscle, or even force of arms, for the operation to succeed. He was going to need a local agent who could lure John Price away from the safety of abolitionist Oberlin. But who? Anson Dayton could accomplish nothing undercover, even if he had wanted to. Likewise, neither Chauncy Wack nor Postmaster Edward Munson, the town's other most prominent Buchananites, would have been willing to jeopardize his already shaky status in town, even for a handsome payday. Jennings therefore made other inquiries among the anti-abolitionists gathered in the tavern, and the consensus was that he ought to seek the assistance of General Lewis Boynton, a prosperous farmer – and a militant Democrat – who lived several miles from Oberlin.

Jennings and Lowe visited the Boynton farm the next day. Despite his military title, General Boynton was not a fighter (his rank turned out to be honorary, awarded during his brief tenure in the Ohio militia). He declined to become personally involved but, surprisingly, he offered the services of his thirteen-year-old son Shakespeare. The young Boynton was as bold as his father was reticent, and he impressed Jennings with his audacity and quick wit. With the general's approval, Jennings quickly struck a deal with "the little boy to come and get the nigger out of town" for a payment of $20.[16] If all went according to plan, Monday, September 13, would be John Price's last day of freedom in Ohio.

TWELVE

THE OBERLIN RESCUE

On Monday morning, September 13, 1858, young Shakespeare Boynton drove his father's wagon to the home of John Price. He first offered the black man a job digging potatoes, but Price declined because he was feeling under the weather. The resourceful Shakespeare quickly changed tacks, inviting Price to join him for a ride in the country. "The fresh air must feel good you," the boy said, promising the unsuspecting laborer that he would "bring you back again."[1] Price had no reason to mistrust a child, so he climbed into the buggy without realizing that he was heading into an ambush.

They had only driven for about ten minutes – perhaps traveling a mile from town – when they were met by a buggy carrying Mitchell, Lowe, and Davis. (Jennings had remained behind to avert suspicion.) The three slave catchers quickly overpowered John, forcing him at gunpoint from the farm wagon into their own buggy. With the frightened John Price wedged between them, a knife placed firmly at his neck, the slave hunters headed toward Wellington, almost ten miles distant, which was the nearest town with the necessary railroad connection.

Shakespeare Boynton's part in the betrayal was not quite complete. Once Price was securely in the custody of the slave hunters, the young man turned his wagon around and returned to Oberlin, where he informed Jennings – still waiting at Wack's – of the successful capture. Pleased by the good news, Jennings paid Shakespeare $20 and immediately departed for Wellington, where he was to meet up with his colleagues and their prisoner. From Wellington, their plan was to proceed by train to Columbus – where they expected to obtain a perfunctory rendition hearing before Commissioner Crittenden – and ultimately to Kentucky.

Price at first had seemed to acquiesce, telling his captors "I'll go with you" after only the briefest of struggles.[2] In fact, he was biding his time, and he soon had an opportunity for resistance. Within a few miles, another buggy passed in the opposite direction, and Price called out loudly for help. Fortunately, the driver of the second buggy was a young man named Ansel Lyman – an Oberlin student and staunch abolitionist who had once served with John Brown's Free-state militia in Kansas. Lyman heard Price's cry of distress and realized what was happening. He resolved to come to the black man's assistance, but he also saw that he was outnumbered and therefore took no immediate action.

Assuming that Price's shouts had been ignored, the kidnappers saw no reason for haste or concern, as they continued on the road to Wellington. Lyman, however, had other ideas. He sped his buggy into town in order to raise the alarm that a black man had been seized in the heart of Oberlin. Arriving in the town, Lyman "immediately aroused the people," who came rushing out of stores and homes upon hearing the shocking news.[3] Everyone had believed that it was impossible for a fugitive to be "stolen" from Oberlin, and the constant presence of runaways was an open secret in town. Only a week earlier, on September 6, Oberlin professors James Monroe and Henry Peck had barely bothered to conceal their assistance to five fugitives who were traveling from Medina to the nearest Lake Erie port and then on to Canada.[4] The audacity of the kidnappers was therefore as wrenching to the community as it was calamitous for the slave.

As word of the kidnapping spread, a crowd of outraged Oberliners gathered in the central square, amid cries of "rescue" and "they can't have him."[5] At least a hundred of them – both white and black – soon set off on the trip to Wellington, some in wagons or on horseback, and some even walking. Although most of Oberlin's white religious leaders were committed to nonresistance, many of the black men armed themselves.[6] As one participant put it, "revolvers slid quietly into their place, rifles were loaded and capped, and shot-guns, muskets, pistols and knives bristled or peeped on every side.[7] It is more likely that the weapons peeped than bristled, as no other observer recounted such an open display of armaments, but there is no doubt that the African-Americans in the crowd were especially prepared to fight if necessary.

Despite his fiery temper, Charles Langston was a cautious man at heart, more inclined to persuasion than confrontation. Still, he was well aware that slave hunters and their allies almost always carried weapons. Several years earlier, when on a speaking tour of small Ohio towns, Langston had been attacked by a gang of pro-slavery ruffians who chased him from his hotel at midnight. He had carried a gun ever since that night, figuring that to be a prudent measure for a black abolitionist, and he made sure it was tucked in his waistband when he headed to Wellingon.[8] Lewis Leary and his brothers-in-law, Wilson and Henry Evans (who were also John Anthony's uncles), set off together for Wellington. Henry was armed with "a small rifle."[9] The Evanses had a low opinion of John Price – they thought him lazy, as the middle classes often regard the less industrious poor – but that was no reason to tolerate his return to slavery.[10]

John Anthony Copeland also rushed to the aid of John Price. The identities of the slave catchers were yet unknown, but everyone in Oberlin suspected that Anson Dayton had a hand in the kidnapping. John Anthony therefore decided to bring a more threatening weapon than a hickory staff. He carried a revolver in his jacket, which he would draw at a crucial moment in the rescue.

Meanwhile, none of the kidnappers realized that they had been observed. Lyman's silence had lulled the men in the buggy into a false sense of security, and Jennings had departed Oberlin – assured by young Shakespeare that all had gone smoothly – well before Lyman arrived to sound the alarm. By 1:00 that afternoon, all of the slave hunters were in Wellington, congratulating each other on a job well done. The next train for Columbus was not scheduled to depart until 5:13, so the four white men took their prisoner to Wadsworth's Hotel, located on the town square, only two blocks from the railroad station. They expected to enjoy a leisurely meal in the dining room, oblivious to the storm that would soon build around them.

THE OBERLINERS BEGAN TO REACH WELLINGTON about an hour after the slave hunters had settled into their dinner. The crowd grew by the minute, joined by a smaller number of Wellington residents. Starting at the railroad station, frantic men ran from building to building, looking for the slave catchers and calling to one another as the frustrating search continued. The shouts grew louder, alternately cheering (for new arrivals) and cursing (when the slave hunters could not be found), until Jennings and company realized they had been followed.[11] Jacob Lowe, the deputy marshal from Cleveland, was the first to notice the commotion, which he drew to the attention of his companions. From the window of Wadsworth's, they saw a mob of abolitionists far larger and more dangerous than the one that had thwarted Jennings in Painesville the previous month. If the Kentuckian had been intimidated then by veiled threats of a beating, he must have been badly rattled by the sight of so many black men with rifles.

It would be another three hours until the southbound train arrived, and the path to the railway station was impassable in any event. Luckily for Jennings, however, the hotel owner – Oliver Wadsworth – was a pro-slavery Democrat, who offered to shelter the posse in a garret accessible only by a ladder from the second floor. As the slave hunters hurried their prisoner up the stairs, Wadsworth stationed his employees at the hotel's front and back entrances. Although the hotel was hardly a fortress, Jennings felt reasonably secure in the attic while he tried to figure out an escape plan.

It did not take long, however, for the Oberliners to discover that Jennings and company were hiding in the hotel. Eventually, at least 200 people – some estimates were much greater – surrounded the building, calling on the slave hunters to release their prisoner. Charles Langston would later be accused of leading the rescue, but in fact the mob was disorganized and leaderless. There was certainly no agreement about tactics: Should they storm the hotel, or merely demand proof that Price had been legally seized? Could a local judge or constable order an arrest of the slave hunters under Ohio law, or would they have to defer to the federal Fugitive Slave Act? Tempers grew hotter, both inside and outside the hotel, as the standoff entered its second hour.

Jennings was confident in the validity of his documents – he was holding a power of attorney and a federal warrant, both of which named Price as a runaway – and he made a bold decision to attempt to calm the mob by appealing to the law. Stepping out onto a balcony in the rear of the hotel, he waved his papers while loudly declaring that "this boy is mine by the laws of Kentucky and the United States [and] the boy is willing to go to Kentucky." That only made things worse, as almost nobody in the crowd cared a whit about the legality of Jennings's warrant. They were there to rescue a black man, and whether he had been born free or enslaved made no real difference. As one participant later explained, "the only fugitive law for which the people of Oberlin [had] any respect, is that recorded in the fifth book of Moses: 'Thou shalt not deliver unto his master the servant which is escaped from his master unto thee; he shall dwell with thee even among you.'"[12] Thus mindful of the biblical verse, someone shouted the rebuke that "there are no slaves in Ohio," while someone else threatened that they "would have the boy or pull the house down."[13]

Many in the crowd demanded that Price himself be brought onto the balcony. "Bring him out! Bring out the man! Out with him," they called.[14] To the surprise of the mob, Jennings complied. He ducked back into the hotel and returned to the balcony with John and the three other slave hunters. Visibly frightened, John was prodded by his captors to tell the crowd that he "supposed" he would have to return to Kentucky because Jennings "had got the papers for him." Many of the participants and observers of the rescue – both pro- and anti-slavery – would later recount in detail the events at Wadsworth's Hotel, but that coerced statement of grim resignation stands as the only record of Price's own words. The obvious intimidation of the poor slave only made the crowd angrier, and people began shouting for Price to jump to freedom. Perhaps Price eventually would have jumped if the shouting had continued long enough, but he never had a chance to act.[15]

John Anthony Copeland began waving a pistol in Jennings's direction, calling on Price to make his escape and promising "to shoot the damn rascal" if anyone interfered.[16] Copeland had more recent experience confronting slave catchers than anyone else in the crowd, although the only weapon he had actually used thus far had been the hickory cane with which he had beaten Anson Dayton. He was not averse to violence, but the show of arms at Wadsworth's was no doubt intended only to frighten Jennings while assuring Price of protection. Copeland had never yet shot at a man, and it is unlikely that he would have fired at Jennings in front of so many witnesses. But Jennings did not know that, and the mere sight of an armed black man was enough to panic the Kentuckian, who then dragged Price back into the hotel.

Now desperate for a solution, Jennings sought a representative of the crowd with whom he could negotiate. One of his henchmen fortuitously recognized Charles Langston, who had once worked as a schoolteacher in Columbus. The deputy vouched for Langston as "a well-disposed, law abiding, and reasonable man," and Jennings therefore invited him to the garret in the hopes of ending the impasse.[17] As it turned out, however, there was no middle ground.

Langston proposed that the slave hunters immediately free Price in exchange for safe passage to the railroad, but that offer was quickly rejected. Jennings had not come that far simply to give up his prize (and the prospect of his fee). Instead, Jennings proposed that an Oberlin delegation accompany the posse to Columbus for the purpose of witnessing what he promised would be a fair trial. Langston knew far too much about the Fugitive Slave Act to accept that deal. A "fair trial" meant only that Price would be "removed" to Kentucky under the authority of the federal government, and Langston wanted no part in facilitating slavery, legal or otherwise. He refused the offer and cautioned Jennings that the mob outside could not be forestalled forever, as they were "bound to rescue the boy at all hazards."[18] Jennings took that as a threat of violence, which would later be the basis for Langston's prosecution.

Langston was right, of course, that no deal short of Price's freedom would have satisfied the crowd outside the hotel; nor was there a leader who could have accepted such a compromise, even if Langston had recommended it. He walked out of the hotel with no hope of a peaceful resolution, and word quickly spread that the negotiation had failed. The siege of Wadsworth's had now lasted for hours, and the crowd's anger – already stoked by Jennings's callous exhibition of his prisoner – could no longer be contained. Talk had failed; action came next.

Two groups of young men simultaneously stormed the hotel. Without apparent coordination, one contingent rushed up the front steps while another entered through the back. The frontal charge was led by the white Oberlin students Ansel Lyman, William Lincoln, and Richard Winsor.

John Anthony Copeland had remained in the rear of the hotel, stationed beneath the balcony where he had so badly frightened Anderson Jennings. He and several other young black men from Oberlin – including Lewis Leary and the harness maker John Scott, as well as an escaped slave named Jeremiah Fox – began an assault of their own. Seeing a construction ladder nearby, they slapped it against the balcony rail and climbed up to the second floor. Ever the faithful "Buchananeer," Wadsworth ordered his employees to stop the rescuers, but the workers wisely backed off when a shot was fired into the ceiling, and Copeland and his friends easily pushed them aside.[19] The black men entered the second-floor landing only seconds behind Lyman, Lincoln, and the other white men.

Copeland and Lincoln clambered up to the attic, soon joined by Winsor, where they banged furiously on the door of Jennings's redoubt. They loudly demanded that the Kentuckian release his prisoner. Jennings again refused, pointlessly insisting that his legal documents entitled him to custody of Price. Jennings realized that the law offered scant protection at that moment, and he had taken the precaution of securing the door with a stout rope, which he held fast with the assistance of the three other slave catchers. For a few moments, the standoff continued, with the posse and the rescuers now separated by only a few feet of space and an infinite gulf in understanding. Jennings claimed refuge under the statutes of Kentucky and the United States, but Copeland and his friends were acting under authority of a much higher law.

Then Lincoln noticed a hole in the wall where there had once been a stovepipe. Standing on a chair, he reached through the gap and managed to knock Jennings off his feet. The stunned Kentuckian briefly loosened his grip on the rope, and the door suddenly swung open. Winsor raced into the tiny room, with Copeland on his heels – John Anthony would later be celebrated as "the second man through" – causing consternation among the overwhelmed slave catchers.[20] Grabbing Price by the arm, Copeland and Winsor hustled the fugitive through the hallway and down the stairs, while Jennings and company could only watch in frustration. There had been no need for gunplay, or even for staves. A single punch to the head – delivered at an awkward angle – had been sufficient to defeat an armed posse.[21]

The rescuers hoisted John Price onto their shoulders and carried him out of the hotel, "huzzaing at the top of their lungs."[22] With more enthusiasm than tenderness – as seemed necessary in the still dangerous circumstances – they threw him into the bed of the nearest wagon, driven by an Oberlin bookstore clerk named Simeon Bushnell. Now at the head of an exultant crowd, Bushnell sped furiously to the presumed safety of Oberlin. John Anthony made his way back to Oberlin as well, where he would as much as anyone ensure that Price's hard-won freedom would never again be endangered.

John Mercer Langston had not been in Oberlin when Ansel Lyman raised the alarm. Like most small-town lawyers in the nineteenth century, he often had to travel to other villages to find business, and his day's work had kept him away from home until late that afternoon. Unaware of the day's dramatic events, he got back to Oberlin just as the rescuers themselves were arriving, and he soon joined "the returning hosts, shouting, singing, rejoicing in the glad results of their brave, defiant, successful enterprise." The celebration stretched late into the night, with a torchlight rally featuring "speeches in denunciation of slavery, the Fugitive Slave Law, slaveholders, and all those who sympathized with and would aid them." John Mercer Langston gave a fiery speech decrying the "dark and frightful methods" of the slave catchers. He expressed the hope that his words might somewhat compensate for "what he had failed to accomplish in deeds on that eventful day," although in truth no one had begrudged his absence.[23]

The crowd applauded John Mercer's eloquence, but they really wanted to hear from the day's heroes. William Lincoln spoke, as did

Simeon Bushnell and Richard Winsor. Then the call went out for "Charlie, Charlie, Charlie Langston," who was greeted by a loud ovation when he ascended the platform. The exuberant addresses continued with speaker after speaker, one of whom led "three glorious cheers for liberty" and "three terrific groans" for the federal government. Anson Dayton was condemned for his assistance to the kidnappers. The reviled deputy, however, was nowhere to be seen, having by then prudently fled Oberlin for his own safety. There would be time enough for a reckoning with Dayton, and his misdeeds were for the time being overshadowed by the sheer joy of liberation. As everyone finally grew exhausted from cheering, the rally concluded with the community's solemn pledge that "no fugitive slave should ever be taken from Oberlin and returned to his enslavement."[24]

SIMEON BUSHNELL MADE AN IMPORTANT STOP ON HIS WAY to the triumphant rally. He drove his wagon to the home of his brother-in-law James Fitch, who owned the bookstore where Bushnell worked, where he quietly escorted John Price through the back door. Like many Oberliners, Fitch had welcomed fugitive slaves in the past, and he gladly showed Price to the "secret room" that he had constructed for that very purpose. Fitch knew, however, that he could not shelter Price for long. He was a prominent abolitionist – even by Oberlin's extraordinary standards – and his house would naturally be one of the first places that slave hunters would come in search of Price. Fitch therefore got in touch with Professor James Monroe, who was known to have smuggled five runaways to freedom only one week earlier.

Monroe was ready and willing to open his own home to the fugitive, but his house had the same high visibility as Fitch's. The two men therefore decided to approach Professor James Fairchild for assistance. Fairchild, as we have seen, was equally vocal in his anti-slavery sentiments, but he was also a prominent "non-resistant." As much as anyone in Oberlin – save perhaps President Finney – he was well known for his adherence to the law. Fairchild endorsed the use of "casuistry" or subterfuge to thwart slave hunters, but he had always drawn the line at force or violence.[25] As Fitch's daughter later put it, Fairchild was the last person ever to be "suspected of doing such a thing as breaking one of the Laws of the United States."[26]

Fitch and Monroe showed up unannounced at Fairchild's doorstep later that evening, requesting that he harbor the slave until more permanent arrangements could be made. Fairchild immediately agreed, acknowledging that he was ready for the first time to expose "myself to penalties of imprisonment and fines [under the] tender mercies of the Fugitive Slave Law."[27] As Fitch and Monroe went to retrieve Price from hiding, Mary Fairchild herded the couple's six children into the parlor and closed the door. She explained the events of Price's capture and rescue – although by then the older children were surely aware of the town's rejoicing – and warned them to tell no one that the fugitive would be concealed in their home. "You must never tell anyone in the world that John is here," she cautioned. And for the rest of your lives, she added, "it will never be safe to betray the fact that we have sheltered in our house a runaway slave."[28] Mary might truly have believed that her family had undertaken a lifelong risk – although plenty of Oberliners had housed fugitives over the years, with virtually no untoward consequences – but it is more likely that she was simply trying to impress the importance of silence on her children, who might otherwise be inclined to brag about their secret houseguest.

In any case, James escorted Price to a second-floor bedroom where the fugitive could be kept out of sight. The door was always locked, and the duly frightened children kept mum when they saw their father "going up to a back room carrying food."[29] James Fairchild wrote a memoir of these events, as did a daughter of James Fitch, but neither they nor any of the other participants thought to provide a description of Price's emotional state, which must have been bewilderment if not outright shock. As a fugitive, Price had drawn the attention of the entire community; but as a person, he seemed to hold no interest at all.

John Price was reasonably safe for the time being, but he could not remain locked in a bedroom forever, and he certainly could no longer live openly in Oberlin. He would have to be taken to Canada as soon as possible. Ordinarily, that would have been accomplished simply by bringing him to a cooperative captain in a nearby Lake Erie port, as so many fugitives had been delivered before, but Price's notoriety, and his very likely traumatized condition, made that too risky. Instead, he would have to be accompanied all the way to Canada.

It was a daring mission, and it seems that John Anthony Copeland was precisely the right man for the job.

THIRTEEN

"THE BLACK MECCA"

JOHN ANTHONY COPELAND "was in the habit of going up to Canada" even before the rescue in Wellington.[1] He was among the many Oberliners who traveled back and forth between the colonies of freedmen and escaped slaves who had settled in what is now Ontario. Some such visits were social and some were commercial, but others were for the purpose of escorting or settling fugitives. In 1836, Reverend Finney had dispatched Hiram Wilson, a recent graduate of the theology department, as an emissary to Canada West for the purpose of reporting on the circumstances of runaway slaves. Five years later, Wilson helped establish the British-American Institute on the outskirts of Chatham, where fugitives could be taught productive trades. Oberlin contributed Bibles and teachers for the institute, as well as assisting with the arrival of a steady stream of newly escaped slaves.[2] As Wilson himself wrote to a colleague at the college, "Those six fugitives who were in Oberlin when we left all got over safe into Canada by the next Monday."[3] They were far from the only ones.

John Anthony's earlier involvement in the northward traffic made him a logical candidate to shepherd John Price across the border. Conducting fugitives was no longer a lighthearted matter, as Oberliners had regarded it for so many years. It was one thing to deflect the attentions of amateur slave hunters but quite another to flout a valid federal warrant, not to mention abusing a deputy U.S. marshal in the process. Only one week earlier, Professor James Monroe had been nonchalant about receiving five slaves who were en route from Medina to the Sandusky harbor, but now the ground had clearly shifted. John Anthony had shown aggressiveness in confronting Marshal Dayton, and courage in breaking through the door at Wadsworth's Hotel, but he was also known for his Christian faith, which was no small matter to the Oberlin theologians who had taken charge of John Price's deliverance. As Copeland himself later said, the rescue of "at least a few of my poor and enslaved brethren" was "the commandment of my God in doing for others as I would have them do to me."[4] If ever a task called for both audacity and devotion, this was surely it.

The arrangements had to be completed with the utmost care, and Price was therefore required to hide for "three days and nights in a back chamber" of the Fairchild home until it was decided that the coast was clear.[5] There had been every expectation that federal authorities would launch a search of Oberlin in the aftermath of the rescue, but Anson Dayton was sensibly afraid to show his face, having been warned that he would have some "serious groaning to do" if he dared make a move.[6] Marshal Matthew Johnson was not so easily intimidated, but he was biding his time while awaiting further instructions from Washington, D.C. The Oberliners sensed that a storm was brewing – as indeed it was – and after three calm days it seemed that the time was right to finish the job that the rescuers had begun at Wadsworth's Hotel.

It is certain that John Price departed Oberlin for Canada on or about September 16, 1858. There is no documentation that he was accompanied by John Anthony Copeland – which is understandable, given the clandestine nature of the journey – but the evidence is compelling. Elias Toussaint Jones was positive that Copeland was the man who took Price to Canada, and two of Copeland's siblings – his sister Mary and his brother Fred – said so as well.[7] Just as tellingly, Copeland disappeared from Oberlin in mid-September, and he was not seen again in Ohio until the following summer. Borrowing from the language of legal argument, Copeland had the motive, means, and opportunity to escort Price to Canada, and that appears to be exactly what he did.

There were three major Canadian destinations for fugitive slaves in Ohio, all of which are located in what is now Ontario. To the west, a crossing could be made from Detroit to Windsor. At the eastern end of Lake Erie lay St. Catharines, with a large community of former fugitives, including many who had been led to freedom by Harriet Tubman. (Anthony Burns would also settle there some years later.) It is most likely, however, that Copeland and Price headed for Chatham. Not only was it the shortest distance from Oberlin – the Lake Erie crossing from the docks of Lorain or Sandusky was only about forty miles – but Chatham was also a well-known terminus of the Underground Railroad, often called the "Black Mecca" of British North America. By 1858, African-Americans, including many fugitives, comprised a quarter of Chatham's population.[8] Most significantly for John Anthony, Oberlin had a long-standing connection to

Chatham, and a number of well-known former Oberliners had prospered there in the black community.

In 1853, James Monroe Jones had moved to Chatham, where he had established himself as a metalsmith specializing in both silver engraving and gun making. He earned the respect of his fellow citizens, both black and white, and acquired the affectionate nickname "Gunsmith Jones." John Anthony had known Gunsmith Jones virtually his entire life – first as a child in Raleigh, then in the emigrant wagon train to Ohio, and finally in Oberlin, where Copeland was a schoolmate and close friend of Jones's younger brothers. John Anthony would have been familiar with the Jones home – which had been built by his father – as well as with Allen Jones's forge, where young men were entertained by the blacksmith's rich singing and the stories of his self-emancipation. In a town where life centered on education, James Monroe Jones's 1849 achievement as one of the first African-American graduates of Oberlin College would have impressed every black youth, including those as ultimately unstudious as John Anthony. Given the assignment of taking Price to Canada, it is almost unimaginable that Copeland would have passed up an opportunity to seek out his old friend and traveling companion.

Even as Copeland and Price were making their way to Canada, Marshal Matthew Johnson had embarked on a plan to bring an end to the anti-slavery resistance in Oberlin. Within a few days of the rescue, he showed up in town on an ostensible peacekeeping mission. He met with "a number of leading citizens [and] sought to allay the indignation of the people." He assured them that Anson Dayton's cooperation with slave hunters had been completely unauthorized in both Oberlin and Painesville. In fact, Dayton had already resigned, said Johnson, and good riddance. "I didn't like the looks of him," from the beginning, "but appointed him because he was so well recommended by Postmaster Munson," he added. Johnson swore that he disapproved of the Fugitive Slave Act and promised that he would personally serve any outstanding fugitive warrants in the future, but only after first providing advance notice to "enable the fugitive to escape."[9] That was a lie. Johnson had obtained his job by promising fealty to the pro-Lecompton (and most ardently pro-slavery) wing of his party, and he had no intention of facilitating the escape of fugitives from Oberlin or anywhere else in northern Ohio.

Johnson was not yet well known in Oberlin, however, so his "smooth and honeyed words" made a temporarily "favorable impression in the minds of the citizens." It would not be long before the extent of his deception was discovered. Upon learning that he had been repudiated by his boss, Dayton produced a letter from Johnson that exposed the whole scheme. Dayton had indeed offered to resign, but only out of fear for his safety and not at the behest of his boss. "You must not resign," Johnson had written, explaining that "I am not disposed to be driven by the violators of the laws and Constitution of the United States." Johnson dismissed the threats against Dayton as "bravado – an attempt to scare you into resignation," and insisted that his deputy remain on the job.[10]

In fact, there had been an ulterior motive for Johnson's visit to Oberlin, and it had nothing to do with providing an advance warning to fugitives. Instead, Johnson met secretly with the few Democrats in town – including innkeeper Chauncy Wack and Postmaster Edward Munson – for the purpose of gathering information that could be used to indict the rescuers. Wack (who had followed the crowd to Wellington, first out of curiosity and then as a spy) and Munson (who had taken notes of the speakers at the postrescue rally) readily cooperated, providing names and descriptions that Johnson would quickly relay to the federal prosecutor in Cleveland. It would be months before anyone in Oberlin would realize that Wack and Munson had betrayed them.[11] Johnson's "duplicity and double-dealing" would also be revealed, and he would be exposed as a "cunning and heartless dissembler."[12] But by then it was too late.

A FULL ACCOUNT OF THE OBERLIN RESCUE had probably not reached Chatham ahead of Copeland and Price. In any event, Jones would have been keen for news from home, and especially the particulars of Price's escape to freedom, even if he was learning about it for the first time. Jones himself had been born a slave and had remained one for the first eight years of his life. He had grown to adulthood in Raleigh, where he had been able to observe the treatment of Southern slaves, and, unlike John Anthony, Gunsmith Jones was already a young man during their families' exodus from North Carolina to Ohio. He therefore would have been intensely aware of the dangers presented by slave hunters and pattyrollers, which might well have escaped nine-year-old John Anthony, and he would have been eager to hear the story of Price's escape from Kentucky and rescue in Wellington.

In return for details of the rescue, Jones would surely have told Copeland about his recent encounter with the celebrated John Brown. Already famous for leading the anti-slavery resistance in Kansas, Brown had been in Chatham only a few months earlier. His "good abolition convention" had been supported by former Oberliners Gunsmith Jones and William Howard Day – the former as a delegate to the convention, the latter having printed the key document – and reports of Brown and his provisional constitution would still have been circulating in late summer, when Copeland and Price arrived.[13]

Jones had played an important role in the Chatham conference, ultimately signing the provisional constitution. Several of the preliminary meetings were held in his shop, and one of Brown's lieutenants – John E. Cook, with whom Copeland would later spend nearly two months in a Virginia jail – boarded in Jones's home for several weeks before and during the conference. Cook and Jones shared a love of fine firearms, and together they burnished and engraved some of the weapons that would be used at Harper's Ferry.[14] If Copeland stayed at Jones's home in September – as was surely possible, given their old friendship – he might well have eaten at the same table, and perhaps slept in the same bed, as Cook had several months earlier. If Copeland visited Jones's shop, he could have seen the tools used to repair and engrave the very rifle that he would later shoulder in Brown's small army.

The Chatham connection between John Brown and John Anthony Copeland –with Gunsmith Jones as the link – is ultimately conjectural but very well founded. Moreover, it appears certain that Copeland spoke of Brown when he finally returned to Oberlin. His brother and sister both recalled that John Anthony had first met Brown in Chatham, and Elias Jones believed so as well.[15] That could not have happened, as Brown was long gone from Canada by the time of the Oberlin Rescue. But Elias and the Copeland siblings could easily have mistaken John Anthony's stories of Brown – gathered from Gunsmith Jones and perhaps William Howard Day – as the report of an actual encounter. In any case, it is quite likely that Copeland's first opportunity to learn of Brown's plan to invade the South would have occurred in September 1858.

EVENTS IN OHIO MOVED INEXORABLY FORWARD even as Copeland and Price made their way to Canada. Marshal Johnson reported back to U.S. Attorney George Belden in Cleveland, who was already working on an indictment at the instruction of his superiors in Washington, D.C. President Buchanan had been deeply offended by the rescue, and he had instructed his attorney general, Jeremiah Black – a fellow Pennsylvanian and pro-slavery Democrat – to take all necessary measures. They briefly considered bringing treason charges – which would have carried the death penalty – but reason prevailed, and they directed Belden to prepare an indictment for violations of the Fugitive Slave Act.[16] Belden soon compiled a list of targets, most of them identified by Johnson's investigation, with the assistance of Dayton, Wack, and Munson.

Matthew Johnson did not forget the pro-slavery commitment he had made when seeking office from President Buchanan, and he proved his worth time and again in the course of the prosecution. In an era long before the random selection of jurors, it was the marshal's job to summon men for service on grand and petite juries. In theory, the jurors were supposed to be chosen for their integrity and standing in the community – it was not then considered antidemocratic to favor the prominent – but in truth they were invariably handpicked for political reliability. It was therefore expected that Johnson would favor administration Democrats when assembling the grand jury, but even so it was shocking that he was unable to find even a single Republican fit for service, in a region where Republicans strongly outnumbered Democrats. More shocking still was the selection of Lewis Boynton as a grand juror.[17] Johnson knew full well that Boynton had colluded with the slave hunters and had offered his son Shakespeare as a decoy in Price's arrest, but that was evidently not a disqualification for grand jury service. As John Mercer Langston bitterly observed, "The son betrays, and the father indicts."[18]

The indictment, of course, was a foregone conclusion, which was made painfully clear by U.S. District Judge Hiram Willson's charge to the grand jury. A loyal Democrat, Willson had nonetheless opposed the Fugitive Slave Act before taking the bench, but he had long since fallen into line with his party's strategic deference to Southern rights. It was speculated that his change of heart on the slavery issue – or apostasy, as some put it – was the "condition upon which his appointment" had been made by the president.[19]

In keeping with his newfound sentiment, Judge Willson's instructions to the grand jury left little to the imagination. He focused not only on the events of the rescue but also on the rescuers' motives, deriding their "declared sense of conscientious duty" and belittling Oberlin's commitment to "higher law":

> There is, in fact, a sentiment prevalent in [Oberlin] that arrogates to human conduct a standard of right above, and independent of, human laws; and it makes the conscience of each individual in society the test of his own accountability to the laws of the land.
>
> While those who cherish this dogma claim and enjoy the protection of the law for their own lives and property, they are unwilling that the law should be operative for the protection of the constitutional rights of others.

Far from favoring freedom, Willson explained, the rescuers were actually "characterized by intolerance and bigotry" against Southern property rights, and sympathy for the slave should therefore "find no place or favor in the Grand-Jury room." It was every person's duty to uphold the Fugitive Slave Act, which secured the reciprocal protection of all citizens "whether residing north or south of the Ohio River."[20] Of course, Willson was only concerned about the rights of white citizens, which hardly needed to be said in the courtroom.

Following testimony from numerous witnesses, the grand jury returned its predictable indictments on December 6, 1858. Thirty-four defendants were charged with violating the Fugitive Slave Act, of whom twelve were African-Americans from Oberlin. The black indictees included John Anthony Copeland and his uncles, Henry and Wilson Evans, as well as Charles Langston and his brother-in-law Orindatus S. B. Wall, and five men who were believed to be fugitive slaves themselves. The white indictees included Simeon Bushnell, Ansel Lyman, Richard Winsor, and William Lincoln.

Johnson's informants had done their work well, having identified and secured testimony against nearly everyone who could be singled out at the rescue. In fact, they had gone further. A separate indictment named three prominent Oberliners who had not even gone to Wellington: bookseller James Fitch, who had briefly hidden John Price, although that was unknown to the grand jury and played no part in the indictment; Henry Peck, an Oberlin professor of sacred rhetoric and moral philosophy; and attorney Ralph Plumb. The latter three were accused of "aiding and abetting" the rescue by having urged the Oberliner mob to embark on the road to Wellington.[21] There was scant proof of that charge, but that was not the point. The purpose of the prosecution was not merely to punish the actual rescuers but also to suppress the growing abolitionist movement in northern Ohio by intimidating its leaders. Not for the last time, the Buchanan administration had badly underestimated the resolve of the anti-slavery movement.

MARSHAL MATTHEW JOHNSON KEPT his promise never again to entrust the execution of legal process to Deputy Dayton, although not out of any sympathy for fugitive slaves or their friends. Instead, he realized that Dayton's rare combination of notoriety and fecklessness would render him wholly ineffective in Oberlin, which left the task of law enforcement to the marshal himself. It took less than a day following the return of the grand jury indictments for Johnson to prepare "a huge packet of warrants," which he promptly brought to Oberlin on Tuesday, December 7, 1858.[22]

Johnson went first to the home of Professor Henry Peck. On a different morning, Peck might well have been sheltering fugitives in his attic, as he had been only a few days before the rescue of John Price. On that particular Tuesday, however, it appears that Peck had nothing to hide. He accepted the warrant without protest and graciously agreed to help Johnson locate the other indictees. Within an hour or so, Peck and Johnson "called on fifteen gentlemen and left them each" with a warrant "inviting them to appear before the court forthwith."[23] Far from the rude treatment experienced by Deputy Dayton, Marshal Johnson was greeted with "the utmost courtesy and good feeling." Having encountered "no excitement and no attempt to resist the process of law," Johnson refrained from arresting his targets and accepted their promises to appear in court the following morning.[24] The civility of the Oberliners may have come as a surprise in some quarters, given the town's reputation as "the headquarters and hot-bed of negro fanaticism in the North." The pro-slavery *Cleveland Plain Dealer* denounced it as a ploy, intimating that the "Higher Law dignitaries, their dusky mates and theological satellites" would eventually fail to keep their obligations.[25]

In fact, not every defendant was available to cooperate with the prosecution, and Johnson failed to execute ten of his twenty-five warrants.[26] Several of the Oberliners were simply out of town at the time, including William Lincoln and Richard Winsor, who had led the charge through Wadsworth's front door. Others, however, laid low. Three of the indictees were fugitive slaves and had no intention of submitting themselves to the law. Likewise impossible to find that day, or any other, was John Anthony Copeland, who would never be arrested.

Johnson's warm feelings toward the surrendering defendants, whom he praised as "gentlemen in every respect," did not extend to the missing African-Americans. He was deeply frustrated by his inability to locate all of his black targets, presciently accusing them of having "cut for Canada" rather than post bail for their appearance in court.[27] Johnson's guess was more accurate than he could have realized, given that at least Copeland had already reached Canada, as had probably some or all of the unfindable fugitives. Johnson was accustomed to losing track of runaway slaves – that was a daily occurrence in antebellum Cleveland – but Copeland was quarry of a different sort, having played a leadership role during the rescue in Wellington. Although he could not yet have known that Copeland had accompanied Price to Chatham, Johnson would not forget that John

Anthony had evaded his grasp. When the opportunity arose the following year, Johnson would pursue Copeland relentlessly, for hundreds of miles beyond his jurisdiction. And when he finally confronted Copeland in a Virginia jail, Johnson would recall the time he had been dodged by the man he derisively called "a Canada negro."[28]

ANSON DAYTON HAD BEEN HAPPY TO SEE his boss deliver the warrants to the Oberlin indictees, naively believing that Johnson's intervention would protect him from retribution. In that he was badly mistaken, as his continued presence as a deputy marshal in Oberlin – even one who refrained from all official duties – was a source of constant displeasure. Merely living in the vicinity, according to one source, made Dayton "obnoxious to his neighbors." Hostility toward Dayton mounted during the months following the rescue; a shot was fired at his house one night, although no harm appears to have been done. Even greater anger erupted, however, within hours of Johnson's arrival with writs in hand. Not every black person in Oberlin calmly acceded to the prosecution of the rescuers, and many assumed "that Deputy Marshal Dayton has been the instigator" of the indictments.[29]

Acting on their suspicions, a group of black men met secretly to plot how best to put an end to Dayton's "man-stealing propensity." They decided that intimidation, and perhaps another beating, would be needed to discourage the deputy, and the sooner the better. Armed with clubs, they approached his house after nightfall and banged clamorously on the door. As it happened, Dayton was not home, and his terrified wife – alone with her small children – implored the intruders to leave. The black men, however, insisted on searching the house. Mrs. Dayton at first refused, but she soon realized that she could "not prevent their coming in," and she reluctantly consented to the search. She had been telling the truth; Dayton was nowhere to be found.[30] The African-Americans departed, but they left little doubt that they might be back at any time. We do not know the names of the members of the ad hoc enforcement committee – Copeland was still away from Oberlin, but it may have included Lewis Leary and Elias Jones or one of his brothers – but we do know that their tactic worked. Dayton and his family left town within a week.[31]

Cleveland's Democrats considered the assault on Dayton to be an affront even worse than the rescue of Price. "If the white people of Oberlin do not restrain these negroes from such lawless acts," the pro-slavery

Plain Dealer editorialized, "there will be worse trouble than that arising from rescuing fugitives."[32] The anti-slavery press, needless to say, saw things differently. Before Dayton's arrival, the black residents of Oberlin had "educated their children, accumulated property, paid their taxes, and conducted themselves in all respects as good citizens." With Dayton's appointment, however, "the official war on Oberlin was commenced." It was only natural that African-Americans would retaliate against the man "who has brought terror, distress, and misery" to so many homes. "Their forbearance is the greater marvel."[33]

FOURTEEN

THE FELONS' FEAST

JOHN ANTHONY COPELAND WOULD NEVER BE APPREHENDED for his involvement in the Oberlin Rescue, but most of his codefendants had no interest in eluding the law. Quite the contrary, they saw their indictment as an opportunity to place slavery itself on trial, and thus very nearly a cause for celebration. Such politicized trials – where the defendants take the offensive – have now become commonplace, but the tactic was novel and untested in the late 1850s. As with many other aspects of the anti-slavery movement, Oberlin was destined to play a leading role. Resistance to the Fugitive Slave Act would not be denied, but rather extolled in the name of "higher law."

The leading defendants therefore did not hesitate to turn themselves in as they had promised Marshal Johnson. On the morning of Wednesday, December 8, ten of the indicted rescuers departed Oberlin by train, amid the cheers of their supporters. By 2:00 that afternoon, they were in the courtroom of U.S. District Judge Hiram Willson, who had earlier castigated their motives in his charge to the grand jury. The prosecutor, U.S. Attorney George Belden, was there to receive the defendants, who were represented by three prominent lawyers, all of whom were devoted abolitionists who had volunteered their services. The chief attorney for the defendants was Rufus Spalding, a former justice of the Ohio Supreme Court, who was assisted that day by Albert Gallatin Riddle, a former state legislator, and Seneca Griswold, a young Oberlin graduate.[1]

The defense strategy quickly became apparent when Spalding called for an immediate trial. The unexpected demand shook the courtroom like a "respectable sized torpedo," as prosecutor Belden had assumed that the defendants, "like other criminals," would seek postponement. His main witnesses, Belden sputtered, were in Kentucky, and he would need at least two weeks to bring them to Ohio. Judge Willson granted the postponement, despite outraged objections from the defense. In truth, the defendants were not ready for trial – the majority of the indictees had not yet even appeared in court – but their point had been made. The case against them had been brought for political "effect at Federal headquarters," and the judge and prosecution were aligned on the side of the Kentucky slave hunters. Already backed into a corner by the demand for trial, Judge Willson released the defendants on their own recognizance, as he would do for the other rescuers, including Charles Langston and the Evans brothers, who would turn themselves in over the course of the next several weeks.[2]

The defendants returned to Oberlin in triumph, eager to take advantage of the opportunity to spread their denunciations of the Fugitive Slave Act. On January 11, 1859, they held a great communal banquet, which they dubbed the "Felons' Feast." The purpose of the occasion was both to celebrate the indictments and to publicize their avowed resistance to slavery and slave catching. The banquet table demonstratively included both blacks and whites, with seating assigned irrespective of color. With many wives in attendance, it was inevitable that black men would sit next to white women, an arrangement infuriating to the pro-slavery Democrats but that drew no particular notice in Oberlin.

The benediction was given by Reverend John Keep, who twenty-four years earlier had cast the deciding vote in favor of Oberlin's integration. "Father Keep" was followed by speaker after speaker, some reciting prayers, some reading letters of congratulation from abolitionist dignitaries, and some delivering stem-winders of their own. One speaker mocked the federal government's efforts to prosecute the rescuers "for their faithful observance of the higher law," and another promised that the "bloodhounds of slavery" would meet stern resistance if they ever again entered the environs of Oberlin. A third speaker vowed that the Fugitive Slave Act "never could be enforced" anywhere in the Western Reserve and that "no fines it can impose or chains it can bind upon us, will ever command our obedience to its unrighteous behests." The exultant mood was typified by James Fitch's challenge to the prosecution. "Will it subdue us?" he cried. "Can it crush us out?" "No, no, no!" came the replies from his friends and neighbors. Fitch then drew laughter when he opined that there could have been no cause for his indictment – he had not even been to Wellington that day – other than his "poor prayers in behalf of the oppressed."[3]

The cheers and laughter then quieted when Ralph Plumb invoked the name of Frederick Brown, the son of John Brown, who had been murdered by border ruffians in Kansas in 1856. The Brown family was well known in Oberlin. Owen Brown – John Brown's father and Frederick's grandfather – had been one of the early trustees of the college, and John Brown himself had once been employed as a land agent on behalf of the school. The "famous Ossawatomie" Brown, as Plumb put it, would be proud of the work that had been accomplished by the rescuers.

Making good use of the momentary hush, Plumb then read "a thrilling letter of sympathy" from John Brown, Jr., who had been his father's lieutenant during the battle for Kansas. The younger Brown extolled the "honored thirty-seven indictees" and then warned that "step by step the Slave power is driving us on to take one or the other horn of the dilemma, either to be *false* to *Humanity* or *traitors* to the *Government.*" Having been "*forced* into the *attitude of resistance to the government,*" he continued, he was actually glad to see the prosecution in Ohio. "This is bringing the war home," he said, with more prescience than anyone realized.[4] Professor Henry Peck's assessment was hardly less militant: "The fire which this outrage has kindled . . . will not go out till an effort has been made to teach these arbitrary and insolent officials that freemen know what their rights are."[5]

The banqueters did not forget to mention John Price, whose freedom had set the affair in motion, although the references were oblique. Little had been known about Price while he lived in Oberlin, and even less was known now that he had been spirited across Lake Erie. Brag as they did about the rescue, neither James Fitch nor any of his confidants said a word about the details of the fugitive's flight to Canada. They were ready to taunt the federal government, but not to help the prosecutor prove his case. Nonetheless, John Mercer Langston did not doubt that "John Price walks abroad in his freedom, or reposes under his own vine and fig tree with no one to molest him or make him afraid."[6]

John Anthony Copeland was not in attendance at the Felons' Feast, nor were ten of the other indicted rescuers. The cryptic explanation at the time was that the missing defendants were "away on business," which in fact was true for some of them. Charles Langston, for example, was on a speaking tour to raise funds for the Ohio State Anti-Slavery Society, and William Lincoln was teaching school in Dublin, Ohio. It was not considered politic to mention the three fugitive slaves who had been indicted – Jeremiah Fox, Thomas Gena, and John Hartwell –although they had obviously chosen wisely to remain unseen.

John Anthony, of course, had been away on the business of escorting John Price to freedom, and it appears that he had not returned to Oberlin by the time of the banquet. The greatest likelihood is that Copeland was still in Canada, although there are other possibilities. He might have been hiding somewhere in Ohio, perhaps in an abolitionist stronghold such as Painesville or Ashtabula. He might even have been living secretly in Oberlin, if not with his parents then with one of the Joneses.

The most fascinating possibility, however, is raised by a mysterious letter from J. Copeland to Gerrit Smith, dated January 10, 1859, and purportedly written from Bloomington, Kansas. Smith was then one of the most prominent abolitionists, and one of the wealthiest men, in the United States. He was an early sponsor of Oberlin College, the 1848 presidential candidate of the Liberty Party, and was elected to Congress in 1852 as a Free-Soiler. Smith bankrolled a number of projects that involved John Brown, including an experimental community for African-Americans in North Elba, New York. He declined Brown's invitation to attend the Chatham conference, although he would later provide financial support for the raid on Harper's Ferry.[7]

There is no other known connection between Copeland and Smith, although their paths might have crossed indirectly in several ways. Smith was a fervent opponent of the Fugitive Slave Act, and he contributed funds to the defense of rescuers in Syracuse and Boston. He was also a strong supporter of the Free-state settlers in Kansas, who included many Ohioans and Oberliners as well as New Englanders. Smith's generosity, especially toward fugitives, was well known in Oberlin. Among many other highly visible acts of charity, he helped pay the tuition for Anthony Burns, the famous runaway who attended the preparatory department with John Anthony, and he provided Bibles for Oberlin's outposts in Chatham and elsewhere in Canada.[8] Copeland was certainly aware of Smith's anti-slavery philanthropy, and it is not unreasonable to think that John Anthony might have written to Smith – as so many supplicants did – for advice or support, or simply to express admiration.[9]

The body of the Kansas letter is intriguing, containing reasons both to believe and to doubt that it was written by John Anthony. It mentions "Bro. Fox," which appears to be a reference to Jeremiah Fox, one of the fugitive slaves who was indicted (though never arrested) for participating in the Oberlin Rescue. The letter also advises Smith that "Capt. John Brown [is] in the field," which makes sense if Copeland had followed

Brown's path from Chatham to Kansas. In fact, Brown had been in the vicinity only three weeks earlier, when he stayed at the cabin of Samuel and Florilla Brown Adair, his half-sister and her husband, both of whom were Oberlin graduates. On the other hand, the letter's main subject is the settlement of a $100 debt to Smith – to be achieved through the sale of a "piano forte" – which is not suggestive of John Anthony. And it also refers to the death of the writer's father, although John Copeland, Sr., was very much alive at the time.[10]

There are several plausible explanations. The simplest, of course, is that the Kansas letter was written by a J. Copeland who was not our John Anthony Copeland. This, however, would not explain the reference to Jeremiah Fox, and it was not the belief of the anonymous archivist of the Gerrit Smith Papers at Syracuse University, who cataloged the sender as "Copeland, J[ohn] [A. Jr.]."

Alternatively, the letter might have been written in code, which was a common practice among John Brown's comrades. Rescuing slaves was sometimes called "digging coal" or the "wool business," and weapons were "sacks of wheat." There is no telling what a "piano forte" might have represented, but the reference is quite similar to a coded letter that Brown's adjutant John Kagi later wrote to Oberlin attorney Ralph Plumb, seeking money "to save his father's land." Surprisingly enough, even coded letters were known to carry real names. The Kansas letter itself refers to "Capt. John Brown" by name, even though he was using the pseudonym Shubel Morgan at the time. Likewise, the "J. Copeland" signature does not rule out the inclusion of a secret message elsewhere in the text.[11]

It is therefore possible that Copeland was already in touch with Brown by late 1858, perhaps via a connection made in Chatham, and that he was writing to Smith at Brown's direction (which is a service that Brown was known to have requested of his followers).[12] Even so, that would not mean that Copeland was actually in Kansas, as the origination point of the letter might have been coded, as well as the contents.

If Copeland really was in Kansas in late 1858, which cannot be ruled out (especially given his likely contacts with other Oberliners who had joined the Free-state cause), that would provide a second link to John Brown in advance of his recruitment for the Harper's Ferry mission. The best we can reliably say about the Gerrit Smith letter, however, is that it provides some additional support for the quite evident conclusion that John Anthony was somewhere other than Oberlin in late 1858 and early 1859.

We may have to speculate about Copeland's whereabouts at the end of 1858, but we definitely know where John Brown was at the time.

BROWN HAD DEPARTED CHATHAM IN MAY 1858, believing that he had enlisted the nucleus of an army for an invasion of Virginia that he intended to launch later that year. His plan was disrupted, however, by the treachery of one of the few men whom Brown had trusted with the details of his plan. Brown had engaged a British soldier of fortune named Colonel Hugh Forbes, who had promised to provide military training for the abolitionist troops. Forbes was in some part an idealist – he had fought on the side of Garibaldi during the 1848 revolutions in Europe – but he was also a mercenary who expected to be paid for his work at the rate of $100 per month. The arrangement failed for multiple reasons. Brown had no real army at the time and very little money, and Forbes did not have as much expertise as he had claimed. The two men had a falling out, each claiming that the other had defaulted on his obligations. They parted ways in stubborn acrimony, which Brown naively believed would mark the end of their entanglement.

Forbes turned out to be as vindictive as he was ineffective. Shortly after the Chatham conference, just as Brown was readying for action, Forbes leaked word of Brown's Virginia plan to publisher Horace Greeley and a number of anti-slavery political leaders, including Republican senators William Seward and Charles Sumner. Forbes even went so far as to approach Senator Henry Wilson on the floor of the U.S. Senate. Despite the unmistakable whiff of blackmail in the exposure, Forbes later claimed that his intentions had been honorable, aimed only at deterring Brown from a suicidal mission that would be "fatal to the anti-slavery cause."[13]

Whatever Forbes's motives, the impact of the betrayal was almost immediate. Men who had agreed to finance Brown's activities in Kansas withdrew their support, unwilling to see their money and supplies used in the South. Senator Wilson insisted that Brown's weaponry be confiscated and turned over to "some reliable men" in Kansas, and others of Brown's backers agreed.[14] Brown was devastated by the news, but he realized that he had no choice but to postpone his ultimate goal. It is necessary "to delay further action *for the present*," he wrote to his son Owen. "Hasty or rash steps" would have to be avoided for the immediate future, and the suspicions raised by Forbes had to be given time to die down.[15]

Brown was facing twin dilemmas as a consequence of Forbes's perfidy. He needed to conceal his ultimate goal by distracting attention from Virginia, but he also needed to convince his backers that he could mount a successful operation somewhere in slave country. As one of his confidants later explained, "[T]here was a lack of confidence in the success of his [Virginia] scheme. It was, therefore, necessary that a movement should be made in another direction, to demonstrate the practicability of the plan."[16] Brown chose to return to Kansas, arriving in June 1858. There he embarked on a plan that would, through unforeseeable twists and turns, eventually lead him to John Anthony Copeland.

Brown spent the summer and early fall exploring means to "take the war into Africa" by rescuing slaves from the South. His "heaven sent" opportunity came in late December, when he learned that a Missouri slave was seeking help to prevent his wife and children from being sold to a Texas slave trader.[17] Recognizing "the most ready and effectual way . . . to meddle directly with the peculiar institution," Brown assembled a force of twenty men for a rescue operation.[18] He led his troops into Vernon County, Missouri, on the night of December 20, 1858.

Under cover of darkness, Brown's men raided the farms of three slave owners, killing one who attempted to resist. The other slaveholders wisely surrendered their human property without a fight, allowing Brown to liberate eleven slaves while also confiscating "horses, mules, oxen, bedding, and two old Conestoga wagons."[19] Brown believed that the appropriated property rightfully belonged to the slaves, who were merely claiming the "fruits of their industry" after years of unpaid labor – but, in any case, he needed the draft animals and wagons in order to make his escape to Kansas and beyond.[20] One of his first stops was at the Adair cabin on Christmas Eve, where Samuel and Florilla extended an Oberlin welcome to Brown and the newly emancipated slaves.[21]

Under Brown's leadership, the wagon train of abolitionists and former slaves embarked on a daring journey of over 1100 miles, traveling over frozen roads in Kansas, Nebraska, and Iowa, and then by rail into Illinois, Indiana, and Michigan. Brown brazenly dared the authorities to pursue him, vowing that he could "not be taken." President James Buchanan and Governor Robert Stewart of Missouri both announced rewards for Brown's arrest, but the offers were in vain. Neither local posses nor federal troops were able to capture Brown, who at one point defeated a U.S. cavalry unit that appeared to have him cornered.[22]

After a very public stop in Chicago, the group finally arrived in Detroit in mid-March 1859. Brown said farewell to his liberated friends – of whom there were now twelve, following the birth en route of a healthy boy, who was aptly named after John Brown – and escorted them to a ferry bound for Windsor. As with the entire operation, there was nothing secret about the final crossing into freedom, and the anti-slavery press proudly reported that "Brown's rescued negroes" had landed in Canada.[23]

At last, Brown could declare that he had "forcibly taken slaves from bondage."[24] His previously skittish financial backers were reinvigorated by the triumph of the Missouri incursion, including Gerrit Smith, who immediately sent Brown a congratulatory contribution. Smith's was only one contribution of many, and Brown's plans for Harper's Ferry would soon be back on track.

The next step, however, was to dispose of the remaining property – two horses and a mule, the rest having been sold in Iowa – that Brown had requisitioned from the Missouri slaveholders. For that purpose, he headed to Cleveland, hoping to get a better price for the liberated livestock while also raising funds from the many abolitionists in the Western Reserve.

Fortuitously, Brown arrived in Cleveland at the outset of the Oberlin Rescue trials. Given his roots in Ohio and his affinity for Oberlin, Brown identified strongly with the rescuers, and he had followed the case closely, even as he trekked across the Midwest. Always on the outlook for recruits, Brown hoped to persuade some of the rescuers to enlist in his command. His long and winding travels had taken him from Missouri to Ohio, where he would meet Lewis Leary and finally send word to John Anthony Copeland.

FIFTEEN

VOTARIES OF THE HIGHER LAW

PRELIMINARY MANEUVERING IN THE OBERLIN CASE ended up taking considerably longer than the two weeks requested by U.S. Attorney Belden in December, and the case did not actually reach trial until March 1859. The prosecutors elected to try the defendants one by one, leading off with Simeon Bushnell, the unassuming Oberlin bookstore clerk who had been seen driving the getaway wagon. The evidence against Bushnell was overwhelming, as many witnesses had seen him leaving Wellington with John Price. Nonetheless, conviction was not a foregone conclusion. Anti-slavery juries in Boston had been known to acquit defendants in rescue cases, essentially nullifying the Fugitive Slave Act by refusing to enforce it. Cleveland, like the entire Western Reserve, was thick with abolitionists, and it would only take one recalcitrant juror to create a mistrial by refusing to return a guilty verdict out of disgust with slave catching.

Fortunately for the prosecution, Marshal Matthew Johnson was again in charge of assembling the panel from which the trial jury would be selected, and he approached the job with characteristic devotion to the needs of the Buchanan administration. Only a few months earlier, Johnson and other Buchananites had founded a newspaper to serve as the administration's editorial voice in northern Ohio. The *National Democrat*, as it was pointedly called, was intended to rival the pro-Douglas *Cleveland Plain Dealer*, which of course meant taking even more fervent aim at Republicans and abolitionists.[1] Acutely aware of Ohio's political realities, the marshal enthusiastically embraced the task of rigging Bushnell's jury.

Although Johnson's official reach extended across the entire northern half of the state, he artfully gathered a forty-man venire without a single member from Lorain County. Man hunting in the Oberlin environs, it appears, extended to suspected slaves but not to potential jurors. Johnson did include ten Republicans on the panel – which was far fewer than their proportion in the district – but that was just for show. Each side was allowed twelve peremptory challenges, which prosecutor Belden effectively used in the process of producing a Republican-free trial jury.

But even that was not the end of the chicanery. Having already seated Lewis Boynton on the grand jury, Johnson managed to place one of his own deputies – who was also the editor of the Democratic *Cadiz Sentinel* – on the trial jury. "Was packing ever better systematized?" complained the anti-slavery *Cleveland Morning Leader*. Even the fiercely pro-Southern *Plain Dealer* objected to the anti-defense bias, observing that "an officer of the court was very much out of place sitting as a Juror."[2]

Johnson had again performed well, and Bushnell's fate was sealed as soon as the jury was seated. Nineteen prosecution witnesses testified to the events of John Price's escape and Bushnell's crucial role in the rescue. Bushnell's lawyers valiantly attempted to mount a defense, questioning the identification of the alleged fugitive – had he been "decidedly black" or "copper colored" – while raising technical defects in the Kentuckians' warrant. But it mattered little in the end.

The prosecutor's summation hardly bothered to mention Bushnell, focusing instead on the entire town of Oberlin. He assailed "the saints of Oberlin," while dismissively ridiculing "sub-saint Bushnell." He argued that "slaves were not fit for freedom," and defended the necessity of the Fugitive Slave Act. "When the Oberlin men went down to Wellington," he said, "they proclaimed that they did so under the Higher Law, for they knew they were outraging the law of the land."

Stunningly, defense attorney Albert Riddle took up the challenge in his own closing argument. He virtually admitted that his client had participated in the rescue, boldly adding

> And now, as to the matter referred to, the so-called dogma of the Higher Law . . . I am perfectly frank to declare, *that I am a votary of that Higher Law*.[3]

Riddle's announcement had its intended effect. The courtroom fell silent, as spectators and participants realized the impact of what they had just heard. The ideal of higher law had been preached from pulpits and repeated in the streets for almost a decade – ever since Senator William Seward had opposed the Fugitive Slave Act by appealing to a "higher law than the Constitution" – but it had never been raised as a legal defense in court. Now, however, attorney Riddle had crossed a barrier, calling the federal Fugitive Slave Act the "sum of all villainies," and urging the jurors to congratulate Bushnell, rather than convict him, for his open defiance of "this unutterably loathsome [and] wicked Act of 1850."[4]

The defense team had entered uncharted territory with an audacious and unprecedented tactic, but it did not impress the court. Judge Willson instructed the jury that higher law had no bearing outside of an "ecclesiastical tribunal." To the court's surprise, and Marshal Johnson's astonishment, at least some of the handpicked jurors appeared to have doubts. They deliberated for over three hours – an unusually long time in that era – before returning a verdict of guilty.

The Bushnell case had only been a warmup. The real test of the higher law would come in the trial of Charles Langston, which was set to begin the following day. The case against Langston was weak, both factually and legally, but it was of the utmost political importance to the Buchanan administration. Although he was militant in his views, Langston's involvement in the rescue had actually been as a peacemaker. He had played no role in the assault on the slave catchers' garret but had only sought to negotiate the voluntary release of the prisoner. He was, however, an important leader of the Ohio State Anti-Slavery Society, and his conviction would therefore serve as a warning to Ohio's free black population. Even nonviolent resistance to the Fugitive Slave Act was going to be met with severe punishment.

One way to secure a conviction, of course, was to depend on a reliable jury, such as the one that had already convicted Bushnell. The defense expected to empanel a new jury, hoping for one that was slightly less biased, but the court and the prosecution had another plan. Judge Willson announced that the Bushnell jury had already been "selected for the term, and it was proper that they should try all the cases."[5] This brought howls of protest from the defense attorneys – who declared it a "monstrous proceeding, the like of which had never been known since courts were first in existence."[6] Judge Willson was not swayed by the extravagant outburst and, as the prosecutors grinned in approval, he ordered the case to proceed before the twelve jurors already in the box.

The defendants felt themselves backed into a corner, facing the prospect of trial before jurors who had already made up their minds. Seeing no way out, attorney Rufus Spalding therefore announced that the prosecutor "could call the accused up as fast as he pleased and try them" but that his clients would flatly refuse to "appear by attorney before such a jury," adding that they would "give no bail, enter no recognizance, and make no promises to return to the Court." U.S. Attorney Belden was more than happy to call Spalding's bluff. "Very well," he said, "then I ask the Court to order these men all into the custody of the marshal."[7]

Judge Willson complied, revoking the defendants' releases on recognizance and commanding Marshal Johnson to take them into custody. The defendants might have backed down at that point, but they declared themselves unwilling "to have *even an appearance of submission* to a tyrannical power" for fear that it would be seen as compliance with the "diabolical Fugitive Slave Act."[8] They were ready to go to jail to prove their point, although they did not yet appreciate the full implications of their obstinacy. Johnson was eager to comply, but he had one small problem. There was no federal jail in Cleveland, and he was dependent on the local sheriff to house his prisoners. Cuyahoga County Sheriff David Wightman, however, was an abolitionist Republican, and it was not immediately certain that he would agree to cooperate with the federal authorities.

Johnson need not have worried. The defendants themselves saw a benefit to imprisonment, which would only heighten their claims of persecution. They willingly presented themselves at the county jail – known as Wightman's Castle – where the sheriff welcomed them with enthusiasm. "I open my doors to you, not as criminals, but as guests," he said. "I cannot regard you as criminals for doing only what I should do myself under similar circumstances."[9] Wightman gave his prisoners free rein of the jail, allowing them visitors – including wives and children – and facilitating interviews with journalists. The defendants took full advantage of the situation, publishing a newspaper called *The Rescuer* and even addressing a rally convened beneath the jailhouse wall. Sympathy for their cause only grew as time passed, leading abolitionist leader William Lloyd Garrison to remark that their sacrifices would "give a fresh impetus to our noble cause."[10] Still, there were hardships. The defendants had initially anticipated spending at most a few days in jail, but Belden and Willson refused all compromises that might have led to their release. In the end, they were incarcerated for nearly three months.

The rescuers would still be in Wightman's Castle when John Brown arrived in Cleveland later that spring. If Sheriff Wightman had been screening visitors, even he might have balked at opening his jail to a man with a price on his head. But in fact the defendants were allowed to receive whomever they wished, which provided the entrée to Oberlin that Brown had been seeking.

Charles Langston's trial began the following morning. Surprisingly, Judge Willson had changed his mind overnight, deciding that the defendant was entitled to a new jury after all. He directed Marshal

Johnson to bring in a new panel, and recessed court until the afternoon. It took Johnson very little time to find another twenty potential jurors, naturally seeking out his cronies. U.S. Attorney Belden exercised no peremptory challenges, having been satisfied that no member of the panel sympathized with fugitive slaves. Langston's attorneys attempted to remove a juror who was already convinced that "the boy was a slave," which undermined one possible defense, but the court ruled that such evident prejudgment was not a sufficient basis for disqualification. The resulting jury was little better than the first one, comprising "nine Administration men, two Fillmore Whigs, and one Republican who had no objection to the Fugitive Slave Law."[11] The presence of two Fillmore Whigs demonstrated the lengths to which Marshal Johnson had gone to locate pro-slavery men in Cleveland. The Whig Party had collapsed in 1854, and Millard Fillmore – the president who had signed the Fugitive Slave Act of 1850 – had been out of office for six years.

The case against Charles Langston hinged on his alleged threat to the slave hunters during the parlay in the attic. On that basis, the prosecutors claimed that he had been the leader of a conspiratorial mob and therefore responsible for everything that followed. There was no shortage of witnesses against Langston, as everyone in the garret – and a good many who were not there, including the oleaginous Chauncy Wack – claimed to have heard him warn the Kentuckians of imminent violence if they did not release John Price.

In a modern trial, the defendant could take the stand to deny the accusation, but that was not possible in 1859. Like every U.S. jurisdiction at the time, Ohio adhered to the "interested party rule," which prohibited a criminal defendant (whether white or black) from testifying on his own behalf. The defense could point out the defects in Jennings's Kentucky papers and the jurisdictional flaw in his Ohio warrant, but the central charge against Langston could not be refuted or explained by the defendant himself. Although several witnesses testified that they had never themselves heard Langston utter the fateful words, it was ultimately impossible to prove the negative – that the defendant had never made any incriminating statements to anybody.

The prosecution's closing argument predictably focused on the "agency Langston had in the rescue," describing him as "very cunning and very hypocritical, very shrewd, but very deceiving."[12] It was obviously the prosecutor's intention to criminalize even peaceful resistance to the Fugitive Slave Act, especially by black men, and he underscored his point by calling Oberlin "a buzzard's nest [where] negroes who arrive over the underground railroad are regarded as dear children." "The students who attend that Oberlin College," he said, "are taught sedition and treason."[13]

Defense counsel met the charge head on, directly confronting the issue of race. Referring to the holding of the despised *Dred Scott* decision – that even free black men could not be citizens of the United States and had "no rights which the white man was bound to respect" – the defense attorney explained that the law gave Langston "no equality, no rights, except in being amenable to the penal statutes." Rather than convict the defendant, counsel argued, the jury should rejoice "over the escape of a brother man from bondage." In other words, the defense again called on the jury to nullify the Fugitive Slave Act for the sake of a black man who was "inspired by the noblest of motives."[14]

True to form, Judge Willson did his best to undermine the defense, instructing the jurors that Langston's efforts at negotiation on behalf of the crowd made him "a party to every act which may afterward be done by any of the others." Following those instructions, the all-white jury had little choice but to convict the defendant, but that turned out to be far from the final word in the case.

Having been found guilty, Langston was at last allowed to address the court – and the nation. Judge Willson was required by law to ask if the defendant had anything to say before sentencing, but he could not have anticipated the impact of Langston's response.

"I know that the courts of this country are so constituted as to oppress and outrage colored men," the defendant began. "I cannot, then, expect, judging from the past history of the country, any mercy from the laws [or] from the Constitution." Langston described the many Kentucky slave hunters who had plagued Ohio, "lying hidden and skulking about, waiting for some opportunity to get their bloody hands on some helpless creature to drag him back – or for the first time – into helpless and life-long bondage." Offering no apology or remorse, Langston made it clear that he intended to continue rescuing fugitives, including those who were lawfully slaves:

> And there were others who had become free – to their everlasting honor I say it – by the exercise of their own God-given powers – by escaping from the plantations of their masters, eluding the blood-thirsty patrols and sentinels so thickly scattered all along their path, outrunning bloodhounds and horses, swimming rivers and fording swamps, and reaching at last, through incredible difficulties, what they, in their delusion, supposed to be free soil.

Every person, said Langston, has the "right to his liberty under the laws of God," no matter what was required to secure his freedom. And that included violent resistance. "If ever a man is seized near me, and is about to be carried Southward as a slave," he declared, "then we are thrown back upon those last defences of our rights, which cannot be taken from us, and which God gave us that we need not be slaves." And still more, he announced,

> I must take upon myself the responsibility of self-protection; and when I come to be claimed by some perjured wretch as his slave, I shall never be taken into slavery. . . . I stand here to say that I will do all I can, for any man thus seized and held.[15]

Never before had a black man so thoroughly defied a prosecutor, rebuked a judge, challenged a criminal statute, and declared his intention to resist the law. Newspaper reports wired the astonishing story across the country. Charles Langston had become an abolitionist hero, but at what cost would it come when Judge Willson pronounced the sentence?

Once again, the courtroom was hushed, and this time the surprising words came from the bench. "You have done injustice to the Court," said Judge Willson, "in thinking that nothing you might say" could affect sentencing. "I see mitigating circumstances in the transaction which should not require, in my opinion, the extreme penalty of the law. . . . On reflection, I am constrained to say that the penalty in your case should be comparatively light."[16]

Willson then sentenced Charles Langston to twenty days in prison and a fine of $100. That was virtually the minimum possible sentence, and it came as a deep disappointment to the prosecution and the Buchanan administration. It was the first time that a U.S. court had even partially recognized the legitimacy of civil disobedience in resistance to the Fugitive Slave Act, and it was certainly the first time that a black man's act of defiance was considered a "mitigating circumstance" by a pro-slavery judge.

The most enduring consequence of Langston's eloquent plea, however, had yet to be realized. John Brown was among the many Americans who looked at Langston's example and had taken it to heart.

SIXTEEN

"THE BRAVEST NEGROES"

JOHN BROWN AND SOME OF HIS COMRADES arrived in Cleveland in March 1858, just as the proceedings in the Oberlin trials were set to begin. Brown and his men took rooms at the City Hotel, located only a few blocks from the courthouse, and placed their animals in the adjacent stable. The trek across the Midwest had depleted Brown's always meager funds – he arrived in Cleveland looking as disheveled as "a melancholy brigand" – and he hoped to raise money by selling the remaining Missouri livestock, as well as by charging admission for a public lecture. As he had done throughout his travels from Missouri, Brown made no secret of his presence in Cleveland. He advertised the mule and horses in a local newspaper, promising potential buyers that they were "Southern animals with northern Principles; once pro-slavery Democrats they are now out and out abolitionists." He was even more brazen about his lecture, announcing that "Old Brown, of Kansas, the terror of Border-Ruffiandom, with a number of his men, will be in Cleveland [to] give a true account of the recent troubles in Kansas, and of the late 'invasion' of Missouri and rescue of eleven slaves."[1]

Marshal Matthew Johnson responded with his usual combination of bluster and inaction. He mounted huge posters around the city announcing that rewards for Brown had been offered by President Buchanan and Missouri Governor Stewart. "In great, black lines of display type," Johnson emphasized the total of $3250 that "might be gotten . . . for Brown's arrest and detention." Johnson himself, however, "never took one step toward arresting Brown," even though the fugitive boldly walked directly past the marshal's office on a daily basis.[2] Such audacity did not escape notice. Humorist Charles Farrar Browne, then an editor of the *Cleveland Plain Dealer* and writing under the pen name Artemus Ward, observed that Brown was cool enough to "make his jolly fortune by letting himself out as an Ice Cream Freezer." Brown indeed had little reason to fear the federal marshal. Public sentiment in Cleveland strongly favored the Missouri rescue operation, and Johnson already had his hands full managing the Oberlin trials. All rewards aside, Johnson was a backstabber, not a street fighter, and it took only one look for him to realize that Brown was too tough for him to handle. As Artemus Ward put it, Brown appeared as though "he could lick a yard full of wildcats before breakfast and without taking off his coat."[3]

Ever defiant, Brown openly taunted Johnson. Commenting on the reward posters, he said that there would be "immediate trouble" if any person should attempt his arrest. He singled out Johnson – pronouncing the marshal's name "with great distinctness" – while threatening to "settle all questions on the spot" if Johnson or any of his deputies attempted to take him into custody.[4] Johnson had no choice but to endure the affront, although he made a mental note to seek revenge should that ever become possible. His only previous arrests of abolitionists had been in Oberlin, however, where the defendants had cooperatively surrendered themselves. Even then, he had been unable or unwilling to track down fugitives such as John Anthony. Now he had to watch Old Brown flout the law. The experience was humiliating, and Johnson would not forget it the following October, when he finally had the opportunity to repay his tormentors.[5]

Apart from embarrassing Marshal Johnson, Brown's lecture was not a success. No more than fifty people attended – at an admission price of twenty-five cents for adults and fifteen cents for children – raising barely enough money to cover the rental of the hall. Brown spoke for only a few minutes before taking questions, some of which he found discomfiting. One of the first questions to Brown was whether he had ever killed anyone in Kansas. The audience was startled at such an obvious reference to the Pottawatomie massacre, but Brown gave an evidently well-rehearsed answer. He declared that "he had never, during his connection with Kansas matters, killed anybody," and that "all newspaper statements to the contrary were false." The questioner pressed, and Brown added that "his young men . . . had done the business," which by then had become his standard deflection of responsibility for the killings.[6]

There were several Oberliners in Brown's Cleveland audience, including Lewis Leary, who later shared his admiration of Brown with John Anthony, his friend and colleague in the Oberlin Anti-Slavery Society.[7] As it turned out, the lecture was a turning point for both men, who were inspired by Brown's promise to continue rescuing slaves from the

South and impressed by his threat to drive slave owners "like fence-stakes into the ground."[8] It would not be long before both Copeland and Leary agreed to join Brown's command, which they understood to be for the purpose of "running off slaves," perhaps again from Missouri or perhaps from Kentucky or elsewhere in the South. Brown was noncommittal at his Cleveland lecture, refusing as always to disclose his future plans.[9]

JOHN BROWN HAD BEEN DEEPLY AFFECTED by the Oberlin Rescue, which had occurred three months before his own foray into Missouri. Seeing the rescuers "wildly cheered throughout Ohio's Western Reserve" further convinced him that others shared his belief that "stealing slaves" was the kind of action that abolitionists must be "ready to take at any moment."[10] Most impressive to him had been the participation of armed black men such as John Anthony, which he saw as a model for his own future army of liberation. As historian Benjamin Quarles observed, the African-Americans of Oberlin were neither meek nor deferential, and they reaffirmed everything Brown "wanted to believe about the militancy of blacks."[11] He had long complained that too many Northern blacks had been unacceptably reticent to fight for their rights, having "tamely submit[ed] to every species of indignity, contempt & wrong." But he had now found the sort of men he had always been seeking, who had nobly resisted "the brutal aggressions" of slavery.[12]

It was coincidental that Brown arrived in Cleveland in time for the rescuers' trials, but he was never one to miss an opportunity at recruitment. He praised the rescuers in his lecture, saying that it was "the duty of every man to liberate slaves whenever he could do so."[13] He compared their exploits to his own Missouri incursion – commending "the Oberlin people for rescuing the slave, because I have myself forcibly taken slaves from bondage" – and he took note of their defiance of the feckless Marshal Johnson.[14] Brown sought out Charles Langston and several other defendants, attempting to enlist them in his army. He remained secretive about his true plans, sticking to the story that he intended only to repeat the Missouri rescue. Declining to reveal his ultimate target, Brown would say only that "it will depend upon circumstances."[15] The rescuers, for their part, were busy mounting their own defense, and none of them accepted the invitation to join Brown's enigmatic enterprise.

Brown departed Cleveland with little money and no new troops. He had not even been able to realize much profit from the sale of his horses and mules. Potential buyers were wary of purchasing stolen livestock, although Brown declared that his right to the animals was better than any title a slave master ever had to his slaves. He made an obviously hollow promise to defend purchasers from interference "by any Missouri claimant," and he was ultimately forced to hold an auction – acting as his own auctioneer – with winning bids that totaled less than $100.[16]

Despite the disappointment, Brown was not ready to abandon his efforts in Ohio. He instructed his adjutant John Kagi to remain in Cleveland for the next two months, with directions to continue fund-raising and recruitment. Only twenty-four years old, Kagi was a native Ohioan who had been appointed "Secretary of War" by the delegates to the Chatham conference. A veteran of Brown's Kansas militia, he had participated in the Missouri rescue and fought in pitched battles against border ruffians. Despite his youth, Kagi had also worked as a lawyer and a journalist, and he had obtained an assignment to cover the Oberlin trials for the *New York Tribune*.[17]

Kagi attended the trials of Simeon Bushnell and Charles Langston, and he exploited his status as a journalist to visit the rescuers in jail following the court's mean-spirited revocation of their releases on recognizance. Kagi met with both Langston brothers, commending John Mercer for his legal work and suggesting to Charles that he organize a mass jailbreak. The latter offer – which Kagi rashly promised "would release them all at once" – was politely declined, as the rescuers were more than willing to remain in custody for the sake of their political point.[18] Kagi stayed in Cleveland until the very end of Langston's trial and sentencing, and he was in the crowd for a massive rally at the jailhouse gates protesting the convictions.[19]

Although he was legitimately filing stories with the *Tribune*, Kagi's true purpose was to continue Brown's importuning. He approached William Lincoln and several of the other prisoners, but he was especially interested in recruiting Charles Langston, whom he described as "a sharp fellow and the leader of the rescue."[20] Kagi was in the courtroom for Langston's dramatic speech at sentencing, which only enhanced his reputation for militancy. Although by then long gone from Ohio, Brown was also profoundly moved by Langston's speech, and he continued to hope that Langston would join him. But Langston was already forty-two years old, and he could not be convinced to ride off into the unknown.[21] Even in Wellington, he had refrained from violence, leaving that to younger men such as Copeland, and the prospect of invading a distant Slave state – whether Missouri, Kentucky, or Virginia – did not appeal to him. Langston did agree to introduce Kagi to several more youthful and energetic Oberliners, eventually providing the final step linking Brown and Copeland.[22]

Langston and the other rescuers were released from jail on July 6, following a compromise with the prosecution in which charges were dismissed against the remaining defendants.[23] Kagi had by then departed Cleveland to undertake other missions for his commander, and Brown himself made a reconnoitering trip to Harper's Ferry, where he arrived on July 4.

Still woefully short of black troops, Brown continued to hope that Charles Langston would assist his recruitment of African-Americans. To that end, Brown sent another messenger to Oberlin, with instructions to pursue every possible contact. Traveling incognito, the envoy arrived in late August 1859.

JOHN MERCER LANGSTON WAS WORKING at his desk on a warm morning when he heard a knock at his office door. Langston was not surprised to see a stranger standing there, as new clients frequently called on him for representation or legal advice. The man introduced himself as "John Thomas" and asked if Langston could see him later that day. Never one to turn away business, the attorney readily agreed to meet at noon, which was the dinner hour in Oberlin. When the appointed time arrived, the stranger cautiously placed his hand on Langston's shoulder and asked for an assurance of confidentiality.

"Then I will give you my real name," said the white man, "so far I have not done so."

Langston had suspected as much, and he nodded in agreement.

"My name is not Thomas. It is John Brown, Jr., and I have called to see you upon matters strictly secret." The younger Brown explained that he and his father admired the "noble white and colored men" who had been imprisoned for the rescue of John Price, and they hoped that Langston could help them "in securing one or more men" who were ready "to leave even home and family, to strike and die for the American bondsman."

Like his older brother, John Mercer Langston was not a man of violence. He declined young Brown's implicit invitation – explaining many years later his belief that such a raid would drive away the enslaved "rather than draw them in needed numbers" – but he readily agreed to provide an introduction to Lewis Sheridan Leary and John Anthony Copeland. The two young men were summoned to Langston's parlor, where the younger Brown provided a general outline of his father's plans. This meeting was Copeland's first known appearance in Oberlin since a few days after the rescue in Wellington. It is possible that he had only recently returned (from either Canada or Kansas), or that he had been living underground in Oberlin for some time. The federal case against him had been dismissed on July 6, along with all of the others, but he may have thought it prudent in the meantime to maintain a low profile as a precaution.

Copeland and Leary were ready for adventure – with Leary the more enthusiastic of the two – and they were already familiar with the elder John Brown's exploits in Kansas and Missouri. Copeland would also have known something of the Chatham conference, but not about the intended invasion of Virginia. Both men agreed to join Brown's band, although they had little idea of what truly lay ahead. According to Langston, John Brown, Jr., provided "a full statement of the purposes" of the raid, but he did not disclose the details of the plan. Recalling the elder Brown's Cleveland lecture, both Copeland and Leary believed that they had been recruited to rescue slaves from a Southern state and take them to Canada. They would not learn the full extent of their mission until they arrived at the outskirts of Harper's Ferry later that year. John Mercer Langston applauded their decision, assuring John Brown, Jr., that he had secured the assistance of "two of the bravest negroes that this country has produced."[24]

FOR THE TIME BEING, Copeland and Leary remained in Oberlin, awaiting the instructions that were to come by mail. Leary was extremely keen to leave Oberlin, and he took the leading role in making the arrangements to join John Brown. That was somewhat unexpected, given Copeland's much earlier exposure to Brown and his far greater experience in resistance to slavery. It was Copeland who had beaten Anson Dayton with a hickory staff on the steps of the Palmer House; it was Copeland who threatened the Kentucky slave hunters with a pistol; it was Copeland who had led the charge into the garret at Wadsworth's Hotel; and it was Copeland who escorted John Price to Canada. Leary had been at most a supporter or spectator at these events, and yet he was now far more eager than his kinsman to rush off to battle. Perhaps he was simply trying to match Copeland's accomplishments, or perhaps he had more personal reasons to make a hasty departure. Leary's hotheadedness had already caused him to flee one hometown, and his domestic situation in Oberlin may have been more unsettled than anyone has ever been willing to acknowledge.

John Brown, Jr., wrote to Leary within a few days of their meeting, and his letter was followed by one from John Kagi a week later. Copeland and Leary were surprised to learn that they were expected to finance their own travel, which presented great difficulty. Leary wrote back to Kagi on September 8, explaining that "want of means" prevented their departure. Both he and Copeland were ready "to dig coal," but someone would have to furnish their "tools." Continuing in code, Leary hoped that he could "get an outfit from parties interested in our welfare in this place," and he mentioned a Mr. P. (meaning either Ralph or Samuel Plumb) as a possible benefactor.[25]

Leary approached the Plumb brothers in mid-September, seeking funds to use "in aiding slaves to escape." Ralph Plumb had been indicted for the Oberlin Rescue, spending over eighty days in the Cuyahoga jail along with the others. A short and balding man, with a beard that today would be described as "Lincolnesque," he was excessively formal, favoring a top hat and frock coat even when he was not conducting business. Plumb later testified that Leary had been "very chary" about disclosing his precise plans and had given no indication of a connection to John Brown, but Plumb's ignorance was almost certainly feigned. He had been visited in jail by Kagi the previous spring, and Kagi had written a coded letter to him in early August, asking for money to "save his father's land." Pleading financial extremis owing to his incarceration, Plumb had replied that Kagi would have to visit "other places" to raise the necessary amount. Plumb had also encountered John Brown, Jr., whom he had known for years, during the latter's recruiting visit to Oberlin only a week or so earlier, and it must have been quite obvious to him that Leary's request was somehow related to John Brown's future plans. As a lawyer, of course, Plumb recognized the danger of asking too many questions. He collected a total of $17.50 from his brother and several friends, and gave the money to Leary and Copeland with good wishes and a promise of silence. It was "our custom" in such situations, he said, "to give the money and say nothing."[26]

Copeland and Leary said almost nothing to anyone about their intention to leave Oberlin and join John Brown. John Anthony told his parents that he was going to Detroit, where he intended to teach for a term in a "colored school." He could not disclose his true destination, but filial devotion required him at least to account for his absence from home. Accustomed to their son's frequent travels, the elder Copelands suspected nothing until they received the alarming news from Harper's Ferry.[27]

The raffish Lewis Leary was far less solicitous of his family. He confided in his employer, harness maker James Scott, that he was going on an expedition to "free the slaves" in the South, but he told no one else. Instead, Leary simply disappeared one night, leaving his wife to nurse their infant daughter while wondering why her husband had vanished. Scott undertook the unpleasant task of explaining to Mary Leary that Lewis had embarked on a rescue mission, but that provided little consolation at the time, as she contemplated the challenge of supporting herself and her child.[28] Mary heard nothing more of her husband until word of John Brown's raid reached Oberlin.

As callous as it was, Leary's abandonment of his wife and daughter was not inconsistent with the behavior that had apparently estranged him from his parents in North Carolina. Many excuses were made for Leary following his martyrdom at Harper's Ferry, but they all ring fairly hollow. African-American journalist William Cooper Nell believed, with scant evidence, that Leary cherished his "young wife and babe," but "the tender words of conjugal love, and the winning smiles of helpless infancy, could not change his purpose to do and dare nobly, for the deliverance of his brethren."[29] Thirty years later, John Mercer Langston recalled that Leary had spoken movingly of his family during the meeting with John Brown, Jr., declaring that "I am ready to die! I only ask that when I have given my life to free others, my own wife and dear little daughter shall never know want." Langston's admiring view of Leary, however, was obviously affected by wishful thinking. He also recalled that the recruitment of Copeland and Leary had occurred only three days before the Harper's Ferry raid, thus justifying the immediacy of Leary's precipitous departure.[30] In fact, the Oberlin meeting was held sometime between August 28 and September 2 – at least six weeks before the raid.[31] Leary had plenty of time to tell Mary of his plans – he spent the intervening weeks writing to Kagi and fund-raising from the Plumb brothers – and the timing of his midnight desertion had surely been caused by something other than the urgency of Brown's call for troops.[32]

Mary Leary was eventually able to forgive her husband, although it may have taken many years. In a 1909 interview, she recalled that Lewis had "wept like a child over their baby" and appeared "shaken with grief" on his last evening at home.[33] Perhaps so, although such memories are often unreliable, and it is likely that she was as much idealizing Leary as she was recalling true events. Mary's grandson had been born only six years earlier, in 1903, and we know that she would raise him on grandmotherly stories of Leary's heroic sacrifice.[34] In any case, Mary herself could be excused for remembering her husband more generously than he may have deserved. Several of Brown's other raiders – including one of his sons and a son-in-law – left orphans or widows, so Lewis Leary was not the only man who placed his ideals ahead of his family. Or perhaps he had only indulged a selfish need to escape the tedium of parenthood, whether or not Mary Leary could bring herself to admit it.

SEVENTEEN

THE INVISIBLES

On a single summer afternoon in Oberlin, John Brown, Jr., had enlisted more black volunteers than his father was able to attract on any other occasion during the entire eighteen months that he was actively seeking troops for the Harper's Ferry operation. For the most part, the elder Brown failed badly in his efforts to recruit African-Americans. Both Harriet Tubman and Frederick Douglass declined to join him, and only one of the thirty-four black signatories of the Chatham Constitution eventually showed up at Harper's Ferry. Even Richard Richardson, a runaway slave who had joined Brown in Kansas and had participated in the Missouri rescue, remained in Canada rather than participate in the invasion of Virginia.[1]

Brown had figured heavily on the availability of black troops, depending on them to inspire local slaves to join his rebellion. As he proposed to Frederick Douglass, Brown had a "special purpose" in mind for his black comrades. "When I strike, the bees will begin to swarm, and I shall want you to help hive them." Douglass demurred, later explaining that either "my discretion or my cowardice made me proof against the dear old man's eloquence."[2] But even without Douglass or another famous African-American, Brown was hopeful that ordinary black foot soldiers would guide an anticipated "swarm" of slaves to his emancipatory banner. Apart from Copeland and Leary, however, there would be only three blacks in Brown's small army.

Why was the younger Brown so much more successful than his father at enrolling black men in their cause? Why did Copeland and Leary respond so readily when so many others equivocated or balked? Of course, we can only speculate – although we can surely assume that it was not a matter of superior persuasiveness, given the old man's renowned eloquence and charisma – but some tentative answers do suggest themselves. Oberlin, as we know, was a unique environment in the antebellum United States, combining an ideology of racial egalitarianism with an exceptional reverence for the rescue of slaves. Black men had intervened forcefully on behalf of fugitives in other cities – most famously at the 1851 "Jerry rescue" in Syracuse and the 1854 attempt to rescue Anthony Burns in Boston – but they had always encountered fierce condemnation from leaders of the surrounding white population. In most of the North, slave rescues were risky in every dimension – politically, socially, and legally.

In Oberlin, however, the redemption of John Price had been almost universally celebrated among both whites and blacks. Charles Langston had been heartily cheered when he returned with the news from Wellington, and guests were seated at the Felons' Feast without regard to color. Oberlin's African-Americans, including many runaways who had "self-emancipated," had become well known for their "touch-me-if-you-dare" attitude toward slave owners, which set them apart even from many militants in other communities.[3] In perhaps no other place would two young black men have been more likely to see themselves as soldiers in an underground army of liberation. John Anthony Copeland, moreover, had already participated in one armed rescue, and he appears to have known something of Brown's Southern strategy for over a year before he agreed to enlist.

John Anthony was not impulsive and must at least have suspected the reason he was called to John Mercer Langston's office to meet the younger Brown. The last time he had received such a summons, it had been to escort John Price to Canada, and he was probably quite ready to undertake another anti-slavery mission even before the proposition was raised to him. In contrast, Lewis Sheridan Leary was rash, and he seems to have had a strong inclination to absent himself from Oberlin, although his reasons remain obscure. Dissimilar as they were, the two kinsmen might well have reinforced one another, Copeland providing cool dedication to abolitionism and Leary providing the necessary degree of recklessness. They would not have been the first (or last) pair of young men to have hastened each other into a dangerous mission that neither might have undertaken alone. Nor should it be forgotten that both Copeland and Leary expected only to rescue slaves in a relatively risk-free operation such as Brown had led in Missouri. Those are at best incomplete answers, teased out from the partial recollections – in both senses – of the survivors. One thing is certain. John Brown owed a debt of gratitude to the Langston brothers for introducing him to Copeland

and Leary. Without the two black Oberliners, he would have had almost no one even to attempt hiving the anticipated bees.

Copeland and Leary left Oberlin on Monday morning, October 10, 1859, with the cash they had received from the Plumb brothers and only vague instructions for reaching John Brown. Their first stop was in Cleveland, where they stayed overnight at the home of Isaac and Amanda Sturtevant. Well known locally for their abolitionism, the Sturtevants had "invited and cordially welcomed" the elder Brown and Kagi to their home the previous spring for a fund-raising meeting where Brown regaled the attendees with the story of his Missouri slave rescue. Although the event seems to have generated little if any money, the Sturtevants agreed to act as a mail drop for Brown, receiving letters in double envelopes and then resending the contents to the ultimate addressee after obtaining a Cleveland postmark.[4] One such letter from the younger Brown was forwarded to Copeland and Leary, directing the pair to the Sturtevants' house on Walnut Street.

At age twenty-five, John Anthony found a confidant in Amanda Sturtevant, who was only twenty-nine years old and quite a firebrand.[5] Her highly visible activism had led the Democratic press to label her a "working woman," which was intended as a searing insult. Amanda, however, embraced the epithet, boldly declaring "myself such, especially in the cause of human-freedom," and adding that "while my strength remains I shall aid it by such means as I may command." Like most Ohio Republicans, Amanda Sturtevant held Marshal Matthew Johnson in special contempt, considering him a sycophant and a dishonorable hireling of the Buchanan administration. She no doubt shared that sentiment with John Anthony during their evening conversation, in the course of which he told her about his intention to join "John Brown's company" in Virginia. Mrs. Sturtevant later denied any advance knowledge of the Harper's Ferry operation, which was probably true. But she and her husband nonetheless knew that their African-American houseguests were intent on "running off slaves," and they were more than pleased to facilitate the effort.[6]

The onward journey continued on Tuesday, when the Sturtevants escorted Copeland and Leary to the railroad station, where they caught the evening train to Pittsburgh and points east. By midday on Wednesday, the travelers had arrived in Chambersburg, Pennsylvania, where

Brown had established a transfer point for men and supplies. Nearly all of Brown's foot soldiers passed through Chambersburg at one time or another, as did the firearms and pikes he intended to use in the raid. Brown and Kagi themselves were frequently in Chambersburg during summer and early fall 1859, usually staying at a rooming house operated by Mary Ritner, who was a staunch abolitionist. She was the daughter-in-law of former Pennsylvania governor Joseph Ritner, known for his anti-slavery sentiment, and her late husband had been active with the Underground Railroad. But even in Pennsylvania, the tenor of the times did not allow black men to stay overnight in a white woman's boarding-house.[7] Consequently, Brown's "colored hands" were lodged with families in Chambersburg's substantial free black community.[8]

Copeland and Leary did not remain in Chambersburg for long. By Thursday, October 12, they had arrived at Brown's headquarters, a small farm on the Maryland side of the Potomac River, about five miles from Harper's Ferry.[9] Using the alias Isaac Smith, Brown had rented the farm from the estate of Dr. Booth Kennedy the previous July, on the pretext that he was planning to prospect for minerals in the area. The ruse must have seemed plausible at first, when Brown was staying on the farm with only his sons Owen and Oliver, but the situation became dodgier as additional recruits arrived throughout the summer.

Eventually, Brown had to adopt a strict secrecy policy, requiring his men to stay indoors at all times during daylight hours. Brown enlisted his daughter Anne and his daughter-in-law Martha – both in their teens – to keep house for the men and to present a facade of normality to the outside world. Under Brown's rules, only he and the two young women were allowed to interact with the local populace. Brown spent his days reconnoitering the environs and meeting with his spy, John Cook, who had been living in Harper's Ferry for over a year. He shopped for supplies and received mail in town, waiting every afternoon at the post office for the newspapers from Baltimore and New York. He even attended several nearby churches, on one occasion delivering a sermon to the only anti-slavery congregation in the area.[10] Anne and Martha had the job of deflecting nosy neighbors and alerting the "invisibles," as Anne called them, to the approach of strangers. The "prisoners," as they called themselves, remained only moderately disciplined, filling their time with singing and Bible study, although some could not resist the temptation to sneak into town after nightfall.[11] Nonetheless, the pretext held remarkably well as summer turned to fall. If anyone in Harper's Ferry suspected the odd goings on at the Kennedy farm, they had not yet begun to investigate or ask questions. Anne Brown praised her invisibles for their ability to remain hidden in trying circumstances. "I never saw such men," she later said to Thomas Wentworth Higginson.[12]

By the time Copeland and Leary reached the Kennedy farm, there were already nineteen men living at Brown's headquarters, sixteen of whom were white. The most recently arrived was John Cook, although he had only a short distance to travel. Cook had been sent to Harper's Ferry in June 1858, shortly after the Chatham conference, with instructions to take a census of slaves and compile detailed floorplans of the federal armory and arsenal. Cook had been assured that the operation would begin within a few months, but the treachery of Hugh Forbes delayed Brown's plans and extended Cook's clandestine posting well into the following year. A notorious libertine, Cook took advantage of the situation by seducing his landlady's daughter, whom he impregnated and then honorably married. By the time Brown arrived in Harper's Ferry in July 1859, Cook was the father of a son and a fairly well-known figure in the region. Cook continued spying from his home base throughout July, August, and September, but Brown called him and his family to the farm on October 6. Cook's wife and child were escorted to Chambersburg and deposited at Mary Ritner's boardinghouse, and Cook remained at the Kennedy farm until the night of the raid.[13]

In addition to Brown himself, the other white men at the farm included five of his family members – three sons and two in-laws – as well as a number of militia veterans from Kansas. John Kagi was there, as was the quick-tempered Mexican War veteran Aaron Stevens, who served as Brown's drillmaster, Charles Tidd, a rough-edged lumberjack from Maine, and two Quaker brothers from Iowa who had been recruited when Brown stopped at their settlement during his wintertime flight from Missouri. One more white man, the erratic but wealthy Francis Merriam, would show up a day later with a much needed $600 in gold, bringing the unit to its final complement of twenty-two men, including Brown, with only five African-Americans. The group was disappointing to Brown in both size and composition, but he evidently believed, as others did after him, that you go to war with the army you have.[14]

THE THREE BLACK MEN who preceded Copeland and Leary to the Kennedy farm were Dangerfield Newby, Oswald Perry Anderson, and Shields Green. Newby's story was the most affecting, and in many ways the least well understood. He was a former slave from Virginia who had been living in Ohio for the past several years. His wife and children, however, remained enslaved in Virginia, and Newby was determined to obtain their freedom. He had diligently saved over $700 for that purpose – an impressive sum for a recently freed slave – but Harriet Newby's master refused to sell his human property.[15] In the wake of that bitter disappointment, Harriet sent several plaintive letters to her husband. "Oh dear Dangerfield, com this fall without fail monny or no Monny," she wrote, "I want to see you so much that is the one bright hope I have before me."[16] A few weeks later, Harriet wrote again, "Dear Dangerfield, you cannot amagine how much I want to see you. It is the grates Comfort I have is thinking of the promist time when you will be here oh that bless hour when I shall see you once more."[17]

Newby met some of Brown's men in summer 1859, in circumstances that are unknown. Newby's brother later assumed that he had met John Brown in Oberlin, although that was impossible given what we know of Brown's whereabouts. It is more likely that Newby encountered either Kagi or John Brown, Jr., or perhaps another of Brown's operatives, somewhere near Belmont County, where he was known to have lived. Newby appears never to have discussed with anyone the details of his recruitment, although he probably believed that he was only joining another rescue mission, similar to Brown's lightning foray into Missouri.

We do know, with great certainty, that Newby was desperate. Harriet's master "was in want of money," and he was threatening to sell her and the children to another owner. "I want you to buy me as soon as possible," she had written, "for if you do not get me some body else will."[18] Seeing little alternative, Dangerfield joined up with Brown in the hope of rescuing his family. He arrived at the farmhouse in late August, and he was already "impatient to have operations commenced," as Anne Brown observed, "for he was anxious to get them."[19] At age thirty-nine, Newby was older than any of the other men at the farmhouse, save Brown himself. He was tall and muscular, "a quiet man, upright, quick-tempered, and devoted to his family."[20] He impressed the young Anne Brown as "a smart and good man for an ignorant one."[21] In fact, Dangerfield was literate – as was Harriet, which was even more unusual for a woman in slavery – and he was far from ignorant. Nonetheless, his dream of rescuing his wife and children was tragically unrealistic. Despite whatever well-intentioned assurances John Brown had made to Dangerfield, the army of liberation would never get anywhere close to the plantation where Harriet and the children were enslaved.

Brown's recruitment of Shields Green was also fortuitous, linked as it was to his much greater effort to enlist Frederick Douglass. Brown had tried mightily to persuade Douglass to join him, beginning with a visit to the black abolitionist's Rochester home in early 1858. It was in Rochester that Brown first drafted his provisional constitution for the encampment "he intended to found in the mountains of Virginia," and it was in Rochester that Douglass first expressed his disapproval of the scheme.[22] Shields Green was an escaped slave from South Carolina, about twenty-five years old, who was then living with Douglass while earning a living as a clothing cleaner. Green made a deep impression on Brown, who saw at once the dignity and "stuff" that provided Green's nickname of "The Emperor." Brown confided his "plans and purpose" in Green, but the fugitive remained in Rochester for the time being.[23]

Brown continued his pursuit of Douglass, finally convincing the black abolitionist to meet him on the outskirts of Chambersburg in August 1859. Brown specifically asked that Green join them for the rendezvous, which was held secretly at an abandoned quarry. Douglass again rejected Brown's proposal, which he predicted would lead his friend into a "perfect steel-trap" from which "he would never get out alive." Surprisingly, however, Green accepted Brown's invitation, saying, as Douglass later reported, "I b'l'eve I'll go down wid de old man."[24]

Green still had to be taken from Chambersburg to the Kennedy farm, which was a risky trip for a fugitive slave. Brown entrusted the assignment to his son Owen, who escorted Green first in a covered wagon and then on foot after they were spotted by a band of slave hunters. The journey was arduous, completed mostly at night and taking the companions across rivers and mountains. Owen's later account of the mission was wildly exaggerated, emphasizing improbable heroics on his own part, but there is no doubt that he successfully delivered Green to the Kennedy farm, where they were welcomed with the applause and cheers of their comrades.[25]

Osborne Perry Anderson, who had been born free in Pennsylvania, was working as a printer in Chatham when Brown arrived in April 1858. An enthusiastic abolitionist, Anderson shared Brown's view that slavery amounted to "a state of perpetual war against the slave," who therefore had "the right to take liberty, and to use arms in defending the same."[26] He was elected secretary of the Chatham conference, and he was later offered a commission as a captain in Brown's army (which he declined, believing that he lacked sufficient military experience to accept the post). Like the other Chatham signatories, Anderson expected the Virginia operation to occur in 1858; unlike all of the others, he remained ready to participate when the call finally came in summer of the following year.

Anderson left Chatham on September 13, 1859, arriving in Chambersburg three days later. His first assignment involved handling 3000 pounds of freight – comprising many sealed boxes of weapons – that had to be moved from railcars to Brown's wagon for transfer to the farmhouse. That required multiple round trips over fifty miles of country roads, and Anderson therefore remained in Chambersburg until September 24. He then walked as far as Middletown, a village on the Maryland border, where he found Brown waiting in a wagon to take him the rest of the way. As did "all the colored men at the Ferry," Anderson "made the journey from the Pennsylvania line in the night."[27]

BROWN'S INABILITY TO ATTRACT more black soldiers has been the subject of considerable scholarly attention, in large part because Brown himself had considered African-American recruits essential to his plans. According to historian Benjamin Quarles, Brown's failure resulted from a combination of overestimation, obsessive secrecy, and poor timing.

Brown sincerely "expected that all the free negroes in the Northern States would immediately flock to his standard," but that was simply unrealistic. His experience among militant black leaders had led him to "universalize the characteristics of the Negroes he knew," especially their willingness to take up arms.[28] Brown's friends and associates – including stalwarts such as Harriet Tubman, William Wells Brown, Lewis Hayden, and Jermain Loguen – had all voiced "strong and incendiary anti-slavery sentiments. Frederick Douglass, for example, had inveighed against the Fugitive Slave Act, saying that the surest way to make it a "dead letter is to make a half dozen or more dead kidnappers."[29] But Douglass and others who expressed similar views throughout the 1850s were speaking of self-defense, not an armed invasion of the South. Brown's great error was to mistake their righteous anger for tacit agreement with his planned foray into Virginia.[30]

Brown's efforts were not helped by his fixation on secrecy. Even as he was attempting to recruit black men to his side, he remained maddeningly cryptic about his intentions. For African-Americans who were accustomed to mistrusting white men, Brown's cageyness provided a serious barrier. Life was risky enough without rushing into the unknown behind a man who fashioned himself as "Moses, whom God has sent to conduct the children through the Red Sea."[31] To his credit, Brown was no more forthcoming with his white financial backers in Boston, who complained that "the Captain leaves us much in the dark concerning his destination and designs."[32] The Bostonians, however, were solicited only for money, while the black men were asked to venture their lives. As historian Tony Horwitz put it, "Brown's vision and ardor inspired more admiration for him than confidence in his chances of success – or in the chances of anyone who went with him."[33]

Nonetheless, Brown might have been able to recruit more black men to the Harper's Ferry operation had it not been for two instances of disastrously bad timing. When he left Chatham in May 1858, Brown had the signatures of thirty-four black men on his provisional constitution, signifying their agreement to join his campaign. Some of them had no doubt signed up halfheartedly, or in the flush of the moment, but many were truly enthusiastic, and they expected to join Brown's command within a month or two. Brown, however, was forced to postpone the raid for over a year, owing to his betrayal by Hugh Forbes, during which time "the zeal of most of the black participants had abated."[34] Brown continued his efforts, sending emissaries to black communities in Canada West, Ohio, Michigan, New York, and Pennsylvania, but only Copeland, Leary, Green, Anderson, and Newby responded. It is possible that others were yet on their way, only to be caught by surprise when Brown "struck prematurely" on October 16. According to Franklin Sanborn, one of Brown's confidants, the original plan had been to strike over a week later, on October 24 or 25 – and several would-be recruits were forced to abandon their travels when they learned that the raid had already been launched. More improbably, it was also said that several full companies of black militia had to abort their mission for the same reason.[35]

TWENTY-TWO MEN DID NOT FIT comfortably in the Kennedy farmhouse. In the best of times, it was crowded, ill furnished, muggy, and plagued by "unmercifully numerous" fleas.[36] Anne and Martha were sent home at the end of September, and the house must also have become filthy and poorly provisioned following their departure. The men were unaccustomed to housekeeping, and Brown was occupied with logistical matters far more important than stocking the larder at a headquarters that he would soon abandon.

Copeland and Leary were probably appalled at the squalor of the farmhouse. With no beds, little food, and sealed windows, it was a stark contrast from the well-appointed homes they had left only a few days before. And they were no doubt curious about their new comrades, both black and white, who ran the gamut from Quaker to roughneck and fugitive to heir. If Copeland got to know any of the other men well, it was Dangerfield Newby. Both African-Americans who had left the South for Ohio, Copeland and Newby at one point shared their stories and aspirations with one another. Copeland later reflected on Newby's determination "to try to free his wife from the cruel hands of her master."[37] But aside from that poignant conversation, the Oberliners had precious little time to become acquainted with either their surroundings or their fellow troops. On Sunday, October 16, barely seventy-two hours after Copeland and Leary had arrived, Brown called a meeting of his men. The revolution was about to begin.

EIGHTEEN

THE WAR DEPARTMENT

John Brown began handing out military commissions on Saturday, October 15, 1859, designating the Kennedy farm as "Head-Quarters War Department, Near Harper's Ferry," and naming several of his most trusted men either captains or lieutenants in the battle against slavery. Both Brown and Kagi signed the documents, the former as "Commander in Chief" and the latter as "Secretary of War."[1] Even at that late date, however, many of the men did not realize the scope of the operation that was about to begin.

On Sunday morning, Brown finally revealed his plan in full. Rising even earlier than usual, he called the men together for a meeting at which he read aloud a Bible verse about the condition of slaves and "offered up a fervent prayer to God to assist in the liberation of the bondmen in that slaveholding land." As Osborne Anderson later recalled, "a deep solemnity pervaded the place," as everyone realized that the long-awaited moment was at hand.[2]

Following breakfast, a council was convened with Anderson as chair. The position was symbolic, as Anderson was the only black man present who had signed the provisional constitution in Chatham, which Brown proceeded to read out loud. Many of the men were already familiar with the document, but others had no idea that they had enlisted in an effort to establish a permanent base of operations in the Virginia mountains. According to Anne Brown, "it seemed to be the impression of most of the men that they had come there to make another [Missouri-type] raid, only on a larger scale."[3] Likewise, John Cook recalled that "there were six or seven in our party who . . . were also ignorant of the plan of operations until the Sunday morning previous to the attack. Among this number were . . . John Copeland and Leary."[4] Even fewer of the men had known that Brown planned to capture the federal armory and arsenal at

Harper's Ferry, and to take prominent hostages, whom he intended to trade for the freedom of local slaves.

Having visited Chatham in 1858, John Copeland would have had some inkling of Brown's constitution, although certainly none of the details, which he might or might not have shared with Lewis Leary during their travels from Ohio to the Kennedy farm. Still, he insisted for the rest of his life that he had signed up only for a rescue mission such as Brown had conducted in Missouri, with no foreknowledge of the extent of Brown's invasion. Expecting to be involved in a lightning strike – freeing slaves and then speeding them to the North or to Canada – Copeland and Leary must have been stunned to realize that they had actually joined what amounted to an army of occupation.

Even the men most familiar with Brown's intentions – adjutant John Kagi, drillmaster Aaron Stevens, and Brown's three sons – were surprised about the timing. They had been led to believe that the attack would not begin for at least another week, as Brown was still hoping for "reinforcements from the North and East."[5] In fact, several of Brown's Kansas comrades later claimed that they had been en route to Harper's Ferry in mid-October, expecting to join the men at the farmhouse, only to learn from the newspapers that Brown's raid had already begun.

Why did Brown launch the attack when he did – with only twenty-one men behind him – rather than wait as expected for additional volunteers? Brown himself never explained the precipitous decision, and his reasons have been ever after the subject of conjecture. Osborne Anderson, who was closest to the scene, believed that word of Brown's plot had leaked out to "prying neighbors" and that Brown had heard of plans "to have a search instituted in the early part of the coming week."[6] Richard Hinton, one of the Kansas veterans who claimed to have been headed to Harper's Ferry, later suggested that Brown had learned of government orders "to remove a large number of arms" from the arsenal, which would have thwarted Brown's plan to obtain the rifles for his own use.[7]

The calculation must have been torturous for Brown. Should he wait for more men and risk discovery and the loss of weapons, or should he "strike a blow immediately" with the small army he had already assembled?[8] As of Wednesday, October 11, he had evidently resolved his doubts in favor of waiting, but then two much anticipated events occurred in short succession that made the decision easier. Brown had known about Copeland and Leary for some time – calling them the "Cleveland friends" in a note to Kagi – but he had no idea when, or if, they would actually reach the Kennedy farm.[9] When Copeland and Leary did arrive on

Thursday, October 12, Brown must have been greatly relieved finally to have a respectable number of black men for the operation.

Brown had been much more closely in touch with Francis Merriam, the unsteady scion of a wealthy New England family, who had recently been referred to him by Lewis Hayden, a prominent black abolitionist in Boston. At a last-minute meeting with Merriam in Philadelphia, Brown had agreed to accept the frail young man into his ranks on the condition that he provide an infusion of funds. Merriam readily agreed, arranging a rendezvous in Chambersburg with Kagi, who then escorted him to Brown's headquarters. Merriam arrived at the farm on October 15, bearing $600 in gold, and Brown at last had the money necessary for an extended occupation of Virginia.

Of the two events, the arrival of the black Oberliners may well have been the more strategically important. Brown could have managed without the money – indeed, he left several hundred dollars in gold in Merriam's possession – but he did not want to lead a white army, and it seems much less likely that Brown would have proceeded with only three black men in his command. John Anthony Copeland may not be the entire key to the puzzle of Brown's timing, but it does appear that he again had been in the right place – as he had been in Wellington – at a crucial moment in time.

THE HOURS AFTER THE SUNDAY MORNING MEETING were spent in preparation, as the men cleaned and checked their weapons and loaded the wagon that Brown had so often used on his trips to and from Chambersburg. It might have alarmed some of the men to notice that Brown had not included any food in the supplies – evidencing the precipitousness of his decision to embark on the raid – but it does not appear that anyone raised an objection. In any case, it was too late to back out. Many of the men had expressed misgivings during the weeks and months they had spent at the farmhouse, and others, including Copeland, later claimed to have been misled into joining an insurrection when they had only intended to rescue slaves, but they all appeared to be united that evening when Brown gathered them for a final admonition:

> And now gentlemen, let me press this one thing on your minds, you all know how dear life is to you, and how dear your lives are to your friends; and in remembering that consider that the lives of others are as dear to them as yours are to you; do not, therefore, take the life of

> any one if you can possibly avoid it; but if it is necessary to take life in order to save your own, then make sure work of it.[10]

Brown then delivered eleven operational orders, detailing the initial tasks for each of his soldiers. Three of the men – his son Owen, Francis Merriam, and an Iowa Quaker named Barclay Coppoc – were to remain at the farmhouse, owing to their physical disabilities, with instructions to guard Brown's weapons cache for later transfer to a forward location. The eighteen others were assigned duties that included cutting telegraph wires, guarding the bridges in and out of Harper's Ferry, and taking hostages. At eight o'clock on Sunday evening, Brown put on "his old Kansas cap" and announced, "Men, get on your arms; we will proceed to the Ferry."[11]

John Brown and his eighteen men, with a single horse and wagon, stepped into the night, ready to begin the war against slavery. John Cook, the spy, was in the lead, which only made sense given his greater familiarity with the local country roads. He was followed closely by lumberjack Charles Tidd, whose stormy temperament was matched by his strength and dedication. It is not known exactly where the five black men figured in the line of march, but given Brown's egalitarianism, it seems certain that he would not have placed them at the rear.

After nearly two hours of deliberate marching, the procession reached the Potomac River bridge, which crossed into Virginia. Cook and Tidd followed their orders to cut the telegraph lines linking Harper's Ferry to the outside world, as the others traipsed silently toward the sleeping town. The first Virginian they encountered was the bridge watchman, William Williams, who was startled to see so many men at that late hour. He was even more startled when Kagi and Stevens took him prisoner, forcing him into the wagon as it rattled across the span.

With two men – Watson Brown and an Iowan named Stewart Taylor – left behind to guard the bridge, Brown led his troops to the U.S. armory, which hugged the river a short distance from the bridge. They easily overpowered the sole watchman, pried open the gate, and seized the armory. Now in control of his prime objective, having faced no meaningful resistance, Brown announced to his men and prisoners, "I came here from Kansas, and this is a slave State; I want to free all the negroes in this State; I have possession of the United States armory; and if the citizens interfere with me I must only burn the town and have blood."[12]

Brown then dispatched his troops to their assignments. Two men were sent across the street to seize the federal arsenal, and two more were ordered to seize the Shenandoah bridge on the other side of the town's small central district. Six men, under the command of Aaron Stevens and guided by John Cook, headed into the countryside to take hostages. That contingent included three African-Americans: Dangerfield Newby, Shields Green, and Osborne Anderson. Brown especially wanted black men present when prominent slave owners were forced to surrender.

Finally, John Copeland and John Kagi (later joined by Lewis Leary) were sent to Hall's Rifle Works, about 800 yards distant from the armory, with instructions to take and hold the factory. They quickly subdued the unarmed guard, and then waited for the in-gathering of slaves, which Brown had promised would occur as soon as word of the liberation spread.

ANY MISGIVINGS AMONG THE ABOLITIONIST TROOPS were dispelled during the first hours of the operation. Brown's men had not only seized the federal compound and rifle works. They had also taken control of the main routes in and out of Harper's Ferry, cutting the telegraph lines that might have been used to summon help. Resistance had been almost nonexistent, and victory seemed for the time being to be well within reach.

The hostage-taking party met with yet more success. Cook led the expedition to the home of Colonel Lewis Washington, who was a great-nephew of George Washington, reaching it at about midnight. During his life as a spy, Cook had scouted the property, a 670-acre plantation known as Beallair, and he was familiar with the layout. He had also falsely befriended Washington and learned the location of several famous artifacts that Washington had inherited from the first president – and which Brown greatly prized for symbolic value – including a sword that had been a gift from Frederick the Great.

By the light of a flambeau, the group broke down the door to the house and roused Washington from his sleep. In his own account of the event, Washington claimed to have bravely defied the intruders, but Osborne Anderson reported that the slave owner was "blubbering like a great calf" at the prospect of losing his property.[13] Stevens demanded Frederick the Great's sword, and Washington ruefully complied. The plantation owner trembled, in both fear and disgrace, when Osborne Anderson stepped forward to receive the sword. Brown had instructed his men not only to kidnap Washington but also to humble him in the process.

Stevens seized several other weapons from Washington, including a shotgun and a small rifle, while Cook surreptitiously filched an antique dueling pistol (which he hid from Brown and kept for himself) that had been a gift to George Washington from the Marquis de Lafayette. Exiting the house with their prisoner, the raiders commandeered Washington's carriage and farm wagon. They liberated three of his male slaves and headed back toward Harper's Ferry. The company stopped en route to capture two more slaveholders – a father and son, both named John Allstadt – and liberate seven more slaves, arriving back at the armory well before dawn.

Brown was delighted to receive the captives and greet the freed slaves, introducing himself as "Ossawatomie Brown, of Kansas," to ensure that there could be no mistaking his identity or his cause.[14] He armed the newly arrived black men with pikes, and he gathered the hostages in the armory's stout engine house, where they joined a number of others who had been unceremoniously snatched from the streets of Harper's Ferry. Brown dispatched Cook to retrieve his weapons cache and then turned his attention to his prisoners.

Once again, Brown placed great value on symbolism. He told Colonel Washington that "I wanted you particularly for the moral effect it would give our cause, having one of your name as a prisoner," and he boldly fastened the revolutionary sword around his own waist.[15] To drive home his point, Brown assigned a black man – this time, Shields Green – to guard the hostages. Washington later complained that Green had been "rather impudent," meaning that the black man had dared to exercise authority over whites. In fact, all of the hostages, including Washington, had been treated courteously while in Brown's custody. He secured food for them from a nearby hotel, and he made sure they were housed in the safest part of the armory compound. Several of the hostages later testified for Brown's defense, saying that he had never mistreated them.[16]

Although it was not apparent at the time, Brown's position had already started to deteriorate. About an hour after midnight on Monday morning, as Stevens and his crew were trundling their captives back to the armory, an eastbound Baltimore & Ohio train approached the Potomac bridge, where Watson Brown was standing guard. Concerned about the unexpected absence of lights on the bridge, the engineer stopped the train, and a conductor named A. J. Phelps set out on foot to investigate. Rattled by the situation, Watson fired at the conductor, causing him to retreat while the engineer backed the train away from the bridge. The sound of the gunshots drew other workers to the scene, including the baggage handler, a free black man named Hayward Shepherd. Watson fired again, this time hitting Shepherd in the back and inflicting a wound that exited just "under the left nipple."[17] The noise awakened Dr. John Starry, who raced to the scene and futilely attempted to minister to Shepherd's injury. It was no use. The free black man died within a few hours, making him, in the words of biographer David Reynolds, "the first casualty of the war for Black liberation."[18]

Harper's Ferry had been attacked, although the true nature of the invasion was still unknown. Dr. Starry called for church bells to begin ringing the alarm, and local militiamen grabbed their rifles and headed into the streets. The town itself, however, was still isolated. Brown had cut the telegraph lines, and his men controlled both railroad bridges. But then Brown made a fateful misjudgment. Withdrawing his men from the Potomac bridge and consolidating them at the armory, he allowed Conductor Phelps to continue eastward. The train crossed into Maryland in the early morning and then stopped at the Monocacy Junction, about twenty miles beyond the Potomac River. There, Phelps sent a telegram to railroad headquarters in Baltimore, advising his superiors that 150 abolitionists had taken Harper's Ferry. The message was received with some skepticism – who could imagine an abolitionist invasion of Virginia? – but it was eventually relayed to President James Buchanan, Secretary of War John Floyd, and Governor Henry Wise of Virginia, at which point Brown's fate was all but sealed.

By midmorning on Monday, the armory compound was surrounded by a dozen local militia companies, who poured fire onto Brown's position. Concerned for the safety of his hostages, who by then numbered close to forty, Brown moved Washington and the others into the sturdy engine house while ordering his men to knock slits in the armory wall so that they could return fire with fire. Brown's troops fought bravely, but the odds were overwhelmingly against them.

In fearful symmetry, the first casualty on Brown's side was also a black man, Dangerfield Newby, who was racing back to the armory from a posting on one of the bridges. Newby had just reached the gate when he was struck in the neck by a six-inch "smoothing iron" that had been fired from a muzzle loader. He died instantly, although death was not punishment enough to mollify the angry Virginians. Newby's corpse was beaten and mutilated. His genitals were cut off, and pieces of his ears passed around as trophies. His body was left in the street, where rooting hogs crowded "around the corpse and almost literally devour[ed] it" while locals watched the scene with ghoulish delight. Several men proudly claimed credit for firing the fatal shot, and one eyewitness observed that nearly the entire community applauded "the hogs for their rough treatment of the invader."[19] Harriet Newby's dreams of freedom died with her husband. Her heartbreaking letters were found in his pockets and were later turned over to the Virginia authorities. "You mus write soon and say when you think you can come," she had implored him in her final letter. "If I thought I shoul never see you this earth would have no charms for me."[20]

The fighting continued throughout the day, with Brown's men steadily getting the worst of it. One by one, they were killed or captured. Brown attempted to negotiate a cease-fire, sending out emissaries under a flag of truce, but the messengers were either shot down or taken prisoner. Even the captured raiders were not safe from retribution. William Thompson – whose brother was married to one of Brown's daughters – was taken on the Shenandoah bridge, where he was tied on the trestle and "riddled with bullets." His lifeless body fell into the river, only to be used for target practice by the militia. His corpse "could be seen for a day or two after, lying at the bottom of the river, with his ghastly face still exhibiting his fearful death agony."[21]

The abolitionists fought back, killing several Virginians, including Harper's Ferry Mayor Fontaine Beckham, and wounding others, but it soon became apparent that the situation was hopeless. Brown's vision of inspiring a mass defection of slaves was fading by the moment, and even his effort to obtain safe passage for his surviving men – in exchange for releasing his hostages – came to naught.

Although the militiamen defending Harper's Ferry were impassioned and brutal, they were poorly organized and much less than fully effective. By Monday afternoon, many of them were also drunk, and their furious assault began to lose some steam. For a time, it seemed as though Brown's main position at the armory might remain relatively secure. Amid the chaos and gun smoke, even a brief lull in the fighting brought welcome respite to Brown's exhausted troops, who had barely slept or eaten for twenty-four hours.

The weary men inside the compound had no way of knowing it, but matters took a decided turn for the worse on late Monday evening, when Colonel Robert E. Lee arrived with a detachment of ninety U.S. Marines, who had been stationed in Washington, D.C.[22] Lee ordered his troops to surround the armory, which he determined to be occupied by a "party of Banditti," and did his best to calm the boisterous and inebriated militiamen. As a chilly rain fell on Harper's Ferry, Lee made ready for the assault he planned to initiate the following morning. There were too many hostages in the armory to risk a nighttime attack.[23]

John Brown had no reason for optimism when he reviewed his troops at sunrise on Tuesday, October 18. Only a few of his own eighteen men were in fighting shape; the others had been killed, captured, or had fled. Brown's son Oliver had succumbed to wounds during the night, and his son Watson lay dying on the ground. Brown did not yet know the fate of the men who had been taken prisoner, nor could he have known the whereabouts of the five men he had tasked with retrieving weapons from his Maryland headquarters. He had last seen Kagi, Copeland, and Leary when he posted them to Hall's Rifle Works, but it had been many hours since the last gunfire had been heard from that direction. The six slaves whom Brown had ostensibly freed and armed with pikes milled about the yard, showing varying degrees of enthusiasm for the battle that had been thrust upon them. Taking grim stock of his circumstances, Brown turned toward his dying son, hoping that he might "endure a little longer" and "die in a glorious cause."[24]

At dawn, Colonel Lee sent his second-in-command, Lieutenant J. E. B. Stuart, to the armory gate under a flag of truce. Speaking through a slight opening in the solid wooden gate, Stuart addressed Brown, whom he recognized from his earlier posting in Kansas.

"You are Osawatomie Brown," said Stuart.

"Well, they do call me that sometimes," came the reply.

Stuart then delivered Lee's terms for surrender, promising to take Brown and his men into federal custody and thus protect them from lynching by the furious Virginians. Recognizing that hanging was sure to follow arrest, Brown repeated his earlier demand for safe passage across the Potomac. "You must allow me to leave this place with my party and prisoners for the lock-house on the Maryland side," he said. "There I will release the prisoners, and as soon as this is done, you and your troops may fire on us and pursue us."[25]

With no authority to negotiate anything other than unconditional surrender, Stuart stepped away from the gate and waved his hat in the air, giving a prearranged signal to a waiting party of twelve marines. Using a heavy ladder as a battering ram, the federal troops quickly broke through the door. They were greeted by gunfire, which killed one man and wounded another, but they soon overcame the resistance. Two of Brown's men were killed by bayonets and two were captured, while Brown himself stood bravely in the middle of the yard, still wearing George Washington's sword. Lewis Washington was impressed by Brown's sangfroid – calling him "the coolest man I ever saw in defying danger and death" – but he still had the presence of mind to point him out to the advancing troops. "There's Brown," he shouted, "this is Ossawatomie."[26]

Lieutenant Israel Green, the leader of the storming party, raced toward Brown with his sword in hand. "Quicker than thought," he slashed Brown across the head, followed by a "thrust in the left breast." To Green's surprise, however, the sword bent. He later realized that he had mistakenly worn his dress sword that morning, which was too dull to inflict a serious wound. Had Green worn his combat saber, Brown no doubt would have been killed.[27] As it was, the old man was beaten into unconsciousness and taken into custody. "The whole was over in a few minutes," wrote Robert E. Lee in his official report to his superiors in the U.S. War Department.[28]

NINETEEN

HALL'S RIFLE WORKS

COPELAND AND KAGI HAD TAKEN THEIR STATION at Hall's Rifle Works a few hours before midnight on Sunday, as part of Brown's initial occupation of Harper's Ferry. Brown later sent Leary to reinforce them, after his other men returned from the hostage-taking mission at Colonel Washington's. Soon, however, the factory came under constant fire, and one more man could not possibly make a difference against the steady assault of the assembled militia. Kagi sent a note to Brown, seeking permission to retreat, but Brown ordered them to hold firm.

The three abolitionists continued fighting as best they could, repelling as many as seven attacks, but their ammunition ran low by midafternoon on Monday, and their position became impossible to defend. As Virginians crashed through the entrance to the factory, Copeland, Leary, and Kagi fled through the back door, where they discovered that the "only means of escape if any" was to cross the Shenandoah River. Copeland and the others "turned and fired one round" before wading into the shallow waters, but they hit no one. Some of the Virginians plunged in after the raiders, while almost fifty others stood on both banks and, as Copeland later put it, "opened a hot fire on us from all sides."[1]

Kagi was hit after he crossed midstream, taking multiple shots in the head and body. According to Mary Mauzy, a local woman who watched the scene, he briefly rose "above the water," only to be shot again "like a dog" and then "dragged . . . out a corpse."[2]

Leary swam to a rock in the middle of the river, where he was "shot through the body" before he could gain purchase. Unable to move, he was later pulled ashore and carried to a cooper's shop, where he lived in agony for another ten or twelve hours. Interviewed by a reporter, Leary asked that news of his fate be sent to his wife and child in Oberlin "to inform them of the manner of his death."[3] If Mary Leary ever received such a message, it would have been the first word from her husband since he disappeared a week earlier.

Copeland fared better than his comrades, reaching an outcropping where he was momentarily able to hide in a clump of bushes. At first, the militia believed he had been killed and that his body was floating downriver. He was soon spied, however, by the men who had come to retrieve the mortally wounded Leary. A Virginian named James Holt splashed through the water in pursuit of Copeland and soon stood face to face with him. Both men raised their rifles, but their powder was wet and neither could fire. As militia encircled the small island, Copeland realized that he had no chance at escape. He threw down his useless gun and surrendered to Holt, who escorted his captive to shore.

Copeland was quickly surrounded by an angry mob bent on lynching. Some of the Virginians started to make a rope of knotted handkerchiefs and looked for a sturdy hanging tree, while others debated shooting him. Copeland's life was saved by the intervention of Dr. John Starry, who berated the mob for being "such cowards as to want to kill a man when disarmed and a pris[o]ner."[4] Spared from death for the time being, Copeland was tied up and taken to a guardhouse to await his fate in a Jefferson County courtroom.

Following Tuesday morning's assault on the armory, Robert E. Lee was able to account for most of the insurgents who had invaded Harper's Ferry. In addition to Copeland, Lee held four other prisoners who had been taken in various circumstances: John Brown had been captured by Lieutenant Green; Edwin Coppoc, one of the Quaker brothers from Iowa, had surrendered when the marines crashed into the armory yard; Shields Green had likewise been captured at the armory, although he had initially dropped his rifle and attempted to disguise himself among the slaves; Aaron Stevens, the Mexican War veteran, had been savagely shot down while attempting to negotiate under a flag of truce, but he had miraculously survived and was now in custody. Ten of the invaders were known to have been killed. Lee also believed that four of Brown's men had escaped for the time being, including John Cook, who had been recognized and identified by Lewis Washington and erroneously assumed to be Brown's second in command. The others who had been identified but not captured were Maine lumberjack Charles Tidd, black Chatham printer Oswald Perry Anderson, and a Pennsylvanian named Albert Hazlett. In addition, three others had successfully fled, although they were at the time unknown to Colonel Lee: Owen Brown, the oldest of Brown's children who had come to Virginia; Barclay Coppoc, whose brother had been captured; and Francis Merriam, the wealthy but infirm Bostonian.[5]

The prisoners were gathered in the armory paymaster's office. Brown and Stevens, who were bleeding badly, were given straw pallets. The three others, who were uninjured, were simply bound hand and foot. Brown, of course, was the center of attention, and he was soon besieged by a crowd of reporters and political figures, including Virginia Governor Henry Wise and Senator James Mason, and Ohio Congressman Clement Vallandingham (who was coincidentally en route from Washington, D.C., to Dayton). Robert E. Lee gallantly offered to protect Brown from interrogation, but the old man appeared more than willing to explain his goals. In lawyerly fashion, Governor Wise even cautioned Brown against saying "anything from him that he did not willingly . . . feel disposed to communicate," adding that his fate "would not in any degree, and could not, be affected by anything he told."[6] But the warning was pointless. Brown was eager to talk. Alexander Boteler, the newly elected congressman from Harper's Ferry, began by asking how Brown had expected to capture the town with so few troops.[7]

"I expected help," was the reply, from "here and elsewhere." Brown was cagey about his intentions, refusing to admit that he planned to spark a slave rebellion, and adamant about shielding the identities of his financial backers. "I planned it all myself," he insisted.[8]

Senator Mason soon took over the questioning, intensely interested in the source of Brown's funding. "Can you tell us who furnished money for your expedition?" he asked.

"I furnished most of it myself," said Brown. "I will answer freely and faithfully about what concerns myself," he continued. "I will answer anything I can with honor – but not about others."

Clement Vallandingham interceded at one point. A pro-slavery Democrat with strong partisan views, the thirty-nine-year-old Vallandingham was a dapper man with dark hair, who wore wispy chin whiskers but no mustache. He would later be Lincoln's greatest congressional antagonist during the Civil War, and his efforts to subvert the war effort ultimately led to his trial before a military tribunal and deportation to the Confederacy. On that day in 1859, however, Vallandingham was still a loyal Unionist, and he was especially keen to implicate his political enemies in crimes against the nation. He questioned Brown about his recent lectures in Cleveland, and whether he had met with abolitionists in the Western Reserve. Hoping to pin something on at least one detested Republican, Vallandingham asked if Brown had consulted Representative Joshua Giddings about his plans to invade the South.

Brown refused to say "anything that would implicate Mr. Giddings" or anyone else. Instead, he changed the subject to his own intentions, which he was eager to explain. "I want you to understand," he said, "that I respect the rights of the poorest and weakest of colored people, oppressed by the slave system.... This is the idea that has moved me, and that alone." Speaking directly to the journalists in the room, and through them to the nation, Brown began a public relations campaign that would eventually transform the debate over slavery. The Southerners were guilty of "a great wrong against God and humanity," he said, and he had no apologies for attempting "to free those [they] willfully and wickedly hold in bondage."

The questioning continued for over an hour, as the interrogators traded turns at attempting to pry information out of Brown. But other than repeated condemnations of slavery, they obtained almost nothing. "You may dispose of me very easily," Brown said, "I am nearly disposed of now; but this question is still to be settled – this negro question I mean – the end of that is not yet." As prosecutor Andrew Hunter later put it, "whenever we touched upon any one that had not been captured he was 'mum.'"[9] Aaron Stevens was also interrogated that day, although he was almost incoherent owing to pain from his wounds.

Copeland was questioned at least twice shortly after his capture. Andrew Hunter, who later served as Virginia's prosecuting attorney, claimed to have interrogated Copeland on Monday, soon after he was saved from lynching. Although Hunter later maintained that he had learned "certain facts" from Copeland about the nature of Brown's organization, he evidently reduced nothing to writing.[10] Copeland was interrogated again the following day, at the direction of Colonel Lee. According to Governor Wise, the frightened Copeland then "offered to betray all persons involved in the affair if spared," but that observation was in the context of contrasting the perceived courage of the white prisoners with the faintheartedness of the blacks.[11] Wise had every reason to reassure his constituents that the black men had all been cringing cowards, even if that involved making up the offer of a confession. In fact, Lee's official report includes no mention of any admissions by Copeland or Green.

At most, it appears that Lee learned only that Copeland and Leary were from Oberlin, which became burning news in the Ohio press.[12]

In Cleveland, Marshal Johnson greeted the word of Copeland's arrest with grim satisfaction. He had been deeply opposed to the deal that ended the Oberlin prosecutions, considering it, as did most Cleveland Democrats, a pitiful capitulation to "the rebellious Higher Law creed."[13] At least Charles Langston and Simeon Bushnell had been convicted, and Johnson had made certain that they served out every day of their sentences even after the bargain had been struck. But Copeland, to Johnson's great annoyance, had never been apprehended and therefore, unlike the other rescuers, had not spent even a single night in jail. Now, with Copeland in custody, Johnson had an opportunity to settle old scores – not with Copeland himself, who was sure to hang, but with other Ohio abolitionists, whom Johnson hoped to entangle in the Harper's Ferry conspiracy.

Virginia was far beyond Johnson's jurisdiction, but that made no difference to the obsessive federal marshal, who was still smarting from Brown's taunts the previous spring.[14] Acting with renewed energy and deliberate speed, he caught a train headed south, arriving in Virginia within a week of the insurrection. Johnson was convinced that Copeland and Leary had not been the only Oberliners complicit in Brown's plot, and he had few scruples about acquiring the necessary proof.

In the meantime, Copeland and the other prisoners had been taken from Harper's Ferry to Charlestown, the Jefferson County seat, where they would face trial. Relocating the prisoners had not been easy. Despite the quick victory of the federal troops, Harper's Ferry remained filled with hundreds of unruly militiamen, many of them drunk and all of them outraged at the bedraggled prisoners. Four Virginians had been killed by Brown's men – in addition to a U.S. Marine who was shot down when storming the engine house – and nine others had been wounded. It was unsurprising that the orderly administration of justice was nearly the last thing on the minds of Harper's Ferry's incensed citizenry.

The local anger was also stoked by fear. Brown's claim that he had expected help "from here and elsewhere" caused many frightened Virginians to imagine that another abolitionist army – this one much larger, and no doubt including armed slaves – was lurking somewhere in the hills. Such rumors inevitably inspired panic, and soon a story spread that the fugitive John Cook had led a massacre in nearby Pleasant Valley. Cook had immediately become the bête noir of Harper's Ferry, and his former neighbors, feeling a profound sense of betrayal, now believed him capable of anything. He had indeed escaped into the hills, as had six others, but none of them had any intention of staging a retaliatory raid, then or ever. Although skeptical of the reported violence, Lee sent a detachment to investigate the rumor. As he suspected, the "alarm proved false," but that did little to assuage the roiling tempers in Harper's Ferry.[15]

Colonel Lee was determined to protect his prisoners from lynching, and Governor Wise issued a strong warning that vigilantes would be punished. That had been enough to calm the mob, although just barely. The makeshift jail in the paymaster's office was far from secure, however, and it was not certain how long the gangs of militiamen would remain peaceful. It was therefore imperative to remove Brown and the others as soon as possible, and that is exactly what Lee ordered at noon on Wednesday, October 19. A jeering crowd lined the street as the prisoners made the short trip to the railroad station, where a train was waiting to take them to Charlestown, the county seat. Brown and Stevens, both badly injured, rode in a wagon while Copeland, Green, and Coppoc walked behind them.

One observer reported that the two black men appeared terrified, with their eyes "almost bursting from their sockets," while the three white men seemed preternaturally calm.[16] The contrast may have been nothing more than a racist caricature – bulging eyes were commonly attributed to black men as a sign of cowardice – and the supposed fearfulness of African-Americans was a staple stereotype in Southern mythology. Governor Wise, who had already praised John Brown's bravery and integrity, calling him "a man of clear head, of courage, fortitude, and simple ingenuousness," had been immediately dismissive of the two black men, describing Green as "cowardly and false" and pronouncing Copeland a "crouching craven."[17] Both Copeland and Green would have been well justified to fear lynching, which had been a fact of life for black men in the South, or even mutilation, as had been inflicted on Dangerfield Newby. But in fact there is no real evidence that they reacted any differently from their white comrades – other than Brown, who had indeed shown astonishing courage and composure. In any event, the military escort was vigilant, and the transfer was accomplished without incident.

There was more at stake than transportation. The removal of the prisoners to Charlestown also had the effect of transferring them from U.S. custody into the sole hands of the Virginia authorities. The switch was important to Governor Wise, who was eager to vindicate Virginia's honor, and it concerned President Buchanan hardly at all. He later described the change in jurisdiction as "a matter quite indifferent to me."[18] Buchanan had evidently given little thought to the implications of ceding prosecution to the Virginians, but his decision would have significant consequences for Brown, Copeland, and the nation.

COPELAND AND THE OTHERS WERE LODGED in the Jefferson County jail, under the superintendence of Captain John Avis. The jailor was an ardent Virginia patriot with no sympathy for abolitionism, but he also had a profound commitment to decency. Although he occasionally dealt in slaves and had led a company of volunteers in the siege of the armory at Harper's Ferry, Avis was determined to treat all of his prisoners – including the blacks – with integrity and compassion.[19] First and foremost, Avis was concerned for the safety of his prisoners, but he also attended to their comfort. He furnished them with lamps and candles for nighttime writing, and he allowed them to keep pens, pocketknives, and other personal effects. He provided them with food from his own kitchen, and he would later facilitate visitors for Brown and the others. Soon after arriving at the jail, Copeland received a visit from a local white minister, with whom he "got down on the cold floor" to "pour out his soul" in prayer.[20]

But even Avis had his limits. The men were kept shackled and segregated, with Copeland and Green sharing a cell in which they were chained to a ring in the floor.[21] And the jailor readily cooperated with the prosecutors when the occasion arose, realizing that he was bringing his prisoners closer to the gallows.

Avis was therefore accommodating when Marshal Matthew Johnson showed up at his jail on October 26, accompanied by U.S. Marshal Jefferson Martin of Virginia and a deputy sheriff named Andrew Kennedy. The lawmen were ushered into Copeland's cell, where Johnson at last faced the man who had eluded him for over a year. Unlike the gallant treatment afforded Brown, there were to be no admonitions or warnings in this interrogation. Perhaps Johnson lacked Governor Wise's sense of legality or Colonel Lee's sense of honor, or perhaps he understood that a black man in Virginia had no rights that a white man was bound to respect. In any case, Johnson was set on obtaining a confession that he could use to pursue his unfinished business in Oberlin, whether or not Copeland was ready to speak with him.

Copeland was a brave and dedicated man, but he was understandably disoriented by the time Johnson confronted him in the Jefferson County jail. In the past few days, he had endured a nighttime march, come under withering fire at the rifle factory, watched his companions "shot like dogs," and experienced a near lynching. He was now in custody facing virtually certain execution, and he had not come anywhere close to rescuing slaves as he had expected upon leaving home. However much resolve he was able to muster, it wilted in the face of Johnson's determination "to ferret out testimony implicating the other parties" in Ohio who could be blamed for the Harper's Ferry raid.[22]

TWENTY

"HIS NEGRO CONFESSION"

MATTHEW JOHNSON WAS BY TURNS a wheedler and a bully, and he put both of those talents to use in obtaining a confession from John Anthony Copeland. In one account, Copeland's confession was "extorted by threats," though in another it was "wormed" out of him. In either event – or both – Copeland's resolve quickly buckled. It did not take long for Marshal Johnson to get what the Ohio press later called "his Negro Confession."[1]

Both Virginia and federal authorities had been eager to implicate leading abolitionists and prominent Republicans in Brown's conspiracy, but Johnson's interests were more parochial. Rather than act as a "mere imitator of Vallandingham," he took aim not at congressional figures but rather at his local enemies in the Western Reserve.[2] Johnson's first question to Copeland was whether he was "the same person who was indicted last year at Cleveland for rescuing the slave 'John.'"

The interrogation continued in that vein, as Johnson demanded to know who had supplied Copeland's funds and where he had stayed during his stopover in Cleveland. Copeland admitted that the Plumbs had given him $15 – slightly less than Ralph Plumb later acknowledged – and he named the Sturtevants as his hosts in Cleveland. Johnson demanded more details, and Copeland added that Plumb and both Sturtevants had known where he was going. Johnson pointedly asked whether Charles Langston had conferred with Copeland and Leary in Cleveland. "He did," replied Copeland, "and knew that I was coming on to John Brown's company." One more question tied everything back to the rescue, as though Johnson intended to revive the prosecutions: "Did you hear Ralph Plumb, on the day the slave 'John' was rescued, urge persons to go to Wellington?" The inquiry had no connection at all to the Harper's Ferry raid, but Copeland answered that he had indeed heard Plumb's instructions "in front of Watson's grocery" in Oberlin.

Johnson showed only minimal interest in the Harper's Ferry operation itself. He asked only if Copeland knew of any attempt "to raise an insurrection" in another state, to which the prisoner replied that he'd heard of "a movement of that kind in Kentucky about the same time." Copeland might have been humoring Johnson by feeding him answers that supported the Democrats' claim of a much wider conspiracy. Alternatively, the answer might have reflected some confusion on Copeland's part. Perhaps, when first recruited, Copeland had believed he was headed for Kentucky, which was a more likely destination for a lightning incursion from Ohio. Once he had been sent to Virginia, Copeland might then have assumed that the parallel Kentucky "movement" had been abandoned or postponed.

Copeland was certain of one thing. He had not meant to participate in an insurrection – much less to have anything to do with "murder or any crime analogous to it" – and he had been unaware of the scope of Brown's plans even during the Sunday night march to Harper's Ferry. "I did not understand at any time, until Monday morning after the fight had commenced, that anything else than running off slaves was intended." He insisted to Johnson that he had never killed anyone, nor wanted to.[3]

Shields Green was also interrogated – by Johnson and others – although no record was made of his responses. There is no doubt, however, that Green resisted providing the details of his recruitment in the abolitionist army, and that he never mentioned having been introduced to Brown by Frederick Douglass. Any incrimination of Douglass would have been a bombshell, certain to have been trumpeted by the Virginia authorities and reported widely in the press. Instead, it is evident that Green shielded his friend and, in fact, Douglass's meeting with Brown remained unknown until years later, when Douglass revealed it himself.[4]

Before heading home, Johnson bragged to reporters that he had obtained a "full confession" from Copeland, identifying "many persons in Northern Ohio [who] are directly implicated" in Brown's conspiracy. He also said that he had a bundle of letters "implicating Gerrit Smith and a number of prominent men of Oberlin . . . and when the facts are made public a sensation may be expected." The sensation would have to wait a while, however, as Johnson claimed to have promised to withhold both the confession and documents for the upcoming trials, at the request of Governor Wise.[5]

Johnson's pledge of secrecy lasted only until he returned to Cleveland on October 29. He quickly wrote up an account of his interview with Copeland – he had not bothered to have anything written or signed in

Charlestown – which he published in his newspaper, the *National Democrat*, on October 31. The response in Ohio was explosive, from every quarter.

The anti-slavery press was predictably outraged. Even before Johnson had published the confession, the *Cleveland Daily Herald* called him "disreputable" and castigated him for "corner[ing] a poor, dispirited negro" and taking advantage of a man "in duress." Johnson's "intermeddling in what does not concern him," continued the *Herald*, "will only secure the contempt of all high minded men, and scare nobody either."[6]

The *Herald*' editors might have been right about high-mindedness, but they were wrong about fear. The Plumbs and Sturtevants were understandably frightened by Johnson's accusations, and they quickly took steps to distance themselves from Copeland and Brown. Both Plumb brothers published "cards" (the nineteenth-century equivalent of a letter to the editor) in the *Cleveland Morning Leader*, denying "the truth of the statements made by the negro Copeland in his confession" and asserting – quite falsely – that they "had ever given Copeland money for the purpose named, or for any other purpose," and that neither one had "ever had a word of conversation upon the Harper's Ferry insurrection or any other insurrection." Ralph Plumb denounced Johnson for extorting the confession through "threats and promises," and insisted – this time, accurately – that it was all part of a plot to even the score for the Oberlin Rescue.[7]

Taciturn by nature, Isaac Sturtevant responded directly to the *National Democrat*. He prudently denied "all knowledge of Brown's revolutionary movements," especially the "plot which was carried into effect at Harper's Ferry," without actually addressing his connection to Copeland. His fiery wife was much more assertive. In a lengthy card, published rather aggressively in the pro-slavery *Plain Dealer*, Amanda Sturtevant expressed compassion for "poor Copeland" while refusing to condemn him. Her invective was reserved for Marshal Johnson. She rebuked the "shameful and unjust attempt on the part of a public officer" to sully her family's reputation, and she scolded the marshal and his "hireling editor" at the *National Democrat* for spreading "false rumors." Ever defiant, Amanda Sturtevant concluded by announcing that she would never stop fighting slavery and instead would "carry the war into the enemy's camp, and kill forever the hydra-headed monster which is threatening our existence as a nation."[8]

The *Morning Leader* accused Johnson of pumping Copeland "with leading questions" in order to "implicate the men of Oberlin he had before officially labored with signal discomfiture to 'crush out.'" The Republican editors of the *Morning Leader* evidently decided that they could best defend their Oberlin friends by discrediting Copeland, whose life was surely forfeit in any case. Copeland was therefore described as "chattering with fear in a blanket on a pallet of straw," and willing to lie in order to save his life. The equally anti-slavery *Herald* challenged Copeland in still nastier terms, although it is difficult to tell whether the word choice was racist (a common fault among abolitionists) or merely ironic (a characteristic of journalists then as now). "Mr. Marshal Johnson," said the *Herald*, "your nigger Copeland is played out; call another witness." Even the fiercely egalitarian *Oberlin Evangelist* questioned Copeland's veracity – no doubt as a means of protecting Langston and the Plumb brothers – saying that his confession was "worthy of no confidence."[9] Copeland was more to be pitied than censured, but no one yet was calling him a hero.

The campaign against Johnson in the abolitionist press was unsurprising. Over a period of weeks, he was accused of everything from coercion, to blackmail, to attempting to drum up circulation for his *National Democrat*. What was surprising, however, was the reaction in certain pro-slavery quarters, where Johnson also came under heavy criticism. Both the *Cleveland Plain Dealer* and the *Cincinnati Enquirer* – Ohio's two leading Democratic newspapers – were highly critical of the marshal's foray into Virginia. The *Enquirer* counseled that Copeland's confession "should be received with great caution" owing to the "beggarly character of the negro [who] no doubt told what he thought would be palatable to the party pumping him." The *Plain Dealer* put it more plainly, assailing the "character of the man who wormed out" the confession. The marshal's account could not be trusted, "especially when written down, not by the negro himself, but by such a person as Johnson."[10]

JOHNSON WAS UNDETERRED BY THE OPPROBRIUM. He had indeed pressured Copeland into confessing, but that was a cause for pride, not embarrassment. Johnson sincerely believed that Copeland's statements were all true – including the supposed invasion of Kentucky – and he simply did not care about the fulminations of the press. The Republican *Morning Leader* and *Herald* were run by his sworn enemies, and the *Enquirer* and *Plain Dealer* were published by the pro-Douglas wing of his own party, which made them semi-enemies as well. Rather than worry about his reputation, Johnson therefore set about assembling his further case against Oberlin.

Mendacious to the end, Johnson began by sending a letter to John Anthony's grief-stricken parents. Feigning sympathy, his true purpose was to enlist them in the prosecution of the Plumbs and others. Johnson assured the Copelands that their son was receiving kind treatment from the jailor, Captain Avis, whom he described as "an honorable, humane gentleman." Getting more to his point, Johnson told the elder Copelands that John Anthony had "complained sorely of those who induced him to enter into this enterprise," thereby intimating that he held the Plumbs and Langstons responsible for his predicament. Seeking to ingratiate himself further, Johnson added that he had given John Anthony some money and, most significantly, that he had intervened "in his behalf to the Court officers." Portraying himself as John Anthony's advocate, Johnson repeated the point. "Everything that I could say in his behalf I did."[11]

Johnson's letter was filled with falsehoods, both trivial and grotesque. He had no respect for Avis, for example, and in fact he later warned the Virginia authorities that the jailor had been too accommodating to Brown. Far more treacherously, Johnson had lied about seeking clemency for John Anthony. To the contrary, he expressed to the Virginia prosecutor his "hope that your authorities will not [be] led into the fatal error of extending any mercy" to Brown's men "in the way of commutation."

In secret correspondence with Andrew Hunter in Virginia, Johnson made it clear that his intention was to exploit the Copeland family for his own purposes. He implored the prosecutor to "obtain from Copeland before his execution another statement confirming the one made to me," explaining that "after Copeland is executed we expect some developments from his relatives."[12]

Before there could be executions, there would have to be trials. Governor Wise was under considerable pressure to hold a drumhead court-martial, to be quickly followed by hangings. (Some of his advisors argued that even a court-martial was unnecessary, in which case the hangings could commence at once). Having already averted a lynching, however, Wise realized that Virginia's honor would be best served by providing at least a semblance of due process to the captured invaders.

In consultation with his counsel, Wise agreed to observe "all the judicial decencies," although they would proceed "at double quick time."[13] The case would be pursued in the Circuit Court of Jefferson County, where the outrage had been committed and where the insurgents were housed in Captain Avis's jail.

Jefferson County's elected district attorney was Charles Harding, a notorious alcoholic best known for his pointless, vulgar, and long-winded declamations. Governor Wise sensibly recognized that the clownish Harding was not up to the job of managing a complex case, and he therefore appointed Andrew Hunter as his special representative. Hunter was everything that Harding was not: well bred, courtly, and above all else, effective before the bench. His "distinguished bearing [and] vigorous Southern personality were well-matched to his vigorous, deliberate courtroom style."[14]

Hunter got right to work, procuring a four-count indictment of the prisoners on October 26, less than a week after the collapse of the insurrection (and, coincidentally, the day that Johnson arrived in Charlestown to interrogate Copeland).[15] The indictment alleged that Brown and the others had committed murder (both directly and by aiding and abetting, thus alleged in separate counts), and had conspired with slaves "to make insurrection against their masters and owners." Most important to Wise and Hunter was the treason count, which asserted that the Harper's Ferry raid had not been an ordinary crime but rather had victimized the entire Commonwealth of Virginia. In the baroque language of nineteenth-century legal documents, the first count of the indictment alleged that Brown and the four others had "attempted to make rebellion and levy war" against Virginia,

> together with divers other evil minded and traitorous persons to the jurors unknown, not having the fear of God before their eyes, but being moved and seduced by the false and malignant counsels of other evil and traitorous persons, and the instigations of the Devil.[16]

The case was to be tried before Judge Richard Parker, the scion of an old Virginia family, whose ancestors included judges, political figures, and other aristocrats. Parker commanded great respect in Jefferson County, both for his lineage and his probity. Short and stout, with a bulbous nose and a grim mien, Parker exerted firm control over his courtroom by sheer force of character. He was known as "an able, sound, and efficient judge" who, despite his "intensely pro-Southern views," was firmly committed to law and sound procedure.[17] Parker had no sympathy for Brown or

Copeland, both of whom he expected to hang, but there would be no executions without at least the outward trappings of justice.

Nor would there be trials without defense lawyers. Early in the proceedings, Parker asked Brown if he was represented by counsel. As it happened, Brown had already written to supporters in the North, asking them to find an "able and faithful" attorney for himself and "the young men prisoners," although he specified that they should "not send an ultra Abolitionist."[18] Seizing the first of many opportunities to confront Virginia justice, Brown told Parker,

> I have had no counsel; I have not been able to advise with anyone. I know nothing about the feelings of my fellow prisoners, and am utterly unable to attend in any way to my own defense.... There are mitigating circumstances that I would urge in our favor, if a fair trial is to be allowed us, but if we are to be forced with a mere form – a trial for execution – you might spare yourselves that trouble.[19]

It went virtually unnoticed that Brown had included Copeland and the three other prisoners – using the first-person pronouns "our," "us," and "we" – in his challenge to the court. It was simply assumed on all sides that Brown spoke for the other defendants, whose own views were seldom sought or considered.

Parker declined to take Brown's bait. He named a local lawyer, Lawson Botts, as defense counsel, in what he must have considered an act of great magnanimity. There were few lawyers in Charlestown more revered than Botts, whose grandfather had represented Aaron Burr and whose father had been a general in the Virginia militia. Botts himself had attended the Virginia Military Institute, and he had participated in the fighting at Harper's Ferry. Nonetheless, he saw no conflict in representing Brown and the others. Apparently without consulting his potential clients, Botts informed the court that he was "prepared to do his best to defend the prisoners." (Botts was later joined on the defense team by Thomas Green, the mayor of Charlestown. Green was a slaveholder and a relative of Senator James Mason, but at least he had not been on the scene at Harper's Ferry, which provided him with a veneer of objectivity.)[20]

Brown was unconvinced by Botts's assertion of professionalism. He pressed for a continuance so that Northern attorneys would have time to arrive. "I have applied for counsel of my own, and doubtless could have them," he argued, "if I am not, as I said before, to be hurried to execution before they can reach me."[21] Pressed to accept the appointed lawyers, Brown equivocated: "If they had designed to assist me as counsel, I should have wanted an opportunity to consult them at my leisure."

The court interpreted Brown's ambivalence as assent and at last turned to the four other prisoners, all of whom evidently agreed to accept the representation. Aaron Stevens spoke up, surprisingly saying that he did "not desire to be defended by Northern counsel" (although he would later change his mind). Shields Green, who was illiterate, remained seated and impassive, looking baffled by the proceedings. John Anthony Copeland rose from his chair. Tilting his head intently toward the bench, he stared piercingly at the judge. There was no mistaking the scowl on his face, but no one thought to record what he said.[22]

TWENTY-ONE

NOTHING LIKE A FAIR TRIAL

CHARLESTOWN WAS FILLED WITH FEAR AND LOATHING when Brown and his comrades arrived from Harper's Ferry, and calls for reckoning did not always differentiate between lynching and the law. The headline on one local newspaper fully captured the sentiment of the locals: "The Infernal Desperadoes Caught, And the Vengeance Of An Outraged Community About To Be Appeased."[1] The Virginia militia patrolled the streets, both to discourage mob violence and to protect against a renewed abolitionist invasion or armed rescue, both of which were rumored to be in the works. In that atmosphere, the trials of the prisoners were set to begin.

John Brown's case was called on Thursday, October 27, barely a week after he had been taken prisoner at the armory. Still weak from his injuries, Brown was carried into the courtroom on a cot, on which he would lie for the duration of his trial. His repeated pleas for time to obtain counsel from the North had all been denied, and he grudgingly acceded to representation by Botts and Green. The two Virginians were both slaveholders, with no sympathy for Brown and less reason to want him acquitted, but they were also sincere professionals who would represent their client to the best of their ability. Of course, they could not defend Brown's ideals, much less justify his actions, but within the confines of their own principles, Botts and Green intended to spare no effort on Brown's behalf. Thus, even before a jury could be chosen and sworn, they revealed the only strategy that seemed feasible to them.

To the surprise of nearly everyone in the courtroom, defense counsel moved to introduce a telegram from one of Brown's Ohio neighbors, stating that "insanity is hereditary" in his family and offering to produce witnesses to that effect. That was an incisive move in strictly legal terms, as an insanity plea was Brown's only realistic hope of avoiding execution, but the defendant wanted nothing to do with it. Brown refused to "put in the plea of insanity," and he objected to his lawyers' efforts to raise such "a miserable artifice and pretext." He viewed the entire strategy with contempt, and he rejected "any attempt to interfere in my behalf on that score." Botts was obliged to inform the court that the issue had been raised without his client's "approbation or concurrence," and the question of Brown's sanity would not come up again during the trial.[2]

The rest of the morning was taken up with opening statements, and the first witness was not called until after the noon recess. Dr. Starry testified to the murder of the black baggage man Hayward Shepherd, and conductor Phelps then testified to the blockade of his eastbound train, as well as his return to Harper's Ferry in time to hear Brown's statements in the paymaster's office. The star witness for the prosecution, however, was Colonel Lewis Washington, who recounted the story of his kidnapping by Stevens and his experiences as Brown's hostage in the armory compound.

Botts and Green conducted searching cross-examinations, but the best they could do was to establish that Brown had treated his hostages courteously and that he had ordered his men not to fire at anyone who was unarmed. Washington added that "all the Negroes were armed with spears while in the armory yard," but none appeared to have taken up arms voluntarily. As the end of the day's session approached, defense counsel again requested a delay, this time announcing that Hiram Griswold, a lawyer from Cleveland, had agreed to represent Brown and was ready to depart for Virginia. Parker was unswayed. He adjourned court for the day without granting a continuance.

The midnight train brought two important passengers, both of whom would have an impact on the Charlestown trials, although in markedly different ways. The first was George Hoyt, a young lawyer from Boston, who had been dispatched by New England abolitionists to provide assistance to Brown. Only twenty-one years old, Hoyt had no trial experience, but that did not matter. He had been sent not as an advocate but rather as a scout. Although most of the Virginians' fears – of attack or rescue – were imaginary, some of Brown's friends had indeed plotted "a scheme for his deliverance."[3] Thus, it was Hoyt's quixotic mission to learn "the location and defenses of the jail [and] the opportunities for a sudden attack and the means of retreat" in order to "consult as to some plan of attempt at rescue."[4] The youthful Hoyt had no real background for such an intrigue, and he must have been shaking when he ran into Andrew Hunter at the train station. "A beardless boy came in last night," the perceptive prosecutor wrote to Governor Wise. "I think he is a spy."[5]

Hunter had come to the railroad station that night to meet a far more notorious arrival. The infamous John Cook had been captured two days earlier on the outskirts of Chambersburg and extradited to Virginia pursuant to a requisition from Governor Wise. Cook had already indicated his willingness to make a confession that would implicate Brown's financial backers, and Hunter wanted to personally escort his promisingly cooperative prisoner to the jail.

HOYT WAS INTRODUCED TO THE COURT the following morning and temporarily admitted to practice in Virginia, although with the understanding that he would not "take part in the case."[6] His status, however, would allow him to sit at counsel table and later to meet privately with Brown in his cell. For the time being, Botts and Green would continue as Brown's trial counsel, as the prosecution continued to call witnesses and present evidence. In all, seven other witnesses testified about various aspects of the raid, including the murder of Mayor Beckham and the death of a marine, Private Luke Quinn, who was shot when Stuart's men burst through the armory gate. Hunter also offered a series of documents that had been found at Brown's Maryland farm, including a copy of the provisional constitution and letters from Gerrit Smith and Frederick Douglass. More than satisfied with the evidence, Hunter then rested the prosecution case.

Brown had instructed Botts and Green to subpoena nine witnesses, whom he expected to testify to his solicitous treatment of his hostages. As it happened, only five of the witnesses appeared in court, and their testimony was not always helpful. One defense witness even volunteered that Brown had threatened to "burn the town and have blood."[7] Four of the subpoenaed witnesses did not show up, leaving Botts and Green with no obvious alternative other than to rest the defense case.

As George Hoyt later wrote to Thomas Wentworth Higginson, the performance of defense counsel had been "as good for Brown as the circumstances of their position permitted," but the defendant himself was far from satisfied with the defense.[8] "The old hero rose painfully and slowly" to his feet to deliver a "stinging rebuke" to his own lawyers and to make a larger point – really addressed to the many reporters in the room – about the quality of Virginia justice:

> I discover that, notwithstanding all the assurances I have received of a fair trial, nothing like a fair trial is to be given me. I gave the names . . . of

> the persons I wished to have called as witnesses ... but it appears that they have not been subpoenaed. ... I have no counsel, as I have before stated, in whom I feel that I can rely.[9]

Botts and Green had been willing to represent Brown, but they were not willing to endure his insults. Speaking on behalf of both attorneys, Thomas Green asked permission to "withdraw from the case, as we can no longer act in behalf of the prisoner, he having declared here that he has no confidence in the counsel who have been assigned him."[10]

Botts and Green evidently decided that their disagreement with Brown extended to Copeland and the others as well, although none of them had ever spoken ill of their attorneys (indeed, they had probably never spoken to them at all). Judge Parker agreed, allowing a blanket withdrawal. That left the neophyte George Hoyt as the only lawyer for John Brown, and it left John Copeland with no lawyer at all.

Hoyt huddled with Brown in the jail on Friday night, explaining that he had come to Charlestown as a spy rather than a lawyer. Brown, however, declined any suggestion of rescue, having recognized that martyrdom fit his goals far better than escape. "I am worth inconceivably more to hang," he later said, "than for any other purpose."[11] Realizing that Brown's "fortitude was sublime and his resignation absolute," Hoyt resolved to spend the night preparing for the first trial of his young career.[12]

Fortunately for both men, the long-sought legal reinforcements reached Charlestown just as the local lawyers were quitting the case. Brown's Northern friends had retained two experienced attorneys – Hiram Griswold and Samuel Chilton – who arrived in time to conclude the trial. The two attorneys could not have been more dissimilar in their backgrounds and politics. Hiram Griswold was an abolitionist from Cleveland who had been extensively involved in Ohio's anti-slavery movement. He was a cousin of Seneca Griswold, who had represented the Oberlin rescuers, and he was eager to represent Brown as a matter of principle. Samuel Chilton, in contrast, had no use for either Brown or abolitionism. A native Virginian, Chilton had more in common with Jefferson County slaveholders than he did with his client. Although he had relocated his practice to Washington, D.C., Chilton remained a pro-slavery Southerner in his outlook, and he accepted Brown's case only after Northern abolitionists promised him an enormous fee of $1000.[13]

Griswold and Chilton vigorously defended their client, calling witnesses on his behalf and presenting energetic closing arguments. Their defense, however, depended entirely on desperate technicalities. Griswold argued forcefully for dismissal of the treason count on the premise that Brown had never been a citizen, or even a resident, of Virginia. Speaking in a pronounced – and perhaps exaggerated – Southern accent, Chilton added that Brown had not personally committed any of the killings at Harper's Ferry. He sought to blame the murders on the other defendants – including John Copeland and Shields Green, whom he did not represent – while arguing that Brown's own acts had been undertaken without legal malice.[14] While admitting that Brown's goal had been to free the slaves, neither Griswold nor Chilton questioned the morality of slavery, for fear of diminishing the vanishingly small chance of saving their client's life.

Judge Richard Parker sent the case to the jury shortly after noon on Monday, October 31, with the expectation that the verdict would be "a mere matter of form." Indeed it was. The jury deliberated for only about forty-five minutes – most of which was spent reading through the seven-page indictment – before pronouncing Brown "Guilty of treason, and conspiring and advising with slaves and others to rebel, and murder in the first degree."[15]

Brown had interjected objections and comments throughout his trial, but he had not been allowed to testify. As did every other state in 1859, Virginia adhered to the "interested party" rule, which prohibited criminal defendants (and all parties in civil cases) from testifying under oath. Odd as it seems today, the rule was then considered necessary to remove a perceived incentive to commit perjury, but it also denied a defendant such as Brown the opportunity to explain his motives or defend his own actions. It was evident that Brown was frustrated by his compelled silence during the trial, but that would change when he appeared for sentencing.

Judge Parker had other matters to resolve on the day following Brown's conviction, so sentencing was not held until Wednesday morning, November 2. As Brown stood stiffly before the bench, Parker directed his clerk to read the obligatory question: Was there anything the defendant wanted "to say why sentence should not be pronounced upon him?" That was the moment Brown had been waiting for. With dignity and defiance – and in words that echoed Charles Langston's own memorable speech at his sentencing in Cleveland – he seized the moment:

> In the first place, I deny everything but what I have all along admitted, of a design on my part to free slaves....
>
> This Court acknowledges, too, as I suppose, the validity of the law of God ... which teaches me that all things whatsoever I would that men should do to me, I should do even so to them. It teaches me further to remember them that are in bonds, as bound with them. I endeavored to act upon that instruction....
>
> I believe that to have interfered as I have done, as I have always freely admitted I have done, in behalf of His despised poor, I did no wrong, but right. Now, if it is deemed necessary that I should forfeit my life for the furtherance of the ends of justice, and mingle my blood further with the blood of my children and with the blood of millions in this slave country whose rights are disregarded by wicked, cruel and unjust enactments, I say let it be done.[16]

Unimpressed by Brown's oratory, Judge Parker observed that "no reasonable doubt could exist of the guilt of the prisoner," and he sentenced Brown to be executed by public hanging on Friday, December 2, 1859.

The effect was far different outside the courtroom. Reporters quickly transcribed Brown's extraordinary speech, and it was published the next day in many major newspapers, to be followed by republication around the country. Spreading with the speed of telegraphy, Brown's heartfelt denunciation of slavery had an enormous impact on the Northern public, "unleashing powerful imagery that would vastly deepen the meanings of his puny act of physical rebellion."[17] Although many abolitionists had initially condemned the Harper's Ferry raid – calling it the act of a madman – they now found themselves in awe of Brown's steadfast dedication and refusal to request mercy in the face of execution. As to the dispensers of Virginia's slaveholding justice, Wendell Phillips was not alone when he proclaimed that "John Brown has twice the right to hang Governor Wise as Governor Wise has to hang him."[18]

The Southern prosecutors may have won the legal case, but it soon became obvious that Brown had taken control of his fate, if not his life, by placing slavery itself on trial. Although condemned as a murderer, Brown had managed through sheer force of eloquence to transform himself into a martyr who would, as Ralph Waldo Emerson soon put it, "make the gallows glorious as the cross."[19] It was a remarkable victory for the old abolitionist, in which he had gotten scant help from his lawyers, who had done their best to keep the explosive issue of slavery out of the trial.

BROWN'S SENTENCING had been delayed for a day so that the court could attend to other business, which meant the nearly perfunctory trial of Edwin Coppoc. The young Iowa Quaker had shown considerable composure following his capture, perhaps in part because he knew that his brother Barclay had managed to escape. He told one journalist that he was "prepared to bear his fate like a man," although his apparent resignation may have been for show. Another reporter noted that Coppoc had been biting "his under-lip . . . as if striving to repress his quivering."[20]

Botts and Green had abandoned Coppoc when they withdrew from representing Brown, but the idealistic Hiram Griswold stepped into the breach for the trial, which, as always, Judge Parker was unwilling to delay. (Samuel Chilton, who was in it only for the money, was never known to take a case pro bono.) Much of the prosecution's evidence repeated the case against Brown, although at a faster pace, and two additional witnesses "swore positively that it was Coppoc who shot and killed Mayor Beckham."[21] Coppoc would always deny shooting Beckham, but Virginia's rules of evidence did not allow him to testify in his own defense, and Griswold's spirited cross-examinations were not sufficient to sway the jury. Following the court's instructions, it took the jurors only a matter of minutes to return the predictable guilty verdict, and Judge Parker set Coppoc's sentencing for Thursday, November 10.

Five of Brown's imprisoned comrades remained to be tried. The gravely wounded Aaron Stevens was not expected to live, making the case against him something less than urgent. The spy John Cook was busy writing a longhand confession that held great promise for the prosecutors, who had seemingly agreed to transfer his case to federal court. Another Harper's Ferry refugee, Albert Hazlett, had recently been captured in Pennsylvania but had not yet been extradited to Virginia; he had assumed the name William Harrison, and he could not be tried until his identity was firmly established.

That left Shields Green and John Copeland as the two defendants whose cases presented the fewest complications for the prosecution. Or at least it appeared that way until another lawyer arrived from Boston.

TWENTY-TWO

AN ABOLITION HARANGUE

Six lawyers had come and gone from John Brown's case by the time attorney George Sennott made his presence known in Charlestown on November 2. Finding the two African-Americans unrepresented, Sennott filed his appearance on behalf of Copeland and Green and began to prepare a startling defense.[1]

Sennott was an outsized character – in terms of height, girth, and personality – whose appearance at first occasioned outright ridicule in Charlestown. The local newspapers took turns deriding him. One reporter sneered that "George Sennott has come to us upon a mission of great bigness, and his size, so far as latitude is concerned, shows him fully up to the immortal standard of envoys extraordinaire." "When he is out of Boston," another journalist scoffed, "we presume lager beer has an opportunity to accumulate."[2] Sennott was indeed a man of large appetites, but he was also an outstanding lawyer. He was an anti-slavery Democrat – an identification that was vanishing in the North and nonexistent in the South – which may have contributed to the scorn he attracted in Charlestown. One courthouse wag opined that Sennott's representation of the black defendants was intended just "to waste time" by a lawyer who was "either a fool, crazy, or drunk."[3] But never was an insult more misguided.

Sennott had taken a circuitous route to abolitionism. Born in Vermont, he had come to Boston as a young man in order to read law in the office of Rufus Choate, who was widely regarded as the finest trial lawyer in New England. Choate was a consummate professional, meaning that he had broad connections but few fixed principles when it came to clients. He was therefore the lawyer of choice for Boston's merchants and bankers, many of whom owed their wealth to goods produced by slavery. Choate had served in both the House of Representatives and the

Senate as a Whig, and he had endorsed Daniel Webster's support for the Fugitive Slave Act of 1850. Unlike most Boston Whigs, however, Choate did not become a Republican when the Whigs collapsed in the wake of the Kansas-Nebraska Act. Rather, he joined the Democrats, taking his protégé, George Sennott, with him.[4]

Through Choate, Sennott became acquainted with activists in what has sometimes been called the Moral Reform Movement, which encompassed an untidy array of causes, including spiritualism, temperance, women's rights, pacifism, the Cult of Domesticity, health food, and abolitionism, all of which more or less derived from "the principle of perfect and entire equality."[5] Many prominent abolitionists – including Lucy Stone and the Grimke sisters – were also active in Moral Reform, and Sennott embraced the movement with the same eclectic disposition that allowed him to reconcile his anti-slavery views with his party affiliation. In late June 1858, he was invited to give the keynote speech at a "Free Convention" in Rutland, Vermont, that attempted to unite the various strands of the movement.

Addressing an audience of over 3000, Sennott stressed the importance of abolitionism – condemning the "South-side view of slavery" as "a hell-side view of God" – while devoting the bulk of his remarks to "Woman's Part in Reform." He argued that no woman is free who "is taught from babyhood that all God made her for was to be an appendage to some man." He argued that women should be allowed to vote, to serve on juries, to hold elective office, and to practice trades and professions, including law. Even more controversially, Sennott observed that the existing status of women – especially in marriage, where "the wife's identity is lost in that of the husband" – was bound to lead to "a hated marriage-bed, and an unwelcome, inharmonious offspring, to plague the world with physical and moral maladies."

The assembled Moral Reformers understood perfectly well that Sennott was advocating women's sexual independence, which he made even more explicit by predicting that "one week of women's freedom" would do more to combat prostitution "than has ever been done before in a century."[6] The audience applauded enthusiastically, but proper Bostonians were soon appalled. As word spread among his clients and neighbors, Sennott was accused of shamefully advocating "Free Love," which obliged him to publish a partial retraction in the *Boston Courier*. Sennott explained that his ideal of female freedom could be realized only within a "true and natural marriage" as an expression of "exclusive conjugal love" between a husband and wife.[7] Nonetheless, he held to his other positions, including voting rights and jury service for women.

For the rest of his life, Sennott's friends and colleagues would marvel at his "brilliant qualities" while fretting that "his impulses often got the better of his judgment." There would always be "a good deal of the Pagan in his nature," which led him to eschew convention in both New England and Virginia.[8] The reactions to Sennott's controversial views in Boston, however, were nothing compared to what greeted him in Charlestown when he proved to be most outspoken on the subject of slavery.

ALTHOUGH JOHN BROWN'S LAWYERS – the courtly Samuel Chilton and the cautious Hiram Griswold – had been unwilling to challenge the legitimacy of slavery, George Sennott showed no such reluctance on behalf of Green and Copeland. With rare audacity, he announced that it was an honor to represent the two black men, and he boldly declared to the court that "the system of Slavery is illogical and absurd." That claim caused outrage in every corner of the Old Dominion, where no such "Abolition harangue" had ever before been heard in a court of law.

Sennott later complained about his treatment in Charlestown, saying that he had encountered "an excitement and a suspicion that looked like insanity." He was trailed whenever he ventured onto the street, and repeatedly questioned by both authorities and self-appointed locals, whom he considered "the most absurd and offensive advocates" of slavery. On at least one occasion, he was prohibited from entering the jail, and he was forced to appeal to Judge Parker to "remove all obstacles and restore him to his just position as counsel."[9] The constant abuse, however, did not deter Sennott from doing his job. His skill and determination would eventually earn grudging respect, and even admiration, among the locals. One Charlestown newspaper was forced to admit that Sennott was "doing his damndest" for the black defendants, and there was even a chance that he might secure their acquittals.[10]

Green's case was called first. Local journalists did not know what to make of the "out-and-out tar colored darky," known to his friends as the Emperor, whose decorous bearing contradicted their image of an obsequious slave.[11] But mysterious demeanor aside, there was no doubt that the prosecution's evidence against Green was overpowering. The chief witness against the defendant was the plantation master Lewis Washington, who described Green's participation in the kidnapping party. Washington also testified that Green – who was carrying a rifle, a pistol, and a butcher knife – had been placed in charge of guarding the white hostages at the armory and that he had fired "a good many" shots in the course of the siege.

Far worse in Washington's eyes, however, had been Green's "impudent manner" in addressing his betters, a crime that the Virginia aristocrat considered more threatening than gunfire. To prove his point, Washington explained that Green had spotted a sniper standing in a window across the street from the armory and had called out "shut that window, damn you; shut it instantly."[12] Shouting commands at a white man – even one who was about to shoot him – was simply unforgivable in Washington's far from humble opinion. Of course, it was unusual for a man born in slavery to act with such self-confidence in Virginia, and it is understandable that Emperor Green appeared "impudent" in the eyes of a slave master. But the reality was, as Frederick Douglass put it, that Green's "courage and self-respect made him quite a dignified character."[13] Lewis Washington, however, was constitutionally incapable of recognizing dignity in a black man, and he was especially offended that Green had presumed to oversee the white hostages.

Washington also called Green a coward. When Jeb Stuart's men made their final assault on Brown's position at the armory, Green wisely threw away his arms and tried to lose himself among the local slaves. Despite Washington's condescending characterization, there was nothing really cowardly about attempting to escape capture or death. In fact, Green showed considerable bravery both during and after the raid. Even under intensive interrogation, Green never implicated Douglass or anyone else in Brown's conspiracy (nor did he identify Albert Hazlett when he arrived in jail claiming to be William Harrison). As befit nobility, the Emperor was fully faithful to the end.

It was during Green's trial that Sennott first displayed his considerable legal talents, taking full advantage of the analytical skills he had learned from Rufus Choate. Seizing every possible opportunity, he engaged in "a sort of guerrilla warfare [in which] he attacked the indictment on all points." As Sennott defended his client with "unflinching persistence," the spectators first "listened, then laughed, then fell to whispering, and then unbridled their irritation," before finally realizing the acuity of his "keenly-drawn arguments."[14] To the consternation of the prosecution, Sennott moved to dismiss the treason count "on the strength of the *Dred Scott* decision, which deprives negroes of citizenship, and consequently of their treasonable capabilities." In the *Dred Scott* case, decided only two years earlier, Chief Justice Roger Taney had infamously concluded that a black man had "no rights which the white man was bound to respect."[15] It was impossible for an abolitionist – indeed, for a humanist – to find any redeeming virtue in the *Dred Scott* case, but Sennott had sensed a way to turn it to his clients' advantage.

Sennott's argument was elegant in its simplicity and ironic in its effect. A treason conviction had to be premised on a breach of allegiance, but the Supreme Court had ruled that no black man, whether free or slave, could ever be a citizen of the United States. Consequently, Shields Green could never have owed any possible duty of loyalty to the Old Dominion. Having thus exposed the hypocrisy of both slavery and the Virginia indictment, Sennott argued that the treason count was therefore invalid. The spectators gasped in "amazement at the utterance of 'Abolition sentiments' in a Virginia Court of justice," but Judge Parker astutely realized that he had been backed into a corner.

The prosecutor sputtered an objection to Sennott's daring motion, but the logic of the defense argument was inescapable. The treason count was dismissed by the court.[16] Sennott's other bold efforts were not equally successful. He sought dismissal of the remaining counts on several technical grounds – including a truly visionary challenge to the exclusion of free black men from the jury venire – but Judge Parker denied every motion. It took the jury only a few minutes to return guilty verdicts on the counts of murder and conspiracy.

WHEN JUDGE PARKER TOOK THE BENCH the following morning for the trial of John Copeland, he looked out across a disorderly courtroom. As they had throughout the earlier proceedings, the spectators in the gallery were boisterous – laughing, eating, and smoking, and freely discarding chestnut shells on the floor. Reporters from the North had initially been shocked by the lack of decorum, but they had by now become almost inured to the unruly atmosphere. Still, it always came as a shock when the lawyers' footsteps made the sound of "trampling on glass" owing to the broken shells that filled the aisles.[17] The crowd in the seats expected to be entertained by another clash between the trim Andrew Hunter, every inch a Virginia gentleman, and the rotund George Sennott, whose intemperate ways were thought to be so foreign and outlandish. As the lawyers settled in at their seats, Parker did his best to preserve order from his perch on a specially raised platform that had been installed only the previous week. He, too, seemed to anticipate novel arguments from counsel, as he had brought with him "a chaos of law-books, papers and inkstands" and held "upon his knees a volume bigger than all the rest."[18]

TWENTY-THREE

ONLY SLAVE STEALING

COPELAND AND SENNOTT MADE AN ODD PAIR when they rose to face the court. The defendant was youthful and wiry, with an appearance so neat that one Southern journalist remarked that "he would make a very genteel dining-room servant."[1] Almost twenty years his client's senior, Sennott overshadowed Copeland in almost every way. His disheveled dress and eccentric personality drew everyone's attention (which was probably beneficial to the silent defendant), and his great size and odd proportions dwarfed nearly everyone in the room. One observer likened him to a "table with an apple on top," and she did not have a small table in mind.[2]

Sennott immediately moved to strike the treason count, as he had the previous day. This time, the prosecution made no objection and voluntarily dismissed the charge. The case would be tried only on the murder and conspiracy counts, but first a jury had to be selected. "Twenty four freeholders" were summoned by the sheriff, who was instructed to exclude citizens of Harper's Ferry. Needless to say, there were no black persons on the panel, although there were many slave owners. As far as Judge Parker was concerned, the only test for impartiality was whether a prospective juror "had expressed an opinion which would prevent [him from] giving the prisoner a fair and impartial trial," although the court took precautions not to reject anyone who might mistakenly have shown too much sympathy for the prosecution. In one typical exchange, Parker continued the questioning until he got the right answer:

JUDGE: Have you heard the evidence in the other cases?

JUROR: (Eagerly) yes, sir.

JUDGE: I mean, if you have heard the evidence, and are likely to be influenced by it, you are disqualified here. Have you heard much of the evidence?

JUROR: No, sir.[3]

Once the jury was seated, two witnesses described Copeland's flight from the rifle works and his arrest in the Shenandoah River, adding that he had been armed with a rifle and a spear. The story of the spear was obviously an embellishment – whether prompted by the prosecutor or simply invented by the witness – intended to tie Copeland to the pikes that Brown had distributed at the armory. Also invented, or perhaps extorted at the scene, was Copeland's purported admission that "he had been placed in charge of Hall's rifle factory by Capt. Brown."[4] In fact, Kagi had always been in command of the outpost, and there was surely no reason for John Anthony to have exaggerated his own authority.

The embroidered testimony was for the most part unnecessary. Copeland had given an actual confession, which Hunter read aloud, insisting that it was sufficient to support convictions for both murder counts, as well as the charge of inciting servile rebellion. Sennott, however, had not exhausted his store of creative motions. He argued that the confession could not be admitted as evidence because "it had been made under influence as well as threats." Although Sennott's contention was undeniable – beyond Virginia's borders, even Democrats recognized that Copeland had been coerced by Marshal Johnson – Judge Parker ruled in favor of the prosecution. Antebellum Virginia law simply could not accept the proposition that any black man was entitled to refuse the demands of white authorities.

Undaunted, Sennott had yet another original argument at the ready. If the confession were to be admitted, he contended, it would have to be taken as a whole. Copeland, however, had admitted only to an attempt to "run off slaves," claiming that he "did not know that Brown was going to create an insurrection."[5] As Sennott explained, that constituted at most the crime of slave stealing, punishable only by imprisonment, as opposed to the capital offenses of rebellion and murder. And yet, Sennott added, no count for slave stealing had been included in the indictment, which should be fatal to the prosecution. Having drafted the charges, the prosecutors now "could not be allowed to contradict their own story."[6] If the court accepted Sennott's interpretation of the confession, Copeland would be ineligible for the death penalty. Even the ordinarily hostile *Richmond Enquirer* conceded the defense counsel had made his point zealously and well.[7]

To the consternation of most observers and the horror of the prosecution, Judge Parker, for the first time in any of the Charlestown trials, seemed favorably inclined toward the defense. He complimented Sennott for the cogency of his argument, and visibly hesitated before ruling. The judge was clearly troubled by the inconsistency between the indictment and the proffered proof, and he could not find an immediate answer in the law books that cluttered the bench. Recognizing that his capital case was on the line, the prosecutor fumed that Sennott's "ingenious pleading" should be disregarded. The other evidence had established a common purpose among the raiders, he claimed, which was quite enough to support a murder conviction. Nonetheless, Parker continued to waver, which caused a collective shudder among the Virginians who packed the courtroom.

Finally, the judge ruled that mere "evidence of a conspiracy to run off slaves did not and would not support the indictment." This time, the court's pronouncement was greeted by shocked silence. It took exceptional courage for a judge to rule in favor of a black defendant and against the Commonwealth, however, and it quickly became apparent that Parker was not that fearless (or foolhardy). He immediately backtracked by allowing that the jury could nonetheless consider whether there had been adequate proof of a "common design [of rebellion and murder] chargeable upon all the conspirators."[8]

Parker thus handed the decision to the jury. But even with that fateful instruction, the outcome of the case was not yet determined. A surprisingly loud and spirited discussion was heard coming from the jury room, unlike anything that had occurred in the three preceding trials. Could it be that Sennott's argument had succeeded in raising doubts? Alas, not for long. The jurors evidently resolved their misgivings and returned a verdict of guilty on each of the three remaining counts. Notwithstanding his high regard for Sennott, Judge Parker seems not to have been surprised. He had kept extensive notes about the progress of Brown's trial, but he made only two entries in his journal concerning John Copeland: "Nov. 4 – John Copeland's trial commenced," and "Nov. 5 – Verdict guilty."[9]

THERE WERE THREE MORE DEFENDANTS in the Charlestown jail, but only John Cook would be brought to trial that term (the cases against Stevens and Hazlett were deferred until the following spring). Next to Brown himself, Cook was the most notorious of the raiders. As a spy, he had been the betrayer of Lewis Washington; as a fugitive for ten days, he had been the most hunted man in the United States, with a $1000 bounty on his head. Now as a prisoner, Cook was known to be working on a written confession that held great promise for the prosecution while terrifying many of Brown's financial backers, who feared that Cook would provide evidence against them.

Cook's sister was married to Ashbel Willard, the Democratic governor of Indiana. Willard was a strong supporter of the Fugitive Slave Act, with no patience for Cook's abolitionism, but he felt a strong familial obligation to come to the aid of his errant brother-in-law. Willard therefore recruited Daniel Voorhees – the U.S. attorney for Indiana, and one of the finest trial lawyers in the Midwest – to act as defense counsel, and the two men reached Charlestown just as Cook was arriving at the jail. Seeing no hope of mounting an actual defense, Willard and Voorhees immediately facilitated an interview with the prosecutors, having persuaded Cook (who needed little convincing) "to make a full confession of all he knew connected with the affair at Harper's Ferry" as his only hope of avoiding the gallows.[10]

Cook and his counsel then spent the better part of a week collaborating with Andrew Hunter on a confession – later published as a pamphlet – that implicated Frederick Douglass, Gerrit Smith, Samuel Howe, and Thaddeus Hyatt, all of whom had been closely associated with Brown. Voorhees believed that he had concluded an arrangement with Hunter in which Cook would ultimately be transferred to federal jurisdiction with the expectation of a pardon or commutation from President Buchanan (who was looking forward to Willard's support in the 1860 election). As it turned out, however, Cook's implication of Douglass and the others was insufficiently detailed to satisfy Governor Wise, who backed out on the deal.[11]

Hunter was deeply embarrassed by the double cross, but Wise was his boss and he had no choice but to bring Cook to trial. Perhaps to salve his conscience, Hunter did agree to dismiss the treason charge, but the murder and conspiracy counts remained intact when Cook faced the court on Monday, November 7. The prosecution introduced Cook's confession, in which he had detailed his extensive participation in Brown's conspiracy. He had spied on the citizens of Harper's Ferry, reconnoitered Colonel Washington's property in the guise of friendship, and later shot several rounds at the militia in a futile attempt to draw fire away from Brown's position. The star witness was once again Lewis Washington, who testified to his betrayal by Cook as well as the spy's later role in his abduction.[12]

Daniel Voorhees made an impassioned plea for his client's life, emphasizing Cook's youth and guilelessness. The defendant, claimed Voorhees, had been badly misled by Brown, who had taken advantage of the "poor, deluded boy." Indeed, "John Brown was the despotic leader and John E. Cook was an ill-fated follower of an enterprise whose horror he now realizes and deplores."[13] As if to emphasize the extent of Cook's remorse, Voorhees then attempted to show that Brown's raid had actually strengthened the institution of slavery by conclusively demonstrating that the slaves themselves had repudiated abolitionism. "The bondsman refuses to be free; drops the implements of war from his hands; is deaf to the call of freedom; turns against his liberators; and, by instinct, obeys the injunction of Paul by returning to his master." Voorhees's argument was directed as much to Governor Wise, in the hope of clemency, as it was to the jury in the hope of acquittal. Wise had earlier boasted that the slaves liberated by Brown "had refused to take up arms against their masters," and Voorhees well understood that the archetype of the happy and contented slave was essential to every Virginian's peace of mind.[14]

The defense oration continued in that vein for hours, always returning to the theme of Cook as "a wayward child" who now renounced abolitionism "as false, pernicious, and pestilential." Several jurors were seen to be weeping by the time Voorhees concluded, but they evidently dried their eyes in the jury room. Cook was convicted of murder and conspiracy. Judge Parker recessed court until the next day, when Cook would be sentenced along with Copeland, Coppoc, and Green.

When court convened at noon on Thursday, November 10, the two white men were accompanied by friends and lawyers. The two black men were alone; their families would not have been allowed to enter Virginia, and their lawyer had returned to Boston some days earlier.

The court clerk directed the prisoners to stand. Reading from a Virginia statute, he asked whether any of them "had anything to say why sentence according to the terms of the verdict, should not now be passed."[15] Each of the white prisoners spoke emotionally in a last-ditch effort save his own life. Both men said they regretted joining the insurrection, claiming they had been deceived by Brown into thinking that Virginia's slaves were longing for freedom. John Cook was especially voluble, speaking at considerable length and with great passion.

According to several newspapers, "the negroes declined saying anything" at the sentencing hearing. In another account, "Shields Green said he had nothing to say, whilst Copeland remained mum."[16] The implication was that the court offered Green and Copeland an opportunity to speak on their own behalf, and they remained silent out of either fear or hopelessness. But those reports may not have been quite accurate.

John Copeland had not grown up in a Southern atmosphere of intimidation and illiteracy. He was accustomed to speaking at meetings in Oberlin, and there was much he might have said about the mitigating circumstances of his recruitment. Despite his commitment to freeing slaves, he had earlier explained to a reporter that he "had no notion of coming here to fight," which of course was true.[17] It would have been uncharacteristic for Copeland to have remained mute if he had been offered an opportunity to provide the same explanation to the court. It is therefore entirely possible, or even likely, that Judge Parker simply did not allow the black prisoners any meaningful occasion to speak at sentencing, although he may have momentarily glanced in their direction following the allocutions of Coppoc and Cook.

It is easy to understand how a perfunctory nod to Green and Copeland could have been reported as though the court had given them an actual invitation to speak. Most journalists, especially those from the South, showed markedly little interest in Green and Copeland throughout the course of the Harper's Ferry trials. The national coverage focused on Brown, of course, but there were also many stories about the other white men. In contrast, almost none of the local or national newspapers devoted significant space to Green and Copeland – the only exception having been stories about Copeland's confession, which implicated white men – typically limiting their reports to one or two perfunctory paragraphs. And no reporter appears to have been much interested in Shields Green, other than to disparage him as appearing "so woe-begone that there was small room for his looking worse."[18]

Judge Parker was "obviously laboring under much feeling" when the time came to pronounce sentence. He had been moved by the youth of the white defendants, and he had taken much solace in the myth – as first announced by Wise and then emphasized by Voorhees – that the slaves of Jefferson County had repudiated Brown:

> Happily for the peace of our whole land, you obtained no support from that quarter whence you so confidently expected it. Not a slave united himself to your party, but, so soon as he could get without the range of your rifles, or as night gave him opportunity, made his escape from men who had come to give him freedom, and hurried to place himself once more beneath the care and protection of his owner.[19]

In truth, a number of slaves had accepted weapons from Brown, and a few had also helped prepare the defenses of the armory. All had dropped their arms and professed loyalty once Jeb Stuart's men controlled the compound, but that was proof of prudence more than docility. No

Charlestown slave could have openly voiced support for Brown in the aftermath of the raid, but many quietly expressed interest in the trials. "People say what they please of the indifference of the negroes to the passing events, but it is not true," wrote Ned House of the *New York Tribune.* "They burn with anxiety to learn every particular, but they fear to show it."[20]

His congratulatory encomium to slavery completed, Parker turned to Cook and Coppoc, speaking with regret. "In spite of your offences against our laws," he said, "I cannot but feel deeply for you, and sincerely, most sincerely, do I sympathize with those friends and relations whose lives are bound up in yours."[21] The court said nothing at all to the black men, and certainly gave no indication of sympathy. But racial solidarity aside, Parker had an obligation to fulfill. "To conclude this sad duty," he continued, "I now announce that the sentence of law is that you, and each one of you . . . be hanged by the neck until you be dead." The court set the execution date for Friday, December 16, two weeks after Brown himself was scheduled to be hanged.

The sheriff was ordered to hang the two black men "between the hours of eight in the forenoon and twelve noon," with the two white men to follow "in the afternoon of [the] same day."[22] Even in death, Virginia demanded strict segregation of the races. The *Virginia Free Press* observed that "the negroes, Green and Copeland, made no response" when the court ruled that they were not fit to die alongside their white comrades.[23]

Barely three weeks had passed since the collapse of Brown's insurrection, and the Virginia courts had swept through five trials and delivered five death sentences. Although all of the defendants had been condemned to hang, there were important differences in the bases of their convictions. Under Virginia law, the governor's sole authority to issue "pardons and reprieves" did not extend to convictions for treason, in which cases grants of clemency additionally required an affirmative vote of the legislature. In other words, Governor Wise could not act alone to pardon either Brown or Coppoc, both of whom had been convicted of treason, although he could pardon Copeland, Green, or Cook. As it turned out, the lawyers had made a difference. George Sennott's strategy, premised on the *Dred Scott* decision, had created an opening that might conceivably save his clients' lives, and Andrew Parker's guilty conscience had done the same for Cook.

Despite the complications created by the treason conviction, Brown's friends and sympathizers immediately besieged Governor Wise with letters urging him to commute the death sentence, arguing either that Brown was insane or alternatively that his martyrdom would only encourage further abolitionist violence. The efforts of Brown's supporters were all for naught. Governor Wise – who harbored an ambition to obtain the Democratic presidential nomination in 1860 – had no desire to initiate a controversial legislative debate over Brown's future. He confided in the prosecutor that he did not intend to pardon Brown, and he soon leaked word to the *Richmond Enquirer* – edited by his son – that the old man's fate "may be considered as sealed."[24]

The clemency efforts on behalf of Cook and Coppoc appeared more promising. Cook was from an influential family – with both wealth and political connections – and his attorneys secured a private audience with Governor Wise, where they presented their case for executive clemency. Because Cook had been acquitted of treason, his fate was entirely in Wise's hands. The lawyers renewed the argument that Cook was a naive youth (although in fact he was already thirty years old) who had been misled by the villainous John Brown. Wise, however, was unmoved, and he let it be known that no "unbiased mind" could possibly "desire the pardon of this man."[25]

Coppoc's case was more complicated. Having been convicted of treason against Virginia, he could not be reprieved without the prior consent of the state legislature. Coppoc did, however, have the support of the Quaker communities in Ohio, Iowa, and elsewhere, which generated considerable sympathy in Virginia. At one point, a committee of the state senate actually recommended a pardon for Coppoc, but the full legislature rejected the proposal when it was discovered that he had written an inflammatory letter to John Brown's wife in which he referred to Virginians as "the enemy."[26]

John Copeland and Shields Green had neither formidable friends nor influential communities to petition for their lives. Nonetheless, many free blacks of the North, powerless and disenfranchised as they were, did their best to aid the black prisoners. Among the entreaties to Governor Wise was a deferential letter from a "committee of colored persons" in Philadelphia, who respectfully sought clemency for Copeland and Green. "We plead," they wrote, for "the intervention of your executive influence in behalf of these poor, miserably misguided men. Recognizing the delicacy of their position, the Philadelphians admitted the guilt of Green and Copeland but suggested that Wise take account of their mitigating circumstances:

> Whatever may have been the impulse that moved them to this desperate act of self destruction, it must be remembered that they are of an identity of interest, complexion, and of *national proscription* with the men whose liberty they sought to secure.
>
> All these things may have operated on their minds as an incentive, driving them into the ranks of Capt. Brown, [so] do they not present strong arguments in the extenuation of their guilt, and may they not justly claim the interposition of Executive clemency in their behalf?

There was no chance, of course, that Wise might accept such an argument. An "identity of interest" with Virginia's slaves could never be considered a valid reason for joining Brown's abolitionist insurrection. The Philadelphians therefore added a far more modest request to their petition:

> We therefore humbly ask that you will grant to us, in the event of their being hung, the bodies of Shields Green and John Copeland, to be transmitted to us for a respectable interment.[27]

In Virginia, black men could not even be assured the decency of proper burial without the intercession of the governor.

Unexpectedly, a faint glimmer of support came from Thomas Devereux, whose wealthy family had once employed Delilah Evans Copeland in North Carolina. Upon learning that "one of the criminals now in custody at Charlestown" was a black man "known by the name of Copeland," Devereux took it upon himself to write to Governor Wise in order to put him "in possession of the antecedents" of the prisoner. While disclaiming any specific knowledge of John Anthony, Devereux assured Wise that his family had been "most respectable" and "well disposed" in Raleigh. That was a humane gesture on Devereux's part – although he stopped far short of suggesting clemency – given that virtually all other Southerners were then clamoring for Copeland's immediate execution. Wise, however, was unmoved by Devereux's kind words. "This is an instance to show how impolitic it is to allow free negroes to go north from slave states," he remarked in response.[28]

Many decades later, both Judge Richard Parker and lead prosecutor Andrew Hunter praised Copeland in their memoirs, calling him "manly" and "respectable," which they evidently meant as high compliments for "the son of a free nigger." In 1888, Hunter told a journalist that "Copeland was the cleverest of all the prisoners," adding "if I had had the power and could have concluded to pardon any, he was the man I would have picked out." Parker expressed a comparable sentiment, saying that "Copeland was the prisoner who impressed me best [because] there was a dignity about him that I could not help liking."[29] The two Southerners deeply regretted, or so they claimed, that a reprieve or pardon for Copeland had been precluded by a treason conviction. In reality, of course, the treason charge against Copeland had been dismissed following George Sennott's inspired invocation of the *Dred Scott* decision. Thus, a clemency recommendation from either Hunter or Parker would certainly have been feasible if either man had actually been inclined to pursue it following the trial. In truth, both Parker and Hunter were pitiless toward Copeland, and neither had given any thought to sparing his life.

Parker's notes of the Copeland trial comprise only two lines – "trial commenced" and "verdict guilty" – which said nothing favorable about the defendant's dignity or manliness.[30] In a post-trial letter to Hunter, he referred to the importance of punishing the defendants for their "great offence... of advising and encouraging slaves to make insurrection," again with no mention of regret at Copeland's fate.[31] Hunter himself left a much longer paper trail, also with no indication that he had given any consideration to clemency. His report to Wise expressed satisfaction over Copeland's conviction and said nothing about the advisability of a pardon, even though he was well aware at the time that dismissal of the treason charge conferred plenary authority on the executive. Nor did Hunter object when Marshal Johnson urged him to reject "the fatal error of extending any mercy" to Copeland "in the way of commutation."[32]

Long after the Civil War, the trial judge and prosecutor evidently came to wish that they had spoken up on Copeland's behalf – if only for the sake of their own postbellum reputations – but their belated protestations of sympathy were obviously contrived. At the time when it mattered, no Virginian advocated mercy for Green or Copeland. Governor Wise himself had publicly branded the two black men as craven cowards, and he was completely unmoved by the petition from the African-Americans of Philadelphia, to whom he never bothered to reply. The death sentences were allowed to stand.

Copeland's father had written to him soon after he learned of his son's arrest and imprisonment. Obviously aware that incoming mail would be read by the authorities, the elder Copeland did his best to exonerate his son. "We do not believe you were aware of the object of the gathering at Harper's Ferry," he wrote, "or that you intended from the first to act the part you have been induced to act." Of course, John Anthony's father knew full well that there was no hope of mercy from the slaveholding commonwealth. "Your mother's sorrow knows no bounds," he added, "though it would be worse than useless to offer our bitter regrets." He closed by asking his son to "write us fully," and he signed the letter with a mark.[33]

John Anthony did not reply for nearly a month, explaining that his "silence has not been occasioned by any want of love" but only because he had "wished to wait & find out what my doom would be." He promised his mother and father that he had taken consolation in the Bible and had sought "forgiveness from my God," and he told them that he had gone to Virginia in a "holy cause." Without mentioning Brown, he assured his grief-stricken parents that "if I must die, I die in trying to liberate a few of my poor & oppressed people from a condition of servitude which God in his word has hurled his most bitter denunciations."[34]

TWENTY-FOUR

THIS GUILTY LAND

All of Jefferson County had remained uneasy in the weeks following the Harper's Ferry insurrection, but Charlestown had increasingly turned into an armed camp as the date for Brown's execution approached. The rumors of an abolitionist rescue mission had never abated, and a mysterious series of barn fires gave renewed life to the story that a rebellion of armed slaves was still about to commence. In response, Governor Wise had ordered the mobilization of over 3000 militia and cadets to guard the approaches to Charlestown. Strangers were questioned and searched, and sometimes detained if they were not able to provide reassuring answers upon interrogation.

The defensive operation was under the command of state militia general William Taliaferro, with the assistance of a contingent of cadets from the Virginia Military Academy led by Professor Thomas Jackson (who would not be revered as "Stonewall" until the beginning of the Civil War). President Buchanan believed that the extensive preparations were unnecessary, but he prudently assigned a few dozen federal troops, again under the leadership of Colonel Lee, to join the ranks at Charlestown.

Many Northerners ridiculed the obsessive suspicions of the Virginians, but others fed the hysteria. In Ohio, the incorrigible Marshal Johnson was still doing his best to ensnare his nemeses in Oberlin. He persuaded the Cleveland postmaster – a fellow Democrat and Buchanan appointee – to monitor the Sturtevants' mail, although nothing incriminating was ever discovered. More pointedly, he advised Andrew Hunter that "some movement is on foot to rescue if possible Brown and his Confederates," involving as many as "9000 desperate men" from the Western Reserve. Johnson therefore offered to "put a watch on the depot at Oberlin" and to "instantly communicate by telegraph" if it appeared that an armed mission was about to depart for Virginia.[1] The proposal was ridiculous. There were not nine men in Ohio – even counting John Brown,

Jr., then living in Ashtabula – who were likely to reinvade the South, let alone 9000, but Governor Wise took seriously even the most outlandish threats. "An attempt will be made to rescue the prisoners," he warned his skittish constituents, "and if that fails, then to seize the citizens of this State as hostages and victims in case of an execution."[2]

A scaffold was erected without incident on the morning of December 2, and Brown was informed that he would be allowed to visit with his comrades before proceeding to the hanging ground. His first stop was at the cell shared by Copeland and Green, where he shook hands with the "two faithful colored men." Maintaining his stern military character, Brown had not quite forgotten their complaints that they had been misled. "Stand up like men," he admonished them, adding that they should "not betray their friends." Then softening, he handed each man a twenty-five-cent piece, saying that "he had no more use for money."[3] The particular gift seems odd today, but it was surely intended at the time as a gesture of reconciliation. Brown had no other way to express his affection for the two men who had offered their lives in his cause, and perhaps he meant also to suggest that they might yet be pardoned. In any case, Copeland and Green accepted the quarters as meaningful keepsakes from their commander.[4]

Brown next visited the cell of Coppoc and Cook. He gave a third quarter to the young Quaker before turning angrily to Cook. Brown might have forgiven Cook's confession, which had been extracted under pressure from his brother-in-law, but he could not overlook the scurrilous legal defense that had justified the institution of slavery. Brown had "nothing but sharp & scathing words" for his former spy, whom he accused of "falsehood & cowardice."[5] Cook halfheartedly attempted to defend himself, but Brown had the last word. "We had gone into a good cause," he said, and Cook should not "deny it now."[6]

The old man then said one last farewell to Aaron Stevens, whom he had known and valued since their days together in Kansas. Still suffering from his wounds, Stevens trembled with emotion when he also received a twenty-five-cent piece from Brown. "Good bye, Captain," said the former drillmaster. "I know you are going to a better land." The religious sentiment was meaningful to Brown. "I know I am," he replied. Brown declined to see Albert Hazlett, who was still pretending to have been wrongly identified. Any hint of recognition could cost Hazlett his life, and Brown therefore "had always persisted in denying any knowledge of him."[7]

In a final act of humanity, Captain Avis took it upon himself to escort Brown from the jail to the wagon that would carry him to the execution site. Pausing for a moment on the steps, Brown handed a hastily written note to a nearby guard. The message had the cadence of an elegy:

> I, John Brown am now quite *certain* that the crimes of this *guilty land*: *will* never be purged *away*; but with Blood. I had *as I now think*: *vainly* flattered myself that without *very much* bloodshed; it might be done.[8]

It took only a few minutes to reach the gallows, where Brown's legs were tied and a hood was fastened over his head. He remained perfectly composed, even when the noose was placed around his neck. Spectators had been kept far away from the scaffold, but the many military cadets and militia guards – one of whom was John Wilkes Booth – were able to observe the old man's preternaturally calm demeanor. One such witness was an aging secessionist firebrand who had attached himself to Jackson's cadets. Although he despised all that Brown represented, he approved of the old abolitionist's fortitude, recording in his journal that Brown stood "erect & as motionless as if he had been a statue," giving no indication that he was "either terrified or concerned."[9] The diarist was Edmund Ruffin, who would later be given the honor of firing the first shot at Fort Sumter. He was also the cousin of North Carolina jurist Thomas Ruffin, who had prepared the papers to free Gunsmith Jones thirty years earlier and had thereby set events in motion that would eventually bring John Anthony Copeland to Harper's Ferry.

At last, Colonel J. T. L. Preston ordered the hangman to spring the trap, shouting, "So perish all such enemies of Virginia! All such enemies of the Union! All such foes of the human race!"[10]

John Brown's martyrdom became perfect on the day of his death. In the North, the event was observed by the ringing of church bells – especially in black congregations – as well as by mass meetings and public prayer. A typical observance was held at an African-American church in Pittsburgh, where Brown was blessed as "a hero because he was fearless to defend ... those in bonds."[11] In Cleveland, Charles Langston addressed a great rally in honor of "the revolutionists of Harper's Ferry." To the chagrin of Marshal Johnson and his fellow Democrats, Langston called on his listeners to emulate "the heroic old man because he labored, lived and died for the outcasts, the friendless, the oppressed, the poor." Langston threw down the gauntlet: "Liberty and slavery will not, cannot live together in harmony."[12] Even the pacifist William Lloyd Garrison, at a meeting of thousands at Boston's Tremont Temple, spoke approvingly of the Harper's Ferry operation. "I am a non-resistant," he declared, "yet, as a peace man – an 'ultra' peace man – I am prepared to say, 'Success to every slave insurrection in the South.'"[13]

As would be expected, the Southern reaction was more than equal and aggressively opposite. The outrage at Brown was exceeded only by the sheer fury over the torrent of sympathy that had poured forth from his Northern admirers. Even more than the Harper's Ferry invasion itself, the lionization of Brown was regarded as an existential threat to slavery, which only bolstered the call for disunion. If an insurrectionist like Brown was a Northern hero, went the argument, what hope could there be for sectional reconciliation? Speaking on the floor of the U.S. Senate, Jefferson Davis declared that the federal government could no longer be trusted to defend the property of slaveholders. "To secure our rights and protect our honor," he vowed, "we will dissever the ties that bind us together, even if it rushes us into a sea of blood."[14] Or as Edmund Ruffin put it, "This robber & murderer, & villain of unmitigated turpitude ... is now the idol of the abolitionists, & perhaps of a majority of all the northern people." He condemned the "northern traducers and worshippers of Brown," whose treachery would only hasten what he termed "the coming struggle" for Southern independence.[15]

In the two weeks that remained before their execution date, the other condemned men drew closer together. Resentments were set aside, and commitments to abolitionism were renewed. Edwin Coppoc made amends with his cellmate John Cook, who by then had rediscovered his anti-slavery ideals (although only after Governor Wise made clear, in an anonymous article in the *Richmond Enquirer*, that Cook's family connections would not secure a pardon).

Facing death, Copeland no longer lamented his recruitment by John Brown. After weeks of imprisonment with his comrades, he had sincerely come to regret his confession, writing to his parents that there had "been misrepresentations of things which I have said." In fact, Copeland's words had been accurately reported, but he still felt the need to make amends. There were "matters I would give most anything to have settled & made right," he explained, and "if I can, I shall correct them."[16] He thus spent his remaining days writing a series of letters to friends and relatives in Oberlin, reaffirming his faith – in both Christianity and abolitionism – and praising the character of his late commander. A week after Brown's execution, Copeland wrote to his brother Henry, explaining that he was not "shattered" by his own impending death. Instead, Copeland expressed his willingness to die for a cause that "would induce true and honest men to honor me." He described Brown as "a General no less brave [and] glorious" than George Washington, and he condemned slave owners as "cruel and unjust men" in a "great but slavery-cursed country."[17]

Copeland wrote another letter on the same day to Addison Halbert, a friend from Oberlin, in which he provided the details of the events surrounding the battle at the rifle works and his eventual arrest. Returning to his constant theme, Copeland said that he was about to die for "obeying the commandments of my God" and giving "freedom to at least a few of my poor and enslaved brethren." Understandably, Copeland did not reflect on the fact that his sacrifice had, as of then, freed no slaves. In fact, he may not even have met any of the slaves whom Brown had briefly liberated, but he was nonetheless passionate in his devotion to those who had been "most foully and unjustly deprived of their liberty."[18]

Just one day later, Copeland wrote a short letter to the Oberlin Anti-Slavery Society, recalling the meetings that he had attended for years. He assured his old colleagues that he still felt deeply for their cause and that he took pride in having fought at Harper's Ferry. Copeland again praised Brown, this time calling him "as noble a defender of human rights as God in his wisdom" had ever created. He exhorted his colleagues to remain true and faithful, and asked them to remember him "as a brave man who dies in a good and glorious cause."[19]

Perhaps because he had already written to the Anti-Slavery Society, Copeland's letters to two dear friends were for the most part personal and religious. To his schoolmate and longtime companion Elias Toussaint Jones, Copeland wrote that the gallows would open "the road to bliss and happiness above with angels in heaven." The letter was in a shaky hand, for which John Anthony apologized. He might well have been overcome with emotion, as the letter contemplated his own death, but he attributed his unsteadiness to writing "on the back of a book on my knee." He prayed that he would meet his friend again in heaven, and he sent his love to Elias's father, sister, and brothers (one of whom, of course, was Gunsmith Jones).[20] Copeland wrote in the same vein to his friend Solomon Grimes, urging him to "do all you can to comfort my poor mother," and to "serve your God and meet me in heaven."[21]

Only on the very day of his execution did John Anthony write again to his mother and father. In his longest letter of all, he remarked that he had seen the sun "declining behind the western mountains for the last time." He was prepared to meet God, he told his parents. Other than that "your hearts will be filled with sorrow at my fate," he continued, "I could pass from this earth without a regret." John Anthony seemingly knew that his final letter would soon be published, as he wrote admiringly of "that great champion of human freedom, Capt. John Brown." He did not protest his lot, but only that "such an unjust institution should exist as the one which demands my life." Echoing words of a resolution at Oberlin's Liberty School, he denounced "the demands of the cruel and unjust monster Slavery," and called on his parents to "attach no blame to anyone for my coming here."[22]

Copeland's reconciliation with Brown and abolitionism was complete. Three of his letters were published in cities around the country, including Cleveland, Boston, New York, and of course Oberlin, all of them extolling Brown's courage and saintliness. John Anthony fully endorsed Brown's image as a selfless liberator, with no suggestion of his earlier misgivings at having been ensnared in a conspiracy that he never intended to join.

In turn, Copeland's confession was all but forgotten. The *Cleveland Morning Leader*, for example, published what it called "Copeland's Farewell Letter" without any reference to its earlier disparagement of his motives for implicating the Plumbs and Sturtevants. Likewise, both *The Liberator* and the *Oberlin Evangelist*, which had previously doubted Copeland's reliability, now proudly reproduced his jailhouse letters, the latter adding that "everything at Charlestown was noble."[23] If anything, Copeland's conduct at that point in his incarceration was nobler than the Northern newspapers realized. Along with the others, he kept Albert Hazlett's secret, feigning complete unfamiliarity with the man who still insisted that his name was William Harrison.

In the eyes of the abolitionist community, in Oberlin and elsewhere, John Anthony Copeland had become a hero of Harper's Ferry.

In one letter, John Anthony told his parents that "all three of my poor comrades who are to ascend the same scaffold" were prepared to meet their God.[24] That was also the observation of the many journalists who visited the Charlestown jail during the weeks before the execution date. All of the prisoners were seen to pray and to accept visits from members of the Charlestown clergy. Cook and Coppoc, in particular, announced their "unqualified assent to the conviction of religious truth" in the company of at least four local ministers.[25] Less was written about Copeland and Green, as even the anti-slavery press was little concerned about the routines of the black men. The reporter for the *New York Tribune*, for example, was Edward "Ned" House, a man of such strong abolitionist convictions that he felt compelled to remain incognito during his entire assignment in Charlestown. Even so, his preexecution comment on Copeland and Green was only that "the negroes had nothing to say of special interest."[26] Notwithstanding the indifference of journalists, we know from Copeland's letters that he spent much of his time in sincere prayer.

As it turned out, however, Cook and Coppoc had been praying only as a subterfuge. In the evenings, they had been chipping through the outside wall with a knife they had borrowed from Shields Green, concealing the hole with their bedding and hiding the debris in their stove. On the night before their execution, Cook and Coppoc made their escape. Climbing through a small opening, they descended unnoticed into the building's courtyard and managed to climb the high external wall. At that point, their luck ran out. A sentry – appropriately named Thomas Guard – happened to be making his rounds at that precise moment. He spotted the two fleeing prisoners and called on them to stop. Coppoc jumped back into the courtyard, but the intrepid Cook continued to head over the wall. Guard fired a warning shot in Cook's direction, loudly announcing his "intention of impaling him on his bayonet." Cook surrendered, bringing to an end the final act of the Harper's Ferry resistance.[27]

Shortly after dawn on Friday, December 16, the streets of Charlestown began to fill with soldiers who were assigned to escort the four prisoners to the gallows. Although the first executions would not occur until midmorning, preparations would take hours to complete. The scaffold had to be built, the condemned men had to be readied, and the town had to be scoured for possible spies and infiltrators. Gawkers from near and far began to arrive at first light, only to be intercepted by the edgy soldiers who patrolled the outskirts of town. Security was especially tight following the previous night's escape attempt, and strangers who could not "get some citizen to vouch for them" were confined in a guardhouse until after the executions. Most of the morbid entertainment seekers were allowed into town, but bad weather put a damper on the expected carnival atmosphere. "The heavens were overcast, the air raw and bitter," and an "equinoctial storm" seemed about to engulf the entire Shenandoah Valley.[28]

A deputation of Charlestown clergy came to the jail, hoping to inspire expressions of remorse. They went first to the cell of Copeland and Green, who were due to be hanged that morning (with the now contrite Cook and Coppoc to follow in the afternoon). As always, the Northern press took little notice of the black prisoners, preferring to concentrate on Cook, who had become even more notorious for his near jailbreak. The *New York Tribune,* for example, mentioned only that the ministers led a short religious service in Green and Copeland's cell. There was more to the scene than that, however. Although Brown himself had repeatedly refused to meet with Southern clergymen, defiantly saying, "I do not want prayers of any man that believes in slavery," the black prisoners were less rigid and more ecumenical.[29] Both accepted the consolations offered by a Methodist minister named George Leech, with Green expressing a strong desire "to pray and prepare for another world."[30] John Anthony joined the prayers, but not without adding a rebuke of his own. "This is but the beginning of the matter," he warned the minister, adding that he and his comrades were giving their lives "for a great principle that will not die."[31]

As befit an Oberlin abolitionist, John Anthony was outspoken to the end. In his last known words, he told a reporter for the *Shepherdstown Register,* and anyone else who might hear him, "If I am dying for freedom, I could not die in a better cause – I would rather die than be a slave."[32]

TWENTY-FIVE

THE COLORED AMERICAN HEROES

GENERAL WILLIAM TALIAFERRO ARRIVED AT THE JAIL shortly after 10:30 on the morning of December 16, leading a contingent of two dozen troops. The armed men formed a hollow square as the jailor and county sheriff led Green and Copeland out of their cells and down the jailhouse steps. An open wagon pulled into the square, carrying two rough poplar caskets. With their arms tied behind their backs, Green and Copeland were helped onto the wagon and seated on their coffins. The two prisoners appeared frightened and downcast, and "wore none of that calm and cheerful spirit evinced by Brown under similar circumstances." Soon the grim parade was under way. Reverend Leech walked slowly behind the wagon, with riflemen flanking the procession as it passed through the streets of Charlestown. It took only five or ten minutes to arrive at the hanging ground, where the condemned men were escorted up the scaffold steps. Copeland stood calm and silent on the gallows, but Green appeared to shiver while praying out loud.[1]

After yet another minister delivered an obligatory prayer, Copeland attempted to step forward to speak to the crowd. It was common in the nineteenth century for condemned men to be allowed a final address, so Copeland reasonably expected to make one last denunciation of slavery. But that routine privilege could not be extended to a black insurrectionist in Virginia. The hangman literally choked off Copeland's speech, abruptly pulling a hood down over his head and tightening the rope around his neck. Copeland did not struggle but instead appeared to endure the ultimate indignity with "firm and unwavering fortitude."[2]

The trap was drawn at a few minutes after eleven o'clock, and the two men were "launched into eternity." Green appeared to die instantly, his neck having been broken by the fall, but Copeland was slowly strangled, and he "writhed in violent contortions for several minutes."[3]

In Oberlin, the extended Copeland family had assembled in their parlor to wait for the "fatal moment when their first-born son and oldest brother . . . would lay down his life." As one of their neighbors observed, John, Sr., and Delilah had lived in a Slave state "and knew full well the bitterness of the cup the poor slave is doomed to drink." They reflected on the story of Moses, recalling that he "had looked upon the afflictions of his people and had his compassion so moved that he slew one of the oppressors." John Anthony, they consoled themselves, was a hero in the biblical mold, having done the same "to free the slaves at Harper's Ferry." Much good would yet come of John Anthony's sacrifice, they believed. "American slavery had been shocked to its very center" by the invasion of Virginia, and it was now a "doomed system, though it might, as with the slaves of Egypt, require forty years" finally to die.[4]

The Copelands had not yet received John Anthony's final letter, written only hours earlier, in which he assured his family that they would meet again in heaven, but they shared his faith. They knelt in prayer as someone read aloud from the very passage in the New Testament in which Jesus gave the same assurance to his disciples:

> Let not your heart be troubled: ye believe in God, believe also in me. In my Father's house are many mansions: if it were not so, I would have told you. I go to prepare a place for you. And if I go and prepare a place for you, I will come again, and receive you unto myself; that where I am, there ye may be also.[5]

Delilah Copeland then stood and turned toward her bereaved husband and children. "If it could be the means of destroying slavery," she said, "I would willingly give up all my men-folks."[6]

Green and Copeland were left hanging for half an hour. The corpses were then cut down so that they could be pronounced dead by Dr. Starry, who had come from Harper's Ferry for the occasion. Governor Wise had refused to make any plans for the respectable interment of the bodies, which were instead hastily buried near the gallows. Even those graves were shallow, however, because Green and Copeland were not expected to remain there long. A delegation of students from the Winchester Medical College had attended the execution, and it was understood that they already had plans for the black cadavers.[7]

After John Cook and Edwin Coppoc were executed later that day, their families had no difficulty securing their remains. Coppoc was put into a walnut casket, supplied by the local undertaker, to be sent to his mother in Iowa. Cook's family had provided an even more elegant coffin, replete with brass fittings, with instructions that it be shipped to his wealthy sister and brother-in-law in Brooklyn. Brown's corpse, too, had been shipped north at the request of his wife. Governor Wise assured Mary Brown that the body would be "protected from all mutilation," and he instructed that it be delivered to her promptly in "a plain, decent coffin."[8]

Shields Green had no known relatives to claim his body, but John Copeland's father made great efforts to obtain a decent burial for his son. In the weeks before the execution, the elder Copeland had repeatedly beseeched Governor Wise for consent to retrieve John Anthony's body so that he could "lay it by the side of his friends." On December 4, he sent Wise a letter asking permission to "send a messenger to Charlestown to take charge of the body and bring it to me," assuring the governor that he "never had the slightest knowledge of the intention of my son before going to Harper's Ferry."[9] When Wise did not answer, the elder Copeland sent a telegram. "Will my sons body be delivered," he pleaded, "please answer by telegraph."[10]

This time Wise replied, though sharply and dismissively. "Yes: to your order to some white citizen. You cannot come to this state yourself."[11] With little time to spare, the Copelands attempted to arrange for the body to be shipped to the custody of A. N. Beecher, the mayor of Oberlin.[12] Wise instructed his staff to make "no reply" to Beecher's telegram; instead he passed the appeal along to General Taliaferro, who was in charge of the execution.[13] Taliaferro then simply ignored the request. With no one present to take custody of the corpses, he ordered them to be buried immediately on the hanging ground.[14]

With the tacit permission of the Virginia authorities, Green and Copeland were allowed to "remain in the ground but a few moments, before they were taken up and conveyed to Winchester for dissection." The dean of the medical school would later ask Wise for permission to place the skeletons on display in the college's anatomy museum, which was apparently necessary because legally available skeletons were scarce and none of the hospital's indigent patients were reliably close to death. Wise gave his assent, on the premise that the bodies had not been "demanded by their proper relatives."[15]

But John Copeland's "proper relatives" had never given up, telling their friends that the inability to bury their son was "the last drop in the cup of agony."[16] On the day after the execution, John and Delilah Copeland sought the assistance of James Monroe, an Oberlin professor and a member of the Ohio state senate. News had by then reached Ohio that the bodies of the black prisoners had been turned over to the medical school for dissection, and the Copelands implored Monroe to "go promptly to Winchester [to] endeavor to recover the body of their son." The professor was firmly opposed to slavery – he had hidden "five slaves from the House of Bondage" only a few days before the Oberlin Rescue – but he was at first reluctant to undertake such an expensive and potentially dangerous mission. He explained to the Copelands that it was probably too late and that hostility in Virginia was likely to make the task impossible. Delilah Copeland, however, "exhibited such intense suffering" that Monroe relented.[17]

Preparation for the journey was not simple. Monroe first procured a letter from attorney Hiram Griswold, who had represented Brown in the Charlestown trial, introducing him to Judge Richard Parker, who happened to live in Winchester. He next obtained the telegram that Governor Wise had sent the Copelands allowing them to send a white man to retrieve their son's remains. Mr. Copeland then executed an affidavit appointing Monroe as his agent for the purpose of "receiving the body." All that was missing was money. The Copelands had none, and Monroe was a self-described "impecunious" academic. Fortunately, members of Oberlin's abolitionist community were able to raise $100 – largely through door-to-door solicitations – which was sufficient to cover Monroe's expenses.

Monroe departed Oberlin by rail on Wednesday, December 19, reaching Winchester late Friday evening. Although more than two months had passed since Brown's raid, Northerners were still treated with suspicion in Virginia, and Monroe was interrogated by both railroad officials and fellow passengers. Still, he arrived in Winchester without incident (other than a lengthy delay owing to snowfall in the Alleghenies), and he headed directly to the Taylor House for lodging.

AT THE HOTEL, MONROE WAS INFORMED that he had to provide his name and address in the registration book, which was evidently open for inspection by a group of "rough and rather *spirituous*" looking young men, who eyed the stranger in the lobby with barely concealed hostility. It came as no surprise that conspicuous Northerners risked violence in Virginia. Monroe knew, for example, that Boston attorney George Hoyt, on a mission to retrieve John Brown's belongings, had recently been forced out of Charlestown by threats of mob action.[18]

And another ominous story from Virginia struck even closer to home. Only a few weeks earlier, Ohio congressman Harrison Blake – who represented the Oberlin district – had been intimidated into abandoning his own attempt to visit the prisoners awaiting execution in the Charlestown jail. As Blake explained in a letter to Monroe, he had encountered constant harassment as soon as his train crossed the state line into Virginia. The railroad tracks were lined with militia troops, and at every stop "passengers had to undergo the scrutiny of an officer who passed through the cars to see if he could find, as they said, 'a damned abolitionist.'" In Cumberland, Blake saw two "peaceable" Ohio farmers arrested when they were overheard saying "something the Slave power did not like." A devoted advocate "of the rights of colored people," Blake himself was circumspect (and tight-lipped) enough to successfully pass through the gantlet until the train reached Martinsburg, where he fortunately ran into Virginia congressman Alexander Boteler, who represented the Harper's Ferry district.[19] Boteler graciously offered to protect his fellow congressman for the rest of the journey, and they reached Harper's Ferry without further incident.

At that point, however, it was necessary to change to another line for the onward trip to Charlestown. Boteler and Blake took their seats on the new train, but it was soon "whispered around" that a congressman "from the Oberlin district" was on board. Angry passengers confronted Boteler and warned him that he would have to "answer for the consequences" if he and Blake insisted on proceeding to Charlestown. Recognizing the seriousness of the threats, Boteler advised Blake that he could no longer guarantee his safe passage and urged him to abandon his trip. The Ohioan was resolute, but he was not foolhardy, and he quickly saw the wisdom in his colleague's advice. The two congressmen prudently abandoned their seats, and Boteler remained with Blake until he could catch an outbound train to Washington, D.C. Blake wrote to Monroe from the safety of the capital, inveighing against the "sin and shame of slavery" while warning his friend that the outraged Virginians had been unwilling to tolerate even "the presence of one unarmed Republican."[20]

Having been alerted to Blake's unsettling experience, Monroe wisely hesitated to see "Oberlin written upon the pages of the register." As he later explained to his students, with characteristic understatement, Monroe feared that mere mention of his famously abolitionist hometown "might produce a degree of excitement unfavorable to my object in visiting the place." The cautious professor therefore signed in as "James Monroe, Russia," substituting the name of Oberlin's adjacent township for the village itself. Sure enough, the inebriated toughs immediately scrutinized the registration book for any sign of abolitionism, but they decided to leave the "Russian" visitor in peace.[21]

Monroe's first stop the following day was at the home of Judge Richard Parker, where he presented his letter of introduction. Parker received Monroe with great courtesy, and expressed sincere sympathy for Copeland's "afflicted father and mother." The judge offered to arrange a meeting between Monroe and the medical school faculty, to be held that day following afternoon tea.[22]

Professor Monroe was no stranger to faculty meetings, and he was evidently quite persuasive in such familiar environs. The Winchester medical faculty "unanimously agreed that the body of Copeland should be... returned to the home of his parents," and the college undertaker volunteered to work through the night in order to prepare the corpse, now six days postmortem, so that the "sorrowful freight should be decently prepared for delivery at the express office the next morning." The only discouraging note was sounded by one of the medical school professors, who cautioned Monroe not to mention their meeting when he returned to his hotel. Already wary of disclosing his mission, Monroe assured the physician that he would keep mum, and he returned to the Taylor House quite satisfied that his sad duties would soon be successfully completed.[23]

Monroe was therefore stunned when a committee of medical students arrived at the hotel early the next morning. He was accustomed to deference from his own students, many of whom were seminarians, but this group was highly agitated and disrespectful. Their leader was a tall, red-haired young man from Georgia who refused Monroe's invitation to sit down. Instead, he insisted on standing while delivering an ultimatum in a pronounced Southern drawl:

> Sah, this nigger that you are trying to get don't belong to the Faculty. He isn't theirs to give away. They had no right to promise him to you. He belongs to us students, sah.... [F]or the faculty to attempt to take him from us, is mo' 'an we can b'ar.[24]

If the cadaver belonged to anyone – other than John and Delilah Copeland – it could only have been the Commonwealth of Virginia, and Monroe was holding unquestionable legal authorization from the governor to take the corpse to Ohio. The medical students, however, had no interest in legal niceties. Although aware that Monroe carried Wise's authorization "to come into this State and get this nigger," they denied the governor's "authority over the affairs of our college [and repudiated] any interference on his part." In case the implicit threat was not sufficiently clear, the students' leader warned Monroe,

> You must see, sah, and the Faculty must see, that if you persist in trying to carry out the arrangement you have made, it will open the do' for all sorts of trouble.... Now, sah, that the facts are befo' you, we trust that we can go away with your assurance that you will abandon the enterprise on which you came to our town. Such an assurance is necessary to give quiet to our people.[25]

To his great credit, Monroe did not give up. He sought out the assistance of a medical school professor, in the hope that he might still be able to claim Copeland's body. Although ostensibly willing to help, the professor informed Monroe that his quest had become "impractible." The students had already broken into the college dissecting room and removed the cadaver, hiding it "at some place in the country." Any further effort to recover the body would only lead to violence.[26]

Shields Green's body, however, had been left behind; no one had ever tried to claim the corpse, and the students correctly assumed that its custody would not be contested. A medical school professor made a point of exhibiting the cadaver to Monroe, perhaps as proof that the faculty retained some slight control over their own institution. Monroe, however, saw only tragedy in Green's condition. He was especially moved by the dead raider's "unclosed, wistful eyes staring wildly upward, as if seeking, in a better world, for some solution of the dark problems of horror and oppression so hard to be explained in this."[27]

Monroe prepared to depart Virginia that day, settling his hotel bill and also paying a considerable sum to the college mortician whose work had been interrupted by the unruly students. Owing to the infrequent rail service in Winchester, it was necessary for him to travel by carriage to Martinsburg, where he could catch a train to Ohio. Just before he left, however, he was warned to stay out of sight in Martinsburg. There was going to be a militia review that day, including many of the troops who had attended Brown's execution. The town would therefore be filled with "many violent and half-drunken men... whom it would be well for me to avoid."[28]

Shields Green and John Copeland were dead and unburied, but they were not forgotten. Upon Monroe's return to Oberlin, a mass meeting was held – on Christmas Day – to commemorate the lives of the two black men. Monroe addressed the rally, explaining to the crowd of thousands that his mission had been both a failure and a success. He had failed in his attempt to repatriate Copeland's body, but the community of Oberlin had succeeded in demonstrating a sense of duty to all of its citizens, regardless of color. Mr. and Mrs. Copeland also expressed gratitude to their neighbors, taking comfort in the knowledge that "every reasonable effort had been made in their own behalf, and in behalf of the memory of their son." In a moving eulogy, Professor Henry Peck – one of the indicted Oberlin rescuers – praised John Copeland as a "firm, heroic, and Christlike champion" of his race, comparable to "the immortal John Brown."[29]

IN 1851, A COMMITTEE OF PROMINENT African-Americans, led by journalist William Cooper Nell, had presented a petition to the Massachusetts legislature seeking the erection of a monument to the memory of Crispus Attucks, whom they called "the first martyr of the American Revolution." Nell appeared personally before a legislative committee, accompanied by Wendell Phillips, where he argued that Attucks should be memorialized because he "was of and with the people" on "the day which history selects as the dawn of the American Revolution." The legislators, however, rejected the petition because a white boy, Christopher Snyder, had been killed one day earlier by British troops. Nell was deeply disappointed by the snub. Snyder had been killed in a "very different scene" that did not offset "the claims of Attucks," whose status as a "colored patriot" well deserved official recognition.[30] The sacrifice of Attucks, Nell believed, proved that the Revolution had been fought for the sake of universal freedom. Thus, the site of Attucks's death "was the spot which was first moistened with American blood in resisting slavery."[31]

In early 1860, Nell tried again. Seeing a profound connection between Boston's Attucks and Oberlin's Copeland and Leary, he began raising funds for a monument in honor of the men he called "the colored American heroes" of Harper's Ferry and to provide support for their survivors.[32] This effort also stalled, however, and Nell settled instead on writing a series of periodical articles.

In the meantime, John Anthony Copeland was remembered warmly by the people who had known him. In Oberlin, his name was invoked during the Civil War, by Elias Jones and others, as the inspiration for black men to join the Union Army.[33] In Chatham, the *Provincial Freedman* circulated a handbill titled "Letters of John A. Copeland, One of the Colored Heroes of Harper's Ferry!"[34]

In 1865, the town of Oberlin erected a memorial to John Anthony Copeland and Lewis Sheridan Leary.[35] The inscription on the cenotaph reads, "These colored citizens of Oberlin, the heroic associates of the immortal John Brown, gave their lives for the slave. *Et nunc servitudo etiam mortua est, laus deo.*"

The Latin phrase means, "And now slavery is indeed dead, thanks be to God."

EPILOGUE

JOHN COOK AND EDWIN COPPOC went to the gallows on the afternoon of December 16, 1859, only a few hours after the execution of John Anthony Copeland and Shields Green. Coppoc's last known words regretted the "parting from friends, not the dread of death." Cook was more expressive, perhaps to make amends for his earlier betrayal. He denounced slavery as a sin and predicted that it "would be abolished in Virginia in less than ten years."[1] The trials of Aaron Stevens and Albert Hazlett were delayed until the following spring. Both men were convicted and sentenced to death. They were hanged on March 16, 1860.

Five of the Harper's Ferry raiders escaped to the North: Owen Brown, Charles Tidd, Barclay Coppoc, Francis Merriam, and Osborne Perry Anderson. Tidd headed for Boston, where he met with Thomas Wentworth Higginson. He later enlisted in the Union Army, dying of disease in 1862, on the eve of the Battle of Roanoke Island. Barclay Coppoc returned to Iowa. His extradition was sought by the Virginia authorities, but Iowa's Republican governor refused to comply. He, too, enlisted in the Union Army, dying in 1861 when his troop train was derailed in Missouri by Confederate saboteurs. Francis Merriam served in the Civil War as a captain of the Third South Carolina Colored Infantry. He survived the war, despite being wounded in combat, and succumbed to illness in late 1865. Owen Brown lived until 1889, spending most of his life as a recluse. He gave occasional interviews, in which he defended his father's life and principles.

Osborne Perry Anderson was the only black man to survive service in John Brown's army. He escaped on foot from Virginia, eventually reaching his home in Chatham, where he set to work on a short book recounting his experience at Harper's Ferry.[2] Anderson's memoir – titled *A Voice from Harper's Ferry* – was published in 1861. He returned to the

United States during the Civil War to assist in recruiting African-American troops for the Union Army. He died of pneumonia in 1872.

Ever loyal to the Buchanan administration, Marshal Matthew Johnson continued hounding abolitionists in Ohio's Western Reserve. In late 1859, he was assigned the task of serving subpoenas for the U.S. Senate committee – chaired by Virginia's James Mason – that was investigating the "invasion and seizure of property at Harper's Ferry." Johnson successfully located Joshua Giddings and Ralph Plumb, who later testified before the committee, but he was unable to serve John Brown, Jr., who was then living in Ashtabula. Johnson claimed that he had been thwarted by the interference of Brown's friends, who "constantly bearing arms [did] proclaim and declare that he shall not be arrested." The more mundane truth was that Johnson left the subpoena at Brown's home, and Brown simply ignored it.[3] President Lincoln removed Johnson from office in early April 1861, only a few weeks after his inauguration.

Anson Dayton foolishly attempted to return to Oberlin in February 1860, only to be surrounded by a "party of five active colored men," including John Anthony's brother Henry, who threatened him with a beating if he did not leave town. With "trembling voice and shaking knees," Dayton pled "eloquently for quarter," which was granted on the condition that he resign his office immediately. Dayton's "confession" was published in the abolitionist press, including his promise, albeit under duress, "that I will never go to Oberlin again."[4]

As she had feared, Harriet Newby was sold to a Louisiana slave dealer along with her children. After she was freed by the Union Army, she remarried and moved back to Virginia, where she lived the rest of her life in freedom.

The Winchester Medical College was burned to the ground by the Union Army in May 1862. With it were destroyed whatever remained of the corpses of Shields Green and John Copeland. The school was never rebuilt.

James Monroe Jones lived and prospered in Chatham, where he became renowned as one of the finest gunsmiths in Canada. In 1860, he was commissioned to make a set of silver-plated derringers for the visiting Prince of Wales (the future King Edward VII), and in 1874 he was given a lifetime appointment as justice of the peace. His daughter Sophia became the first African-American woman to graduate from medical school at the University of Michigan. "Gunsmith" Jones died in 1905. Elias Toussaint Jones remained in Oberlin, where he taught school. He died in 1917.

Delilah and John Copeland, Sr., remained with their family in Oberlin. Their son Henry moved to Lawrence, Kansas, where in 1863 he joined John Brown, Jr., in defense of the Free state capital against the murderous bushwhackers of William Quantrill.[5] Another son, William, also joined the Union Army. He studied law after the war and relocated to Arkansas, where he served two terms in the state legislature. William became the first black police detective in Little Rock, where he was killed in the line of duty.[6] In 1881, James Fairchild, by then the president of Oberlin College, spoke in tribute to the Copelands at the celebration of their fiftieth wedding anniversary. Delilah Copeland died in 1888 and John, Sr., passed away in 1893.

Collections were taken up in Boston and Oberlin to support Mary Leary and her daughter after the news was received of Lewis's death. Mary returned to her studies at Oberlin for two years while working as a milliner. In 1869, she married Charles Langston, who was over twenty years her senior. The couple later moved to Lawrence, Kansas, where Mary gave birth to a daughter named Caroline. Caroline was briefly married to James Nathaniel Hughes of Missouri. In 1902, Caroline gave birth to a son, whom she named after her father's family. The young man grew up to be the poet and playwright Langston Hughes. Mary Patterson Leary Langston told her grandson many stories of the brave men who died at Harper's Ferry, and he later recalled holding a shawl "full of bullet holes" that was said to have been Lewis Leary's.[7] One of Langston Hughes's most memorable poems is "October the Sixteenth," commemorating the date on which John Brown first attacked Harper's Ferry, with Copeland and Leary at his side. It begins:

> Perhaps
> You will remember
> John Brown.
>
> John Brown
> Who took his gun,
> Took twenty-one companions,
> White and Black,
> Went to shoot your way to freedom.[8]

In July 1905, the great scholar and activist W. E. B. DuBois convened a meeting of African-American civil rights leaders just outside Buffalo, at Fort Erie on the Canadian side of the Niagara River. Their purpose was to create an organization that would "work openly and aggressively for equal civil and political rights for the colored people of the country." The group called itself the Niagara Movement and resolved to engage in "fearless agitation" "until every black man in this country knows that he is [entitled to] demand all the duties and privileges of a full-fledged man." The group formed chapters in seventeen states and set about fighting against "Jimcrowism and disfranchisement."[9]

The Niagara Movement held its second annual meeting at Harper's Ferry on August 17, 1906. There was no better place, said one of the conveners, to inspire "the children of ex-slaves; for here at Harper's Ferry, John Brown dealt a death blow to that hydra-headed monster, human slavery." The group spent one day of their conference – calling it "John Brown's Day" – visiting historic sites, including the jail where Brown and Copeland had been incarcerated, the courthouse where they were tried, and the hillock where they were executed. In the afternoon, they gathered for speeches. DuBois himself, who would soon write a biography of Brown, gave a stirring address about the history of American slavery and Brown's role in its demise. "John Brown could not have imagined as he looked through the barred window of his dungeon," said one observer, "that some day such a remarkable tribute would be paid to him on the very ground where he made his gallant stand."[10] Frederick Douglass's son Lewis, who was present on the dais, waved in appreciation but did not speak, while men in the audience shouted approval and women were moved to tears.

Also on the dais was Henriette Leary Evans, the maternal aunt of John Anthony Copeland (and the sister of Lewis Sheridan Leary). As a young woman in 1854, Henriette had fled North Carolina with her family, including her brother, braving the pattyrollers to make a new life in Ohio. In fall 1858, she had celebrated the success of the Oberlin-Wellington rescue, in which her husband Henry had carried a rifle. She learned the shocking news from Harper's Ferry in October 1859, and on December 16 she had prayed with her sister Delilah Copeland as the family held a vigil on the day of John Anthony's execution.

Now in her eighth decade, Henriette had come to Harper's Ferry as a representative of the families of the long-dead heroes. She was asked only to say a few words, and she spoke "in a voice made slender by age." Henriette invoked "the bravery, the love for freedom and the self-sacrifice of her kinsmen in dying as they did for the race," and noted that even their enemies had praised their courage. She might well have added that John Brown's great achievement had depended on the young men who followed him, and there could have been no invasion of Virginia, and no attack on the heartland of slavery, without Copeland and Leary and their comrades. But there was no need to say that on John Brown's Day. As it was, the audience hung on every word, as though drawing closer to the martyrs, and they "went away with more reverence for the memory of those who died for freedom than they ever had before."[11]

Inspired by the stories of Brown, Copeland, and Leary, the delegates dispersed to continue their work, which they believed would "stiffen the backbone of the Negro race" and "arraign the American people before the judgment seat of progressive humanity."[12] Despite their determination, however, the organization did not long endure. Fittingly, the last successful meeting of the Niagara Movement was held in Oberlin in 1908, although some chapter activities continued for two more years. By then, DuBois had become committed to founding a new organization, based on similar principles. In 1910, he brought the remaining members of the Niagara Movement into the National Association for the Advancement of Colored People, of which he became the director of publicity and research.[13] The Oberlin chapter of the NAACP was led by Elias Toussaint Jones, who always honored the memory of his friend John Anthony Copeland.

NOTES

Prologue

1. John A. Copeland, Jr., to Dear Father & Mother, November 26, 1859 (Oberlin College Archives).

2. *Charleston Mercury*, October 31, 1859; Reynolds, *John Brown* at 333.

3. John A. Copeland to Dear Elias [Jones], undated, December 1859 (Library of Virginia).

4. John A. Copeland, Jr., to Dear Father & Mother, November 26, 1859 (Oberlin College Archives).

5. Finney, *Autobiography* at 382; Finney, *Revivals of Religion* at 110.

6. "John A. Copeland to Hiram Bannon, December 11, 1859," *Historia* (December 10, 1909).

7. Although born a New England Quaker, Greene retired after the war to a plantation near Savannah, which he "stocked with good gangs of Negroes." Golway, *Washington's General* at 310.

8. "John A. Copeland to Hiram Bannon, December 11, 1859," *Historia* (December 10, 1909).

9. John A. Copeland to My Dear Brother, December 10, 1859, printed in *Oberlin Evangelist*, December 21, 1859.

10. Hundreds of slaves worked at Washington's Mt. Vernon plantation, including over 100 that he held in his own name, and others that were either leased or the property of his wife. His will provided for their freedom following the death of his widow. Wiencek, *Imperfect God* at 4. For an example of Washington as an icon among black abolitionists, see William Watkins, "Who Are the Murderers?" in *Frederick Douglass' Paper*, June 2, 1854, reproduced in Ripley et al., *Black Abolitionist Papers*, Vol. 4 at 227–29.

11. John A. Copeland to My Dear Brother, December 10, 1859, printed in *Oberlin Evangelist*, December 21, 1859.

12. John A. Copeland to My Dear Brother, December 10, 1859, printed in *Oberlin Evangelist*, December 21, 1859 (italics and noncapitalization original).

13. In Ohio, a black militia regiment named itself the Attucks Guards. Nell, *Colored Patriots* at 11, 13–20.

14. John A. Copeland to Dear Elias [Jones], undated, December 1859 (Library of Virginia).

15. J. Fairchild, *Oberlin* at 117.

16. Fairchild would later serve for twenty-three years as the third president of Oberlin College (1866–89). Swing, *James Harris Fairchild* at 61, 184; "James Harris Fairchild (1817–1902)," Oberlin College Archives, http://www.oberlin.edu/archive/holdings/finding/RG2/SG3/biography.html.

17. J. Fairchild, "Sketch of the Anti-Slavery History of Oberlin," *Oberlin Evangelist,* July 16, 1856 (capitalization original).

18. In fact, the trustees had been equally divided on the resolution, with the deciding vote cast by the board's chair, Reverend John Keep. J. Fairchild, "Sketch of the Anti-Slavery History of Oberlin," *Oberlin Evangelist,* July 16, 1856.

19. J. Fairchild, "Sketch of the Anti-Slavery History of Oberlin," *Oberlin Evangelist,* July 16, 1856. The most famous sign was on Middle Ridge Road, six miles north of Oberlin. Another sign, four miles east of town, showed a slave pursued by a tiger. Burroughs, "Oberlin's Part in the Slavery Conflict," *Ohio Archeological and Historical Quarterly* (April 1911) at 290.

20. Shumway and Brower, *Oberliniana* at 35; Fletcher, *Oberlin College* at 396. In some versions of this story, the decoys themselves were black, though provably free.

21. J. Fairchild, "Sketch of the Anti-Slavery History of Oberlin," *Oberlin Evangelist,* July 16, 1856; J. Fairchild, *Oberlin* at 117.

22. Quarles, *Allies for Freedom* at 88.

23. Nell, "John Anthony Copeland," *Pine and Palm,* July 20, 1861. Nell was among the first to call Brown's black allies "The Colored American Heroes of Harper's Ferry." *The Liberator,* February 24, 1860. See Wesley and Uzelac, *William Cooper Nell* at 606–13.

24. *Pine and Palm,* July 20, 1861. The Copelands had five biological children, including John, Jr., as well as two adopted children (a boy and a girl). Bigglestone, *Oberlin* at 50–51; Greene, *Leary-Evans* at 16, 44.

25. *Oberlin Weekly News,* August 19, 1881.

26. J. Langston, *Virginia Plantation* at 195.

27. Mary Copeland interview, December 9, 1908 (Villard Papers, Columbia University); Elias Jones interview, December 9, 1908 (Villard Papers, Columbia University). According to one Ohio newspaper, Copeland also had "rather straight hair." *Cleveland Morning Leader,* December 23, 1859.

28. Fletcher, *Oberlin College* at 396–97.

29. Clark, *Narratives* at 93. Over 100 fugitive slave narratives were published in the antebellum era, and most of them recounted the stark terror of their escapes, including the constant fear of encountering slave hunters. The actual experience of running away was far different from the "lark" described by the well-meaning Oberliners, and it was well captured in the first novel written by a fugitive slave. Hannah Crafts wrote that she and a companion "trembled at a sound, a shadow filled us with alarm. Trees in the dusky gloom took the forms of men, and stumps and hillocks were strangely transferred into bloodhounds crouching to spring on their prey." Crafts, *Bondwoman's Narrative* at xii, 52. It is now believed that the author of Crafts's semiautobiographical novel was a former North Carolina slave named Hannah Bond, who escaped to the North in 1857. "Professor Says He Has Solved a Mystery over a Slave's Novel," *New York Times,* September 18, 2013.

30. "It is now ten years since any attempt had been made to get possession of fugitives from service in Oberlin." *Cleveland Morning Leader,* September 10, 1858.

31. *Dred Scott v. Sandford,* 60 U.S. 393, 407 (1857).

32. Minardi, *Making Slavery History* at 161–62.

33. *Dred Scott v. Sandford,* 60 U.S. 393, 407 (1857).

34. *Dred Scott v. Sandford,* 60 U.S. 393, 408–12 (1857).

35. I do not mean this as a criticism of other writers, who understandably treated Copeland as a minor figure. Still, it is interesting to consider the omissions and errors in the Brown biographies that have been published since 2000. David Reynolds, in *John Brown, Abolitionist* (2005), barely mentions Copeland's participation in the Oberlin Rescue, giving it roughly half a sentence. In *Midnight Rising* (2011), Tony Horwitz has more to say about Copeland's role at Harper's Ferry, but he also devotes only a couple of lines to his life before meeting John Brown. John Stauffer and Zoe Trodd mention Copeland only four

times in the text of *The Tribunal* (2012), and the Oberlin Rescue not at all. The same is true of Robert McGlone's *John Brown's War against Slavery* (2009). Evan Carton erroneously reports in *Patriotic Treason* (2006) that Copeland had "served time in a Cleveland prison" for his part in the Oberlin Rescue when in fact he was never arrested, much less jailed. Nearly all of the Brown biographies, including *Fire from the Midst of You* (2002) by the extremely knowledgeable Louis DeCaro, have mischaracterized Copeland's family relationship to Lewis Sheridan Leary, another of the participants in the Harper's Ferry raid. Copeland was not Leary's nephew, as is often stated; rather, two of Copeland's maternal uncles were married to Leary's sisters. General histories have also made mistakes about the details of Copeland's life, most recently in J. Brent Morris's excellent *Oberlin, Hotbed of Abolitionism* (2014). Even Benjamin Quarles's masterful *Allies for Freedom* (1974), which provides the most extensive previous account of John Copeland's life and anti-slavery career, allots less than a page to the details of the Oberlin Rescue, while also misreporting that Copeland was jailed afterward.

CHAPTER ONE. The Frozen River

1. Article IX, Constitution of Kentucky (1792). Article IX also guaranteed recognition of "persons deemed slaves by the laws of any one of the United States." Similar provisions were included in all of Kentucky's revised constitutions until the Thirteenth Amendment rendered them ineffective. Kentucky, however, did not ratify the Thirteenth Amendment until 1976.

2. Article VIII, Section 2, Constitution of Ohio (1803). The Ohio Constitution was adopted in 1802 and became effective upon Ohio's admission to the Union the following year. The language on slavery was adapted from the Northwest Ordinance, which provided, "There shall be neither slavery nor involuntary servitude in the said territory, otherwise than in the punishment of crimes." Article 6, An Ordinance for the Government of the Territory of the United States Northwest of the River Ohio (1787).

3. "Recent circumstances have forced the conviction upon us [that] individuals have been and are now held as slaves in this city. The near neighborhood of Kentucky, the numerous family alliances between the citizens of both states, and the continual interchange of population, open various covert ways for the introduction of slavery among us." *The Philanthropist* (Cincinnati), November 11, 1840. The common American practice was contrary to the famous British case of *Somerset v. Stewart,* in which the Court of the King's Bench ruled against the master of a Virginia slave who had voluntarily brought his servant to England. "Slavery," said Lord Justice Mansfield, "is so odious, that nothing can be suffered to support it, but positive law. Whatever inconveniences, therefore, may follow from the decision . . . the black must be discharged." Hochschild, *Bury the Chains.* For the most part, American courts did not tend to enforce the *Somerset* rule. In *United States ex rel Wheeler v. Williamson,* 28 F. Cas. 686 (1855), for example, a federal district judge affirmed "the rights of slave owners passing through" Pennsylvania. See also Brandt and Kroyt Brandt, *Passmore Williamson* at 134–35. There were exceptions, however, such as *Commonwealth v. Aves,* 35 Mass. 193 (1836), and *Lemmon v. People,* 20 N.Y. 562 (1860). In 1856, the Ohio Supreme Court adopted a version of Britain's *Somerset* case, holding that a slave immediately became free once brought into Ohio "by the consent and act of its owner." The court's precise words are worth repeating. Slavery's "manacles instantly break asunder and crumble to dust, when he who has worn them obtains the liberty from his oppressor, and is afforded the opportunity by him of placing his feet upon our shore, and of breathing the air of freedom." *Anderson v. Poindexter,* 6 Ohio St. 622, 630 (1856). Important as it was, however, the provision did not apply to runaways, who continued to be subject to the Fugitive Slave Act. In the 1857 *Dred Scott* decision, the U.S. Supreme Court ruled that slave owners had a constitutional property right under the Fifth Amendment to bring their slaves into federal

territories, and that travel to or through a Free state or territory did not emancipate a slave.

4. The slave owner then sued the captain of the riverboat that had transported the musicians from Kentucky to Ohio, seeking to hold him liable for transporting the slaves without express permission. Unable to deny the essential facts, the defendant argued that the slaves had become free when they had taken an earlier, authorized trip to perform at similar venues in Ohio. If the men were free, there could be no damages for their loss. The case went all the way to the U.S. Supreme Court, where Chief Justice Roger Taney, later the author of the *Dred Scott* decision, held for the master, ruling that "it was exclusively in the power of Kentucky to determine for itself whether their employment in another state should or should not make them free on their return" from Ohio. *Strader v. Graham*, 51 U.S. 82 (1850). Taney's decision, however, did nothing to prevent other slaves from absconding to Ohio, having once obtained "a clear view of life outside of slavery" and the "opportunities that freedom offered." Salafia, *Slavery's Borderland* at 167.

5. Clarke, *Narratives* at 21. Other fugitive slave narratives also recount the horrors of family separation. Jermain Loguen, for example, wrote of the visit of slave traders who came to purchase children on a plantation. The scene might well describe, although on a different scale, John Price's forced removal from his family: "The mothers heard the wail of the children and came running through the fields.... Learning, by the way, that the slave drivers were at the house binding the children, and as they approached, seeing at a distance, a long coffle of little children... marching towards the house, they broke into howls and screams and groans, which filled the air." Loguen, *Narrative of Real Life* at 115–16. Solomon Northup described a similar scene in New Orleans as a slave trader sold a mother separately from her daughter: "'Don't leave me, mama – don't leave me,' screamed the child, as its mother was pushed harshly forward; 'Don't leave me – come back, mama,' she still cried, stretching forth her little arms imploringly. But she cried in vain." Northup, *Twelve Years a Slave* at 87–88. In Kentucky, as many as a third of all slave children "suffered separation from their families through sale." Salafia, *Slavery's Borderland* at 179.

6. Clarke, *Narratives* at 103.

7. Clarke, *Narratives* at 112.

8. Escaping was a difficult challenge for slaves, even those who lived near the border with a Free state. White Southerners frequently complained about "stampedes" of runaways, greatly exaggerating the number of slaves who had successfully reached the North. Abolitionists had their own reasons to overstate the accomplishments of the Underground Railroad. Oakes, *Slavery and Freedom* at 169. According to historian Stanley Campbell, however, the actual number of slaves who reached freedom – as opposed to those who simply "lurked" in the vicinity of their homes before eventually returning to their owners – may never have been much more than 1000 per year. Campbell, *Slave Catchers* at 6, 111. Other estimates – or guesses, as Eric Foner put it – have been higher, but in in either case, "only a trickle... of the millions of Southern slaves [ever] actually escaped to freedom in the North or Canada." E. Foner, *Gateway to Freedom* at 4; Davis, *Age of Emancipation* at 235. In contrast, the *Maysville Eagle* once reported that "*over two hundred*" fugitive slaves had departed from Sandusky to Canada during a single two-month period, and that another forty had embarked from Cleveland in a single week. Harrold, *Border War* at 145 (emphasis in original source). It is evident that the slave dealers of Maysville were greatly exercised over the loss of their human property and eager to read stories of Northern perfidy. But even if Campbell dramatically underestimated the total number of successful fugitives from the entire South, the number departing monthly from Sandusky, or weekly from Cleveland, could not have been even a small fraction of that claimed by the *Eagle*.

9. Brandt, *Town* at 6; McCabe, "Oberlin-Wellington Rescue," *Godey's Magazine* (October 1896).

10. Clarke, *Narratives* at 55–56 (punctuation original).

11. Clarke, *Narratives* at 114 (spelling original). Clarke was speaking here of slave patrols on the Kentucky side of the river; his attitude toward slave catchers in Ohio, including those who attempted to kidnap his brother, was the same. Clarke, *Narratives* at 89–91.

CHAPTER TWO. A GOOD ABOLITION CONVENTION

1. Villard, *John Brown* at 88.

2. John Brown, Jr., to John Brown, May 20 and 24, 1855, quoted in Villard, *John Brown* at 84.

3. John Brown, Jr., to John Brown, May 5, 1855, quoted in Horwitz, *Midnight Rising* at 42.

4. Villard, *John Brown* at 84. DeCaro, *Fire from the Midst of You* at 225.

5. Villard, *John Brown* at 85 (punctuation and capitalization in original).

6. John Brown to John Teesdale, Editor, the *Summit Beacon*, December 20, 1855 (Villard Papers, Columbia University); also reproduced in Clemens, "John Brown," *Peterson Magazine* (March 1898) at 215.

7. Wealthy H. Brown to Louisa C. Barber, March 23, 1856 (Villard Papers, Columbia University).

8. Goodrich, *War to the Knife* at 114–15.

9. Richardson, "Free Missouri II," *Atlantic Monthly* (April 1868) at 498.

10. Jason Brown interview, December 13, 1908 (Villard Papers, Columbia University).

11. Jason Brown interview, December 13, 1908 (Villard Papers, Columbia University).

12. According to one reporter, the five bodies had been left "cold and dead upon the ground, gashed, torn, hacked and disfigured to a degree at which even Indian barbarity would shudder." *New York Herald*, June 10, 1856. For a more favorable account of Brown's actions, see DeCaro, *Fire from the Midst of You* at 234–36.

13. Trodd and Stauffer, *Meteor of War* at 89.

14. Wells, *Dear Preceptor* at 101.

15. Morris, *Hotbed* at 177.

16. Brown's father lived in Hudson, Ohio, about fifty miles from Oberlin, until his death in 1856.

17. Reynolds, *John Brown* at 210–12.

18. Villard, *John Brown* at 248.

19. Dana, "How We Met John Brown," *Atlantic Monthly* (July 1871) at 6. As Dana recorded in his journal, the meeting was on June 23, 1849, well before Brown had become famous for his exploits in Kansas and Virginia. Dana had no idea at the time that his host was a militant abolitionist, but he added a note to his journal in 1864, observing that, "This man became afterwards of world-wide renown [as] the hero of Pottowattomie & the 'John Brown' of Harper's Ferry." Dana, *Journal* at 1:364–65 (spelling original).

20. Brown, "John Brown and the Fugitive Slave Law," *The Independent*, March 10, 1870 (Stutler Collection, West Virginia State Archives). See also DeCaro, *Cost of Freedom* at 133–35; Sanborn, *The Life and Letters of John Brown* at 124–27.

21. Reynolds, *John Brown* at 123. As it happened, Brown's Gileadites were never called to battle.

22. Geffert and Libby, "John Brown's Raid," in McCarthy and Stauffer, *Prophets of Protest* at 169.

23. Quarles, *Allies for Freedom* at 50. Regarding Brown's plan, see DeCaro, *Emancipator* at 82–88.

24. Reynolds, *John Brown* at 264.

25. The money was offered by an "anti-slavery association of colored people" that included Elias Toussaint Jones. Elias Jones interview, December 9, 1908 (Villard Papers, Columbia University).

CHAPTER THREE. THE COLONY AND THE COLLEGE

1. Fletcher, *Oberlin College* at 85.
2. Fletcher, *Oberlin College* at 91.
3. J. Fairchild, "Baccalaureate Sermon," in Ballantine, *Oberlin Jubilee* at 95; E. Fairchild, *Historical Sketch* at 9.
4. Fletcher, *Oberlin College* at 92.
5. Hatcher, *Western Reserve* at 207.
6. J. Fairchild, "Baccalaureate Sermon" at 92.
7. J. Fairchild, *Oberlin* at 4–6; Paragraphs Fifth and Sixth, Covenant of the Oberlin Colony (Oberlin College Archives).
8. J. Fairchild, "Sketch of the Anti-Slavery History of Oberlin," *Oberlin Evangelist*, July 16, 1856.
9. In 1838, Weld married the important abolitionist and suffragist Angelina Grimke. His 1839 book *American Slavery as It Is: Testimony of a Thousand Witnesses*, published by the American Anti-Slavery Society, played an important role in the spread of abolitionism and may have influenced Harriet Beecher Stowe's even more influential *Uncle Tom's Cabin*.
10. Hall, "Education and Slavery," *Western Monthly Magazine* (May 1834) at 266–73, quoted in Fletcher, *Oberlin College* at 156.
11. J. Fairchild, "Sketch of the Anti-Slavery History of Oberlin," *Oberlin Evangelist*, July 16, 1856.
12. Beecher was not free from bigotry, managing to be simultaneously anti-slavery and anti-Catholic. He had "moved his family to Cincinnati to save the West from the Catholic Church." Goldfield, *America Aflame* at 4.
13. Beecher counseled "caution and moderation" in Cincinnati, but his eastern sermons were incendiary, and not in a good way. Fletcher, *Oberlin College* at 156. He was rabidly anti-Catholic, and his appearance in Boston led a mob to burn down an Ursuline convent in Charlestown, Massachusetts. Goldfield, *America Aflame* at 21–27.
14. Fletcher, *Oberlin College* at 162.
15. J. Fairchild, "Baccalaureate Sermon" at 94.
16. Fletcher, *Oberlin College* at 159 (capitalization original).
17. J. Fairchild, "Sketch of the Anti-Slavery History of Oberlin," *Oberlin Evangelist*, July 16, 1856 (capitalization and italics original).
18. J. Fairchild, "Sketch of the Anti-Slavery History of Oberlin," *Oberlin Evangelist*, July 16, 1856 (capitalization and italics original).
19. Fletcher, *Oberlin College* at 170.
20. Fletcher, *Oberlin College* at 172.
21. J. Fairchild, "Sketch of the Anti-Slavery History of Oberlin," *Oberlin Evangelist*, July 16, 1856.

CHAPTER FOUR. "A MOST WELL DISPOSED BOY"

1. United States Census, Schedule of Slave Inhabitants, Raleigh, North Carolina, 1830. Hogg relocated from North Carolina for New York City in 1835, perhaps seeking medical treatment. He prepared a new will before his departure, executing it upon arrival in New York, in which he devised his slaves to his wife, who evidently remained in North Carolina, and then to his son following her death. Last Will and Testament of Gavin Hogg, October 9, 1835 (North Carolina State Archive).

2. Thomas Devereux to Henry Wise, November 10, 1859 (Wise Family Papers, Library of Congress).

3. *Pine and Palm*, July 20, 1861.

4. Bigglestone, *Oberlin* at 71; Greene, *Leary-Evans* at 25.

5. Last Will and Testament of Frances Devereux, December 23, 1847 (North Carolina State Archives).

6. Thomas Devereux to Henry Wise, November 10, 1859 (Wise Family Papers, Library of Congress). It is likely that Delilah's New England travels were in the service of Reverend Leonidas and Frances Ann Polk, the son-in-law and daughter of Frances Devereux, who was the family matriarch. The elder Frances Devereux also owned many slaves, whom she often hired out or loaned to family members, including the Polks. Mrs. Devereux's will bequeathed her field slaves to the Polks while providing more benevolently that her faithful "Female Servant Evelyna" should be sold only "to such a person as she may choose for her Master." Her four other house slaves were not quite as lucky. Although not given the choice of a new master, they were to be sold only to "some person or persons residing within the limits of the State of North Carolina . . . my object being to keep them near their relatives." There were limits to Mrs. Devereux's kindness. One of the house slaves had a seven-year-old daughter, who would be allowed to remain with her mother only "until she is a proper age to be taken from her." Last Will and Testament of Frances Devereux, December 23, 1847 (North Carolina State Archives). Regarding the withholding of wages from free blacks, see Berlin, *Slaves without Masters* at 223–24.

7. Berlin, *Slaves without Masters* at 318.

8. Thomas Devereux to Henry Wise, November 10, 1859 (Wise Family Papers, Library of Congress). Gavin Hogg named his oldest son Thomas Devereux Hogg, further evidencing the strong relationship between the two families and strengthening the likelihood that John, Sr., and Delilah had been introduced as a consequence of their connection to the two white families.

9. *Oberlin Weekly News*, August 9, 1881.

10. Mary Copeland to Katherine Mayo, December 16, 1905 (Villard Papers, Columbia University).

11. Berlin, *Slaves without Masters* at 317. Free blacks in some Southern states were not even allowed to own dogs. Russell, *Free Negro in Virginia* at 97.

12. Franklin, *Free Negro in North Carolina* at 68.

13. Franklin, *Free Negro in North Carolina* at 64.

14. Oates, *Fires of Jubilee* at 98–100; Breen, "A Prophet in His Own Land: Support for Nat Turner and His Rebellion within Southampton's Black Community," in Greenberg, *Nat Turner* at 103; French, *Rebellious Slave* at 33–64; Ford, *Deliver Us from Evil* at 343.

15. Franklin, *Free Negro in North Carolina* at 58, 70, 73; Barfield, *Forgotten Caste* at 126; Ford, *Deliver Us from Evil* at 418.

16. Ford, *Deliver Us from Evil* at 418.

17. Marryat, *Diary in America* at 82.

18. Berlin, *Slaves without Masters.*

19. Franklin, *Free Negro in North Carolina* at 48.

20. Solomon Northup took the sensible precaution of obtaining "free papers" before he departed New York for Washington, D.C., but the document – certified by a U.S. clerk and entered into the memorandum book at the New York customhouse – was stolen from him by the kidnappers who sold him into slavery. Fortunately, the records were still available when Northup was finally able to send word of his enslavement to friends in the North, who were then able to secure his release – but only after he had spent twelve years as a slave on Louisiana plantations. Northup, *Twelve Years a Slave* at 32, 275.

21. There are numerous references to pattyrollers in Belinda Hurmence's *My Folks Don't Want Me to Talk about Slavery*, a collection of oral histories of former North Carolina slaves. For example,

> Then the pattyrollers, they keep close watch on the poor niggers so they have no chance to do anything or go anywhere. They just like policemen, only worser. Because they never let the niggers go anywhere without a pass from his massa. If you wasn't in your proper place when the pattyrollers come, they lash you till you was black and blue. The women got fifteen lashes and the men thirty. That is just for being without a pass.

"Narrative of W. L. Bost," in Hurmence, *My Folks Don't Want Me to Talk about Slavery* at 94–95; see also 1, 8, 30, 42, 46, 76.

22. Franklin, *Free Negro in North Carolina* at 57; C. Wilson, *Freedom at Risk* at 9.

23. Bigglestone, *Oberlin* at 50; Brandt, *Town* at 118.

24. C. S. Hopkins, "Some By-Gone Days," *Oberlin News*, June 17, 1898. The article refers to Allen Jones, who departed Raleigh in a company that included the Copeland family.

25. An Act Concerning Slaves and Free Persons of Color, quoted in Franklin, *Free Negro in North Carolina* at 69 (capitalization original).

26. Berlin, *Slaves without Masters* at 319.

27. The text of the 1854 statute differed slightly:

> If any free negro, who may be a resident of this State, shall migrate and go into any other State, and shall be absent the space of ninety days or more, he shall cease to be a resident and an inhabitant of this State, and it shall not be lawful for him to return to the State. Revised Code of North Carolina, Chapter 107, Sec. 57 (1854).

The fine and servitude provisions were in Section 54 of the act.

28. Delilah's mother was Fanny Evans, born in Virginia in 1785. Greene, *Leary-Evans* at 40. Henry Evans was born in 1817; Wilson Bruce Evans was born in 1824. Bigglestone, *Oberlin* at 69.

29. Berlin, *Slaves without Masters* at 316. As historian David Brion Davis put it, "free blacks . . . provided the key to slave emancipation. D. Davis, *Problem of Slavery* at xiv.

30. T. Wilson, *Black Codes* at 16; Berlin, *Generations of Captivity* at 234.

31. Endorsement of H. A. W. (Henry A. Wise), November 12, 1859, on Thomas P. Devereux to Henry Wise, November 10, 1859 (Wise Family Papers, Library of Congress) (noncapitalization original). See also Bonner, *Mastering America* at 18–19 (slave owners depicted "free people of color as the major threat" to their society).

32. *Oberlin Weekly News*, August 19, 1881.

33. For example, *Alexandria Gazette*, September 9, 1843; *New-Hampshire Patriot*, July 28, 1852. A similar falsehood was frequently told when slaves successfully escaped. "The overseers told us they got killed, reason they never come back." "Narrative of Henry James Trentham," in Hurmence, *My Folks Don't Want Me to Talk about Slavery* at 8. The lies became even more malicious during the Civil War, when liberation was actually at hand. "I was afraid of the Yankees because Missus had told us the Yankees were going to kill every nigger in the South." "Narrative of Hannah Crasson," in Hurmence, *My Folks Don't Want Me to Talk about Slavery* at 20. Indeed, the ploy dated back at least to the Revolutionary War. In 1775, Lord Dunmore offered freedom to any Virginia slave who would fight for the Crown. In response, slaveholders concocted the "wishful legend" that the British intended to resell the slaves in the West Indies. "In speeches to their gathered slaves, masters warned of their West Indian peril and invited a renewed commitment to their servitude in Virginia." For the most part, the trickery did not work, and over 6000 slaves joined the British forces. Although virtually none were sold to the West Indies, about 2000 were returned to their masters after Cornwallis's defeat. A. Taylor, *Internal Enemy* at 25, 28.

34. The western route would take them through Tennessee and Kentucky. The northern route would pass through Virginia and either Maryland or Kentucky.

35. Franklin, *Free Negro in North Carolina* at 53.

36. *Pine and Palm*, July 20, 1861.

37. The Copelands would not have been safe from kidnappers even in the North. Although they could not have known it at the time, the U.S. Supreme Court had recently issued a decision invalidating the personal liberty laws in every Northern state, thus enabling slave hunters to apprehend alleged fugitives without the requirement of a trial in a state court. *Prigg v. Pennsylvania,* 41 U.S. 539 (1842). For a full discussion of the circumstances and consequences of the *Prigg* case, see H. Baker, *Prigg v. Pennsylvania.* See also Reid, "Margaret Morgan's Story," *Slavery and Abolition,* (September 2012) at 359. For additional information on the kidnapping of free blacks, see C. Wilson, *Freedom at Risk.*

38. It is possible that the Copeland and Jones families met while in the employ of Gavin Hogg, the white man who raised John Copeland and who may once have owned Temperance Jones. Although Temperance and her children were freed in 1829, the Joneses appear to have been living on Hogg's property in 1830. John and Delilah Copeland were not married until 1831, so it is probable that John was still living with the Hoggs in 1830.

39. *American Missionary,* October 1856; *National Anti-Slavery Standard,* October 11, 1856.

40. Carol C. Bowie to Mercedes Holden Singleton, October 30, 1960 (Oberlin College Archives). Ms. Bowie, the great-granddaughter of Allen and Temperance Jones, recounted family lore she had heard from her grandfather, Elias Toussaint Jones, who was Allen and Temperance's son. In versions of the story found in other sources, the amount of Allen's stolen savings is $2000 and even $3000, while the perfidy of the swindle is the same. Robinson and Robinson, *Seek the Truth* at 32; *American Missionary,* October 1856. Although it was the undeniable custom to allow slaves to retain money earned in the evenings and on Sundays, Jeffreys was legally entitled to keep all of Jones's earnings under the principle of *quicquid acquiritur servo, acquiritur domino.* Cobb, *Law of Negro Slavery* at 236.

41. The date of Jones's own emancipation is unknown, but it must have preceded the 1829 manumission of his wife and children by a good number of years. Hopkins, "Some By-Gone Days," *Oberlin News,* June 17, 1898. Hopkins, who was an Oberlin contemporary of the Jones children, gave the manumission amount as $3000, which may well have been exaggerated given the $685 price for Jones's own freedom. According to a genealogy in the Oberlin College Archives, Allen Jones also purchased the freedom of his elderly father, who had endured the Middle Passage from West Africa to slavery in America but did not survive to make the journey north.

42. Allen Jones may have had an additional reason for acquiring his wife and children as property. Under North Carolina law, emancipated slaves were required to depart the state within ninety days. Thus, some free blacks purchased family members, rather than purchasing their outright freedom, in order to enable them to remain in the state. There was an exception to mandatory exile for slaves who were freed as a reward for "meritorious service," but that required the approval of the Superior Court. Hurd, *Law of Freedom and Bondage* at 2:87. Thus, even if Tempe's owner could be trusted to emancipate her and the children, there was no guarantee that he would take the additional step of petitioning a court to allow her to stay in North Carolina. The practice of intrafamily ownership was fairly common among free blacks, and overwhelmingly benevolent. Oakes, *Ruling Race* at 47–48.

43. "To the Honorable the Judge of the Superior Court of the County of Wake, Petition for the Emancipation of Slaves," Autumn Term, 1829 (spelling, capitalization, and non-punctuation original) (Superior Court of Wake County, North Carolina). The three lawyers who filed the petition were Thomas Ruffin, George Badger, and (probably) Henry Seawell, all of whom were practicing in Raleigh at the time and had been associated with one another over the years. De Ruelhac Hamilton, *Papers of Thomas Ruffin* at 1:498 and passim. The reference to Tempe's "highly meritorious" service to her former master was legally necessary in order to permit her to remain in North Carolina. Slaves emancipated for any reason other than reward for "meritorious service" were required to leave the state within ninety days. Hurd, *Law of Freedom and Bondage* at 2:87.

44. Yanuck, "Thomas Ruffin and North Carolina Slave Law," *Journal of Southern History* (November 1955) at 461; de Ruelhac Hamilton, "Thomas Ruffin," in Malone, *Dictionary of American Biography* at 16:216–17; Orth, "Thomas Ruffin," in Newman, *Dictionary of American Law* at 471–72; Muller, "Judging Thomas Ruffin and the Hindsight Defense," 87 *North Carolina Law Review* 757 (2009).

45. *Carolina Observer*, November 26, 1829.

46. The facts of the case involved a slave who had been hired out to work, but the holding applied equally to any owner, lessee, or other white person in the position of master. *State v. Mann*, 13 N.C. 263 (1829). See also Yanuck, "Thomas Ruffin and North Carolina Slave Law," *Journal of Southern History* (November 1955).

47. Ruffin might have undertaken the Jones case at the request of his friends Gavin Hogg (who was possibly the original owner of Temperance and her children) or Thomas Devereux (whose family employed Delilah Evans Copeland). Both Hogg and Devereux were lawyers who occasionally referred cases to Ruffin, and they may have had personal reasons to refrain from representing Jones. It appears, however, that Ruffin did not personally handle the matter from beginning to end. Although his handwritten notes state that he felt "interested much in the story," he mistakenly believed at one point that it involved an "attempt to imprison a Free Negro." Trial Docket, November Term, 1829 (Ruffin Papers, University of North Carolina Library). It therefore seems likely, especially given Ruffin's impending elevation to the state supreme court, that he delegated the matter, as he often did, to George Badger or another of his colleagues. See, for example, William Cain to Thomas Ruffin, June 25, 1929; and A. Little to Thomas Ruffin, October 14, 1859 (Ruffin Papers, University of North Carolina Library). Badger himself was later a U.S. senator and Secretary of the Navy. His nomination to the U.S. Supreme Court was rejected by the Senate in 1853. Gavin Hogg, it will be recalled, was the man who raised John Copeland, Sr. The 1830 census has the Joneses, who were by then free, residing on the extensive Hogg property, along with ten white people and seventeen slaves. A connection between the Joneses and the Hoggs would also explain their later association with the Copelands.

48. Several of Jones's sons also gave interviews or left records in which they made no mention of the circumstances of the Petition for Emancipation. Elias Jones, for example, was acutely aware that he had been born free, unlike his older siblings, but he did not realize that the three eldest Jones children had once been their father's slaves. Elias Jones interview, December 9, 1908 (Villard Papers, Columbia University). Likewise, the full story is absent from later Jones family lore. Carol C. Bowie to Mercedes Holden Singleton, October 30, 1960 (Oberlin College Archives).

49. Berlin, *Slaves without Masters* at 316.

50. *National Anti-Slavery Standard*, October 11, 1856; *American Missionary*, October 1856. Jones no doubt would have subscribed to one of the explicitly anti-slavery newspapers if they had been available in the South. That was impossible, however, because "southern newspapers published blacklists of banned, anti-slavery writings." Stauffer, "Fighting the Devil with His Own Fire," in Delbanco, *Abolitionist Imagination* at 75.

51. Bigglestone, *Oberlin* at 123.

52. *National Anti-Slavery Standard*, October 11, 1856; *American Missionary*, October 1856.

53. Ford, *Deliver Us from Evil* at 418.

54. The Copelands' permission letters were dated March 3, 1843. *Pine and Palm*, July 20, 1861. The information on Allen Jones's father is from the Jones family genealogy in the Oberlin College Archives.

55. Greene, *Leary-Evans* at 44.

56. There are varying accounts of James Monroe Jones's birth date. His birth year was listed as 1821 in the Canada Census of 1871, with the notation that it was "estimated." In a handwritten note to the Oberlin Alumni Association, he reported his birthday as January 15, 1821. "To the Alumni of Oberlin College," June 21, 1875 (Chatham-Kent

Black Historical Society). His obituary gave his birthday as January 10, 1821. "Interesting Life" (undated clipping, Chatham-Kent Black Historical Society). Another source, however, reports that he was seventeen in 1843, which would place his birth year as 1825 or 1826. "Oberliniana," *Oberlin Alumni Magazine* (April 1961) at 3. President James Monroe was an odd namesake for the son of a defiant black family. Monroe was a slaveholder who, as governor of Virginia in 1800, had ordered the execution of Gabriel and twenty-six other slaves who had been accused of plotting a rebellion. A. Taylor, *Internal Enemy* at 97.

57. Elias Jones interview, December 9, 1908 (Villard Papers, Columbia University).

CHAPTER FIVE. "I HAVE FOUND PARADISE"

1. *American Missionary*, October 1856.
2. *Oberlin Weekly News*, August 19, 1881.
3. *Oberlin Weekly News*, August 19, 1881; Bigglestone, *Oberlin* at 51. Dresser was not exaggerating. Slave hunters from Kentucky and Virginia operated freely in southern Ohio, and they were not known to distinguish carefully between fugitives and free blacks. A typical story was told by Lewis Williamson, a free black man with a farm located "three miles below Gallipolis." Williamson was lured away from his property by an unscrupulous neighbor, so that slave catchers could seize his wife and children. "At dead of night they entered my little habitation and dragged my wife and three small children from their beds." *The Liberator*, December 10, 1841, quoted in Sterling, *Thunder Tones* at 145. See also D. Davis, *Age of Emancipation* at 245.
4. *Oberlin Weekly News*, August 19, 1881.
5. *Oberlin Weekly News*, August 19, 1881.
6. Blodgett, *Oberlin History* at 29.
7. J. Langston, *Virginia Plantation* at 102 (nonpunctuation in original).
8. Quillin, *Color Line* at 45.
9. It was founded in 1842. Burroughs, "Oberlin's Part in the Slavery Conflict," *Ohio Archeological and Historical Quarterly* (April 1911).
10. Morris, *Hotbed* at 70; J. Langston, *Virginia Plantation* at 101 (noncapitalization in original).
11. Finney, *Revivals of Religion*, passim.
12. Hambrick-Stowe, *Charles G. Finney* at 173. Finney believed that "the destruction of the slave system was a major prerequisite for the coming of the millennium." Essig, "The Lord's Free Man: Charles G. Finney and His Abolitionism," in McKivigan, *Abolitionism* at 319. As historian Andrew Delbanco put it, abolitionists such as Finney "saw slavery as the bolt around which all other evils swung." Delbanco, *Abolitionist Imagination* at 73.
13. Quoted in Ellsworth, "Oberlin" at 26. See also McKivigan, *Proslavery Religion* at 18–35.
14. Many of the oral histories of former slaves included references to preachers who admonished them to obey their masters. "They preached to us that we would go to hell alive if we sassed our white folks," as one put it. "Narrative of Mattie Curtis," in Hurmence, *My Folks Don't Want Me to Talk about Slavery* at 36. Another former slave recognized the role of organized religion in the larger system of subjugation. "They preached to us to obey our master. No nigger was allowed to preach. They allowed us to pray and shout sometimes, but they better not be catched with a book." "Narrative of Parker Pool," in Hurmence, *My Folks Don't Want Me to Talk about Slavery* at 84. Historian Lacy Ford describes "a systematic ideology of white supremacy" in which "whites must always be dominant and superior, blacks always subordinate and excluded from the rights and privileges of republican society." Ford, *Deliver Us from Evil* at 9, 444. Or, as William Wells Brown – fugitive slave, novelist, playwright, and historian – put it, the South was "the land of whips, chains, and Bibles." Brown, "Narrative of William W. Brown," in Y. Taylor, *Born a Slave* at 703. See also Greenspan, *William Wells Brown*.

15. Carol C. Bowie to Mercedes Holden Singleton, October 30, 1960 (Oberlin College Archives); *American Missionary*, October 1856.

16. Hopkins, "Some By-Gone Days," *Oberlin News* (biweekly), June 17, 1898; *Oberlin Weekly News*, November 4, 1881. Also see Book of Exodus 20:2.

17. Blodgett, *Oberlin History* at 32.

18. Hopkins, "Some By-Gone Days," *Oberlin News* (biweekly), June 17, 1898.

19. *Pine and Palm*, July 20, 1861.

20. Hopkins, "Some By-Gone Days," *Oberlin News* (biweekly), June 17, 1898. The Jones brothers in the 1845 scuffle were William and John. Despite his revolutionary middle name, Elias Toussaint was less aggressive than his brothers, and he would remain so throughout his life. The white child who received the beating was Washburn Safford, whose father was among Oberlin's first settlers. The interruption in Washburn's education did not do lasting damage; he later graduated from Oberlin and became a lawyer in Kansas.

21. John Mercer Langston to Henry Howe, April 10, 1854, quoted in Morris, *Hotbed* at 71.

22. E. Fairchild, *Historical Sketch.*

23. Fletcher, *Oberlin College* at 523 (spelling original).

24. Fletcher, *Oberlin College* at 175, 76.

25. Horton, "Black Education at Oberlin College," *Journal of Negro Education* (Autumn 1985) at 481.

26. E. Fairchild, *Historical Sketch.*

27. Fletcher, *Oberlin College* at 524 (spelling in original source).

28. Blackwell, *Lucy Stone* at 47.

29. *Oberlin Evangelist*, September 10, 1851.

30. *American Missionary*, October 1856.

31. "Uncle Tom's Cabin, or Life among the Lowly," by Mrs. H. B. Stowe, *The National Era*, June 5, 1851. Neighbors later compared Allen Jones to "a character meet for the pen of Harriet Beecher Stowe," describing him as "good and gray as Uncle Tom." *American Missionary*, October 1856. "Uncle Tom" was far from a pejorative in the antebellum era, as Stowe's famous character was understood as a heroic example of Christian resistance to slavery. Stowe, *Key to Uncle Tom's Cabin* at 38.

32. Hopkins, "Some By-Gone Days," *Oberlin News* (biweekly), June 17, 1898.

33. John A. Copeland, Sr., to His Excellency Henry A. Wise, December 4, 1859 (Wise Family Papers, Library of Congress). Copeland's shaky signature is in a quite different hand from the body of the letter. The name of the amanuensis is unknown.

CHAPTER SIX. "MY OBJECT IN COMING TO OBERLIN"

1. Ellsworth, "Oberlin" at 78.

2. J. Fairchild, *Oberlin* at 368.

3. Dillon, "John Parker and the Underground Railroad," in Van Tine and Pierce, *Builders of Ohio* at 99.

4. *Prigg v. Pennsylvania*, 41 U.S. 539, 625 (1842). For an excellent discussion of this case, see H. Baker, *Prigg v. Pennsylvania*. Regarding the extent of slave hunting throughout Ohio, see Van Tine and Pierce, *Builders of Ohio* at 103–06.

5. *Ohio Statesman*, March 13, 1841. According to another account – albeit in the antislavery press – there was not even a disturbance, let alone a riot. *The Philanthropist*, March 24, 1841. This accords with Professor James Harris Fairchild's much later recollection of the incident (although he incorrectly placed it in 1840). J. Fairchild, *Underground Railroad* at 111. For a longer account of the event, detailing greater violence from the Southern perspective, see Harrold, *Border War* at 105.

6. Clarke, *Narratives* at 85–86.

7. Clarke, *Narratives* at 91–93. Clarke recalled that he had been represented at the hearing by Salmon Chase, which is highly improbable. Chase lived in Cincinnati at the time, and there is no mention of Clarke in Chase's biographies, journals, or correspondence. Niven, *Chase Journals*; Niven, *Chase Correspondence*; Niven, *Chase Biography*; Blue, *Salmon P. Chase.*

8. Sinha, *Counterrevolution of Slavery* at 73; Bordewich, *America's Great Debate* at 127; Remini, *Edge of the Precipice* at 66; Oakes, *Freedom National* at 29.

9. Jones, *Mutiny on the Amistad* at 14–30.

10. Merrill, *Sarah Margru Kinson* at 7.

11. Merrill, *Sarah Margru Kinson* at 8 (nonpunctuation original); Lawson and Merrill, *Three Sarahs* at 14.

12. "Helen Ferris (later Mrs. Charles G. Bisbee) and the class she taught in the Preparatory Department, fall 1855" (Oberlin College Archives).

13. For a full account of the Anthony Burns case, see Von Frank, *Trials of Anthony Burns*; Stevens, *Anthony Burns*; Maltz, *Fugitive Slave on Trial.*

14. "Narrative of W. L. Bost," in Hurmence, *My Folks Don't Want Me to Talk about Slavery* at 95.

15. As is well known, interracial marriage did not become legal in Virginia until 1967, when the U.S. Supreme Court declared its antimiscegenation statute unconstitutional. *Loving v. Virginia*, 388 U.S. 1 (1967).

16. Lucy Langston had two other children with Ralph Quarles – another son and a daughter – both of whom were also freed and relocated to Ohio. Cheek and Cheek, *John Mercer Langston* at 14–19. The Quarles–Langston relationship was an exception to the usual arrangement, in which owners sexually exploited their female slaves. See McLaurin, *Celia.* A more famous exception was the now-proven relationship between Sally Hemings and Thomas Jefferson. See Gordon-Reed, *Hemingses of Monticello.*

17. Blue, *No Taint of Compromise* at 67–68.

18. *The Liberator*, March 2, 1849.

19. *The Liberator*, March 2, 1849 (capitalization original).

20. J. Langston, *Virginia Plantation* at 195.

CHAPTER SEVEN. NOT A FUGITIVE WAS SEIZED

1. Delbanco, *Abolitionist Imagination* at 12. As historian Edward Baptist put it, the Act made "the federal government the servant of enslavers by helping them to control their property in human beings." Baptist, *The Half Has Never Been Told* at 338.

2. P. Foner, *History of Black Americans* at 3:17; Forbes, *No Country* at 111.

3. *Baltimore Sun*, September 30, 1850 (spelling original).

4. Campbell, *Slave Catchers* at 116fn8; American Foreign and Anti-Slavery Society, *The Fugitive Slave Bill*, reproduced in Finkelman, *Slavery, Race, and the American Legal System* at 1:535.

5. Calhoun, *Lawmen* at 82–91.

6. "National Free Soil Convention, Speech of Frederick Douglass at the Mass Convention at Pittsburg," *North Star/Frederick Douglass' Paper*, August 20, 1852.

7. Cheek and Cheek, *John Mercer Langston* at 188.

8. Slaughter, *Bloody Dawn.* Only one case was brought to trial, that of Castner Hanway, a white miller who had been an observer of the fighting rather than a participant. The prosecution failed for lack of proof, and charges against the other defendants were then dismissed. The black leaders of the resistance, Thomas Parker and his brother-in-law Alexander Pinckney, fled to Canada with their families and were never apprehended. For a longer discussion of the Christiana case, including the trial-losing mistakes by the prosecution, see Lubet, *Fugitive Justice* at 50–131.

9. Application of Jabez Fitch, undated, 1857 (General Records, Department of Justice, National Archives).

10. Early Settlers' Association of Cuyahoga County, *Annals* at 2:154.

11. Alexander, "Willson Era," in Finkelman and Alexander, *Justice and Legal Change* at 15–17. See "An Act to Divide the State of Ohio into Two Judicial Districts, Section 8," United States Code, ch. 73, 10 Stat. 604 (February 10, 1855).

12. Fletcher, *Oberlin College* at 85.

13. Elisha Whittlesey to Jabez Fitch, March 11, 1857 (General Records of the Department of Justice, National Archives); William Anderson to Jabez Fitch, March 11, 1857 (General Records of the Department of Justice, National Archives); Thomas L. Smith to Jabez Fitch, March 11, 1857 (General Records of the Department of Justice, National Archives). See also *Cleveland Morning Leader*, December 14, 1858, observing that Fitch's accounts were "kept in better order and were more promptly settled" than any other marshal's in the United States.

14. Calhoun, *Lawmen* at 55.

15. *Cleveland Morning Leader*, December 14, 1858, April 19, 1859, and April 30, 1859; Cochran, *Western Reserve* at 119.

16. Weisenburger, *Modern Medea*; Frederickson and Walters, *Gendered Resistance*. As is well known, the Margaret Garner case inspired Toni Morrison's Pulitzer Prize–winning novel *Beloved*.

17. *Cleveland Morning Leader*, April 30, 1859. Marshal Robinson himself resigned in October 1856, after little more than a year in office, in the wake of the bitter recriminations that followed his callous handling of the Margaret Garner case.

18. "Abstract of applications for Marshalship of North Dist Ohio," undated, 1857 (General Records of the Department of Justice, National Archives) (capitalization and non-punctuation original).

19. Representative Joseph Burns to Attorney General Jeremiah S. Black, December 19, 1857 (General Records of the Department of Justice, National Archives).

20. Senator G. E. Pugh to U.S. Attorney General J. S. Black, April 4, 1857 (General Records of the Department of Justice, National Archives).

CHAPTER EIGHT. THE NEW MARSHAL

1. Wilentz, *American Democracy*, passim.

2. He would adopt the description himself in his 1859 State of the Union message.

3. Quitt, *Stephen A. Douglas* at 126; Johannsen, *Stephen A. Douglas* at 521–24; Alexander, "Willson Era," in Finkelman and Alexander, *Justice and Legal Change* at 17–18.

4. Johannsen, *Stephen A. Douglas* at 557. Douglas had earlier complained to Buchanan about his "apparent neglect of [Illinois] in the distribution of the Patronage under your administration." Johannsen, *Stephen A. Douglas* at 555.

5. Etcheson, *Bleeding Kansas* at 139; McPherson, *Battle Cry* at 164–65; Harrold, *Border War* at 172.

6. J. Baker, *James Buchanan* at 100.

7. Johannsen, *Stephen A. Douglas* at 586.

8. In addition to the usual lust for office, it was understood that the marshal's next term would be especially lucrative because it would span the 1860 national census. *Holmes County Republican*, May 13, 1858. As the chief "Executive Civil Officer" in northern Ohio, the new marshal would be in charge of conducting the census and would receive a payment based on the number of people "actually enumerated." Calhoun, *Lawmen* at 17, 19. The population of Cuyahoga County alone was nearly 180,000, so the per capita payoff promised to be profitable indeed.

9. See L. W. Hall to James Buchanan, April 16, 1858 (noting his dedication to "the interests of the party"); A. J. Dickinson to the President, April 3, 1857 (stressing "harmony

of the party"); Jacob Stuart to the Attorney General, March 3, 1858 (promoting a candidate "for the sake of harmony"); J. J. Hofman to J. S. Black, February 8, 1858 (promoting himself as furthering "the success . . . of the Democratic Party"); Ezra Dean to James Buchanan, January 30, 1857 (recommending a "firm consistent Democrat"); Democratic Citizens of Wayne County to James Buchanan (recommending the candidate as an "active, influential Democrat"); and Peter East to James Buchanan, February 23, 1857 (recommending "a sterling Democrat of the old Jefferson school") (all in General Records of the Department of Justice, National Archives). See also letters of M. Hoofland to Howell Cobb, March 9, 1857 (supporting the candidate for his "favorable position in the Democratic Party"); William Sawyer to Lewis Cass, March 11, 1857 (endorsing the candidate for his "sound reliable Democracy"), both in General Records of the Department of Justice, National Archives.

10. Democratic members of the Ohio House of Representatives to James Buchanan, January 25, 1858 (supporting a "true & reliable Democrat") (General Records of the Department of Justice, National Archives).

11. Democratic members of the Ohio Senate to James Buchanan, January 25, 1858 (supporting a "Democrat ever ready to devote his undivided energies & means in promoting the interests of the party") (General Records of the Department of Justice, National Archives). Several other aspirants presented petitions from mixed groups of state legislators, such as Democratic Members of the General Assembly to James Buchanan, March 29, 1857 (General Records of the Department of Justice, National Archives). See also Recommendation signed by a Majority of the Democratic members of the Ohio Legislature, undated, 1857; Abstract of recommendation of William Blackburn by members of the Ohio Legislature, undated, 1857; and Democratic Members of the Ohio Legislature to the President of the United States, February 24, 1857 (all in General Records of the Department of Justice, National Archives).

12. A Brief of the Recommendations in Behalf of William H. Gill, undated, 1857 (including Edwin M. Stanton, later President Abraham Lincoln's secretary of war, who was then still a Democrat) (General Records of the Department of Justice, National Archives).

13. Petition of Democratic Citizens of Stark County to J. S. Black, January 19, 1858 (warning against appointment of county probate judge William Burke, lest Governor Salmon Chase replace him on the court with a "Black Republican," and recommending E. J. Loveland in his stead) (General Records of the Department of Justice, National Archives).

14. Letter of Susan A. Clark to the President, January 6, 1857 (extolling her father as "uniformly and devotedly an administration Democrat") (General Records of the Department of Justice, National Archives).

15. Johannsen, *Stephen A. Douglas* at 609. See also Speech of Hon. George E. Pugh of Ohio on the Kansas Lecompton Constitution in the Senate of the United States, Congressional Globe, Senate, 35th Congress, 1st Session (March 15, 1858).

16. William Lawrence to James Buchanan, March 9, 1858 (stating that Johnson had never been "a leading or prominent Democrat") (General Records of the Department of Justice, National Archives). Johnson's only previous office had been as postmaster in Massillon almost twenty years earlier, where he was appointed to remedy the rumored "defalcations" of his predecessor, who had been summarily removed from office. *Cleveland Daily Herald*, December 30, 1839.

17. *Cleveland Morning Leader*, March 15, 1859.

18. *Cleveland Morning Leader*, March 15, 1859.

19. William Lawrence to James Buchanan, March 9, 1858 (General Records of the Department of Justice, National Archives).

20. Abner L. Backus to the President of the United States, March 1, 1858; Paul Edwards to the President, March 11, 1858; Robert Parks to James Buchanan, undated, but circa March 1858; Judge Samuel Starkweather to James Buchanan, March 17, 1858;

and Euceny D. Potter to the President, April 18, 1858 (all in General Records of the Department of Justice, National Archives). Johnson additionally submitted his own memorandum, explaining the history of the bank, the circumstances of its failure, and his own post-bankruptcy efforts to compensate depositors. He also gathered and submitted many of the supporting letters, which was unusually proactive. Matthew Johnson to the President, March 22, 1858 (General Records of the Department of Justice, National Archives).

21. Petition of the Lecompton Democrats of the City of Toledo to James Buchanan, March 25, 1858. In his letter transmitting the petition of the Toledo Lecompton Democrats to the President, Dennis Coghlin, collector for the Port of Toledo, declared that "Mr. Johnson possesses the entire confidence of his fellow Democrats here [who] who took part in the recent meeting here at which the Administration, and more especially its Kansas policy, were emphatically and enthusiastically endorsed and his appointment would give them great satisfaction." (Both letter and petition in General Records of the Department of Justice, National Archives).

22. Richard Mott to the President, March 11, 1858 (General Records of the Department of Justice, National Archives).

23. M. Johnson to the President, March 12, 1858 (General Records of the Department of Justice, National Archives).

24. Sen. G. E. Pugh to the President, April 20, 1858 (General Records of the Department of Justice, National Archives).

25. *Cleveland Morning Leader*, November 15, 1858. A. J. Dickinson to the President, April 5, 1857 (General Records of the Department of Justice, National Archives).

26. Transmittal by William H. Gill to the Attorney General, March 12, 1858, with enclosures of a letter from Rev. William Young Brown to the Attorney General, March 5, 1858, and certificate of J. A. Blocksom, W. M. N. L. [Masonic] Lodge, plus statement of Democratic Citizens of Columbiana Co., Ohio, undated abstracts, circa early March 1858, that, according to Gill, "positively refuted" charges made against Gill's "private character" (General Records of the Department of Justice, National Archives).

27. William H. Gill to Hon. J. S. Black, April 13, 1858 (emphasis original) (General Records of the Department of Justice, National Archives).

28. William L. Clarke to Hon. Gen. J. Burns, March 4, 1857 (emphasis in original) (General Records of the Department of Justice, National Archives).

29. *Holmes County Republican*, May 13, 1858.

30. *New York Tribune*, February 23, 1858. Congressional Globe, House of Representatives, 35th Congress, 1st Session (February 12, 1858); Congressional Globe, House of Representatives, 35th Congress, 1st Session (February 19, 1858).

31. Congressional Globe, House of Representatives, 35th Congress, 1st Session (March 4, 1858).

32. *Holmes County Republican*, August 26, 1858; *Holmes County Republican*, September 2, 1858.

33. *Cleveland Morning Leader*, April 30, 1859.

34. *Cleveland Morning Leader*, December 15, 1858.

CHAPTER NINE. "RECITAL OF THE WRONG AND OUTRAGE"

1. Peeke, *History of Erie County* at 907.
2. *Cleveland Morning Leader*, September 10, 1858.
3. Cheek and Cheek, *John Mercer Langston* at 316.
4. Brandt, *Town* at 47.
5. Prichard, *Episcopal Church* at 16–17, 112–13; Holmes, *Episcopal Church* at 80. As an example of the Episcopal Church's ambivalence over slavery, John McKivigan notes that of eighty-nine officers of the American and Foreign Anti-Slavery Society in the period 1840–54, only two were known to be Episcopalians. McKivigan, *Proslavery Religion* at 77.

6. *Cleveland Morning Leader*, September 10, 1858.

7. Sharfstein, *Invisible Line* at 90; Cheek and Cheek, "John Mercer Langston," in Litwack and Meier, *Black Leaders* at 110.

8. J. Langston, *Virginia Plantation* at 168.

9. Fletcher, *Oberlin College* at 402; *Cleveland Morning Leader*, September 10, 1858. "Locofoco" was a nickname for Democrats, pejorative when used by others but also adopted by Democrats themselves.

10. *Cleveland Morning Leader*, September 10, 1858.

11. Cheek and Cheek, *John Mercer Langston* at 316; *Cleveland Morning Leader*, September 10, 1858.

12. *Cleveland Morning Leader*, December 14, 1858, and April 19, 1859.

13. *Cleveland Morning Leader*, April 19, 1859.

14. Baumann, *Black Education at Oberlin* at 29.

15. *Pine and Palm*, July 20, 1861.

16. *Pine and Palm*, July 20, 1861.

17. *Pine and Palm*, July 20, 1861.

18. J. Langston, *Virginia Plantation* at 194–95.

19. *Pine and Palm*, July 20, 1861.

20. J. Langston, *Virginia Plantation* at 195.

21. Fletcher, *Oberlin College* at 269–70. Fletcher refers to Garrison as having been a "Comeouter" in 1847, but others might disagree. See McKivigan, "The Antislavery 'Comeouter' Sects: A Neglected Dimension of the Abolitionist Movement," in McKivigan, *Abolitionism* at 236. Fletcher also said that Oberliners were quite distinct from comeouters, and others again would disagree. See Padgett, "Comeouterism and Antislavery Violence in Ohio's Western Reserve," in McKivigan and Harrold, *Antislavery Violence* at 200–01, stating that "the institution most closely identified with comeouterism was Oberlin College." The definition of comeouterism has no bearing on the life of John Anthony Copeland, but for what it is worth, Fletcher was certainly well versed in Oberliniana. He graduated from Oberlin in 1920 and, after earning a doctorate in history at Harvard, taught at the college for thirty years. His two-volume history of Oberlin was published in 1943 and remains a definitive source to this day. Padgett's essay, on the other hand, contains many factual errors about Oberlin, including two in the first paragraph.

22. Blackwell, *Lucy Stone* at 184. For another version of the same quotation, see Weisenburger, *Modern Medea* at 172. Neither Stone's intervention nor a spirited defense by anti-slavery lawyers was enough to save Margaret Garner from rendition. The U.S. commissioner ordered her returned to her master.

23. *Dred Scott v. Sandford*, 60 U.S. 393 (1857).

24. Cochran, *Western Reserve* at 117 (capitalization and noncapitalization original).

25. Henriette Evans interview, March 5, 1908 (Villard Papers, Columbia University); Stephen Weeks to Oswald Villard, November 20, 1907 (Villard Papers, Columbia University). Sarah was related to Hiram Revels, who would later become the first black man elected to the U.S. Senate.

26. Greene, *Leary-Evans* at 10.

27. Henriette Evans interview, March 5, 1908 (Villard Papers, Columbia University).

28. Henriette Evans interview, March 5, 1908 (Villard Papers, Columbia University). If Sheridan did indeed emigrate from the United States to Liberia, it was at least ten years after Lucy's 1825 marriage to Matthew Leary. In June 1835, he was a delegate to North Carolina's constitutional convention, at which he argued strongly against the disenfranchisement of Leary and other free blacks. *Carolina Observer*, June 16, 1835.

29. "The Leary Family," *Negro History Bulletin* (November 1946) at 27–28.

30. Henriette Evans interview, March 5, 1908 (Villard Papers, Columbia University) (punctuation original).

31. *Carolina Observer*, June 16, 1835.

32. Henriette Evans interview, March 5, 1908 (Villard Papers, Columbia University). Matthew Leary owned at least three slaves in 1850 – a fourteen-year-old girl and two adult men (ages thirty-eight and forty-five). United States Census, Schedule of Slave Inhabitants, Fayetteville, North Carolina, 1850. Under North Carolina law, manumitted slaves were required to leave the state unless they could show that they had been freed in return for "meritorious service." Thus, it was not unusual for free blacks to acquire slaves as a first step toward emancipation. U. Philips, *Life and Labor* at 172; Hurd, *Freedom and Bondage* at 2:87; Oakes, *Ruling Race* at 47–48.

33. Henriette Evans interview, March 5, 1908 (Villard Papers, Columbia University); Mrs. C. M. Langston (Mary Patterson Leary Langston) interview, July 27, 1908 (Villard Papers, Columbia University).

34. Henriette Evans interview, March 5, 1908 (Villard Papers, Columbia University).

35. Mrs. C. M. Langston (Mary Leary Langston) interview, July 27, 1908 (Villard Papers, Columbia University).

36. Love, "Facts about Lewis Sheridan," *Negro History Bulletin* (June 1943) at 198. The account is highly doubtful. According to the same niece, Leary fled Fayetteville in the dark of night, picking his way "through the thick forests and under brush to the banks of the Cape Fear River," where he found a hidden boat in which he began the onward journey to Oberlin. In fact, as is well documented, Leary departed North Carolina by daylight in the company of his two sisters and their husbands, with the permission of the governor.

37. Henriette Evans interview, March 5, 1908 (Villard Papers, Columbia University); Mrs. C. M. Langston (Mary Leary Langston) interview, July 27, 1908 (Villard Papers, Columbia University).

38. The bequests included fifty cents each for Henriette and Sarah Jane, and one dollar for Lewis's daughter Lois. Matthew left much greater bequests, including his house and real property, to another daughter and son, who remained in Fayetteville. Last Will and Testament of M. N. Leary, February 7, 1880 (North Carolina State Archives).

39. John H. Cook and A. A. McKethan to Gov. David Reid, April 22, 1854, and John M. Kirkland to Gov. David Reid, April 23, 1854, quoted in Greene, *Leary-Evans* at 46–47. The letter on Henry's behalf included his brother and brother-in-law, the latter being Lewis Sheridan Leary.

40. There was no blood relationship or even a close relationship by marriage. Copeland's mother's brother was married to Leary's sister.

CHAPTER TEN. WACK'S TAVERN

1. J. Fairchild, "Baccalaureate Sermon," in Ballantine, *Oberlin Jubilee* at 95; E. Fairchild, *Historical Sketch* at 9.

2. Cochran, *Western Reserve* at 119; Fletcher, *Oberlin College* at 588.

3. Emoluments for M. Johnson, U.S. Marshal for the Northern District of Ohio, July 1, 1858 to January 1, 1859 (Department of the Treasury, Records of the Accounting Officers, National Archives). *Cleveland Morning Leader*, September 10, 1858 (referring to Dayton's acceptance of a third-party fee for slave hunting). United States marshals would not be paid salaries until 1896, and even then their deputies continued to be fee-paid. Parrillo, *Against the Profit Motive* at 508.

4. Obituary Record, Alumni of Oberlin College, 1905–06 (Oberlin College Archives); James Monroe Jones response to Alumni Reunion Questionnaire, June 21, 1875 (Oberlin College Archives).

5. James Monroe Jones responses to Questionnaire for Semi-Centennial Register, 1883 (Oberlin College Archives).

6. In contrast, Allen and Temperance Jones insisted that their children become educated. According to legend, James Monroe had briefly considered leaving school,

discouraged by his slow progress in Greek and Latin. His father took him to the smithy yard and, showing him an ax embedded in a chopping block, explained the hardships he had endured to bring the family to Oberlin. "Now, James," he said, "you take your choice. You go back to college, or you lay your head on this chopping block and I chop it off." "Oberliniana," *Oberlin Alumni Magazine* (April 1961). Allen's descendants recognized the incident as apocryphal, but they continued telling the story to emphasize their ancestors' deep commitment to education. Carol C. Bowie to Mercedes Holden Singleton, October 30, 1960 (Oberlin College Archives).

7. James Henry Scott (Mulatto, Oberlin) interview, December 7, 1908 (Villard Papers, Columbia University). In an early biography of John Brown, Richard Hinton described Leary as "a bright and quite well educated young man." There is no doubt that Leary was intelligent, and he was certainly literate, but there is no reason to believe that he had been educated beyond common school. Perhaps Hinton confused Leary with Copeland, who had at least spent a year in Oberlin's preparatory department. It is more likely, however, that the description of Leary was simply an example of Hinton's creative idealization of Brown and his comrades. Hinton, *John Brown and His Men* at 508.

8. J. Langston, *Virginia Plantation* at 194.

9. J. Langston, *Virginia Plantation* at 194.

10. Cheek and Cheek, *John Mercer Langston* at 356.

11. Nell, "Lewis Sherrard Leary," *Pine and Palm*, July 27, 1861. Nell mistakenly gave Leary's middle name as "Sherrard," and his error has been repeated in numerous other sources.

12. Marriage Index, Lorain County, Ohio, 1824–1865 (Cuyahoga County Public Library). The groom's name is recorded as Lewis L. Lowry and the bride's as Mary L. Patterson, but records were often imprecise in the antebellum era. Based on surrounding circumstances, there is no doubt that this is the marriage of Lewis S. Leary and Mary S. Patterson. For example, a contemporaneous source stated that Mary and Lewis were married "about eighteen months" before the Harper's Ferry raid in October 1859. *Pine and Palm*, July 27, 1861.

13. Hughes, *Big Sea* at 37.

14. Quarles, *Allies for Freedom* at 87; Hughes, *Big Sea* at 12.

15. Sources variously give the Leary girl's name as Lois, Loise, or Louise. Cheek and Cheek, *John Mercer Langston* at 356; Brandt, *Town* at 251; Rampersad, *Langston Hughes* at 1:6. John Mercer Langston's autobiography mentions the Learys' daughter but does not name her. J. Langston, *Virginia Plantation* at 193. William Cooper Nell, the noted African-American reformer and journalist from Boston, referred only to Leary's cherished "babe." *Pine and Palm*, July 27, 1861. To confuse matters, the 1860 census lists Mary Leary's child as a one-year-old boy named Lewis. United States Census Report, June 26, 1860. The census enumerator, however, was Chauncey Wack, who would not have been welcome in Mary Leary's home – or the home of any black Oberliner – in 1860. It is therefore most likely that Wack was less than scrupulous in recording the families of African-Americans; he might have been guessing, or he may not have cared about accuracy. Mary had moved to Kansas by 1870, where the census includes her eleven-year-old daughter (born in Ohio) named Lois S. Learo. Likewise, the 1875 Kansas census includes sixteen-year-old Lous L. Lary in Mary's household.

The child was said to be six months old when Leary departed Oberlin in August or September 1859. *Pine and Palm*, July 27, 1861. That would place her birth in February or March 1859, which is consistent with the couple's May 12, 1858, wedding date. Some sources, including Langston Hughes, state that Mary was pregnant when Lewis departed Oberlin in summer 1859, but that is contradicted by the census report, which indicates that Lois was born no later than June 1859 (otherwise, according to census requirements, her age would have been given in months rather than years). But see Hughes, *Big Sea* at 37 (stating that Mary Leary "was with child in Oberlin when Sheridan Leary went away"), and Rampersad, *Langston Hughes* at 6 (repeating Hughes's recollection that Mary Leary was pregnant when Lewis departed for Harper's Ferry). Of course, Wack could have been mistaken about the child's age as well as her gender, but John Mercer Langston's recollection and William Cooper Nell's nearly contemporaneous account make it virtually certain that Lois had already been born before Leary joined John Brown.

16. *Cleveland Morning Leader*, December 14, 1858.

17. *Cleveland Morning Leader*, September 10, 1858.

18. *Cleveland Morning Leader*, September 10, 1858.

19. *Cleveland Morning Leader*, September 10, 1858; *Cleveland Morning Leader*, December 14, 1858.

20. Shipherd, *Oberlin-Wellington Rescue* at 241–42. The verse suggests that Dayton had three accomplices, but news accounts mention only two.

21. *Cleveland Morning Leader*, September 10, 1858; *Cleveland Morning Leader*, April 15, 1859.

22. Cochran, *Western Reserve* at 121, 123.

23. *Cleveland Morning Leader*, September 10, 1858.

24. Morris, *Hotbed* at 200, quoting *Oberlin Alumni Magazine* (November 1909) at 54–55.

25. *Frederick Douglass' Paper*, June 2, 1854, reproduced in Ripley and Finkenbine, *Black Abolitionist Papers* at 4:220, 229.

26. *Anti-Slavery Bugle*, December 4, 1858, quoted in Cheek and Cheek, *John Mercer Langston* at 339.

27. Shipherd, *Oberlin-Wellington Rescue* at 241–42.

28. *Cleveland Morning Leader*, December 14, 1858; *Cleveland Morning Leader*, November 1, 1859; *Cleveland Morning Leader*, September 10, 1858; *Cleveland Daily Herald*, August 28, 1858; Cochran, *Western Reserve* at 121; Testimony of Ralph Plumb, in United States Congress, *Report of the Select Committee of the Senate* at 179–86.

CHAPTER ELEVEN. A BRACE OF PISTOLS

1. Cochran, *Western Reserve* at 123 (italics original).
2. Cochran, *Western Reserve* at 123 (italics original).
3. Cochran, *Western Reserve* at 124–25 (italics and noncapitalization original).
4. Cochran, *Western Reserve* at 124 (italics and noncapitalization original).
5. Shipherd, *Oberlin-Wellington Rescue* at 77.
6. J. Fairchild, *Underground Railroad* at 94–95.
7. Cochran, *Western Reserve* at 125.
8. *Painesville Telegraph*, quoted in *Cleveland Morning Leader*, September 10, 1858.
9. Clarke, *Narratives* at 90.
10. Shipherd, *Oberlin-Wellington Rescue* at 101.
11. *Painesville Telegraph*, quoted in *Cleveland Morning Leader*, September 10, 1858.
12. Shipherd, *Oberlin-Wellington Rescue* at 16.
13. *Cleveland Daily Herald*, August 28, 1858.
14. Cochran, *Western Reserve* at 121.
15. Shipherd, *Oberlin-Wellington Rescue* at 120.
16. Shipherd, *Oberlin-Wellington Rescue* at 19.

CHAPTER TWELVE. THE OBERLIN RESCUE

1. Shipherd, *Oberlin-Wellington Rescue* at 35.
2. Shipherd, *Oberlin-Wellington Rescue* at 151.
3. Brandt, *Town* at 69.

4. H. G. Blake to James Monroe and Henry Peck, September 6, 1858 (Oberlin College Archives). The Oberliners were acting in response to a letter from Harrison Blake of Medina, a former speaker of the Ohio State Senate, who would soon be elected to the U.S. Congress. Blake had written, candidly and obviously unfearful of exposure, "Gents, here are five slaves from the House of Bondage, that I need not say to you that you will see to them." Most messages on the Underground Railroad were sent in code, but Blake and the Oberliners evidently felt no need to be cryptic.

5. Shipherd, *Oberlin-Wellington Rescue* at 24; *Oberlin News*, March 3, 1899; *The Liberator*, October 1, 1858.

6. Baumann, *Reappraisal* at 28.

7. *New York Tribune*, September 14, 1858.

8. Blue, *No Taint of Compromise* at 67–68.

9. Shipherd, *Oberlin-Wellington Rescue* at 126.

10. McCabe, "Oberlin-Wellington Rescue," *Godey's Magazine* (October 1896). Concerning the mores and attitudes of the black middle classes in the North, see Ball, *Antislavery Life* at 10–36.

11. *The Liberator*, October 1, 1858.

12. *Oberlin Evangelist*, September 29, 1858.

13. McCabe, "Oberlin-Wellington Rescue"; Shipherd, *Oberlin-Wellington Rescue* at 26.

14. *The Liberator*, October 1, 1858.

15. Shipherd, *Oberlin-Wellington Rescue* at 60.

16. Shipherd, *Oberlin-Wellington Rescue* at 105.

17. Shipherd, *Oberlin-Wellington Rescue* at 159.

18. Shipherd, *Oberlin-Wellington Rescue* at 139.

19. *The Liberator*, October 1, 1858.

20. "A Monument," *Anglo-African Magazine*, January 14, 1860.

21. Lincoln, *Personal Reminiscences* (Palmer Collection, Western Reserve Historical Society).

22. *The Liberator*, October 1, 1858.

23. J. Langston, *Virginia Plantation* at 185–86.

24. *New York Tribune*, September 14, 1858; Shipherd, *Oberlin-Wellington Rescue* at 106–07.

25. J. Fairchild, *Underground Railroad* at 96.

26. Fitch, "Wellington Rescue Case" (Oberlin College Archives).

27. J. Fairchild, *Underground Railroad* at 114.

28. McCabe, "Oberlin-Wellington Rescue" at 375.

29. Swing, *James Harris Fairchild* at 190.

CHAPTER THIRTEEN. "THE BLACK MECCA"

1. Elias Jones interview, December 9, 1908 (Villard Papers, Columbia University).

2. Hatcher, *Western Reserve* at 246–48.

3. Hiram Wilson to Hamilton Hill, September 11, 1848 (Oberlin College Archives).

4. John A. Copeland to Friend [Addison] Halbert, December 10, 1859 (Villard Papers, Columbia University Library); also in Black Abolitionist Papers at 1:47–48.

5. Fairchild, *Underground Railroad* at 114.

6. *New York Tribune*, September 14, 1858.

7. Elias Jones interview, December 9, 1908 (Villard Papers, Columbia University); Mary J. Copeland to Katherine Mayo, December 16, 1908 (Villard Papers, Columbia University); Mary Copeland interview, December 9, 1908 (Villard Papers, Columbia University). Fred appears to have been the family's emissary to Oberlin College. In 1908, he responded

to a survey of "non-graduate" students with the details of his brother's death. *Oberlin College – General Catalog – 1908* (Oberlin College Archives). Benjamin Quarles stated without qualification that "it was Copeland who had escorted former slave John Price during the final stages of his flight into Canada." Quarles, *Allies for Freedom* at 88.

8. Shadd, "Chatham's Black Heritage" (Chatham-Kent Black Historical Society) at 8.

9. *Cleveland Morning Leader*, December 14, 1858; *Cleveland Morning Leader*, April 15, 1859; Shipherd, *Oberlin-Wellington Rescue* at 241.

10. *Cleveland Morning Leader*, December 14, 1858; *Cleveland Morning Leader*, April 21, 1859; Shipherd, *Oberlin-Wellington Rescue* at 241.

11. *Cleveland Plain Dealer*, September 24, 1858; *Cleveland Morning Leader*, February 21, 1860.

12. *Cleveland Morning Leader*, April 19 and April 21, 1858.

13. Gunsmith Jones departed Chatham for the West Coast at some point in late 1858; the precise date is unknown. I have speculated that he was still there in mid-September, which seems probable given what we do know about the timing. Among the other indications, Brown's adjutant, John Kagi, reported on attempts to recruit a "coppersmith" from Chatham in October 1858. The unnamed coppersmith is often thought to have been J. G. Reynolds, but the description also fits James Monroe Jones. Hinton, *John Brown and His Men* at 180. Even if Jones was not then in Chatham, however, stories of John Brown would still have been in wide circulation. In addition, another Oberliner, printer William Howard Day, was definitely in Chatham. Day had printed the copies of Brown's "provisional constitution," and he certainly would have shared that story with a visiting abolitionist from Oberlin. Of the white men who attended the convention, Brown's son-in-law Henry Thompson was still in Chatham at least until mid-August 1858, and perhaps later. Henry Thompson to J. H. Kagi, August 16, 1858, Calendar of Virginia State Papers at 11:291.

14. Elias Jones interview, December 9, 1908 (Villard Papers, Columbia University); Hamilton, "John Brown in Canada," *Canadian Magazine* (December 1894) at 8, 15; *Chatham Weekly Planet*, April 28, 1881.

15. Mary J. Copeland to Katherine Mayo, December 16, 1908 (Villard Papers, Columbia University); Mary Copeland interview, December 9, 1908 (Villard Papers, Columbia University).

16. Brigance, *Jeremiah Sullivan Black* at 58–60.

17. *Cleveland Morning Leader*, December 10, 1859.

18. J. Langston, *Virginia Plantation* at 186.

19. *Cleveland Daily Herald*, May 18, 1859.

20. Shipherd, *Oberlin-Wellington Rescue* at 14–15. The reference to "higher law" was a disdainful allusion to Senator William Seward's 1850 speech in opposition to the Fugitive Slave Act, in which he argued that there was "a higher law than the Constitution." Stahr, *Seward* at 124.

21. *Oberlin Evangelist*, December 22, 1858.

22. Shipherd, *Oberlin-Wellington Rescue* at 4.

23. *Oberlin Evangelist*, December 22, 1858.

24. *Cleveland Morning Leader*, December 10, 1858.

25. *Cleveland Plain Dealer*, December 7, 1858.

26. Johnson carried an additional twelve warrants for residents of Wellington, some of which he was able to serve later that day. Brandt, *Town* at 122.

27. *Cleveland Plain Dealer*, December 7, 1858.

28. *Cleveland Daily Herald*, November 5, 1859 (quoting the *Cincinnati Enquirer*).

29. *Cleveland Morning Leader*, December 14, 1858.

30. *Cleveland Plain Dealer*, December 10, 1858; *Cleveland Morning Leader*, December 14, 1858; *Savannah Daily Morning News*, December 21, 1858.

31. Brandt, *Town* at 283.

32. *Cleveland Plain Dealer*, December 10, 1858.
33. *Cleveland Morning Leader*, December 14, 1858.

CHAPTER FOURTEEN. THE FELONS' FEAST

1. *Cleveland Daily Herald*, December 7, 1858; Van Tassel and Grabowski, *Encyclopedia of Cleveland History* at 833; Early Settlers Association of Cuyahoga County, *Annals* at 3:495; Brandt, *Town* at 145.
2. *Cleveland Daily Herald*, December 7, 1858.
3. Shipherd, *Oberlin-Wellington Rescue* at 5–11 (all spellings, punctuation, and emphases in original).
4. Shipherd, *Oberrlin-Wellington Rescue* at 5–11 (all spellings, capitalizations, punctuation, and emphases in original).
5. Peck, "Slave-Rescue Case in Ohio." *The Liberator*, January 28, 1859.
6. J. Langston, "Oberlin-Wellington Rescue," *Anglo-African Magazine* (July 1859) at 1; Cheek and Cheek, *John Mercer Langston* at 319.
7. See Frothingham, *Gerrit Smith*.
8. Hatcher, *Western Reserve* at 629.
9. For example, George Thompson, who had been imprisoned in Missouri for his anti-slavery activities, sought Smith's support for his attendance at Oberlin: "I would be of some help to prosecute my *Studies*, in preparation to preach the gospel to the suffering Poor – *the colored Race* – in this country – or Africa if the Lord permits." Hatcher, *Western Reserve* at 628.
10. J. Copeland to Hon. Gerrit Smith, January 10, 1859 (Gerrit Smith Papers, Syracuse University).
11. J. Copeland to Hon. Gerrit Smith, January 10, 1859 (Gerrit Smith Papers, Syracuse University); DeCaro, *Man Who Lived* at 83; Testimony of Ralph Plumb, United States Congress, *Report of the Select Committee of the Senate* at 179–86. Copeland's post–Harper's Ferry letters have survived in printed or hand-copied form, but there is no extant exemplar of his handwriting.
12. See, for example, Cook, *Confession* at 7.
13. Reynolds, *John Brown* at 247–48. Forbes later denied providing any information to officials of the Buchanan administration, while insisting that his only purpose had been to deter Brown's mission for the good of the abolitionist movement. *New York Herald*, October 25, 1859.
14. Reynolds, *John Brown* at 264.
15. Quoted in Reynolds, *John Brown* at 265.
16. Lawson, *American State Trials* 6:828; Cook, *Confession* at 9.
17. Hinton, *John Brown and His Men* at 218; Soike, *Necessary Courage* at 141.
18. Villard, *John Brown* at 386.
19. Reynolds, *John Brown and His Men* at 278.
20. Grinnell, *Men and Events* at 213.
21. Morris, *Hotbed* at 195.
22. Reynolds, *John Brown* at 279, 285. For the fullest account of these events, see Soike, *Necessary Courage* at 136–57.
23. *New York Tribune*, March 18, 1859.
24. *New York Herald*, October 21, 1859.

CHAPTER FIFTEEN. VOTARIES OF THE HIGHER LAW

1. *Cleveland Morning Leader*, April 19 and April 26, 1859; "Daily National Democrat," in Van Tassel and Grabowski, *Encyclopedia of Cleveland History*. Johnson had earlier purchased

and operated the *New Lisbon Patriot*, another pro-slavery newspaper. *Perrysburg Journal*, June 3, 1858.

2. *Cleveland Morning Leader*, April 15, 1859 (capitalization in original). As the organ of the Douglas Democracy, the *Plain Dealer* might be expected to be critical of Johnson, although certainly not to the point of defending the Oberlin Rescuers.

3. Shipherd, *Oberlin-Wellington Rescue* at 45.

4. Shipherd, *Oberlin-Wellington Rescue* at 62.

5. Shipherd, *Oberlin-Wellington Rescue* at 88.

6. Shipherd, *Oberlin-Wellington Rescue* at 89.

7. Shipherd, *Oberlin-Wellington Rescue* at 89.

8. Shipherd, *Oberlin-Wellington Rescue* at 183 (emphasis original).

9. *Oberlin Evangelist*, April 27, 1859.

10. William Lloyd Garrison to James Monroe, April 22, 1859 (Oberlin College Archives).

11. Shipherd, *Oberlin-Wellington Rescue* at 97.

12. Shipherd, *Oberlin-Wellington Rescue* at 128.

13. Shipherd, *Oberlin-Wellington Rescue* at 166 (noncapitalization in original).

14. Shipherd, *Oberlin-Wellington Rescue* at 141.

15. Shipherd, *Oberlin-Wellington Rescue* at 175–78 (spelling original).

16. Shipherd, *Oberlin-Wellington Rescue* at 178.

CHAPTER SIXTEEN. "THE BRAVEST NEGROES"

1. *Cleveland Morning Leader*, April 29, 1894.

2. *Cleveland Morning Leader*, April 29, 1894; Land, "John Brown's Ohio Environment," *Ohio Archeological and Historical Quarterly* (January 1948) at 26.

3. *Cleveland Plain Dealer*, March 22, 1859.

4. *Cleveland Morning Leader*, April 29, 1894.

5. *Cleveland Morning Leader*, November 28, 1859. M[atthew] Johnson to Hon. Andrew Hunter, November 15, 1859 (Library of Virginia), published in *Virginia Magazine of History and Biography* (July 1902) at 280–82.

6. *Cleveland Plain Dealer*, March 22, 1859; *Cleveland Morning Leader*, April 29, 1894.

7. Quarles, *Allies for Freedom* at 87.

8. *Cleveland Morning Leader*, April 29, 1894.

9. *Cleveland Morning Leader*, April 29, 1894; DeCaro, *Fire from the Midst of You* at 258–59.

10. Reynolds, *John Brown* at 289.

11. Quarles, *Allies for Freedom* at 72.

12. Ruchames, *Making of a Revolutionary* at 71–72.

13. *Cleveland Plain Dealer*, March 22, 1859; *Cleveland Morning Leader*, April 29, 1894.

14. *New York Herald*, October 21, 1859.

15. *Cleveland Morning Leader*, April 29, 1894.

16. *Cleveland Morning Leader*, April 29, 1894.

17. Wayland, *Kagi and Brown* at 89.

18. J. Langston, *Virginia Plantation* at 192.

19. *Cleveland Morning Leader*, April 29, 1894. The demonstrators called on the Ohio Supreme Court to issue a writ of habeas corpus freeing the prisoners, which would have resulted in a confrontation between federal and state authorities. Governor Salmon Chase spoke at the rally, promising to enforce such a judgment by his state's highest court, even if it meant calling out the Ohio militia. To cope with that contingency, Marshal Johnson sought instructions from President Buchanan and Attorney General Black, who directed him to enforce federal law with all necessary force. Matthew Johnson to President Buchanan, April 23, 1859 (Department of Justice, Letters Received, National Archives); Matthew Johnson

to Jeremiah Black, April 20, 1859 (Department of Justice, Letters Received, National Archives); Jeremiah Black to Matthew Johnson, April 26, 1859 (Department of Justice, Office of the Attorney General, National Archives). The potential crisis was averted when the Ohio Supreme Court declined to intervene in the case. *Ex Parte Bushnell*, 9 Ohio St. 77 (1859).

20. Kagi to Dear Tidd, May 8, 1859, Calendar of Virginia State Papers at 11:345–46. Kagi also approached other Oberliners, including Ralph Plumb (from whom he requested funds) and William Lincoln (whom he sought to enlist). R. Plumb to I. Henrie, Esq'r [John Kagi], August 23, 1859, Calendar of Virginia State Papers at 11:314–15; Lincoln, *Personal Reminiscences* (Palmer Collection, Western Reserve Historical Society).

21. Kagi to Dear Tidd, April 22, 1859, Calendar of Virginia State Papers at 11:345.

22. I. H. H. [presumably I. H. Harris] to My Dear I. Henrie [John Kagi], August 22, 1859, Calendar of Virginia State Papers at 11:335.

23. Local authorities in Lorain County had managed to arrest the slave hunters Jennings and Mitchell on charges of kidnapping, which made them temporarily unavailable as witnesses for the remaining federal trials. The Kentuckians were fearful that they would be convicted, as it was impossible for them to prove that the long-absent John Price had actually been a slave. They consequently pressured U.S. Attorney Belden to make a deal in which all prosecutions, state and federal, were dismissed. Belden was resentful of the outcome, given the bogus nature of the kidnapping case, but Oberlin exulted. Lubet, *Fugitive Justice* at 294–314. "At last the Higher Law was triumphant," said John Mercer Langston. J. Langston, *Virginia Plantation* at 190. See Brandt, *Town* at 231–37.

24. J. Langston, *Virginia Plantation* at 193 (noncapitalization in original).

25. L. S. Leary to J. Henrie (John Kagi), September 8, 1859, Calendar of Virginia State Papers at 11:305–06.

26. Testimony of Ralph Plumb, United States Congress, *Report of the Select Committee of the Senate* at 179–86.

27. Article Commemorating the Copelands' Fiftieth Anniversary, *Oberlin Weekly News*, August 19, 1881.

28. James Henry Scott (Mulatto, Oberlin) interview, December 7, 1908 (Villard Papers, Columbia University); Rampersad, *Langston Hughes* at 1:6.

29. Nell, "Lewis Sherrard Leary," *Pine and Palm*, July 27, 1861; Wesley and Uzelac, *William Cooper Nell* at 610–11.

30. J. Langston, *Virginia Plantation* at 190, 192.

31. John Brown, Jr., wrote to Kagi from Sandusky on August 27, saying that he was taking the morning train to Oberlin, a distance of only forty miles. John Smith [John Brown Jr.] to Friend Henrie [John Kagi], August 27, 1859, in "Documents Relative to the Harper's Ferry Invasion Appended to Governor Wise's Message" (Library of Virginia). He again wrote to Kagi on September 2, advising him that "friend L– y [Leary] of Ob– [Oberlin] will be on hand soon." Hinton, *John Brown and His Men* at 263.

32. According to Leary's sister, not until "she saw her brother's name mentioned as one of the killed" at Harper's Ferry did anyone in the family know that "Lewis was a soldier in the anti-slavery cause." Featherstonhaugh, "John Brown's Men," *Publications of the Southern History Association* (October 1899) at 295.

33. Mary Patterson Leary Langston interview, July 27, 1909 (Villard Papers, Columbia University).

34. Hughes, *Big Sea* at 12, 299.

CHAPTER SEVENTEEN. THE INVISIBLES

1. Quarles, *Allies for Freedom* at 74–75.
2. Douglass, *Life and Times* at 279.

3. *Anti-Slavery Bugle*, December 4, 1858, quoted in Cheek and Cheek, *John Mercer Langston* at 339.

4. *Cleveland Plain Dealer*, November 5, 1859.

5. United States Census, 1860 (regarding Amanda Sturtevant's age, not her temperament).

6. *Cleveland Daily Herald*, October 31, 1859; *Cleveland Plain Dealer*, November 5, 1859.

7. Hinton, *John Brown and His Men* at 249. See also Ritner, "Annual Message to the Assembly – 1836," in Reed, *Pennsylvania Archives*.

8. Hinton, *John Brown and His Men* at 272.

9. Tony Horwitz states that Copeland and Leary arrived on Saturday morning, October 15, but that seems an error. Horwitz, *Midnight* Rising at 124. Osborne Anderson, who was present at the time, was certain that they had arrived on Thursday, and Copeland himself said that they reached the Maryland farm two days before the raid, which would have been Friday at the latest. Anderson, *Voice from Harper's Ferry* at 26.

10. DeCaro, *Cost of Freedom* at 72–73.

11. Anderson, *Voice from Harper's Ferry* at 25–26.

12. Higginson, *Contemporaries* at 234.

13. See Lubet, *John Brown's Spy*.

14. Reynolds, *John Brown* at 300.

15. Schwarz, *Migrants against Slavery* at 159–63. Harriet Newby was enslaved in the household of Dr. Lewis Jennings, located in Brentsville, which is roughly sixty miles from Harper's Ferry. Harriet and Dangerfield had between two and seven children (sources vary).

16. Harriet Newby to Dangerfield Newby, April 11, 1859 (spelling original) (Library of Virginia).

17. Harriet Newby to Dangerfield Newby, April 22, 1859 (spelling and punctuation original), Calendar of Virginia State Papers at 11:311.

18. Harriet Newby to Dangerfield Newby, August 16, 1859 (spelling and punctuation original), Calendar of Virginia State Papers at 11:311.

19. "Statement of Annie Brown, Daughter of John Brown, Written November 1886" (Frank Logan/John Brown Collection, Chicago History Museum).

20. Featherstonhaugh, "John Brown's Men," *Publications of the Southern History Association* (October 1899) at 294.

21. Anne Brown to Thomas Wentworth Higginson, November 29, 1859 (Higginson Papers, Anti-Slavery Collections, Boston Public Library); Higginson, *Contemporaries* at 233–34. See also Schwarz, *Migrants against Slavery* at 101, 149–68.

22. Horwitz, *Midnight Rising* at 74.

23. Douglass, *Life and Times* at 276–78.

24. Douglass, "John Brown," speech delivered at Storer College, in Foner and Taylor, *Frederick Douglass* at 633. See also Quarles, *Allies for Freedom* at 64; Ruchames, *Making of a Revolutionary* at 297.

25. "Owen Brown's Story of His Journey from Hagerstown to Kennedy Farm, with Shields Green, a Colored Man" (Horatio Nelson Rust Collection, Huntington Library).

26. Anderson, *Voice from Harper's Ferry* at 9–10.

27. Anderson, *Voice from Harper's Ferry* at 28.

28. Testimony of Richard Realf, in United States Congress, *Report of the Select Committee of the Senate* at 97; Quarles, *Allies for Freedom* at 65.

29. *Frederick Douglass' Paper*, August 20, 1852.

30. Quarles, *Allies for Freedom* at 72.

31. George Gill to Richard Hinton, July 7, 1893 (Richard Hinton Collection, Kansas State Historical Society), quoted in Horwitz, *Midnight Rising* at 92.

32. Alcott, *Journals* at 315–16.

33. Horwitz, *Midnight Rising* at 83.

34. Quarles, *Allies for Freedom* at 74.

35. Quarles, *Allies for Freedom* at 82–83. W. E. B. DuBois believed that Brown's emissaries, including John, Jr., had not been up to the task. "The magic of Brown's presence," he said, might have been enough "to convince men that this was a real chance to strike an effective blow." But Brown was busy making logistical arrangements in Virginia and therefore had to leave most of the recruiting to others. DuBois, *John Brown* at 27.

36. "Statement of Annie Brown, Daughter of John Brown, Written November 1886" (Frank Logan/John Brown Collection, Chicago History Museum).

37. John Copeland to Dear Elias [Jones], undated, December 1859 (Library of Virginia).

CHAPTER EIGHTEEN. THE WAR DEPARTMENT

1. Watson Brown Commission, October 15, 1859, Calendar of Virginia State Papers at 11:324.

2. Anderson, *Voice from Harper's Ferry* at 28.

3. Annie Brown Adams to Richard Hinton, June 7, 1894 (Richard Hinton Collection, Kansas State Historical Society), quoted in Horwitz, *Midnight Rising* at 111.

4. Cook, *Confession* at 11.

5. Anderson, *Voice from Harper's Ferry* at 27.

6. Anderson, *Voice from Harper's Ferry* at 27. Anderson was writing over a year after the event, with reason to rationalize Brown's seemingly hasty decision to launch the attack earlier than planned. John Cook, writing only weeks afterward, provided a different explanation. According to Cook, Brown had received a letter from supporters in Boston "finding fault" with his management and urging him to proceed without "unnecessary delay and expense." Of course, Cook was then trying to save his life through plea negotiations, and he had good reasons to implicate Boston abolitionists to whatever extent possible. Cook, *Confession* at 10.

7. Hinton, *John Brown and His Men* at 278.

8. Anderson, *Voice from Harper's Ferry* at 27.

9. Brown to Kagi, undated memorandum of instructions, Calendar of Virginia State Papers at 11:321.

10. Cook, *Confession* at 12.

11. Anderson, *Voice from Harper's Ferry* at 31.

12. Testimony of Daniel Whelan, United States Congress, *Report of the Select Committee of the Senate* at 21–23 (capitalization in original).

13. Testimony of Lewis Washington, United States Congress, *Report of the Select Committee of the Senate* at 29–40; Lawson, *American State Trials* at 6:826; Anderson, *Voice from Harper's Ferry* at 41.

14. Reynolds, *John Brown* at 311.

15. Testimony of Lewis Washington, United States Congress, *Report of the Select Committee of the Senate* at 34.

16. Testimony of John Dangerfield, Captain Sinn, and Terence Burns, in Lawson, *American State Trials* at 6:767–75.

17. Testimony of Conductor Phelps, in Lawson, *American State Trials* at 6:744.

18. Reynolds, *John Brown* at 316.

19. Barry, *Story of Harper's Ferry* at 82–83.

20. Harriet Newby to Dear Husband, August 16, 1959 (spelling original), Calendar of Virginia State Papers at 11:311.

21. Hinton, *John Brown and His Men* at 309.

22. Korda, *Clouds of Glory* at xvii.

23. Horwitz, *Midnight Rising* at 176.

24. Quoted in Horwitz, *Midnight Rising* at 171.

25. Boteler, "Recollections of the John Brown Raid," *Century Magazine* (July 1883) at 407 (spelling original).

26. *Richmond Enquirer*, October 21, 1859; Green, "Capture of John Brown," *North American Review* (December 1885) (spelling original).

27. Green, "Capture of John Brown," *North American Review* (December 1885); DeCaro, *Emancipator* at 68–81.

28. Col. R. E. Lee to the Adjutant General, October 19, 1859, United States Congress, *Report of the Select Committee of the Senate* at 42.

CHAPTER NINETEEN. HALL'S RIFLE WORKS

1. John A. Copeland to Friend [Addison] Halbert, December 10, 1859 (Villard Papers, Columbia University Library; also in Black Abolitionist Papers at 1:47–48.)

2. Mary Mauzy to Daughter (Eugenia Burton), October 17, 1859 (Stutler Collection, West Virginia Memory Project, West Virginia Archives).

3. Strother, "Late Invasion at Harper's Ferry," *Harper's Weekly* (November 5, 1859).

4. John A. Copeland to Friend [Addison] Halbert, December 10, 1859 (Villard Papers, Columbia University Library; also in Black Abolitionist Papers 1:47–48); Lawson, *American State Trials* at 6:743.

5. Col. R. E. Lee to the Adjutant General, October 19, 1859, United States Congress, *Report of the Select Committee of the Senate* at 42.

6. Testimony of Andrew Hunter, United States Congress, *Report of the Select Committee of the Senate* at 60.

7. Other than as noted, quotations from Brown's interrogation are taken from the *New York Herald*, October 21, 1859; *Richmond Enquirer*, October 21, 1859; or *Boston Traveler*, October 25, 1859. Summaries of the interrogation may be found in Ruchames, *John Brown Reader* at 118–25; Boteler, "Recollections of the John Brown Raid," *The Century Magazine* (July 1883); Lawson, *American State Trials* at 6:711–716; and Shackleton, "What Support Did John Brown Rely Upon," *Magazine of American History* (April 1893). Spellings, punctuation, and capitalization are all original.

8. Boteler, "Recollections of the John Brown Raid," *The Century Magazine* (July 1883) at 410.

9. Hunter, "John Brown's Raid," *Publications of the Southern History Association* (July 1897) at 167.

10. Hunter, "John Brown's Raid," *Publications of the Southern History Association*, (July 1897) at 167.

11. *Richmond Enquirer*, October 25, 1859.

12. "Col. R.E. Lee's Report to Adjutant General," October 19, 1859 (Wise Executive Papers, Library of Virginia), also published in *Virginia Magazine of History and Biography* (July 1902) at 24; A. H., "List of Insurgents," undated, 1859 (Wise Executive Papers, Library of Virginia), also printed in *Virginia Magazine of History and Biography* (January 1902) at 274–75.

13. Shipherd, *Oberlin-Wellington Rescue* at 267; M. Johnson to President Buchanan, April 28, 1859 (General Records, Department of Justice, National Archives).

14. The story of Brown's derisiveness toward Johnson had been written by Kagi and published in the *Cleveland Morning Leader* and elsewhere. Johnson continued to seek a copy of Kagi's notes for the article well into the fall, "as written proof in his own handwriting for my purposes here." M[atthew] Johnson to Hon. Andrew Hunter, November 15, 1859 (Wise Executive Papers, Library of Virginia), published in *Virginia Magazine of History and Biography* (July 1902) at 280–82.

15. *Richmond Enquirer*, October 21, 1859.

16. *New York Herald*, October 20, 1859.

17. *Richmond Enquirer,* October 25, 1859; *Cleveland Morning Leader,* November 1, 1859; *Evening Post,* October 25, 1859; Redpath, *Captain John Brown* at 273.

18. Buchanan, "James Buchanan to Andrew Hunter, December 17, 1859," *Proceedings of the Massachusetts Historical Society* (December 1912) at 245.

19. Col. John T. Gibson to Gov. Henry Wise, October 18, 1859, in "Documents Relative to the Harper's Ferry Invasion Appended to Governor Wise's Message" (Wise Executive Papers, Library of Virginia).

20. "Memoir of Rev. George V. Leech, Baltimore Conference, M. E. Church," undated manuscript (Villard Papers, Columbia University).

21. "Memoir of Rev. George V. Leech, Baltimore Conference, M. E. Church," unpublished manuscript (Villard Papers, Columbia University).

22. *New York Times,* October 27, 1859; *Richmond Enquirer,* November 1, 1859.

CHAPTER TWENTY. "HIS NEGRO CONFESSION"

1. *Cleveland Daily Herald,* October 28 and November 5, 1859; *Cincinnati Enquirer,* November 4, 1859; *Pittsburgh Daily Gazette and Advertiser,* November 8, 1859.

2. *Cleveland Daily Herald,* October 28, 1859.

3. Copeland's confession was published in multiple venues. The most complete versions, including all but one of the quotations here, can be found in the *Cleveland Daily Herald,* October 31, 1859, and the *National Democrat,* October 31, 1859. Copeland's denial of murder or any "analogous crime," which was not included in the published confession, is found in M[atthew Johnson] to John Copeland [Sr.], October 29, 1859 (Villard Papers, Columbia University). Shorter versions of the confession can be found in the *New York Tribune,* October 31, 1859, and Strother, "Trial of the Conspirators," *Harper's Weekly* (November 12, 1859).

4. "Col. R. E. Lee's Report to Adjutant General," October 19, 1859 (Wise Executive Papers, Library of Virginia), also published in *Virginia Magazine of History and Biography* (July 1902) at 24. Brown's friend and first biographer, James Redpath, condemned Johnson as "that vile fellow . . . who tried to pump the colored men." Redpath to Stevens, January 23, 1860 (Stevens Family Papers, Massachusetts Historical Society). See also M. Johnson to Andrew Hunter, November 15, 1859 (Wise Executive Papers, Library of Virginia), also printed in *Virginia Magazine of History and Biography* (January 1902) at 276–77. Regarding Douglass's revelation of his role in Green's recruitment, see Douglass, "John Brown," speech delivered at Storer College, in Foner and Taylor, *Frederick Douglass* at 633.

5. *Cleveland Daily Herald,* October 28, 1859; *Richmond Enquirer,* November 1, 1859.

6. *Cleveland Daily Herald,* October 28, 1859.

7. *Cleveland Morning Leader,* November 1, 1859; *Pittsburgh Daily Gazette and Advertiser,* November 8, 1859.

8. *Cleveland Plain Dealer,* November 5, 1859.

9. *Cleveland Morning Leader,* October 28 and November 1, 1859; *Cleveland Daily Herald,* November 1, 1859; *Oberlin Evangelist,* November 9, 1859. The *Herald* was strongly abolitionist. In the issue that reproduced Copeland's confession, for example, another story argued that slavery "compels its friends to violate the commonest justice [and] it compels the officers of law to become oppressors in office." In an adjacent column, however, the *Herald* twice criticized Marshal Johnson for relying on "the nigger's confession." *Cleveland Daily Herald,* October 31, 1859. The coincidence of abolitionism and racism was not unusual in the antebellum era, although it is difficult to read today.

10. *Cincinnati Enquirer,* November 4, 1859; *Cleveland Plain Dealer,* November 5, 1859.

11. M[atthew] Johnson to John Copeland [Sr.], October 29, 1859 (Villard Papers, Columbia University).

12. M[atthew] Johnson to Hon. Andrew Hunter, November 15, 1859 (Wise Executive Papers, Library of Virginia), also published in *Virginia Magazine of History and Biography* (July 1902) at 280–82.

13. Andrew Hunter to Gov. Henry Wise, October 22, 1859 (Wise Executive Papers, Library of Virginia).

14. Lawson, *American State Trials* at 6:728n29.

15. The actual legal proceedings were complex, requiring first a preliminary hearing before an "examining court" of eight magistrates, as well as deliberations by the grand jury. For a full account, see McGinty, *John Brown's Trial.*

16. Indictment of John Brown et al., October 26, 1859 (John Brown Papers, Circuit Court of Jefferson County).

17. Parker, "The Trial of John Brown: Its Secret History, Revealed for the First Time by the Judge," *St. Louis Globe-Democrat*, April 8, 1886; Lawson, *American State Trials* at 6:710n21; Tucker, "Reminiscences of Virginia's Judges and Jurists," *Virginia Law Register* (July 1895) at 16; Stutler, "Judge Richard Parker," *Magazine of the Jefferson County Historical Society* (December 1953) at 27–33.

18. Sanborn, *Life and Letters of John Brown* at 579; Redpath, *Captain John Brown* at 344; *New York Herald*, October 27, 1859.

19. *New York Herald*, October 26, 1859.

20. Lawson, *American State Trials* at 6:728n31. *New York Herald*, October 26, 1859; *New York Tribune*, October 29, 1859. Parker also named a second lawyer, former congressman Charles Faulkner, who objected to the appointment because he had participated in Brown's initial interrogation. Under the circumstances, Faulkner argued, it would be "improper and inexpedient" for him to take the case. Parker at first refused to release Faulkner, but he eventually relented and allowed him to withdraw. *New York Tribune*, October 29, 1859; *New York Herald*, October 26, 1859.

21. *New York Herald*, October 26, 1859.

22. *New York Tribune*, October 29, 1859; Strother, "Copeland, Listening to the Indictment and Pleadings," October 26, 1859, and "Copeland and Green Listening to the Indictment," October 26, 1859 (West Virginia Historical Art Collection, University of West Virginia).

CHAPTER TWENTY-ONE. NOTHING LIKE A FAIR TRIAL

1. *Charlestown Independent Democrat*, October 18, 1859, quoted in Horwitz, *Midnight Rising* at 199.

2. *New York Herald*, October 28, 1859.

3. Hoyt, "Recollections of John Brown's Trial," *Leavenworth Daily Conservative*, July 31, 1867.

4. Hinton, *John Brown and His Men* at 365–66; Villard, *John Brown* at 480–81.

5. Hunter to Wise, October 28, 1859, quoted in Villard, *John Brown* at 485; Reynolds, *John Brown* at 352.

6. *Richmond Enquirer*, November 1, 1859; *New York Herald*, October 29, 1859.

7. *New York Herald*, October 29, 1859.

8. Thomas Wentworth Higginson to Dear Friends (John Brown's Daughters), November 4, 1859 (Stutler Collection, West Virginia Memory Project, West Virginia State Archives).

9. Hoyt, "Recollections of John Brown's Trial," *Leavenworth Daily Conservative*, August 11, 1867; *New York Herald*, October 29, 1859; Lawson, *American State Trials* at 6:766.

10. *New York Herald*, October 29, 1859; Lawson, *American State Trials* at 6:766.

11. John Brown to Dear Brother Jeremiah (Jeremiah Brown), November 12, 1859, in Ruchames, *John Brown Reader* at 134; DeCaro, *Fire from the Midst of You* at 275.

12. Hoyt, "Recollections of John Brown's Trial," *Leavenworth Daily Conservative,* August 4, 1867; McGinty, *John Brown's Trial* at 178.

13. Lawson, *American State Trials* at 6:766; McGinty, *John Brown's Trial* at 183.

14. Lawson, *American State Trials* at 6:778–99.

15. Barry, *Annals of Harper's Ferry* at 44. The verdict is quoted in Lawson, *American State Trials* at 6:799–800.

16. Lawson, *American State Trials* at 6:801. Judge Parker's remark is from the same source.

17. Fellman, *God and Country* at 40.

18. Phillips, *Speeches, Lectures and Letters* at 272.

19. Reynolds, *John Brown* at 357, 367. Emerson made the "gallows glorious" statement in a lecture titled "Courage," which he delivered in the Boston Music Hall in November 1859. Emerson, "Courage," *Complete Works* at 7:434. Henry Thoreau may have been even more prescient, observing that "when you plant . . . a hero in his field, a crop of heroes is sure to spring up." Quoted in Baptist, *The Half Has Never Been Told* at 395.

20. *Baltimore Sun,* October 31, 1859; *New York Tribune,* November 12, 1859; *Richmond Enquirer,* December 20, 1859; Galbreath, "Edwin Coppoc," *Ohio History* (October 1921) at 448.

21. Lawson, *American State Trials* at 6:806.

CHAPTER TWENTY-TWO. AN ABOLITION HARANGUE

1. Sennott arrived on November 2 in the company of Judge Thomas Russell, also of Boston. Sennott's initial assignment had been to secure Brown's personal property, but he enthusiastically expanded his role when he discovered the greater need for trial counsel. *New York Tribune,* November 12 and 19, 1859. Brown's six previous lawyers were Lawson Botts, Thomas Green, Charles Faulkner, George Hoyt, Samuel Chilton, and Hiram Griswold.

2. *New York Tribune,* November 12, 1859.

3. Cleon Moore to David Hunter Strother [Porte Crayon], November 4, 1859 (Stutler Collection, West Virginia Memory Project, West Virginia State Archives).

4. Matthews, *Rufus Choate* at 190–242. Regarding Choate's excellent advocacy on behalf of the powerful, see Dana, "Cruelty to Seamen," *American Jurist* (October 1839) at 92.

5. Altherr, "Convention of Moral Lunatics," *Vermont History* (Vol. 69, 2001) symposium supplement at 91, 96; Lerner, *Grimké Sisters.*

6. Free Convention, *Proceedings of the Free Convention Held at Rutland, Vermont, July 25th, 26th, and 27th, 1858* at 109–18. The pamphlet is evidently mistitled, as the Free Convention was actually held in June.

7. *The Liberator,* July 9, 1858.

8. *Boston Daily Advertiser,* July 10, 1879.

9. *New York Tribune,* November 19, 1859.

10. *New York Tribune,* November 12, 1859. The local newspaper was the *Spirit of Jefferson,* which was quoted at length in the *Tribune* article. Sennott's reaction is found in "Speech of George Sennott, Esq., before the Virginia Legislature," delivered March 8, 1860, printed in *The Liberator,* April 6, 1860.

11. *Spirit of Jefferson,* quoted in *New York Tribune,* November 12, 1859.

12. Lawson, *American State Trials* at 6:810–11.

13. Douglass, *Life and Times* at 387.

14. *New York Tribune,* November 7, 1859.

15. *Dred Scott v. Sandford,* 60 U.S. 393 (1857).

16. *New York Tribune,* November 12, 1859.

17. *New York Herald*, November 10, 1859; *New York Tribune*, November 12, 1859.
18. *New York Tribune*, November 12, 1859.

CHAPTER TWENTY-THREE. ONLY SLAVE STEALING

1. Strother, "Trial of the Conspirators," *Harper's Weekly* (November 12, 1859).
2. Rebecca Spring interview, September 9, 1908 (Villard Papers, Columbia University).
3. *New York Tribune*, November 19, 1859. The quoted colloquy occurred during one of the other Charlestown trials, but it is typical of the voir dire questions that Parker is known to have used in every case.
4. Lawson, *American State Trials* at 6:810–11.
5. *Cleveland Daily Herald*, November 1, 1859.
6. *New York Tribune*, November 12, 1859.
7. *Richmond Enquirer*, November 11, 1859.
8. *New York Tribune*, November 12, 1859.
9. Parker, "Notes on the trial of John Brown and his associates, 25 October – 14 November, 1859" (Paul Mellon Collection, University of Virginia Library).
10. *Richmond Enquirer*, November 1, 1859.
11. *Baltimore American*, November 9, 1859.
12. *Baltimore American*, November 11, 1859.
13. All quotations from Voorhees's argument are taken from Voorhees, "Defense of John E. Cook," in *Forty Years of Oratory* at 2:379–402. For a full account of Cook's life and trial, see Lubet, *John Brown's Spy*.
14. *Richmond Enquirer*, October 25, 1859.
15. *Virginia Free Press*, November 17, 1859; *Baltimore American*, November 12, 1859.
16. *Virginia Free Press*, November 17, 1859; *Baltimore American*, November 12, 1859; *Dawson's Daily Times*, November 19, 1859; *New York Tribune*, November 19, 1859.
17. *Cleveland Daily Herald*, November 1, 1859.
18. *New York Herald*, November 10, 1859.
19. *Virginia Free Press*, November 17, 1859.
20. *New York Tribune*, November 19, 1859. For more on Brown's African-American supporters, see Libby, Geffert, and Taylor, *John Brown Mysteries*, and Quarles, *Allies for Freedom*.
21. *Dawson's Daily Times*, November 19, 1859; *Virginia Free Press*, November 17, 1859.
22. *Baltimore American*, November 12, 1859; *New York Tribune*, November 19, 1859. Death Warrants for John E. Cooke, Shields Green, and John Copeland, November 10, 1859 (John Brown Papers, Jefferson County Circuit Clerk's Office). There was also a death warrant for Edwin Coppoc, but it has not survived in the records of the court.
23. *Virginia Free Press*, November 17, 1859.
24. McGinty, *John Brown's Trial* at 241–48.
25. *Richmond Enquirer*, November 25, 1859.
26. Villard, *John Brown* at 570; Galbreath, "Edwin Coppoc," *Ohio History* (October 1921) at 428.
27. *New York Tribune*, December 17, 1859. A similar inquiry came from the black citizens of New Bedford. *The Liberator*, December 16, 1859.
28. Endorsement of H. A. W. (Henry A. Wise), November 12, 1859, on Thomas P. Devereux to Henry Wise, November 10, 1859 (Wise Family Papers, Library of Congress) (noncapitalization original).
29. *St. Louis Globe-Democrat*, April 8, 1888. Hunter repeated the claim a decade later, saying, "If it had been possible to recommend a pardon for any of them it would have been for this man Copeland." Hunter, "John Brown's Raid," *Publications of the Southern History Association* (July 1897) at 188 (nonpunctuation in original).

30. Parker, "Trial of John Brown and His Associates" (Paul Mellon Collection, University of Virginia Library).

31. Parker, "Richard Parker to Andrew Hunter, December 26, 1859," *Proceedings of the Massachusetts Historical Society* (December 1912) at 245 (spelling original).

32. Hunter, "John Brown's Raid," *Publications of the Southern History Association* (July 1897) at 188; "The Trial of John Brown: Its Secret History, Revealed for the First Time by the Judge," *St. Louis Globe-Democrat*, April 8, 1886. Andrew Hunter to Henry Wise, November 4, 1859 (Wise Family Papers, Library of Congress). M[atthew] Johnson to Hon. Andrew Hunter, November 15, 1859 (Library of Virginia), published in *Virginia Magazine of History and Biography* (July 1902) at 280–82. In early 1860, Andrew Hunter did describe Copeland somewhat favorably as "a mulatto, a smart, intelligent fellow," but he said nothing about a purported desire for clemency, which he would not mention for another twenty-five years. Andrew Hunter Testimony, United States Congress, *Report of the Select Committee of the Senate* at 64.

33. John Copeland, Sr., to My Dear Son, October 31, 1859 (Villard Papers, Columbia University Library).

34. John A. Copeland, Jr., to Dear Father & Mother, November 26, 1859 (Oberlin College Archives).

CHAPTER TWENTY-FOUR. This Guilty Land

1. G. L. Kile to M. Johnson, U.S. Marshal, November 11, 1859 (Library of Virginia), published in *Virginia Magazine of History and Biography* (July 1902) at 279–80; M[atthew] Johnson to Hon. Andrew Hunter, November 15, 1859 (Library of Virginia), published in *Virginia Magazine of History and Biography* (July 1902) at 280–82.

2. Quoted in Villard, *John Brown* at 523. Some militant abolitionists – including Thomas Wentworth Higginson, Lysander Spooner, and Richard Hinton – had in fact explored various "wild rescue schemes," but nothing ever came of their fanciful plotting. Brown himself discouraged all talk of a rescue. Reynolds, *John Brown* at 379, 389.

3. *New York Times*, December 3, 1859; Sanborn, *Life and Letters* at 625.

4. It was widely reported that Brown had given coins to his comrades, but there were almost no negative comments on the gifts. The one exception was the *Oberlin Evangelist*, which opined that "the giving of a quarter of a dollar apiece to several of his fellow-prisoners on the morning of the execution, *that* was a little *daft*!" *Oberlin Evangelist*, January 4, 1860.

5. Strother, "Eyewitness Account of the Execution of John Brown," unpublished manuscript, December 1859 (Stutler Collection, West Virginia State Archives).

6. Hinton, *John Brown and His Men* at 484–85; Villard, *John Brown* at 554.

7. *New York Times*, December 3, 1859.

8. Hinton, *John Brown and His Men* at 398; Ruchames, *John Brown Reader* at 167.

9. Ruffin, *Diary* at 369–70.

10. J. T. L. Preston, "Execution of John Brown," *The Southern Bivouac* (August 1886).

11. Quoted in Trodd and Stauffer, *Meteor of War* at 214.

12. C. Langston, "Speech in Cleveland," in *Tribute of Respect* at 19, 21.

13. Quoted in Horwitz, *Midnight Rising* at 259.

14. Davis, "Remarks to the U.S. Senate, December 8, 1859," quoted in Trodd and Stauffer, *Meteor of War* at 260. Davis's speech was delivered on the day of Brown's funeral, which was held in North Elba, New York.

15. Ruffin, *Diary* at 366–67, 372.

16. John A. Copeland to Dear Father & Mother, November 26, 1859 (Oberlin College Archives).

17. John A. Copeland to My Dear Brother, December 10, 1859, printed in *Oberlin Evangelist*, December 21, 1859.

18. John A. Copeland to Friend Halbert, December 10, 1859 (Villard Papers, Columbia University Library).

19. John A. Copeland to Oberlin Anti-Slavery Society, December 11, 1859 (Villard Papers, Columbia University Library).

20. John Copeland to Dear Elias [Jones], undated, December 1859 (Library of Virginia).

21. John A. Copeland to Solomon Grimes, December 14, 1859 (Rust Collection, Huntington Library).

22. John A. Copeland to Dear Father, Mother, Brothers Henry, William and Freddy, and Sisters Sarah and Mary, December 16, 1859, *Oberlin Evangelist*, January 4, 1860.

23. *Oberlin Evangelist*, January 4, 1860.

24. John A. Copeland to Dear Father, Mother, Brothers Henry, William and Freddy, and Sisters Sarah and Mary, December 16, 1859, *Oberlin Evangelist*, January 4, 1860.

25. *New York Times*, December 17, 1859.

26. *New York Tribune*, December 3, 1859.

27. *New York Tribune*, December 17, 1859; *Virginia Free Press*, December 22, 1859; *Richmond Enquirer*, December 20, 1859; *Shepherdstown Register*, December 24, 1859.

28. *New York Tribune*, December 17, 1859; *Cincinnati Gazette*, December 16, 1859; George Mauzy to Eugenia Burton, December 18, 1859 (capitalization original) (Stutler Collection, West Virginia Memory Project, West Virginia Archives).

29. DeCaro, *Fire from the Midst of You* at 267. Brown was unyielding, saying that such prayers "would be an abomination to God." Hinton, *John Brown and His Men* at 430.

30. *Baltimore Sun*, December 19, 1859; *Shepherdstown Register*, December 24, 1859.

31. "Memoir of Rev. George V. Leech" (Villard Papers, Columbia University).

32. *Baltimore Sun*, December 19, 1859; *Shepherdstown Register*, December 24, 1859. According to the *Baltimore Sun*, Copeland complied with a request for his autograph from Avis's son, writing "Jno. A. Copeland was born at Raleigh, North Carolina, August 15, 1834" (abbreviation in original).

CHAPTER TWENTY-FIVE. THE COLORED AMERICAN HEROES

1. This chapter is adapted from Lubet, ""Execution in Virginia," 91 *North Carolina Law Review* 1785 (2013).

2. *Richmond Enquirer*, December 20, 1859; "A Monument," *Anglo-African Magazine* (January 14, 1860). Regarding the right of a condemned prisoner to make a final speech from the gallows, see Banner, *Death Penalty* at 24.

3. *Richmond Enquirer*, December 20, 1859.

4. *New York Tribune*, January 6, 1860.

5. *New York Tribune*, January 6, 1860. The Bible quotation is from the Book of John, Chapter 14.

6. *New York Tribune*, January 6, 1860.

7. *Cincinnati Gazette*, December 16, 1859; *Richmond Enquirer*, December 20, 1859; Monroe, *Oberlin Thursday Lectures* at 170–71.

8. Horwitz, *Midnight Rising* at 243.

9. John Copeland to His Excellency, December 4, 1859 (Wise Family Papers, Library of Congress).

10. To His Excellency Gov. Wise, December 12, 1859 (Wise Family Papers, Library of Congress) (nonpunctuation in original).

11. Endorsement by hand of H. A. Wise, December 12, 1859 (Wise Family Papers, Library of Congress).

12. A. N. Beecher to H. A. Wise, December 17, 1859 (Wise Family Papers, Library of Congress).

13. Endorsement by hand of H. A. Wise, December 19, 1859 (Wise Family Papers, Library of Congress).

14. Quarles, *Allies for Freedom* at 140. A more aggressive request came from a group of citizens of Orange, New Jersey, including Oberlin alumna Lucy Stone. Apparently unaware of Copeland's family, and calling themselves "the abolitionists of this town," they petitioned Wise to be given the bodies of Copeland and Green for Christian burial. Wise did not reply. Henry Blackwell and others to His Excellency Henry Wise, December 14, 1859 (Wise Family Papers, Library of Congress).

15. *Cincinnati Gazette*, December 16, 1859; *Richmond Enquirer*, December 20, 1859; Monroe, *Oberlin Thursday Lectures* at 170–71. Wise's statement is in Quarles, *Allies for Freedom* at 141.

16. *Oberlin Evangelist*, January 4, 1860.

17. Unless noted otherwise, the story of James Monroe's journey to Virginia is taken from his 1897 memoir, *Oberlin Thursday Lectures* at 158–84. H. G. Blake to James Monroe and Henry Peck, September 6, 1858 (Oberlin College Archives).

18. Monroe, *Oberlin Thursday Lectures* at 166 (italics in original). The "spirituousness" of the youths referred to their insobriety as well as their rowdiness. See, for example, Rush, *Enquiry into the Effects of Spirituous Liquors*. Concerning Hoyt's ill treatment, see *The Liberator*, November 25, 1859.

19. "Life of H. G. Blake written by himself at request of Capt. Chas. Blake," undated typescript (Gloria Brown Collection, Medina, Ohio).

20. H. G. Blake to James Monroe, December 1, 1859 (James Monroe Papers, Oberlin College Archives); *Medina Gazette*, December 8, 1859; Land, "John Brown's Ohio Environment," *Ohio Archaeological and Historical Quarterly* (January 1948) at 24, 43; Stegmaier, "Ohio Republican Stirs up the House," *Ohio History* 116 (2009) at 62, 65.

21. Monroe, *Oberlin Thursday Lectures* at 167.

22. Monroe, *Oberlin Thursday Lectures* at 167.

23. Monroe, *Oberlin Thursday Lectures* at 168.

24. Monroe, *Oberlin Thursday Lectures* at 170.

25. Monroe, *Oberlin Thursday Lectures* at 171.

26. Monroe, *Oberlin Thursday Lectures* at 172–73.

27. Monroe, *Oberlin Thursday Lectures* at 175.

28. Monroe, *Oberlin Thursday Lectures* at 174.

29. "A Monument," *Anglo-African Magazine* (January 14, 1860).

30. Nell, *Colored Patriots* at 14–15.

31. Nell, *Colored Patriots* at 20. In 1858, Nell successfully organized an observance of the Boston Massacre "for the first time since the Revolutionary War." The event, which recognized Attucks's martyrdom, was held annually until 1865. A monument to the Boston Massacre victims, including Attucks, was finally built in 1888. Minardi, *Making Slavery History* at 162–63.

32. William Cooper Nell to Thomas Wentworth Higginson, February 6, 1860 (Anti-Slavery Collections, Boston Public Library); W. C. Nell to Dear Mr. Editor, June 17, 1861, *Pine and Palm*, July 6, 1861; *The Liberator*, February 24, 1860.

33. *Oberlin Evangelist*, July 30, 1862.

34. Undated handbill, *The Provincial Freedman* (Mary Ann Shadd Cary Papers, Howard University); Quarles, *Allies for Freedom* at 136.

35. Shields Green's name is also on the cenotaph because James Monroe erroneously believed that he had known Green in Oberlin. The mistake was discovered, but it was retained as a gesture of respect for his sacrifice. "A Monument," *Anglo-African Magazine* (January 14, 1860). At one point, the Oberliners also considered including Dangerfield Newby's name on their monument, but it was ultimately decided to include only those who were once believed to have some connection to Oberlin. J. M. Fitch to James Redpath, July 17, 1860 (Richard Hinton Collection, Kansas State Historical Society).

Epilogue

1. *New York Tribune*, December 17, 1859; *Shepherdstown Register*, December 21 and 24, 1859 (spelling original); *Richmond Enquirer*, December 20, 1859.

2. O. P. Anderson to R. J. Hinton, October 13, 1860 (Hinton Collection, Kansas State Historical Society).

3. *Congressional Globe*, Thirty-Sixth Congress, First session (April 16, 1860); *Cleveland Morning Leader*, January 27, 1860.

4. *Cleveland Morning Leader*, February 21, 1860.

5. Mrs. D. E. Copeland to F. G. Adams, July 13, 1887 (Villard Papers, Columbia University).

6. *Oberlin Weekly News*, August 19, 1881; *Oberlin Review*, February 6, 1886.

7. Hughes, *Big Sea* at 12.

8. "October the Sixteenth," in Hughes, *Collected Works* at 2:84.

9. Barber, "Niagara Movement at Harper's Ferry," *Voice of the Negro* (October 1906) at 403, 410 (spelling in original); Rudwick, "Niagara Movement," *Journal of Negro History* (July 1957) at 180.

10. Barber, "Niagara Movement at Harper's Ferry," *Voice of the Negro* (October 1906) at 409–10.

11. Barber, "Niagara Movement at Harper's Ferry," *Voice of the Negro* (October 1906) at 403, 410.

12. Barber, "Niagara Movement at Harper's Ferry," *Voice of the Negro* (October 1906) at 405, 410.

13. The Niagara meeting in Oberlin was held almost fifty years to the day after John Copeland had escorted John Price to Canada, and it was observed by "the few white haired survivors of the Oberlin-Wellington rescue." *Oberlin Tribune*, September 11, 1908. Concerning the transition to the NAACP, see Rudwick, "Niagara Movement," *Journal of Negro History* (July 1957) at 195–98.

BIBLIOGRAPHY

ARCHIVES, COLLECTIONS, AND DEPOSITORIES

Horatio Nelson Rust Collection, Huntington Library, San Marino, CA
Frank Logan/John Brown Collection, Chicago History Museum, Chicago, IL
Richard Hinton Collection, Kansas State Historical Society, Topeka, KS
Records of the Accounting Officers of the Department of the Treasury, National Archives, College Park, MD
Records of the Department of Justice, National Archives, College Park, MD
U.S. Census Reports, 1830–1870, Bureau of the Census, Department of Commerce, Suitland, MD
Anti-Slavery Collections, Boston Public Library, Boston, MA
Stevens Family Papers, Massachusetts Historical Society, Boston, MA
Oswald Garrison Villard Papers, Columbia University Library, New York, NY
Gerrit Smith Papers, Syracuse University, Syracuse, NY
Thomas Ruffin Papers, University of North Carolina Library, Chapel Hill, NC
North Carolina State Archives, Raleigh, NC
Superior Court of Wake County, North Carolina
Palmer Collection, Western Reserve Historical Society, Cleveland, OH
Marriage Index, Lorain County, Ohio, 1824–1865, Cuyahoga County Public Library, Fairview Park, OH
Gloria Brown Collection, Medina, OH
Oberlin College Archives, Oberlin, OH
Paul Mellon Collection, University of Virginia Library, Charlottesville, VA
Henry Wise Executive Papers, Library of Virginia, Richmond, VA
Calendar of Virginia State Papers, vol. 11 (January 1, 1836 to April 15, 1869), State Capitol, Richmond, VA
Wise Family Papers, Library of Congress, Washington, DC
Mary Ann Shadd Cary Papers, Howard University, Washington, DC
John Brown Papers, Jefferson County Circuit Clerk's Office, Charles Town, WV
Boyd B. Stutler Collection, West Virginia Memory Project, West Virginia State Archives, Charleston, WV
West Virginia Historical Art Collection, University of West Virginia, Morgantown, WV
Chatham-Kent Black Historical Society, Chatham, Ontario

Black Abolitionist Papers, bap.chadwyck.com
West Virginia Division of Forestry, www.wvforestry.com

NEWSPAPERS

Alexandria Gazette, Alexandria, VA
American Missionary, New York, NY
Anti-Slavery Bugle, New Lisbon, OH
Baltimore American, Baltimore, MD
Baltimore Sun, Baltimore, MD
Boston Courier, Boston, MA
Boston Daily Advertiser, Boston, MA
Boston Traveler, Boston, MA
Carolina Observer, Fayetteville, NC
Charleston Mercury, Charleston, SC
Charlestown Independent Democrat, Charlestown, VA [WV]
Chatham Weekly Planet, Chatham, Ontario
Cincinnati Enquirer, Cincinnati, OH
Cincinnati Gazette, Cincinnati, OH
Cleveland Daily Herald, Cleveland, OH
Cleveland Morning Leader, Cleveland, OH
Cleveland Plain Dealer, Cleveland, OH
Congressional Globe, Washington, DC
Dawson's Daily Times, Fort Wayne, IN
Evening Post, Philadelphia, PA
Holmes County Republican, Millersburg, OH
Leavenworth Daily Conservative, Leavenworth, KS
The Liberator, Boston, MA
Maysville Eagle, Maysville, KY
Medina Gazette, Medina, OH
National Anti-Slavery Standard, New York, NY; Philadelphia, PA
National Democrat, Cleveland, OH
New-Hampshire Patriot, Concord, NH
New York Herald, New York, NY
New York Times, New York, NY
New York Tribune, New York, NY
North Star/Frederick Douglass' Paper, Rochester, NY
Oberlin Evangelist, Oberlin, OH
Oberlin News, Oberlin, OH
Oberlin Review, Oberlin, OH
Oberlin Tribune, Oberlin, OH
Oberlin Weekly News, Oberlin, OH
Ohio Statesman, Columbus, OH
Perrysburg Journal, Perrysburg, OH
The Philanthropist, Cincinnati, OH
Pine and Palm, Boston, MA
Pittsburgh Daily Gazette and Advertiser, Pittsburgh, PA
Richmond Enquirer, Richmond, VA

Savannah Daily Morning News, Savannah, GA
Shepherdstown Register, Shepherdstown, VA [WV]
St. Louis Globe-Democrat, St. Louis, MO
Virginia Free Press, Charlestown, VA [WV]

BOOKS

Alcott, Amos Bronson. *The Journals of Bronson Alcott*, ed. Odell Shepard. Port Washington, NY: Kennikat Press, 1966.

Alexander, Roberta Sue. "The Willson Era: The Inception of the Northern District of Ohio, 1855–67," in *Justice and Legal Change on the Shores of Lake Erie: A History of the U.S. District Court for the Northern District of Ohio*, ed. Paul Finkelman and Roberta Sue Alexander. Athens: Ohio University Press, 2012. 15–36.

American Foreign and Anti-Slavery Society. "The Fugitive Slave Bill; Its History and Unconstitutionality; With an Account of the Seizure and Enslavement of James Hamlet, and His Subsequent Restoration to Liberty," reproduced in *Slavery, Race, and the American Legal System, 1700–1872*, ser. 2, vol. 1: *Fugitive Slaves and the American Courts: The Pamphlet Literature*, ed. Paul Finkelman. New York: Garland, 1988.535.

Anderson, Osborne Perry. *A Voice from Harper's Ferry*. Freeport, NY: Books for Libraries Press, 1972.

Baker, H. Robert. *Prigg v. Pennsylvania: Slavery, the Supreme Court, and the Ambivalent Constitution*. Lawrence: University Press of Kansas, 2012.

Baker, Jean H. *James Buchanan*. New York: Times Books, 2004.

Ball, Erica L. *To Live an Antislavery Life: Personal Politics and the Antebellum Black Middle Class*. Athens: University of Georgia Press, 2012.

Ballantine, William G., ed. *Oberlin Jubilee, 1833–1883*. Oberlin, OH: E. J. Goodrich, 1883.

Banner, Stuart. *The Death Penalty in American History*. Cambridge, MA: Harvard University Press, 2003.

Baptist, Edward. *The Half Has Never Been Told: Slavery and the Making of American Capitalism*. New York: Basic Books, 2014.

Barfield, Rodney. *America's Forgotten Caste: Free Blacks in Antebellum Virginia and North Carolina*. Bloomington, IN: XLIBRIS, 2013.

Barry, Joseph. *The Annals of Harper's Ferry*. Hagerstown, MD: Dechert, 1869.

______. *The Strange Story of Harper's Ferry: With Legends of the Surrounding Country*. Martinsburg, WV: Thompson Brothers, 1903.

Baumann, Roland M. *Constructing Black Education at Oberlin College: A Documentary History*. Athens: Ohio University Press, 2010.

______. *The 1858 Oberlin-Wellington Rescue: A Reappraisal*. Oberlin, OH: Oberlin College, 2003.

Berlin, Ira. *Generations of Captivity: A History of African-American Slaves*. Cambridge, MA: Belknap Press of Harvard University Press, 2003.

______. *Slaves without Masters: The Free Negro in the Antebellum South*. New York: New Press, 1992.

Bigglestone, William E. *They Stopped in Oberlin*. Oberlin, OH: Oberlin College, 2002.

Blackwell, Alice Stone. *Lucy Stone: Pioneer of Women's Rights.* Boston: Little, Brown, 1930.

Blodgett, Geoffrey. *Oberlin History: Essays and Impressions.* Kent, OH: Kent State University Press, 2006.

Blue, Frederick J. *No Taint of Compromise: Crusaders in Antislavery Politics.* Baton Rouge: Louisiana State University Press, 2005.

———. *Salmon P. Chase: A Life in Politics.* Kent, OH: Kent State University Press, 1987.

Bonner, Robert E. *Mastering America: Southern Slaveholders and the Crisis of American Nationhood.* Cambridge: Cambridge University Press, 2009.

Bordewich, Fergus M. *America's Great Debate: Henry Clay, Stephen A. Douglas, and the Compromise That Preserved the Union.* New York: Simon and Schuster, 2012.

Brandt, Nat. *The Town That Started the Civil War.* Syracuse, NY: Syracuse University Press, 1990.

Brandt, Nat, and Yanna Kroyt Brandt. *In the Shadow of the Civil War: Passmore Williamson and the Rescue of Jane Johnson.* Columbia: University of South Carolina Press, 2007.

Breen, Patrick. "A Prophet in His Own Land: Support for Nat Turner and His Rebellion within Southampton's Black Community," in *Nat Turner: A Slave Rebellion in History and Memory,* ed. Kenneth S. Greenberg, New York: Oxford University Press, 2003. 103–18.

Brigance, William N. *Jeremiah Sullivan Black: A Defender of the Constitution and the Ten Commandments.* Philadelphia: University of Pennsylvania Press, 1934.

Brown, William Wells. "Narrative of William W. Brown, a Fugitive Slave," in *I Was Born a Slave: An Anthology of Classic Slave Narratives,* ed. Yuval Taylor. Chicago: Lawrence Hill Books, 1999. 703.

Calhoun, Frederick. *The Lawmen: United States Marshals and Their Deputies, 1789–1989.* Washington, DC: Smithsonian Institution Press, 1989.

Campbell, Stanley Wallace. *The Slave Catchers: Enforcement of the Fugitive Slave Law, 1850–1860.* Chapel Hill: University of North Carolina Press, 1970.

Carton, Evan. *Patriotic Treason: John Brown and the Soul of America.* New York: Free Press, 2006.

Cheek, William F., and Aimee Lee Cheek. *John Mercer Langston and the Fight for Black Freedom.* Urbana: University of Illinois Press, 1989.

———. "John Mercer Langston: Principle and Politics," in *Black Leaders of the Nineteenth Century,* ed. Leon Litwack and August Meier. Urbana: University of Illinois Press, 1988. 110.

Clarke, Louis Garrard. *Narratives of the Sufferings of Lewis and Milton Clarke, Sons of a Soldier of the Revolution, During a Captivity of More than Twenty Years among the Slaveholders of Kentucky, Dictated by Themselves.* Boston: B. Marsh, 1846.

Cobb, Thomas Read Rootes. *An Inquiry into the Law of Negro Slavery in the United States of America: To which is Prefixed, an Historical Sketch of Slavery.* Philadelphia: T. and J. W. Johnson, 1858.

Cochran, William Cox. *The Western Reserve and the Fugitive Slave Law: A Prelude to the Civil War.* Cleveland, OH: Western Reserve Historical Society, 1920.

Cook[e], John E. *Confession of John E. Cooke, Brother-in-Law of Gov. A. P. Willard of Indiana, and One of the Participants in the Harper's Ferry Invasion.* Charlestown, VA: D. Smith Eichelberger, 1859.

Crafts, Hannah. *The Bondwoman's Narrative*, ed. Henry Louis Gates, Jr. New York: Grand Central Publishing, 2002.

Dana, Richard Henry. *The Journal of Richard Henry Dana*, vol. 1, ed. Robert F. Lucid. Cambridge, MA: Belknap Press of Harvard University Press, 1968.

Davis, David Brion. *The Problem of Slavery in the Age of Emancipation*. New York: Alfred A. Knopf, 2014.

Davis, Jefferson. "Remarks to the U.S. Senate, December 8, 1859," in *Meteor of War: The John Brown Story*, ed. Zoe Trodd and John Stauffer. Philadelphia: Brandywine Press, 2004. 260.

DeCaro, Louis A. *Fire from the Midst of You: A Religious Life of John Brown*. New York: New York University Press, 2002.

———. *John Brown: The Cost of Freedom*. New York: International Publishers Co., 2007.

———. *John Brown, Emancipator*. lulu.com, 2012.

———. *John Brown: The Man Who Lived*. lulu.com, 2008.

Delbanco, Andrew. *The Abolitionist Imagination*. Cambridge, MA: Harvard University Press, 2012.

Dillon, Merton. "John Parker and the Underground Railroad," in *Builders of Ohio: A Biographical History*, ed. Warren Van Tine and Michael Pierce. Columbus: Ohio State University Press, 2003. 99.

Douglass, Frederick. "John Brown," in *Frederick Douglass: Selected Speeches and Writings*, ed. Philip Foner and Yuval Taylor. Chicago: Lawrence Hill Books, 1999. 633.

———. *The Life and Times of Frederick Douglass*. New York: Collier Books, 1971.

DuBois, W. E. B. *John Brown: A Biography*. Philadelphia: G. W. Jacobs, 1909.

Early Settlers Association of Cuyahoga County. *Annals of the Early Settlers Association of Cuyahoga County*, vol. 3, no. 1. Cleveland, OH: Williams, 1892.

Emerson, Ralph Waldo. *The Complete Works of Ralph Waldo Emerson*. New York: Houghton Mifflin, 1903–04.

Essig, James. "The Lord's Free Man: Charles G. Finney and His Abolitionism," in *Abolitionism and American Religion*, ed. John R. McKivigan. London: Routledge, 1999. 319.

Etcheson, Nicole. *Bleeding Kansas: Contested Liberty in the Civil War Era*. Lawrence: University Press of Kansas, 2004.

Fairchild, Edward Henry. *Historical Sketch of Oberlin College*. Springfield, OH: Republic Printing, 1868.

Fairchild, James Harris. "Baccalaureate Sermon: Providential Aspects of the Oberlin Enterprise," in *Oberlin Jubilee, 1833–1883*, ed. W. G. Ballantine. Oberlin, OH: E. J. Goodrich, 1883. 95.

———. *Oberlin: The Colony and the College. 1833–1883*. Oberlin, OH: E. J. Goodrich, 1883.

———. *The Underground Railroad*. Cleveland, OH: Western Reserve Historical Society, 1895.

Fellman, Michael. *In the Name of God and Country: Reconsidering Terrorism in American History*. New Haven, CT: Yale University Press, 2010.

Finkelman, Paul, ed. *Slavery, Race, and the American Legal System, 1700–1872*, ser. 2: *Fugitive Slaves and the American Courts: The Pamphlet Literature*. New York: Garland, 1988.

Finkelman, Paul, and Roberta Sue Alexander, eds. *Justice and Legal Change on the Shores of Lake Erie: A History of the U.S. District Court for the Northern District of Ohio.* Athens: Ohio University Press, 2012.

Finney, Charles Grandison. *Charles G. Finney: An Autobiography.* Westwood, NJ: Fleming H. Revell, 1908.

———. *Lectures on Revivals of Religion.* Cambridge, MA: Belknap Press of Harvard University Press, 1960.

Fletcher, Robert Samuel. *A History of Oberlin College from Its Foundation through the Civil War.* Oberlin, OH: Oberlin College, 1943.

Foner, Eric. *Gateway to Freedom: The Hidden History of the Underground Railroad.* New York: W. W. Norton, 2015.

Foner, Philip S. *History of Black Americans,* vol. 3: *From the Compromise of 1850 to the End of the Civil War.* Westport, CT: Greenwood Press, 1983.

Foner, Philip S., and Yuval Taylor, eds. *Frederick Douglass: Selected Speeches and Writings.* Chicago: Lawrence Hill Books, 1999.

Forbes, Ella. *But We Have No Country: The 1851 Christiana, Pennsylvania Resistance.* Cherry Hill, NJ: Africana Homestead Legacy, 1998.

Ford, Lacy K. *Deliver Us from Evil: The Slavery Question in the Old South.* New York: Oxford University Press, 2009.

Franklin, John Hope. *The Free Negro in North Carolina, 1790–1860.* Chapel Hill: University of North Carolina Press, 1995.

Frederickson, Mary E., and Delores M. Walters, eds. *Gendered Resistance: Women, Slavery, and the Legacy of Margaret Garner.* Urbana: University of Illinois Press, 2013.

Free Convention. *Proceedings of the Free Convention Held at Rutland, Vermont, July 25th, 26th, and 27th, 1858.* Pamphlet. Boston: J. B. Yerrinton and Son, 1858.

French, Scot. *The Rebellious Slave: Nat Turner in American Memory.* Boston: Houghton Mifflin, 2004.

Frothingham, Octavius Brooks. *Gerrit Smith: A Biography.* New York: G. P. Putnam's Sons, 1879.

Geffert, Hannah, and Jean Libby. "Regional Black Involvement in John Brown's Raid on Harper's Ferry," in *Prophets of Protest: Reconsidering the History of American Abolitionism,* ed. Timothy McCarthy and John Stauffer. New York: New Press, 2006. 169.

Goldfield, David R. *America Aflame: How the Civil War Created a Nation.* New York: Bloomsbury Press, 2011.

Goodrich, Thomas. *War to the Knife: Bleeding Kansas, 1854–1861.* Mechanicsburg, PA: Stackpole Books, 1998.

Golway, Terry. *Washington's General: Nathanael Greene and the Triumph of the American Revolution.* New York: Henry Holt, 2004.

Gordon-Reed, Annette. *The Hemingses of Monticello: An American Family.* New York: W. W. Norton, 2008.

Greenberg, Kenneth S., ed. *Nat Turner: A Slave Rebellion in History and Memory.* New York: Oxford University Press, 2003.

Greene, Robert Ewell. *The Leary-Evans, Ohio's Free People of Color.* Washington: Hickman Printing, 1989.

Greenspan, Ezra. *William Wells Brown: A Reader.* Athens: University of Georgia Press, 2008.

Grinnell, Josiah Bushnell. *Men and Events of Forty Years: Autobiographical Reminiscences of an Active Career from 1850 to 1890.* Boston: D. Lothrop, 1891.

Hambrick-Stowe, Charles E. *Charles G. Finney and the Spirit of American Evangelicalism.* Grand Rapids, MI: W. B. Eerdmans, 1996.

Harrold, Stanley. *Border War: Fighting over Slavery before the Civil War.* Chapel Hill: University of North Carolina Press, 2010.

Hatcher, Harlan Henthorne. *The Western Reserve: The Story of New Connecticut in Ohio.* Indianapolis: Bobbs-Merrill, 1949.

Higginson, Thomas Wentworth. *Contemporaries.* New York: Houghton Mifflin, 1899.

Hinton, Richard. *John Brown and His Men.* New York: Funk and Wagnalls, 1894.

Hochschild, Adam. *Bury the Chains: The Struggle to Abolish Slavery.* London: Macmillan, 2005.

Holmes, David. *A Brief History of the Episcopal Church.* Valley Forge, PA: Trinity Press International, 1993.

Horwitz, Tony. *Midnight Rising: John Brown and the Raid That Sparked the Civil War.* New York: Henry Holt, 2011.

Hughes, Langston. *The Big Sea: An Autobiography.* New York: Alfred A. Knopf, 1940.

______. *The Collected Works of Langston Hughes,* vol. 2: *The Poems, 1941–1950,* ed. Arnold Rampersad. Columbia: University of Missouri Press, 2001.

Hurd, John. *Law of Freedom and Bondage.* Boston: Little, Brown, 1858.

Hurmence, Belinda, ed. *My Folks Don't Want Me to Talk about Slavery: Twenty-One Oral Histories of Former North Carolina Slaves.* Winston-Salem, NC: J.F. Blair, 1984.

Johannsen, Robert. *Stephen A. Douglas.* New York: Oxford University Press, 1973.

Jones, Howard. *Mutiny on the Amistad: The Saga of a Slave Revolt and Its Impact on American Abolition, Law, and Diplomacy.* New York: Oxford University Press, 1987.

Korda, Michael. *Clouds of Glory: The Life and Legend of Robert E. Lee.* New York: Harper, 2014.

Langston, Charles H. *A Tribute of Respect Commemorative of the Worth and Sacrifice of John Brown of Ossawatomie.* Cleveland: N.P., 1859.

Langston, John Mercer. *From the Virginia Plantation to the National Capitol.* North Stratford, NH: Ayer, 2002.

Lawson, Ellen NicKenzie, and Marlene D. Merrill, comps. *The Three Sarahs: Documents of Antebellum Black College Women.* New York: Edwin Mellen Press, 1984.

Lawson, John D. *American State Trials,* vol. 6. St. Louis: Thomas Law Books, 1916.

Lerner, Gerda. *The Grimké Sisters from South Carolina: Pioneers for Women's Rights and Abolition.* Chapel Hill: University of North Carolina Press, 2004.

Libby, Jean, Hannah N. Geffert, and Evelyn M. E. Taylor. *John Brown Mysteries.* Missoula, MT: Pictorial Histories Publishing, 1999.

Litwack, Leon, and August Meier, eds. *Black Leaders of the Nineteenth Century.* Urbana: University of Illinois Press, 1988.

Loguen, Jermain Wesley. *The Rev. J. W. Loguen as a Slave and as a Freeman: A Narrative of Real Life.* Syracuse, NY: J. G. K. Truair, 1859.

Lubet, Steven. *Fugitive Justice: Runaways, Rescuers, and Slavery on Trial.* Cambridge, MA: Belknap Press of Harvard University Press, 2010.

———. *John Brown's Spy: The Adventurous Life and Tragic Confession of John E. Cook.* New Haven, CT: Yale University Press, 2012.

Maltz, Earl M. *Fugitive Slave on Trial: The Anthony Burns Case and Abolitionist Outrage.* Lawrence: University Press of Kansas, 2010.

Marryat, Frederick. *A Diary in America: With Remarks on Its Institutions.* London: Longman, Orme, Brown, Green and Longmans, 1839.

Matthews, Jean V. *Rufus Choate: The Law and Civic Virtue.* Philadelphia: Temple University Press, 1980.

McCarthy, Timothy, and John Stauffer, eds. *Prophets of Protest: Reconsidering the History of American Abolitionism.* New York: New Press, 2006.

McGinty, Brian. *John Brown's Trial.* Cambridge, MA: Harvard University Press, 2009.

McGlone, Robert E. *John Brown's War against Slavery.* Cambridge: Cambridge University Press, 2009.

McKivigan, John R., ed. *Abolitionism and American Religion.* London: Routledge, 1999.

———. *The War against Proslavery Religion: Abolitionism and the Northern Churches, 1830–1865.* Ithaca, NY: Cornell University Press, 1984.

McKivigan, John, and Stanley Harrold, eds. *Antislavery Violence: Sectional, Racial, and Cultural Conflict in Antebellum America.* Knoxville: University of Tennessee Press, 1999.

McLaurin, Melton Alonza. *Celia, a Slave.* Athens: University of Georgia Press, 1991.

McPherson, James. *Battle Cry of Freedom: The Civil War Era.* New York: Oxford University Press, 1988.

Merrill, Marlene D. *Sarah Margru Kinson: The Two Worlds of an Amistad Captive.* Oberlin, OH: Oberlin Historical and Improvement Organization, 2003.

Minardi, Margot. *Making Slavery History: Abolitionism and the Politics of Memory in Massachusetts.* New York: Oxford University Press, 2010.

Monroe, James. *Oberlin Thursday Lectures, Addresses, and Essays.* Oberlin, OH: E. J. Goodrich, 1897.

Morris, J. Brent. *Oberlin, Hotbed of Abolitionism: College, Community, and the Fight for Freedom and Equality in Antebellum America.* Chapel Hill: University of North Carolina Press, 2014.

Nell, William Cooper. *Colored Patriots of the American Revolution.* London: Longman, Orme, Brown, Green and Longmans, 1839.

Niven, John. *Salmon P. Chase: A Biography.* New York: Oxford University Press, 1995.

———. *The Salmon P. Chase Papers,* vol. 1: *Journals, 1829–1872.* Kent, OH: Kent State University Press, 1993.

———. *The Salmon P. Chase Papers,* vol. 2: *Correspondence, 1823–1857.* Kent, OH: Kent State University Press, 1995.

Northup, Solomon. *Twelve Years a Slave.* Auburn: Derby and Miller, 1853.

Oakes, James. *Freedom National: The Destruction of Slavery in the United States, 1861–1865*. New York: W. W. Norton, 2013.

———. *The Ruling Race: A History of American Slaveholders*. New York: W. W. Norton, 1998.

———. *Slavery and Freedom: An Interpretation of the Old South*. New York: Alfred A. Knopf, 1990.

Oates, Stephen B. *The Fires of Jubilee: Nat Turner's Fierce Rebellion*. New York: Harper and Row, 1975.

Orth, John. "Thomas Ruffin," in *The Yale Biographical Dictionary of American Law*, ed. Roger Newman. New Haven, CT: Yale University Press, 2009.

Padgett, Chris. "Comeouterism and Antislavery Violence in Ohio's Western Reserve," in *Antislavery Violence: Sectional, Racial, and Cultural Conflict in Antebellum America*, ed. John McKivigan and Stanley Harrold. Knoxville: University of Tennessee Press, 1999. 200–01.

Parrillo, Nicholas R. *Against the Profit Motive: The Salary Revolution in American Government, 1780–1940*. New Haven, CT: Yale University Press, 2013.

Peeke, Hewson Lindsley. *A Standard History of Erie County, Ohio*. Chicago: Lewis Publishing, 1916.

Philips, Ulrich B. *Life and Labor in the Old South*. New York: Grosset and Dunlap, 1929.

Phillips, Wendell. *Speeches, Lectures and Letters*. Boston: J. Redpath, 1863.

Prichard, Robert. *A History of the Episcopal Church*. Harrisburg, PA: Morehouse, 1991.

Quarles, Benjamin. *Allies for Freedom: Blacks and John Brown*. Cambridge, MA: Da Capo Press, 2001 (new edition).

Quillin, Frank Uriah. *The Color Line in Ohio: A History of Race Prejudice in a Typical Northern State*. Ann Arbor, MI: G. Wahr, 1913.

Quitt, Martin. *Stephen A. Douglas and Antebellum Democracy*. Cambridge: Cambridge University Press, 2012.

Rampersad, Arnold. *The Life of Langston Hughes*, vol. 1: *1902–1941: I, Too, Sing America*. New York: Oxford University Press, 2002.

Redpath, James. *The Public Life of Captain John Brown*. New York: William S. Hein, 1860.

Remini, Robert. *At the Edge of the Precipice: Henry Clay and the Compromise That Saved the Union*. New York: Basic Books, 2010.

Reynolds, David. *John Brown, Abolitionist: The Man Who Killed Slavery, Sparked the Civil War, and Seeded Civil Rights*. New York: Alfred A. Knopf, dist. Random House, 2005.

Ripley, C. Peter, and Roy E. Finkenbine et al., eds. *The Black Abolitionist Papers*, vol. 4: *The United States, 1847–1858*. Chapel Hill: University of North Carolina Press, 1991.

Ritner, Joseph. "Annual Message to the Assembly – 1836," in *Pennsylvania Archives*, ser. 4, vol. 6: *Papers of the Governors: 1832–1845*, ed. George Edward Reed. Harrisburg, PA: State of Pennsylvania, 1902. 282–334.

Robinson, Gwendolyn, and John W. Robinson. *Seek the Truth: A Story of Chatham's Black Community*. Chatham N.P., 1989.

de Roulhac Hamilton, Joseph G., ed. *The Papers of Thomas Ruffin*, vol. 1. New York: AMS Press, 1973.

______. "Thomas Ruffin," in *Dictionary of American Biography*, vol. 16: *Robert to Seward*, ed. Dumas Malone. New York: Charles Scribner's Sons, 1935.

Ruchames, Louis, ed. *John Brown: The Making of a Revolutionary*. New York: Grosset and Dunlap, 1969.

______. *A John Brown Reader: The Story of John Brown in His Own Words*. New York: Abelard-Schuman, 1959.

Ruffin, Edmund. *Diary of Edmund Ruffin*, vol. 1, ed. William Kauffman Scarborough. Baton Rouge: Louisiana State University Press, 1972.

Rush, Benjamin. *An Enquiry into the Effects of Spirituous Liquors upon the Human Body, and Their Influence upon the Happiness of Society*. Philadelphia: Thomas Bradford, 1791.

Russell, John Henderson. *The Free Negro in Virginia, 1619–1895*. New York: Negro Universities Press, 1969.

Salafia, Matthew. *Slavery's Borderland: Freedom and Bondage along the Ohio River*. Philadelphia: University of Pennsylvania Press, 2013.

Sanborn, Franklin B., *The Life and Letters of John Brown, Liberator of Kansas and Martyr of Virginia*. New York: Negro Universities Press, 1969 (reprint).

Schwarz, Philip J. *Migrants against Slavery: Virginians and the Nation*. Charlottesville: University Press of Virginia, 2001.

Sharfstein, Daniel J. *The Invisible Line: Three American Families and the Secret Journey from Black to White*. New York: Penguin Press, 2011.

Shipherd, Jacob R., comp. *History of the Oberlin-Wellington Rescue*. New York: Negro Universities Press, 1969.

Shumway, A. L., and C. DeW. Brower. *Oberliniana: A Jubilee Volume of Semi-historical Anecdotes Connected with the Past and Present of Oberlin College, 1833–1883*. Cleveland: Home Publishing, 1883.

Sinha, Manisha. *The Counterrevolution of Slavery: Politics and Ideology in Antebellum South Carolina*. Chapel Hill: University of North Carolina Press, 2000.

Slaughter, Thomas P. *Bloody Dawn: The Christiana Riot and Racial Violence in the Antebellum North*. New York: Oxford University Press, 1991.

Soike, Lowell J. *Necessary Courage: Iowa's Underground Railroad in the Struggle against Slavery*. Iowa City: University of Iowa Press, 2013.

Stahr, Walter. *Seward: Lincoln's Indispensable Man*. New York: Simon and Schuster, 2012.

Stauffer, John. "Fighting the Devil with His Own Fire," in *The Abolitionist Imagination*, ed. Andrew Delbanco. Cambridge, MA: Harvard University Press, 2012. 75.

Sterling, Dorothy, comp. *Speak Out in Thunder Tones: Letters and Other Writings By Black Northerners, 1787–1865*. Garden City, NY: Doubleday, 1973.

Stevens, Charles. *Anthony Burns: A History*. Boston: J. P. Jewitt, 1856.

Stowe, Harriet Beecher. *The Key to Uncle Tom's Cabin*. Port Washington, NY: Kennikat Press, 1968.

Swing, Albert Temple. *James Harris Fairchild, or Sixty-Eight Years with a Christian College*. New York: Fleming H. Revell, 1907.

Taylor, Alan. *The Internal Enemy: Slavery and War in Virginia, 1772–1832*. New York: W. W. Norton, 2013.

Taylor, Yuval, ed. *I Was Born a Slave: An Anthology of Classic Slave Narratives*. Chicago: Lawrence Hill Books, 1999.

Trodd, Zoe, and John Stauffer, eds. *Meteor of War: The John Brown Story*. Philadelphia: Brandywine Press, 2004.

———. *The Tribunal: Responses to John Brown and the Harpers Ferry Raid.* Cambridge, MA: Belknap Press of Harvard University Press, 2012.

United States Congress. *Report of the Select Committee of the Senate Appointed to Inquire into the Late Invasion and the Seizure of Public Property at Harper's Ferry.* Ann Arbor: University of Michigan Library, 2005.

Van Tassel, David, and John Grabowski, eds. *The Encyclopedia of Cleveland History.* Bloomington: Indiana University Press, 1987.

Van Tine, Warren, and Michael Pierce, eds. *Builders of Ohio: A Biographical History.* Columbus: Ohio State University Press, 2003.

Villard, Oswald Garrison. *John Brown, 1800–1859: A Biography Fifty Years After.* Boston: Houghton Mifflin, 1910.

Von Frank, Albert. *The Trials of Anthony Burns: Freedom and Slavery in Emerson's Boston.* Cambridge, MA: Harvard University Press, 1998.

Voorhees, Daniel Wolsey. *Forty Years of Oratory: Daniel Wolsey Voorhees, Lectures, Addresses and Speeches,* vol. 2. Indianapolis: Bowen-Merrill, 1898.

Watkins, William. "Who Are the Murderers?" in *The Black Abolitionist Papers,* vol. 4: *The United States, 1847–1858,* ed. C. Peter Ripley et al. Chapel Hill: University of North Carolina Press, 1991. 227–29. (Originally appeared in *Frederick Douglass' Paper,* June 2, 1854.)

Wayland, John Walter. *John Kagi and John Brown.* Strasburg, VA: Shenandoah, 1961.

Weisenburger, Steven. *Modern Medea: A Family Story of Slavery and Child Murder from the Old South.* New York: Hill and Wang, 1998.

Weld, Theodore D., comp. *American Slavery as It Is: Testimony of a Thousand Witnesses.* New York: American Anti-Slavery Society, 1839.

Wells, Anna Mary. *Dear Preceptor: The Life and Times of Thomas Wentworth Higginson.* Boston: Houghton Mifflin, 1963.

Wesley, Dorothy Porter, and Constance Porter Uzelac, eds. *William Cooper Nell, Nineteenth-Century African American Abolitionist, Historian, Integrationist: Selected Writings, 1832–1874.* Baltimore: Black Classic Press, 2002.

Wiencek, Henry. *An Imperfect God: George Washington, His Slaves, and the Creation of America.* New York: Farrar, Straus and Giroux, 2003.

Wilentz, Sean. *The Rise of American Democracy: Jefferson to Lincoln.* New York: W. W. Norton, 2005.

Wilson, Carol. *Freedom at Risk: The Kidnapping of Free Blacks in America, 1780–1865.* Lexington: University Press of Kentucky, 1994.

Wilson, Theodore Brantner. *The Black Codes of the South.* University: University of Alabama Press, 1965.

PERIODICAL ARTICLES

A. H. "List of Insurgents As Furnished Me by Brown & Stephens at Harper's Ferry." *Virginia Magazine of History and Biography* 10, no. 3 (January 1902): 274–75.

"A Monument." *Anglo-African Magazine* (January 14, 1860).

Altherr, Thomas. "A Convention of Moral Lunatics: The Rutland, Vermont, Free Convention of 1858." Symposium Supplement. *Vermont History* 69 (2001): 90–104.

Barber, J. Max. "The Niagara Movement at Harper's Ferry." *Voice of the Negro* 3, no. 10 (October 1906): 402–11.

Boteler, Alexander. "Recollections of the John Brown Raid by a Virginian Who Witnessed the Fight." *The Century Magazine* 26 (July 1883): 399–410.

Brown, William Wells. "John Brown and the Fugitive Slave Law." *The Independent* (March 10, 1870). Boyd B. Stutler Collection, West Virginia State Archives.

Buchanan, James. "James Buchanan to Andrew Hunter." *Proceedings of the Massachusetts Historical Society* 46 (December 1912): 245.

Burroughs, Wilbur Greeley. "Oberlin's Part in the Slavery Conflict." *Ohio Archaeological and Historical Quarterly* 20, no. 2 (April 1911): 269–334.

Clemens, Will. "John Brown: The American Reformer, Part III." *The Peterson Magazine* (March 1898): 215.

Copeland, John A. "John A. Copeland to Hiram Bannon, December 11, 1859." *Historia* (December 10, 1909).

Dana, Richard Henry Jr. "Cruelty to Seamen: The Case of Nichols and Couch." *American Jurist and Law Magazine* 22 (October 1839): 92–107.

———. "How We Met John Brown." *Atlantic Monthly* 28, no. 165 (July 1871): 1–9.

Fairchild, James Harris. "A Sketch of the Anti-Slavery History of Oberlin." *Oberlin Evangelist* (July 16, 1856).

Featherstonhaugh, Thomas. "John Brown's Men: The Lives of Those Killed at Harper's Ferry." *Publications of the Southern History Association* 3, no. 4 (October 1899): 281–306.

Galbreath, C. B. "Edwin Coppoc." *Ohio History Journal* 30, no. 4 (October 1921): 396–451.

Green, Israel. "The Capture of John Brown." *North American Review* 141 (December 1885): 564–69.

Hall, James. "Education and Slavery." *Western Monthly Magazine* 3 (May 1834): 266–73.

Hamilton, James Cleland. "John Brown in Canada." *The Canadian Magazine* 4, no. 2 (December 1894): 119–40.

Hopkins, C. S. "Some By-Gone Days." *Oberlin News* (June 17, 1898).

Horton, James Oliver. "Black Education at Oberlin College: A Controversial Commitment." *Journal of Negro Education* 54, no. 4 (Autumn 1985): 477–99.

Hoyt, George. "Recollections of John Brown's Trial by One of His Lawyers." *Leavenworth Daily Conservative* (July 31, 1867).

Hunter, Andrew. "John Brown's Raid." *Publications of the Southern History Association* 1, no. 3 (July 1897): 165–95.

Johnson, Matthew. "Letter to Andrew Hunter." *Virginia Magazine of History and Biography* 10, no. 1 (July 1902): 280–82.

Land, Mary. "John Brown's Ohio Environment." *Ohio Archaeological and Historical Quarterly* 57, no. 1 (January 1948): 24–47.

Langston, John Mercer. "The Oberlin-Wellington Rescue." *Anglo-African Magazine* 1, no. 7 (July 1859): 209–20.

______. "The Leary Family." *Negro History Bulletin* 10, no. 2 (November 1946): 27–34.

Lee, Robert E. "Col. R. E. Lee's Report to Adjutant General." *Virginia Magazine of History and Biography* 10, no. 1 (July 1902): 18–25.

Love, Rose Leary. "A Few Facts about Lewis Sheridan Leary Who Was Killed at Harpers Ferry in John Brown's Raid." *Negro History Bulletin* 6, no. 9 (June 1943): 198.

Lubet, Steven. "Execution in Virginia, 1859: The Trials of Copeland and Green." 91 *North Carolina Law Review* 1785 (2013).

McCabe, Lida Rose. "The Oberlin-Wellington Rescue." *Godey's Magazine* 133 (October 1896): 361–76.

Muller, Eric L. "Judging Thomas Ruffin and the Hindsight Defense." 87 *North Carolina Law Review* 757–98 (2009).

Nell, William Cooper. "John Anthony Copeland." *Pine and Palm* (July 20, 1861).

______. "Lewis Sherrard Leary." *Pine and Palm* (July 27, 1861).

"Oberliniana: Testimony to Integration – Saga of the Allen Jones Family." *Oberlin Alumni Magazine* (April 1961).

Parker, Richard. "Richard Parker to Andrew Hunter." *Proceedings of the Massachusetts Historical Society* 46 (December 1912): 245–46.

Peck, Henry. "The Slave-Rescue Case in Ohio." *The Liberator* (January 28, 1859).

Preston, J. T. L. "The Execution of John Brown." *The Southern Bivouac* (August 1886): 187–89.

Reid, Patricia A. "Margaret Morgan's Story: A Threshold between Slavery and Freedom, 1820–1842." *Slavery and Abolition* 33, no. 3 (September 2012): 359–80.

Richardson, Albert. "Free Missouri II." *Atlantic Monthly* 21, no. 126 (April 1868): 498.

Rudwick, Elliot. "The Niagara Movement." *Journal of Negro History* 42, no. 3 (July 1957): 177–200.

Shackleton, Robert. "What Support Did John Brown Rely Upon." *Magazine of American History* 29, no. 4 (1893): 348–59.

Stegmaier, Mark. "An Ohio Republican Stirs up the House: The Blake Resolution of 1860 and the Politics of the Sectional Crisis in Congress." *Ohio History* 116, no. 1 (2009): 62–87.

Strother, David Hunter (Porte Crayon). "The Late Invasion at Harper's Ferry." *Harper's Weekly* (November 5, 1859): 712–14.

______. "The Trial of the Conspirators." *Harper's Weekly* (November 12, 1859): 729–30.

Stutler, Boyd B. "Judge Richard Parker – He Tried John Brown." *Magazine of the Jefferson County Historical Society* 19 (December 1953): 27–37.

Tucker, John Randolph. "Reminiscences of Virginia's Judges and Jurists." Supplement. *The Virginia Law Register* 1, no. 3 (July 1895): 1–47.

Watkins, William. "Who Are the Murderers?" *Frederick Douglass' Paper* (June 2, 1854).

Yanuck, Julius. "Thomas Ruffin and North Carolina Slave Law." *Journal of Southern History* 21, no. 4 (1955): 456–75.

COURT DECISIONS

Somerset v. Stewart, 98 Eng. Rep. 499 (K.B.) (1772).
State v. Mann, 13 N.C. 263 (1829).
Commonwealth v. Aves, 35 Mass. 193 (1836).
Prigg v. Pennsylvania, 41 U.S. 539 (1842).
Strader v. Graham, 51 U.S. 82 (1850).
United States ex rel Wheeler v. Williamson, 28 F. Cas. 686 (1855).
Anderson v. Poindexter, 6 Ohio St. 622, 630 (1856).
Dred Scott v. Sandford, 60 U.S. 393, 407, 408–412 (1857).
Ex Parte Bushnell, 9 Ohio St. 77 (1859).
Lemmon v. People, 20 N.Y. 562 (1860).
Loving v. Virginia, 388 U.S. 1 (1967).

UNPUBLISHED MANUSCRIPTS

Blake, Harrison. "Life of H.G. Blake, at the request of Capt. Charles Blake." Undated typescript, Gloria Brown Collection, Medina, OH.

Brown, Annie. "Statement of Annie Brown, Daughter of John Brown, Written November 1886." Frank Logan/John Brown Collection, Chicago History Museum, Chicago, IL.

Brown, Owen. "Owen Brown's Story of His Journey from Hagerstown to Kennedy Farm, with Shields Green, a Colored Man." Horatio Nelson Rust Collection, Huntington Library, San Marino, CA.

Ellsworth, Clayton. "Oberlin and the Anti-Slavery Movement up to the Civil War." Unpublished dissertation. Cornell University, Ithaca, NY, 1930.

Fitch, Emma Monroe. "The Wellington Rescue Case in 1858." Undated typescript, Oberlin College Archive, Oberlin, OH.

Leech, George V. "Memoir of Rev. George V. Leech, Baltimore Conference, M. E. Church." Undated manuscript. Villard Papers, Columbia University, New York, NY.

Lincoln, William. "Personal Reminiscences with an Account of the Rescue of the Negro Slave John." Unpaginated manuscript. Palmer Collection, Western Reserve Historical Society, Cleveland, OH.

Shadd, Adrienne. "Celebrating the Legacy: Chatham's Black Heritage." Unpublished paper produced for the revised exhibit *Black Mecca: The Story of Chatham's Black Community*. Chatham-Kent Black Historical Society, Chatham, Ontario, 2004.

Strother, David Hunter. "Eyewitness Account of the Execution of John Brown." December 1859. Stutler Collection, West Virginia State Archives, Charleston, WV.

INDEX